AF607965

Selected Correspondence of Bernard Shaw

Bernard Shaw and Gilbert Murray

Selected Correspondence of Bernard Shaw

Bernard Shaw and Gilbert Murray

Edited by Charles A. Carpenter

UNIVERSITY OF TORONTO PRESS
Toronto Buffalo London

Published by University of Toronto Press
Toronto Buffalo London
www.utppublishing.com

ISBN 978-1-4426-4382-6 (cloth)

Library and Archives Canada Cataloguing in Publication

Shaw, Bernard, 1856–1950
[Correspondence. Selections (Toronto, Ont.)]
Selected correspondance of Bernard Shaw

Includes bibliographical references and index
Contents: [v. 8] Bernard Shaw and Gilbert Murray/edited by Charles A. Carpenter.
ISBN 978-1-4426-4382-6 (v. 8 : bound)

1. Shaw, Bernard, 1856–1950 – Correspondence. 2. Dramatists, Irish – 20th century – Correspondence. I. Title.

PR5366.A4 1995 822'.912 C959-301518

University of Toronto Press acknowledges the financial assistance to its publishing program of the Canada Council for the Arts and the Ontario Arts Council, an agency of the Government of Ontario.

Canada Council for the Arts Conseil des Arts du Canada

University of Toronto Press acknowledges the financial support of the Government of Canada through the Canada Book Fund for its publishing activities.

Contents

General Editor's Note

This volume is the eighth in the series entitled *Selected Correspondence of Bernard Shaw.* The first two volumes – *Bernard Shaw and H.G. Wells,* edited by J. Percy Smith, and *Theatrics,* edited by Dan H. Laurence – first appeared in 1995. The third – *Bernard Shaw and Gabriel Pascal,* edited by Bernard Dukore – was published in 1996, and the fourth and fifth volumes – *Bernard Shaw and Barry Jackson,* edited by L.W. Conolly, and *Bernard Shaw and the Webbs,* edited by Alex C. Michalos and Deborah C. Poff – appeared in 2002. The sixth volume – *Bernard Shaw and Nancy Astor,* edited by J.P. Wearing – was published in 2005. The seventh volume – *Bernard Shaw and His Publishers,* edited by Michel C. Pharand – was published in 2009.

The volumes in this series are of two kinds. Percy Smith's inaugural volume represents an example of the first kind: correspondence between Shaw and another individual of distinction in his or her own right. Bernard Dukore's, J.P. Wearing's, my own editions, and the present volume are further examples of this kind. *Bernard Shaw and the Webbs* is a minor variation on this model in that it deals with Shaw' relationship with *two* distinguished individuals.

This approach replicates other editions of Shaw correspondence published before this series: Christopher St John's *Ellen Terry and Bernard Shaw: A Correspondence* (1931) and Alan Dent's *Bernard Shaw and Mrs Patrick Campbell: Their Correspondence* (1931), among others. The advantage of this approach, of course, is that it gives the reader two (or more) voices rather than one, with all the stimulation that can arise from complementary or adversarial views on issues, events, or people. Such an approach also allows for insights into the nature of close personal and professional relationships, with all the emotional and intellectual drama that usually accompanied such Shavian associations. While matching the epistolary Shaw in full flow is a tough challenge, people such as Wells, Pascal, Jackson, the Webbs, and Nancy Astor – hardened professionals all – were not easily intimidated by Shaw's sharp wit, searing logic, or intellectual aggression. Thus, the sparks sometimes fly, from which light as well as heat is generated.

This attempt to capture Shaw's *dialogue* with friends and colleagues differs, of course, from collections solely of Shaw's letters to individuals, be they single individuals, as in C.B. Purdom's *Bernard Shaw's Letters to Granville Barker* (1957) or Samuel Weiss's *Bernard Shaw's Letters to Siegfried Trebitsch* (1986), or hundreds of individuals, as in Dan H. Laurence's monumental edition *Bernard Shaw: Collected Letters* (4 volumes, 1965–88). And both of these approaches differ again from the second kind of volume in this series, Shaw's letter to a variety of individuals *on a particular subject.*

Introduction

When I emailed Sidney P. Albert, one of only two fellow Shavians I knew was familiar with Gilbert Murray, to tell him that I was embarking on this project, he replied: 'I would caution you to consider how daunting a challenge it is ... You will be dealing with writings of two voluminous authors who have written about every subject imaginable. Those who have written extensively about them are dead, dying, or frequenting medical facilities.' What he didn't mention is that if Shaw almost certainly set the world record for most letters written, Gilbert Murray must have finished in the top five. He wrote or co-signed almost 300 letters just to the editor of the London *Times*, although Shaw exceeded him in that respect by far.[1] The present volume includes 171 letters, 86 from Murray, 85 from Shaw (only 30 of them in Dan H. Laurence's edition of Shaw's *Collected Letters*).

The name George Gilbert Aimé Murray, sensibly carved down to Gilbert Murray, will be much less familiar to most readers of this volume than that of George Bernard Shaw, indulgently truncated to Bernard Shaw or G.B.S. While there are more than a dozen biographies of Shaw, there are only two of Murray: Frances West's compact *Gilbert Murray: A Life* (1984) and a much more thorough and scholarly one, Duncan Wilson's *Gilbert Murray, OM, 1886–1957* (1987).[2] Murray's career is well capsulized in the subtitle of one of the very few critical books about him, the collection of essays *Gilbert Murray Reassessed: Hellenism, Theatre, and International Politics.* The editor, Christopher Stray, embellishes it further in his introduction with an (edited) list of the range of his activities: 'Greek scholar, historian of literature and of religion, political activist and polemicist, internationalist, translator, man of the theatre, editor, psychic researcher' (2). He omitted husband, father, son-in-law, and grandfather, which in his case were challenging roles.

Bernard Shaw paraded the impressive range of his own activities so that his first authorized biographer, Archibald Henderson, would 'shew me in the context of my time' rather than focusing heavily on his play-writing: 'I want you to do something that will be useful to yourself and to the world; and that is, to make me a mere peg on which to hang a study of the last quarter of the XIX century, especially as to the Collectivist movement in politics, ethics, and sociology; the Ibsen-Nietzschean movement in morals; ... the Wagnerian movement in music, and the anti-romantic movement (including what people call realism, naturalism, and impressionism) in literature and art.'[3] The next fifty years of his life were still to come, with a new philosophy to disseminate, a revised socialism to propagate, and a host of innovative, brainy 'disquisitory dramas' to create and stage.

Writing in 1915, the popular American essayist John Jay Chapman eulogized the personal qualities of Murray for people unfamiliar with him:

> Professor Gilbert Murray is the best known scholar in the British Empire, and is the most widely beloved scholar of the present epoch ... His enormous literacy and his easy command over the whole book-world appear like a miracle to the general reader ... His suavity, his personal charm, his real humility, his humor, his freedom from dogmatism, the Orpheus-like serenity with which he walks through the Plutonic regions, illuminating scholarship as he goes with the interest of a fairy-tale, make him the adored friend of every reader. ('Professor Gilbert Murray – Oxford,' 97)

J.A.K. Thomson, the man whom Duncan Wilson says knew him best, summed him up more objectively: 'While he was one of the friendliest, he was one of the remotest of men. He had a thousand well-wishers and no intimate.' His characteristics were those of 'an ancient philosopher, ... especially that central serenity and self-sufficiency ... which they so commonly made it their object to attain ... He could see both sides of a case, even a case in which his own feelings were deeply engaged' ('Gilbert Murray, 1866–1957,' 254, 256). In sharp contrast to Shaw, he struck most people as a 'balanced' individual without a touch of exhibitionism in his nature. To assert his more human side, however, he enjoyed putting on a quirky display before visitors: he would lie on the floor 'with a brimming glass of water balanced precariously on his forehead,' and then rise without spilling a drop (Ginden, 221).

The friendship between Shaw and Murray began on 16 July 1895, at the drama critic William Archer's provocation, when the former was already G.B.S. and the latter Professor Gilbert Murray. It ended in 1950, when 94-year-old Shaw died, seven years before Murray, who reached 91. The two long-livers had a great deal more in common than their early excision of 'George' from their names and their later survival power. Both Shaw's and Murray's fathers were hard-drinking Irishmen. In 1876 Shaw left his father's home in Dublin (and further schooling) to join his mother in London; the year after, Murray and his mother left Australia for London, his father having died four years before. Both men were clearly geniuses, both were born teachers, and both were addicted to writing. A tiny but symptomatic parallel: late in life, both sought privacy by writing in a hut on the lawn.

The similarities do not end there, but the contrasts are at least as striking. While Shaw had to endure relative poverty, Murray soon entered the domain of the intelligentsia. Shaw lived off his mother and taught himself to write by trying his hand at fiction, then took an ill-paid succession of jobs as a reporter of one art after another. Murray excelled as a student so conspicuously that he was elected to the professorship of Greek at Glasgow University as a twenty-three-year-old. He was an endearing enough personality for Shaw to exempt him from his habitual contempt for professors, rarely hesitating to tap his friend's vast fountain of erudition for knowledge and perspective on a variety of subjects.

Shaw trumpeted an atheist creed early, attacking Christian ideals and Victorian prudery, but later became the herald of a full-blown religion of creative evolution; Murray, his father a Catholic and mother a Protestant but neither one devout, became a 'Hellenic' agnostic openly tolerant of all religions except evangelical sects. Shaw was a distinctive brand of Fabian socialist from 1885 on; Murray was a prototypical upper-middle-class Victorian – roughly, a capitalist with enough socialist sentiment to call himself a Radical Liberal – until he died. He had married into the family of Lord and Lady Carlisle, who owned Castle Howard, 'a formidable outpost of traditional aristocratic opulence and modern liberal radicalism.'[4] Late in life he limned the divergent political stances of Shaw and himself with wry wit: 'Mary [his wife] sends her love. She is grateful to you for remaining, like her, obstinately Socialist, while I still cling to the noble, if extinct, tribe of Liberals' (Letter 167). He was not entirely joking; earlier in the year he had remarked enigmatically to a friend, 'Rum how right [the Liberals] are and how extinct' (Wilson, 391).

Murray wrote in a late memorial of Shaw: 'I knew him first when I was in my early twenties and he in his thirties, an amazing young man with a red beard, bold views on music and philosophy and most other subjects, and a number of plays which no prudent manager would produce.' He and Shaw, he added, were 'both teetotallers, both vegetarians, both great "world-changers," … but, unlike other world-changers, neither of us at all noticeably grumbly or unamiable.'[5] Their first meeting on that July day in 1895 established two other important things that the two had in common, ambitions as a playwright and strong interest in the drama of Henrik Ibsen. Around 1897 Murray told Lady Carlisle that 'Ibsen rather spoils one for appreciating ordinary plays' (Wilson, 79). Archer had invited Murray to his home to tell him what he had to say about the Professor's first attempt at playwriting, *Carlyon Sahib,* which was partly inspired by Ibsen.[6] At the urging of Charles Charrington and his wife Janet Achurch, it was being considered for production at the Independent Theatre – the very theatre which had presented Shaw's first play, *Widowers' Houses.* Archer had also invited Shaw, then author of *The Quintessence of Ibsenism* and theatre critic for the *Saturday Review.*[7] In a letter to Murray, Achurch said that Shaw had read the play and admires it 'exceedingly.'[8]

The discussion of the play was apparently dominated by Archer's suggestions of various ways to improve it. But Shaw objected. According to Murray's later recollections, Shaw had emphatically declared: 'what's the good of re-writing? It is a good play with bad parts, as it is. So are all good plays! No. Write another and another; when you have written a dozen, you'll know ever so much more about it.'[9] But the Charringtons' interest continued, and the play, after Archer rewrote parts of it, was finally produced at the Kennington Theatre on 18 June 1899. In spite of the fact that it starred the extremely popular Mrs Patrick Campbell and Archer gave it a rave review in the *Manchester Guardian,* performances of the play were terminated after only a fortnight's run (Wilson, 80–3).

Meanwhile, another symptomatic contrast between the two men arose, this time in the political realm. Both Shaw and Murray became preoccupied with the South African War, commonly referred to as the second Boer War, from its inception on 11 October 1899 to its cessation on 31 May 1902. Murray, following his humanitarian bent, quickly became pro-Boer. He was appalled at the public hysteria for crushing Boer resistance to British attempts to annex the gold-rich Transvaal. This stand led to his near-expulsion from the Liberal Party. Essays in which he indirectly attacked British imperialist policy followed: 'The Exploitation of Inferior Races in Ancient and Modern Times' in 1900, 'National Ideals, Conscious and Unconscious,' and 'Intransigence' in 1901. In the meantime he put his usual active role in party politics on hold and joined other academics in sponsoring the South African Conciliation Committee (Wilson, 71–3).

Bernard Shaw revealed his more flexible and nuanced attitude towards the war from the start. When hostilities commenced in 1899, he at once tried to circumvent the disruption it might cause among fellow Fabians. He wrote Edward Pease, secretary of the Society: 'Dont let us, after all these years, split the society by declaring ourselves on a non-socialist point of policy' (letter of 30 October 1899 in *Collected Letters*, 2, 115). Although deploring the conduct of the war – a letter to Murray of 22 January 1902 calls it 'the sensational tragedy now being enacted on the veldt' – he led the opposition to both pro-imperialist and pro-Boer Fabian factions. Taking a thoroughly pragmatic view of the conflict, he acted on the assumption that annexation of the Transvaal was inevitable and encouraged members to support candidates for office whom they considered the best regardless of their attitude towards the war. His letter to Pease continues: 'Our sole business is to work out a practical scheme for securing the mines when we "resume" the Transvaal.'

Shaw's most important contribution to the debate came a year later: drafting the tract *Fabianism and the Empire*, then collaborating with over one hundred Fabians in producing the final version (issued 2 October 1900). As Michael Holroyd explains:

> Very little of Fabianism and the Empire deals with South Africa which, though topical, is seen as part of an historical pattern. The design of socialism

> in this pattern is to turn Empires into true Commonwealths. Shaw's manifesto imagines a Fabianizing of the Empire in the cause of efficiency ... [He] grafts socialism on to Colonialism with such statesmanlike prose and sweeping vision as to reduce the differences of the Fabians to family bickering. (Holroyd 2, 44)

The war continued until overwhelming British power (and ruthlessness) led to the Treaty of Vereeniging on 31 May 1902. Holroyd notes wryly, '22,000 British soldiers had been killed and £223,000,000 spent – but no great shaving had been split off the Fabian Society' (2, 41).

Murray's next step in his dramatic career was to attempt a version of Euripides' *Andromache* more or less freely translated with the aim of contributing indirectly to the enrichment of post-Ibsenite modern drama. It was received respectfully by non-academic spectators, but eventually became a major factor in his decision to restrict himself to translations of Greek plays that would meet an academic standard of accuracy and depend on Euripides to appeal to wider audiences. In this he succeeded, and several were produced at the Royal Court Theatre during its highly influential seasons of 1904–7.

This was of course the legendary period of Shaw's 'reign at the Court.' The very early 1900s led to a rejuvenation of his career as a dramatist. After composing his first ten plays in the nineties and engendering a great deal of interest but little willingness to stage them, Shaw decided to shift his direction toward publishing them. *Plays Pleasant and Unpleasant* and *Three Plays for Puritans* came out in 1898, featuring highly readable prefaces and novelistic stage directions. Finishing the massive discussion play *Man and Superman: A Comedy and a Philosophy* in 1903, he garnished the book-length volume with a long 'Epistle Dedicatory' to a critic, the 'Revolutionist's Handbook,' and 'Maxims for Revolutionists,' and published it with little or no prospect of having the play performed.

However, the book attracted so much attention – equal parts of the magic brew, admiration and vilification – that it spurred a Shaw boom which led indirectly to the Court Theatre's 'almost miraculous renascence' of British drama, as Archer pronounced it in *The Old Drama and the New* (24–5). The main development was the Harley Granville Barker–J.E. Vedrenne series of productions at London's Royal Court Theatre, with Vedrenne the manager and Barker directing. In a letter to Archer of 21 April 1903 Barker said, 'Do you think there is anything in this idea? To take the Court Theatre for six months or a year and to run there a stock season of the uncommercial Drama: Hauptmann – Sudermann – Ibsen – Maeterlinck – Schnitzler – Shaw – Brieux, etc. ... A fresh production every fortnight ... The highest price five or six shillings. To be worked mainly as a subscription theatre' (Salmon, ed., 41–2). Nothing came of this immediately, but in February 1904 Barker, who had directed several plays for the Stage Society, was asked to mount a production of Shakespeare's *Two Gentlemen of Verona* at the Court. He agreed on the condition that he could stage six matinee performances of Shaw's *Candida*; the proposal was accepted (MacCarthy, *The Court Theatre*, 1).

The *Candida* matinees were as successful as anyone could expect from a new venture, with Barker 'near perfection' in the role of Marchbanks (Purdom, 22). This prompted Barker and Vedrenne to launch a series of other plays deemed commercially unpromising or infeasible, the great majority by Shaw. Thus began an enterprise that was to continue at the Court for two and a half years. The epoch became much celebrated in the annals of the English stage; the 1983 edition of the *Oxford Companion to the Theatre* declares that 'its influence on the English theatre was incalculable' (813).

The initial production of *Candida* in April of 1904 is normally considered the starting point of this enterprise. However, in June the lessee of the Court had declared a strong inclination to see Greek drama performed there, and the play that became the first official performance of the venture was Murray's translation of *Hippolytus*. As Eric Salmon states,

> It appears to have been Barker's production of (and playing in) Murray's translation of the *Hippolytus* of Euripides in the following month which really triggered off the scheme ... *Candida* had been a way of getting an example of the 'new drama' into the Court, but *Hippolytus* inspired the idea of using the Court for a whole series of plays – standard works as well as new works – presented in repertory. In a very real sense, Barker's connection with Murray led to the single most important development of his career, and the forming and moulding of that development was the result of the creative impact of their two minds. (*Granville Barker and His Correspondents*, 197)

The Court also mounted Murray's versions of *The Trojan Women* and *Electra.* The alternation between the new plays by Shaw and Euripidean classics made stageworthy by Murray evoked such responses as that of the critic W.H. Salter:

> That Euripides is 'modern' requires no proof. Does he not, with Prof. Gilbert Murray for interpreter, find his natural place on our stage by the side of our newest and brainiest dramatists? Is he not familiar to all Fleet Street as the 'Greek Ibsen,' the 'Attic Shaw'? Are not his plays an inexhaustible mine of tags for the Feminist and other workers for Great Causes? (*Essays on Two Moderns,* 9)

A marvellous merger of the two playwrights occurred in 1905, when Shaw got the idea of modelling the *jeune premier* of his developing playscript *Major Barbara* on the only Greek professor he knew well. The slight, spectacled Cusins would not only be made up to resemble Murray, but would quote passages from his translations of Euripides' *Hippolytus* and *The Bacchae* as if they were his own. To those who knew his mother-in-law, the Countess of Carlisle, Lady Britomart would be an exaggerated but detectable adaptation. Shaw also reworked elements of Murray's *Bacchae* in the first two acts and his version of Aristophanes' *The Frogs* in the third. The play is thus a genuine collaboration of the two close friends quite apart from the specific revisions Murray suggested as Shaw struggled to refashion its third act – never succeeding to his own satisfaction.[10]

The Court Theatre venture endured until late June 1907, when Barker and Vedrenne tried their hand at the West End. The contributions of Murray to its reputation had been an integral part of its good fortune, but it was undeniably the rich offerings by Shaw that were mainly responsible for transforming the current state of the drama, as well as supporting the theatre itself. Of the 988 performances given, 701 of them were of eleven Shaw plays.

A significant obstacle in the evolution of the 'higher drama' was England's long-standing, anomalous policy of requiring playwrights to submit their works to the Lord Chamberlain's office for approval or disapproval by an 'Examiner of Plays.' The official reader followed set guidelines to detect characters, scenes, or language that might be construed as politically, religiously, or morally offensive. In the 1890s Shelley's *Cenci* and Sophocles' *Oedipus Rex* were both 'censored' because they involved incest and parricide, and Shaw's *Mrs Warren's Profession* because it openly discussed prostitution and raised the possibility of incest. Shaw had railed against this policy for years, emphasizing its suppressive effect on dramatic artists who, like himself, felt compelled to supersede the largely conventional, unchallenging drama that had prevailed for years.

Early in 1907, the Examiner of Plays had refused to license *The Breaking Point* by Edward Garnett, which depicted an unmarried mother, and Barker's drama *Waste* because it involved an abortion. His rulings prompted William Archer to urge a large group of literary men to join a campaign for the abolition of this policy. He enlisted Murray, John Galsworthy, and J.M. Barrie to form a provisional committee. They drew up a letter protesting the censorship and had it signed by seventy-one prominent authors, among them Shaw. The letter, published in *The Times* on 29 October 1907, argues the case against 'the power lodged in the hands of a single official – who judges without a public hearing, and against whose dictum there is no appeal.' (The full text of the letter is printed in *Mrs Warren's Profession*, ed. Conolly, 208–9.)[11] The group letter and a deputation to the prime minister's office that followed were the first steps in a concerted campaign, tirelessly stage-managed by Shaw, to end or significantly revise the governmental examination of plays. It was successful only to a degree – an advisory committee to assist the censor was appointed – and the policy itself was not wiped off the books until 1968. Two years after that *Oh, Calcutta!* could be moved from New York to London.

Shaw began to develop his religious philosophy of the Life Force / Creative Evolution towards the end of the 1800s. The germ of it appears in an 1889 letter to Hubert Bland in which he discusses the inverse of the 'ordinary' man as one attempting to 'attain consciousness of himself as a vessel of the Zeitgeist or will or whatever it may be.'[12] It is almost fully developed in his interpretation of 'Godhead' in *The Perfect Wagnerite* as a force that 'organizes itself into all living shapes,' ultimately 'into rare persons who may ... be called gods capable of thought' and who 'perceive that it is only by the establishment of a social order founded on common bonds of moral faith that the world can rise from mere savagery.'[13] He first advertised the concept prominently in the Hell scene of *Man and Superman*. Don Juan's animadversions upon a 'stupid,' trial-and-error cosmic force which is striving, with the help of human brain- and will-power, to attain 'higher organization, wider, deeper, intenser self-consciousness, and clearer self-understanding,' showed dramatically that Shaw was indeed 'in the grip of the Life Force.' He repeated and expanded upon this basic concept in various contexts, including his 1909 'sermon in crude melodrama,' *The Shewing-up of Blanco Posnet.* In that play, a self-styled scorner of the law who believes that God is responsible for everything, even the croup, is pressured (by God, of course) into sacrificing his freedom in order to help a mother whose baby is dying – and does die – from the croup. Several articles and speeches that promote aspects of the idea are reprinted in *The Religious Speeches of Bernard Shaw.* Three lectures supply apt examples: 'The Religion of the British Empire' (1906) defines God as 'this wonderful will of the universe'; 'The New Theology' (1907) challenges accepted theories of evolution by attributing advances (as well as regressions) to 'a force behind the universe ... working up through imperfection and mistake to a perfect, organized being, having the power of fulfilling its highest purposes'; and 'The Religion of the Future' (1911, given before the Heretics Society of Cambridge) emphasizes 'the full consequences of moral responsibility that comes to men with the knowledge that there never will be a God unless we make one.'[14] He wrote many other variations on the same themes. Not incidentally, his letter to Murray of 22 September 1913 contains one of his clearest expositions of the Life Force and its ramifications for humanity.

Gilbert Murray defined himself as a humanistic agnostic tolerant of all but the supernatural beliefs of Christians but highly partial to Hellenic philosophical tenets during the Olympian period. At an extreme, he can denounce the 'pernicious rubbish' that accompanies conventional Christianity.[15] Murray's rejection of conventional Christianity reflects an underlying attitude in the late Victorian vein with a Hellenic colouring: akin to secular humanism with an optimistic cast. Quite surprisingly, it also resembles Shaw's theory of the Life Force to a noteworthy degree.

In a letter of 31 January 1900 to Lady Carlisle, Murray clearly avowed his preference for Hellenic beliefs: 'Greece has a profound and permanent message to mankind, a message quite untouched by "supernaturalism" and revealed religions; it is human rational and progressive, and affects not Art only but the whole of life ... I *have* got a faith and a message; they may be mistaken or vulgar or valueless, but they are there, and

I want to speak them out' (Wilson, 78). His most thorough discussion of these beliefs emerges indirectly in a 1915 essay on the Stoic philosophy, which he heralds as 'the greatest system of organized thought which the mind of man had built up for itself in the Graeco-Roman world before the coming of Christianity.'[16] Stoicism, he declares, 'represents a way of looking at the world and the practical problems of life which possesses still a permanent interest for the human race, and a permanent power of inspiration' (89). Soon he develops his description in terms that are curiously similar to those of Shaw:

> Goodness is performing your function well ... What do we mean by doing it 'well'? Here the Greek falls back on a scientific conception which had great influence in the fifth century B.C., and, somewhat transformed and differently named, has regained it in our own days. We call it 'Evolution.' The Greeks called it *Phusis,* a word which we translate by 'Nature,' but which seems to mean more exactly 'growth,' or 'the process of growth' ... Let us ... accept this conception of a force very like that which most of us assume when we speak of evolution; especially, perhaps, it is like what Bergson calls *La Vie* or *L'Élan Vital* at the back of *L'Évolution Créatrice,* though to the Greeks it seemed still more personal and vivid; a force which is present in all the live world, and is always making things grow towards the fulfillment of their utmost capacity. We see now what goodness is; it is living or acting according to Phusis, working with Phusis in her eternal effort towards perfection ... It means living according to the spirit which makes the world grow and progress ... It is at work everywhere. It is like a soul, or a life-force, running through all matter as the 'soul' or life of a man runs through all his limbs.. It is the soul of the world. (96–7)

Somewhat like Shaw, Murray proceeds to describe this 'life-force' as 'indistinguishable from a purpose, the purpose of the great world-process. It is like a foreseeing, freethinking power,' in this respect 'the nearest approach to a definite personal God which is admitted by the austere logic of Stoicism.' However, he does not conceive of that entity as a trial-and-error force, capable of making the croup or cancer as well as supermen; the power he visualizes 'is always making things grow towards the fulfillment of their utmost capacity.' And he even moves quite noticeably in the direction of conventional Christian doctrine when he asserts:

'Man's soul, being actually a portion of the divine fire, has the same freedom that God himself has. He can act either with God or against him, though, of course, when he acts against him he will ultimately be overwhelmed' (98). A benevolent God named 'Phusis' is still the controlling agent, although the term 'ultimately' leaves a great deal of room for the antics of Nero and Hitler as well as natural disasters popularly called 'acts of God.'

Both Murray and Shaw were much-admired speakers and teachers, Murray in a seminar room or lecture hall, Shaw in a huge variety of venues, from a street corner to the largest auditorium available. Although Shaw's specialty was controversy, the steamier the better, both were endowed with abilities that made them highly attractive as explainers and persuaders. A typical observation from a contemporary should suffice for Shaw, since he quickly became a conspicuous public figure: in just twenty-five years as a prominent member of the Fabian Executive Committee, he gave well over 1000 (unpaid) speeches for the cause. S.K. Ratcliffe, an early member of the Fabian Society, eloquently expressed his judgment in 'Shaw as a Young Socialist':

> Bernard Shaw was by native endowment what the author of Ecclesiastes calls a master of assemblies ... In the laying out of any subject he took for granted that his hearers could follow him through an hour of close exposition and argument ... The address would be a masterpiece of imaginative construction, packed with argument and provocation, and delivered with perfect craftsmanship ... It was the completeness of his technical equipment, the wholeness of his command and self-command, that impressed audiences everywhere. He was a marvellous total phenomenon. In public speech, as in writing, there did not appear to be anything that he could not do.[17]

Shaw's singular habits as a speaker and writer had a conspicuous downside, as nearly everyone recognized. Murray himself became an indirect target of his wrath by favouring the decision of the Foreign Office, led by Sir Edward Grey, to go to war with Germany and its allies in 1914. Shaw issued a controversial diatribe, *Common Sense about the War*, which blamed the decision on the governing classes of England – what Germans call 'Junkers': 'country gentlemen' with strong autocratic tendencies. He declared that the Foreign Office was 'a Junker Club,' and that Grey was 'a

Junker from his topmost hair to the tips of his toes' (*What Shaw Really Wrote about the War*, 18–19). Murray felt obliged to defend Grey in a long pamphlet, and Shaw responded with a scathing review, which left no doubt that Murray fit his notion of a Junker.[18] In a late retrospect that reflects a long-held and quite extreme opinion, Murray contrasted his valued friend with Grey:

> [Shaw] never wrote as a judge, always as an accuser or an advocate. He attacked the things he considered wrong, showed them up as ridiculous, illogical, oppressive; he vividly over-stated his case against them. It was for others to pronounce judgment. I once came away with him from hearing a speech of Sir Edward Grey's. It had been just in Grey's manner; a moderate, unadorned, fair and absolutely convincing statement. Shaw thought it very poor indeed. It had none of the qualities that he valued; no wit, no eloquence, no happy phrase, no new point of view or illuminating paradox. It was, in fact, the just judge speaking, not the brilliant advocate. ('A Few Memories,' 9)

Gilbert Murray began his career as an educator when he was elected as a fellow of New College, Oxford University, just after graduating. His intellectual acumen and articulateness were recognized by an unprecedented honour: appointment, at the age of twenty-three, for the chair of Greek at Glasgow University. Rather fragile physically, he had to resign after ten hectic years of overwork. A series of translations and other publications, largely related to Greek drama, enhanced his reputation so much that in 1908 he was chosen to the most prestigious position in his field, Regius Professor of Greek at Oxford. Two of his students, his ultimate successor in that chair, E.R. Dodds, and another classical scholar who became renowned, C.M. Bowra, recorded complementary views of his teaching, both of them focused on his discussing a Greek play. Dodds writes in his autobiography:

> By far the most exciting intellectual adventure of those years was Gilbert Murray's course of lectures on the *Bacchae* ... His lectures were memorable, not merely for the delicate art with which they were composed or the beauty of the voice in which they were delivered, but because they were a communication of experience; it was this which gave them their quite extraordinary

> quality of immediacy. To hear Murray read aloud and interpret a passage of Greek poetry brought successive generations of his students the intoxicating illusion of direct contact with the past, and to many of them a permanent enlargement of their sensibility. I was one of those many.[19]

Bowra devotes a chapter to Murray in his memoirs. An excerpt:

> His lectures, on Homer and Aeschylus' *Agamemnon*, were by far the best that I heard. He had a charming, musical voice, and he read the majestic Aeschylean choruses with a full sense of their magnificent rhythm. More than this, he really explained what the play was about. He had considerable experience of the stage, and ideas on how the *Agamemnon* must have been acted, but beyond this the poet in him responded to its imaginative and emotional sweep, and he rose to its lofty occasions ... He provided the inspiration that transformed what might have been rather a dull grind into an exalting and exciting experience. He made Greek poetry live and compelled us to feel that we must spare no effort to get at its essence, to understand it fully, and see how it worked.[20]

Shaw tends not to draw such adoration as these men claim for Murray. No one applies the term "delicate art" to him. In fact, his effectiveness as a teacher and propagandistic orator depended to a significant extent upon irritating his listeners and readers to get their attention and make them think. A typical early address before an audience of scientists provoked this report from a newspaperman:

> The dovecots were much fluttered ... by the appearance of a strange and rather startling figure ... [who] calmly denounced as robbers some of the men the world is accustomed to regard as the ornaments of society, the patterns of morality, and the pillars of the church. This was Mr George Bernard Shaw. The whole thing was done, not with the savagery of a wild and illiterate controversialist, but with the light touch, the deadly playfulness, and the rapier thrusts of a cultivated and thoughtful man.[21]

Late in life Shaw declared: 'It is always necessary to overstate a case startlingly to make people sit up and listen to it, and to frighten them into acting on it. I do this myself habitually and deliberately.'[22] The team of

Sidney and Beatrice Webb was the backbone of the Fabian movement, and both were sometimes appalled by their prize ally's anti-academic techniques. Yet the more critical of the two, Beatrice, noted in her diary that he was 'an artist to the tips of his fingers and an admirable *craftsman.* I have never known a man use his pen in such a workmanlike fashion or acquire such a thoroughly technical knowledge of any subject upon which he gives an opinion ... He always translates it into epigram, sparkling generalization or witty personalities' (*Diary of Beatrice Webb* 2, 36–7). An Oxford student's memory of hearing Shaw speak in 1913 may be compared with those of Murray's students:

> For the particular purposes for which Shaw's voice was chiefly employed, the purposes of argument, exposition and demonstration ... I have never heard its equal ... This melodious voice was very pleasant to listen to, so pleasant that it enabled its owner to make assertions which, coming from any other speaker, would have been immediately challenged, and to rebuke and even on occasion outrageously to insult his audience without causing a riot ... It was this habit of his of conveying what were then the most outrageous sentiments – as, for example, that everybody's income ought to be equal irrespective of work done, or that incorrigible criminals or invalids ought to be painlessly eliminated – that first took my breath away ... [But] in retrospect I do not doubt that the owner's intention was to produce precisely the conviction that the voice did in fact produce – namely, that what was so obvious to the speaker must be equally obvious to everyone in the audience who was not a congenital idiot.[23]

The noted historian A.J.P. Taylor found only one thing favourable to say about Shaw: he called him "the greatest arguer there has ever been.[24]

Most of these arguments revolved around Fabianism and its political nemeses, from extreme Conservatism to Gladstonian Liberalism, Murray's inheritance from his background and temperament. In 1902 Murray was invited (by Shaw?) to address the Fabian Society for the sake of comparing the two doctrines. The result was unexpected and illuminating: as Wilson paraphrases a section of the notes,

> The political essence of the talk was an attempt to convince the Fabians that on domestic issues they were more radical than Socialist. Radicals and

> Fabians alike believed in the futility of violent revolutionary policies; they were opposed in common to Tory government, which was in league with the Church, financiers, and the drink trade, and hostile to all but technical education. Liberalism had entirely lost its hold on the rich as a class. Murray professed to think a split more likely between the various kinds of socialists than between Fabians and radicals. They should join together in common political propaganda against 'the cause of Wealth, Force and Inertia ... Personally I expect that in spite of Mr. Webb your party will in the end prefer the principles of Liberalism and Democracy to considerations of symmetry and convenience.' (75)

It is unfortunate that no reply from Shaw seems to be extant. But about this time he had registered his general attitude toward democracy in one of his trenchant 'Maxims for Revolutionists': 'Democracy substitutes election by the incompetent many for appointment by the corrupt few' (*Complete Prefaces* [CPr], 2, 782). A statement written in 1930 elaborates lucidly upon this, and opens the door for his extreme tolerance of anti-democratic regimes:

> Benevolence is not a qualification for rulership at all: capable rulers have often been infernal scoundrels, and benevolent monarchs hopelessly incapable rulers ... The desideratum is a method of government in which the governed choose their rulers and can change them, but in which only capable persons are eligible for choice or change. Hereditary monarchy obviously cannot supply this. The notion that adult suffrage can supply it has been reduced to absurdity by experience. It is worse than hereditary monarchy, which may accidentally and occasionally produce a capable ruler, whereas adult suffrage, through the general dislike of capable rulers, and the popularity of agreeable and extravagant ne'er-do-wells ... positively prevents capable rulers from entering politics.[25]

A notable turning-point in Shaw's attitude as a humanistic Fabian crested from 21 to 30 July 1931 when he visited Russia to tour selected areas and talk to Joseph Stalin, general secretary of the Communist Party at the time. He had anticipated his shift in attitude in a 1930 preface to a new edition of *Fabian Essays in Socialism*, where he heralded the Russian revolution of 1917 as 'a most beneficent event in spite of the incidental horrors which attend all too long delayed revolutions.' He declared that

> the attempt at Liberal constitutional parliamentarism which followed had almost instantly broken down and been swept away and replaced by a ruthless dictatorship of men of action who were also doctrinaire Marxists. These were very soon convinced by their opponents that the establishment of Socialism must be effected not by discussion and vote, but by those who actively desired it killing those who actively objected to it. Which they accordingly proceeded to do, and be done by, with terrific energy. And, far from alienating popular sympathy, they found the country rising to this sort of leadership with … enthusiasm.[26]

Firmly rejecting the humanistic tenet that ends cannot justify means, Stalin's regime was marked by forced agricultural collectivization, hastily instituted industrialization, and brutal treatment of doctrinal rivals. The toll of the executed and imprisoned rose inexorably. Such repressive tactics reached their peak in the 1930s, when Shaw went there to observe the effects of the revolution first-hand. In spite of his awareness of some of these tactics, his wife reported to a friend on 5 August 1931 that he was evidently so enchanted with the Russian experiment that he said 'it all seems like a "splendid, sunny dream"' (letter to William Maxwell in Holroyd 3, 248).

On his return home Shaw described his ecstatic impressions at a meeting of the Independent Labour Party National Summer School, recorded in the *New Leader* on 7 August:

> I have been preaching Socialism all my political life and here at last is a country which has established Socialism, made it the basis of its political system, definitely thrown over private property, and turned its back on Capitalism … The first thing I discovered with great gratification is that the Socialism which has established itself is Fabian Socialism … The Fabians have turned out to be perfectly right … The other thing which I did say quite freely to his [Stalin's] intense and great amusement is that it is a definitely religious system … The whole institution is necessarily religious. It is not saying to the people, 'You will have enough to eat and a shorter working day,' but the people who are managing it are filled with a purely religious

impulse. An irreligious man is a man looking after himself ... A man who is religious is bored with himself and wants to make the world better, who is looking forward to a future better than the past, [who is] working for something greater and larger than himself. That is the essence of religion.

Then he turns to the dark side of the regime and tries to rationalize even the worst elements of the system:

Of course there is no capital punishment ... But ... there is shooting for political offences. If a man begins to sabotage, if he begins speculating, if he tries to take advantage of the system in any way to enrich himself, then that man disappears ... On all these points they are entirely ruthless ... There is no Parliament and no nonsense of that sort. There are bodies which do discuss policy, but when a job has to be done it is always by a dictator. That is, someone is made to do it on his own responsibility. If he goes wrong, he crashes.[27]

Shaw expressed the gist of his recommendation to consider Russia's example seriously in a letter of 8 January 1932 to Augustin Hamon: 'The secret of Stalin is that he is entirely opportunist as to *means*, discarding all doctrinaire limitations, and confident that Russia is big enough to achieve Socialism by itself independently of the capitalist world' (CL 4, 269).[28] On the same day, Beatrice Webb noted in her diary that Shaw seemed to 'hanker for some credo to be *enforced* from birth onwards on the whole population' (*Diary* 4, 249–50). Three years later she summed up what she viewed as his radical transformation:

As a young social reformer, he hated cruelty and oppression and pleaded for freedom. He idealized the rebel. Today he idealizes the dictator, whether he be a Mussolini, a Hitler or a Stalin ... He refuses to discriminate between one dictator and another ... He has no faith in science and very little in a 'peaceful penetration' of goodwill and science. It is the will to power over other mortals that is the creative element in human history. (*Diary* 4, 1 July 1935)

Her statement encompasses Shaw's most thorough and public explanation of his general attitude towards killing as a valid and desirable policy (mentioned as far back as the 1910s), his preface to *On the Rocks: A Political*

Comedy (CP 6, 573–628, dated 22 October 1933). Its recurring theme is 'extermination'; its positive thrust, of which Beatrice seemed unaware, is exemplified in his assertion that 'in the long run the power to exterminate is too grave to be left in any hands but those of a thoroughly Communist Government responsible to the whole community' (583). In due time, incidentally, the Webbs were converted to communism and wrote one of the most definitive studies of its then-current brand.

Unfortunately no letters are extant between Shaw and Murray which give any indication of the reaction of that humanistic Liberal. On 2 July 1932 Murray received a letter from Naomi Mitchison in which, as Wilson summarizes it, 'she described enthusiastically a visit to Soviet Russia, and said that she now realized what fifth-century Athens must have been like' (341), but again, there is no record of a reply. His son Stephen had reacted against his parents' political beliefs by joining the Communist Party along with his wife (Wilson, 342); and his grandson Philip Toynbee drew vitriol from Murray for the characters in his first novel: 'If the young Communists are like that, they are indescribably loathsome' (344). Perhaps what he would have told Shaw is suggested in a letter he wrote early in the Second World War to Francis Cornford, whose children had also joined the party:

> I think that the main thing underlying this Communist attitude in the young is discontent, first with their own prospects and secondly with the civilization which gave them such black prospects. Christopher [Cornford] thinks it ridiculous to expect the world to be reformed by high-minded Liberal intellectuals, but this is to underrate the slow indirect influence of thinkers, and to ignore the lesson of history that you cannot obtain justice by merely killing the people you think unjust. However, these are only truisms. The Bolshevik frame of mind is a symptom of the failure of civilization … I think it will be accompanied by a great recrudescence of superstition. (342)

From the mid-thirties up to 1940 Murray and Shaw were both deeply concerned about the seeming inevitability of another world war, especially since Murray was intensely involved in League of Nations business as chairman and then president of the League of Nations Union, while Shaw followed his urge to immerse the public in his pointedly 'fair' viewpoints on fascist leaders. In several letters Murray tries to involve Shaw in his organization's committees, especially the International Committee on Intellectual Cooperation (CIC), and is met with apologies. In 1929 the Malvern Festival was founded by Barry Jackson for the express purpose of performing Shaw's plays. Among the twenty presented from then until 1939 were the British premieres of *The Apple Cart, Too True to be Good, The Simpleton of the Unexpected Isles, Geneva,* and *In Good King Charles's Golden Days.* The two discussed most of these plays, but of special interest to Murray was *Geneva* (1938) because it crossed the boundary into his most struggling domain, the CIC. *Geneva* focuses critically on its flailing, but finally conveys that one of its key functions could be crucial if it were well administered in the real world: characters representing Mussolini, Franco, and Hitler (Bombardone, General Flanco, and Battler) are summoned by the CIC to submit to hearings before the International Court at The Hague. Murray remarked that he didn't think it was one of Shaw's best plays, but it did put the CIC in the centre of the picture despite being largely neglected by the British government. He was especially pleased that Shaw has the dictators comply with the imaginary summons, even though the tough defences they offer, following Shaw's credo of 'giving the devil his due,' had little appeal to him (see headnote to Letter 114). Later Shaw will tell him, 'The Intellectual Co-operation Committee is an imposing title; but it never meant anything but Gilbert Murray' (Letter 157).

In the 1940s Murray gratified Shaw by spending his few spare hours translating more Greek plays and soliciting comments from him. He worked on Sophocles' *Antigone* and the *The Trachiniae* (with the title *The Wife of Heracles*), as well as Aristophanes' *The Birds*; in between he turned to plays by Menander, *The Rape of the Locks* and *The Arbitration,* which prompted Shaw to analyse their prosody assiduously, even though he considered the earlier Greek plays far superior. In July 1947 Shaw commended Murray's artistry extravagantly, noting that he had just told the manager of the Malvern Festival Theatre that 'when the Festival is resumed next year he should produce Heracles, as yours is the only name and reputation that can give his program the dignity that Shakespeare gives to Stratford' (Letter 157). This did not happen, but the two were able to compare their observations on Gabriel Pascal's successors to the 'hit' film of *Pygmalion, Major Barbara,* and *Cæsar and Cleopatra,* with Murray crediting them as much as he could, and Shaw groping to see beyond the damage that Pascal had inflicted upon them.

Although their last years were largely harmonious, they maintained lifelong political convictions which sum up their variant and changing natures – Murray the Victorian Liberal, ever receding from his 'Radical' beginnings; Shaw the gradualistic Fabian, finally reborn as a full-fledged Stalinist, though not a member of the Communist Party. Among the last letters they wrote to each other are found passages that capsulize this theme. Murray's was prompted by reading Shaw's *Everybody's Political What's What?* in 1944:

> Our main difference is that I, on the whole, think the present or at least the pre-war English civilization about the best there has ever been and you think it almost the worst. But I agree with most of what you say about its absurdities, and particularly about the hopeless absurdity with which people use political terms like 'democracy'. 'freedom'. 'Fascism' 'capitalism' &c. (Letter 146)

Shaw's counter-statement did not emerge for five years, and of course it was much more fulsome than Murray's original. The following excerpts will allow him to have the final say:

> One of the differences between our retrospect of the nineteenth century is that you still accept the Whig view that it was a period of prosperity and happiness, hideously broken up by the wars of the twentieth. My outlook was much the same as yours until at the beginning of the 80ties Marx changed the mind of Europe and, for me, snatched the lid off hell ... The moment Marx got his knife into me, all this faded into an obsolete past; and I was henceforth hated by the Liberals whom I discarded as fossils, and, with Sidney Webb, made the old Socialism, with its Liberal barricaders, constitutional by Fabianism, which is now, by the way, Stalinism in Russia.
>
> The revolutionary change in my Anschauung makes what difference there is between you and me. You are pre-Marx in my estimate of the nineteenth century; but as you are not also pre-Plato or pre-Euripides, we get on pretty well together. (Letter 168)

They did.

NOTES

1 William Bruneau and Russell Wodell, '"Yours obediently, Gilbert Murray": Letters to *The Times*,' in Stray, ed., *Gilbert Murray Reassessed*, 319.
2 Note, however, that Wilson unexpectedly died in 1983, 'leaving a fully annotated manuscript of Murray's life until 1930,' which his wife Elizabeth completed through 1957 with the help of several people ('Preface,' ix).
3 Letter of 10 February 1905 in Laurence, ed., *Bernard Shaw: Collected Letters* (henceforth CL), vol. 2, 511.
4 Whitebrook, *William Archer*, 185.
5 'A Few Memories,' 7.
6 In a letter of 28 March 1895 to Charles Charrington, Archer said: 'I have read Carlyon Sahib & am exceedingly interested in it – so much so that if you can possibly put me in communication with the author I should like to write him in detail about it, or still better to see him. The play is really a great thing in its way, but I should be exceedingly sorry to see it done in its present form, because it would be a fine thing thrown away ... It is the most original and powerful play I have ever come across in manuscript, to my recollection, and I should very much like to see it brought to perfection.' Murray recalled it in 1954 as 'a modern study of an utterly unscrupulous dictator, somewhat like those whom we have seen since, but decidedly less unattractive' ('Friendships at Cambridge,' *The Listener*, 51, no. 1306 [11 March 1954]: 7).
7 On 16 July 1895, Shaw's diary prompted him: 'Archer's at 14½ to meet Murray and discuss his play' (*Diary, 1885–1897*, 1087). Murray had a very different connection to the Independent Theatre Society than Shaw did as one of its first members in 1891. It is curious that they had not already met – or perhaps they had. Later, Murray also became a member of the Stage Society, along with Shaw, at its first meeting on 19 July 1899.
8 Achurch to Murray, 4 February 1895 (Lathem Papers).
9 For other illuminating angles on the topic, see Hugo's 'Britons, Boers, and Blacks' and Pugh's 'Bernard Shaw, Imperialist.'
10 A thorough and penetrating analysis of this collaboration is Albert's '"In More Ways than One": *Major Barbara*'s Debt to Gilbert Murray.' If Cusins was actually named after Gustavus Adolphus, king of Sweden, as Holroyd speculates, Albert missed a rich allusion: the king was a 'brilliant linguist who subsequently mastered the art of war' (2, 107).
11 Shaw had, in fact, begun railing against this policy as far back as 1886, when the Lord Chamberlain's office forbade the Shelley Society from presenting *The Cenci* (*Our Corner*, August 1886). In his 'Appendix' to the

1891 *Quintessence of Ibsenism* Shaw asserted, 'What is wanted is the entire abolition of the censorship and the establishment of Free Art in the sense in which we speak of Free Trade' (*Shaw on Theatre*, 11). The subject comes up again and again in his *Saturday Review* essays, most notably in his lengthy memoir of E.F. Smyth Pigott, for twenty years the examiner of stage plays ('The Late Censor,' 2 March 1895). After *Mrs Warren's Profession* was refused a licence in 1898 by the new examiner, G.A. Redford, he published a major essay, 'The Censorship of the Stage in England,' in the *North American Review* 169 (August 1899): 251–62; repr. in *Shaw on Theatre*, 66–80).

12 Laurence, CL 1, 228.

13 *Major Critical Essays*, 174. Charles A. Berst amplifies this point in 'In the Beginning: The Poetic Genesis of Shaw's God.'

14 *The Religious Speeches of Bernard Shaw*, 6, 18–19, 35. For the development of Shaw's concept of Creative Evolution through *Back to Methuselah* and later see Leary, '*Too True to be Good* and Shaw's Romantic Synthesis,' and Baker, *Bernard Shaw's Remarkable Religion.*

15 Letter of 10 February 1931 to Lionel Curtis.

16 'The Stoic Philosophy,' the Moncure Conway Memorial Lecture, delivered 16 March 1915, repr. in *Essays & Addresses*, 89–106.

17 In *Shaw and Society*, 62–3.

18 'Professor Gilbert Murray's Defence of Sir Edward Grey.'

19 *Missing Persons*, 28.

20 *Memories*, 110.

21 Leader-writer of *The Star* reporting on the meeting of the British Association for the Advancement of Science at Bath on 7 September 1888, repr. in Shaw, *Platform and Pulpit*, ix.

22 Shaw, *Everybody's Political What's What?* 49.

23 Joad, *Shaw*, 30–1.

24 'Shaw the Court Jester,' from the 1956 *Observer*, repr. in his *Politicians, Socialism and Historians* (London: Hamish Hamilton, 1980), 131.

25 From the typescript of Shaw's replies to a questionnaire on *The Apple Cart* from the theatre correspondent of the *Observer*, G.W. Bishop, published 23 March 1930 (Cornell, not yet classified).

26 'Forty Years Later,' repr. in CPr 3, 93–4, 91.

27 Speech to the Independent Labour Party National Summer School ('"We Want a Five-Year Plan Here"'). A British engineer who had worked in Soviet Russia had written in the *Daily Express* in June 1932 that (as Shaw puts it) what he had seen was 'not the real Russia, but an elaborate show staged for my special benefit.' Shaw responded with a detailed picture of the various places and situations he had seen, none of which could have

been indicative of a staged show (Shaw, *Agitations*, 286–9). When Shaw was visiting South Africa with Charlotte in the first months of 1932, he began writing a book based on his deductions of the Russian experiment after his visit. The manuscript was abandoned before they returned, but he had sent sections of it to his secretary to be typed. The typescript, over 100 pages, was edited by Harry M. Geduld and published in 1964 with the title Shaw gave it, *The Rationalization of Russia*. After painting the self-seeking arch-capitalist as the scourge of most modern political systems, he addresses the issue of exterminating the unredeemable bourgeoisie at length, culminating his argument with: 'The plain truth is that all civilized governments exact minimum standards of conduct which they enforce by killing the people who do not attain them. Our question is not to kill or not to kill, but how to select the right people to kill ... Russia, in exterminating a particular sort of undesirable for the good of the rest is doing precisely what we are doing and always have been doing; and ... the essential difference between the Russian liquidator with his pistol ... and the British hangman is that they do not operate on the same sort of person' (112–13).

28 In *Shaw's Controversial Socialism*, James Alexander presents a balanced view of this problematic issue, which he considers the 'crux' of his book's argument: 'There was no shift in the structure of Shaw's thought, or even in his purposes: what there was was an extension of the range of political possibilities he was willing to consider. And this extension was a consequence of the war of 1914–18 and the Revolution of 1917. And the change was that where, earlier, Shaw had tended to distinguish Socialism from both Liberalism and Marxism, now he tacitly accepted that his Socialism, or Fabian Socialism, had no independent entity. He spoke about Socialism as if it were not one doctrine, or belief, or movement, but two – or two-in-one. One was Marxist, one Liberal; one revolutionary, one reformist' (207–8).

Editor's Note

Of the 85 letters from Shaw included in this volume, only 30 are printed in Dan H. Laurence's four-volume selective edition of the *Collected Letters.* Laurence denotes where he discovered the originals of these letters; but some of those locations changed over the years – notably the letters transcribed from the British Drama League, later renamed the British Theatre Association. That folded in 1990, and although it would be difficult to ascertain which institutions assimilated their substantial holdings, it is virtually positive that all their letters from Shaw to Gilbert Murray were placed in the Bodleian Library of Oxford University.

The large majority of the 86 letters from Murray to Shaw are in the British Library, formerly the British Museum. Others to either correspondent are scattered at the Harry Ransom Center of the University of Texas at Austin, the University of Guelph, Bucknell University (one), and Cornell University (one, uncatalogued). Curators of several Shaw repositories examined their holdings at my request and reported that they had no original Shaw / Murray letters: the Berg Collection at the New York Public Library, the Archibald Henderson Collection at the University of North Carolina, the Richard S. Weiner Collection at Colgate University, the Sidney P. Albert Collection at Brown University, the London School of Economics, the National Library of Ireland, the Victoria and Albert Museum, and the special theatre collections at Harvard, Yale, and Princeton. The Bernard Shaw Collection at the University of Delaware has a complete list of letter recipients on its website, and Murray is not one of them.

Many years ago a professor / librarian at Dartmouth College, Edward Connery Lathem, amassed a nearly complete set of transcriptions of Shaw / Murray correspondence for the University of Toronto Press series. He eventually decided not to adhere to the standard format of the series, then unfortunately died before completing a planned edition for another distributor. The set of transcriptions was passed on to me, partly from the copies of letters and notes from 1897 to 1905 that he had sent to the general editor of the series, and the rest (with no notes accompanying them) from the Lathem Papers collection at the Dartmouth College Library. Since these copies gave no indication of the original source but seemed to be transcribed (and proofread) quite accurately, I have printed the very few whose sources I could not discover and indicated the source as 'ECL,' which denotes the Lathem Papers. These are a postcard from Shaw to Murray ('or Lady Murray') on 23 February 1914, a letter from Shaw to Murray on 7 February 1934, and a letter from Murray to Shaw on 13 January 1942. Despite extensive efforts I failed to trace the current owners of these letters. If anyone can inform us of their locations please contact the University of Toronto Press.

Most everyone who consults this volume will be familiar with Shaw's self-styled spelling, which ranges from omitting the 'u' from 'labour,' 'neighbour,' 'armour,' and the like to eliminating apostrophes in contractions (such as 'hadnt') when it will not affect the meaning. (His more radical changes such as 'shew' for 'show' and 'Shakespear' for 'Shakespeare' may first strike one as typos.) These usages have been retained except when the original letters were inaccessible or printed copies altered them. Typographical errors have generally been corrected to avoid frequent occurrences of the editorial '[*sic*],' which is reserved to mean 'Yes, this is what he actually wrote' (e.g., Murray's habitual misspellings of 'Cusins' as 'Cusens').

In line with previous volumes in this series, the letters are numbered consecutively and arranged chronologically. Each letter begins with its number and either **To Gilbert Murray** or **To G. Bernard Shaw**. Headnotes introduce and describe the context where necessary and on occasion supply narrative links to fill significant gaps between the letters of these intimate friends. (The most regrettable of these is the twenty-seven-month hiatus after their sharp dispute over Great Britain getting into the First World War; it seems unquestionable that the exchanges must have continued, but they are either not extant or have not been located.) Following the letters, when necessary and possible, are notes that identify individuals mentioned and clarify references and allusions, with the subject of each annotation in bold type. The addresses of the two men and the dates of their letters have been standardized. No addresses are lacking, and the few missing dates are signalled by a conjectured date in brackets.

Acknowledgments

This section must begin by acknowledging the elder statesman of Shaw / Murray studies, the late Sidney P. Albert, Professor Emeritus of Philosophy, California State University at Los Angeles, whose first and most illuminating article on the specific subject, '"In More Ways than One": *Major Barbara*'s Debt to Gilbert Murray,' appeared in the *Educational Theatre Journal* in 1968, and whose culminating study of the play, *Shaw, Plato, and Euripides: Classical Currents in Major Barbara,* was published last year in the University Press of Florida's Bernard Shaw series. Learning that I had committed myself to edit this volume, he wrote the cautionary letter which I quote at the beginning of the Introduction, and promised all the assistance he could muster in his declining years (he died in 2013 just short of 99). However, he poured all his remaining energy into completing his own superb book rather than ferreting out material that might be useful to me. His sons Alan and Larry examined his personal collection of Shaw / Murray letters, and his assistant, Nettie Coleman, scanned them and sent copies to me. I especially appreciated her help.

Every Shavian, in one way or another, is deeply indebted to the late Dan H. Laurence, indefatigable editor of the four-volume *Collected Letters* and the two-volume *Bernard Shaw: A Bibliography* in the distinguished 'Soho Bibliographies' series. His wide-ranging but cogent headnotes in the *Letters* were an especially rich source of vital information. *Journey to Heartbreak: The Crucible Years of Bernard Shaw 1914–1918,* by the equally indefatigable Stanley Weintraub, yielded a wealth of information and quotations from obscure articles that I could not find elsewhere. I also found A.M. Gibbs's *A Bernard Shaw Chronology* indispensable.

In the early stages of this project I learned that the Rare Books and Manuscripts department of Colgate University's Case Library held many photoduplicates of letters from Shaw to Murray and I requested them. Carl Peterson sent me a full set free of charge (even for postage), and commented that he had done the same for several other people working on volumes in this series. Later I contacted Francesca Livermore in the same department to make sure that the letters were all from the Bodleian Library. Despite her efforts, she could not locate records that would show this, but luckily, I had made a friend of the curator of Shaw's Corner in Ayot St Lawrence, Susan Morgan, and she kindly went to the Bodleian and verified that all of them were held there. I am greatly indebted to these generous individuals.

Michel Pharand, author of *Bernard Shaw and the French*, provided me with an accurate translation of *Sur la pierre blanche*, a novel by Anatole France which Shaw had quoted (from the English translation) on 5 November 1914. He also assisted me in tackling several difficult problems with footnotes that resisted clarification. Bernard F. Dukore, author of many books on Shaw and a great friend, examined my introduction critically, leading to several revisions, and once again incurred my gratitude. Brad Kent, a young professor at l'Université Laval, sent me a document from his current research that recorded the debate among officials after G.A. Redford, Examiner of Plays, recommended that Murray's translation of *Oedipus Rex* be banned from staging. After an exchange of letters in November 1910, his decision was overruled. The most fascinating response to information that I requested came from Andrew Etherington, once a food-service consultant at Whiteley Village, a retirement community in Surrey, about which Shaw had made derisive statements in Letter 168. Consulting his long-term memories, he convincingly refuted most of Shaw's condemning 'facts.'

Permission to publish Bernard Shaw's letters was granted by The Society of Authors, specifically Head of Literary Estates Jeremy Crow, acting for the Estate of Bernard Shaw. Permission to publish Gilbert Murray's letters was freely granted by Alexander Murray, his grandson and literary executor of the Gilbert Murray papers. Permission to publish several letters held by the Harry Ransom Center at the University of Texas was also granted, as were the single letters held by Cornell University (Bernard F. Burgunder Collection of George Bernard Shaw, #4617. Division of Rare and Manuscript Collections, Cornell University Library), and Bucknell

University (Bertrand Library, Special Collections / University Archives, George Bernard Shaw Collection MS70).

Thanks go also to Richard Ratzlaff and Barbara Porter at University of Toronto Press, as well as copyeditor John St James. Thanks too to the two anonymous readers who read the manuscript on behalf of the Press.

Of the many specialist librarians who assisted me in one way or another, the following were helpful:

Binghamton University Library: the Interlibrary Loan Department, Jesslynn Shafer, Director

Bodleian Library: Colin Harris, Curator of Special Collections and Western Manuscripts; Helen Gilio and Samantha Townsend, Imaging Services; and Amanda Flynn, Customer Services

British Library: Jamie Andrews, Head of Modern Literary Manuscripts; Zoe Stansell, Manuscript Reference Service; and Imaging Services personnel

Brown University Library: Tim Engels, Senior Library Specialist: Scholarly Resources: Manuscripts

Bucknell University Library, Isabella O'Neill, Curator, Special Collections / University Archives

Colgate University, Everett Needham Case Library: Carl Peterson, Head of Special Collections and University Archivist, and Francesca Livermore, Rare Books and Manuscripts

Cornell University, Carl A. Kroch Library: Katherine Reagan, Rare Books and Bernard F. Burgunder Shaw collection, and Ana Guimares, Head of Reference Services, Division of Rare and Manuscript Collections

Dartmouth College Library: Peter Carini, Rauner Special Collections Librarian, and Jay Satterfield, Special Collections Librarian

Guelph University, Archival and Special Collections, including the Dan H. Laurence Collection of Shaviana; staff members preferred to be left unnamed

University of Texas at Austin, Harry Ransom Center: Richard Workman, Associate Librarian; Rick Watson, Head of Reference Services; and Emily Roehl, Manuscripts

My own reference collection, with Binghamton University's book and periodical collection and Cornell's vast holdings, were my chief sources of background information – along with *Wikipedia*, of course.

I must express a huge debt to the late Edward Connery Lathem, whose labours beginning in the 1980s I was able to draw upon with great profit to the undertaking and great relief to my schedule and pocketbook. I hope that he would have considered the product of the gift he inadvertently gave me was worthy of his efforts.

On the personal level, I am most indebted to Leonard W. Conolly, general editor of the *Selected Correspondence* series, who had enough confidence in the remnants of an octogenarian's scholarly abilities to offer me the project. I was finishing another daunting task at the time, a huge secondary bibliography of the dramatic writings of Samuel Beckett, which ended up taking much longer than anticipated and therefore delayed work on this volume. As I began to send him the pages I had finished he was perceptive, encouraging, and helpful, consummate editor that he has always been.

A relevant truth is that I had ulterior motives which made me welcome what was to me a brand new type of scholarship that became more and more engrossing as I proceeded: my wonderful second wife had died in 2009, and I craved more all-diverting busywork to plunge into after the Beckett bibliography was completed. Thus, albeit indirectly, this volume owes a great deal to my beloved Martha.

Abbreviations

Type of correspondence

ALCS	Autograph letter-card signed
ALS	Autograph letter signed
ALU	Autograph letter unsigned
APCS	Autograph postcard signed
TEL	Telegram
TLS	Typed letter signed
TLT	Typed letter, typed signature
TLU	Typed letter unsigned

Sources of the correspondence

BL	British Library (Department of Manuscripts)
Bod	Bodleian Library, Oxford University (Department of Special Collections and Western Manuscripts)
Bucknell	Bucknell University Library (Special Collections / University Archives of The Ellen Clarke Bertrand Library)
CL	*Collected Letters*, 4 vols, ed. Dan H. Laurence
CP	*Collected Plays with Their Prefaces*, 7 vols, ed. Dan H. Laurence
CPr	*Complete Prefaces*, 3 vols, ed. Dan H. Laurence and Daniel J. Leary
Col	Colgate University (Rare Books and Manuscripts, Case Library)
Cornell	Cornell University (Bernard F. Burgunder Collection,

	Division of Rare and Manuscript Collection, Carl E. Kroch Library)
ECL	Edward Connery Lathem (personal collection of transcripts)
Guelph	University of Guelph, McLaughlin Library (Archival and Special Collections; Dan H. Laurence collection)
HRC	Harry Ransom Humanities Research Center, University of Texas at Austin
SPA	Sidney P. Albert (personal collection of transcripts)

Letters

1 / To Gilbert Murray Pitfold, Haslemere
19th September 1898

[ALS: CL 2]

Shaw, newly married to Charlotte Payne-Townshend on 1 June 1898, had moved with her nine days later to a house at Pitfold, near Haslemere and Grayshott in Surrey. He was recuperating from a bone infection in his left foot, finishing The Perfect Wagnerite, *and writing* Cæsar and Cleopatra *in the months before the following letter. In October the Shaws moved to a larger house near Hindhead, 'Blen-Cathra.' Murray's early impression of Charlotte, disclosed in a letter of 6 July, is revealing of all three people: 'I like his wife decidedly: she corrects & even contradicts his statements when necessary, & he bears the process with respect & patience; at the same time she has an undisguised belief in his towering genius and wisdom. This combination seems to me to show the proper spirit in a wife. She also wants him to sit still and write the great work – philosophica.' (Bod).*

Meanwhile, Shaw's Plays Pleasant and Unpleasant *had been published on 19 April. Before that date Murray had received a pre-publication copy from William Archer, and he commented on them briefly in two letters of 16 April to his wife, Lady Mary (Bod). In the first, he noted 'Very interesting, though not good plays'; in the second, he characterized* Mrs Warren's Profession *as 'Very original & powerful, though cold, hard and "unpleasant,"' adding in Greek what the 'profession' is.*

In the British general election of 1895, the Tories had soundly trounced the Liberal party, which had advocated the widespread adoption of a 'Local Option' to address the controversial 'Drink Question.' The House of Commons had passed a Local Option Resolution in 1888, granting 'a legal power of restraining the issue or renewal of Licences for the Sale of Intoxicating Liquors' to 'the persons most deeply interested and affected, namely, the inhabitants themselves' (House of Commons debate of 27 April). In 1898 the village of Grayshott lacked a public house and exercised the option to establish one before a private interest could do so. Shaw had written to Lady Mary Murray on 1 September 1898 setting forth his views on the Drink Question as it bore on the Local Option. After urging her to relax her 'moral attitude,' he added: 'I throw myself on the Professor for support' (CL 2, 59–61). Her husband wrote to Shaw at length (the letter is apparently not preserved), instituting their long-lasting correspondence. It evoked the following reply from Shaw.

My dear Murray

I must say a word on your long letter in reply to mine, for which I am much indebted to you, as I want to get pulled over the subject by somebody. The point on which the facts strike me quite differently to you, is your estimate of the political force of Teetotalism – or let us say Local Optionism. At the last general election the Liberal party, which had survived Home Rule, was practically wiped out by Local Option. The result was quite unprecedented: nothing worse could have happened to a government which had lost a Sedan. Since then, I have never dreamt of counting Local Option as a live political factor. It seemed obvious that the Liberals must drop Local Option, and that they must drop the Drink Question altogether unless they could hit on some acceptable form of Drink Legislation. I confess I am altogether taken aback by your contention that Local Option must be accepted because the voters are determined to have it, rightly or wrongly. My view of the situation is that it must be abandoned because the voters are determined to have none of it, wrongly or rightly, and have, in fact, already voted in that sense, with unparrallelled (never could spell it) unanimity. This leaves us staring at one another, wondering which of us is politically blind. And there, for the present, I stick.

As to Grayshott, your handsome concession encourages me to sit on your head to the extent of urging that except in the few cases where a village is wholly owned by a teetotal despot, the case must always arise as a choice between a tied house and an untied one. The alternative of having no pub at all does not present itself.

We have just heard from Archer, who has returned from his travels, and will come to Pitfold with brother Charles on some day to be fixed hereafter.

I am sorry to hear that Tilford is not agreeing with you. Is country air, then, a fraud like all the other things? Why not try vegetarianism? It will amuse you for a while, anyhow.

yrs sincerely,
G. Bernard Shaw

Shaw's statement that 'nothing worse could happen to a government which had lost a **Sedan**' refers to the government of Emperor Napoleon III during the Battle of Sedan (France) on 1 September 1870, which decided the Franco-Prussian war in favour of Prussia and its allies and ended the emperor's reign. His capture also ended the Second French Empire, the last monarchy in France. Shaw mentions the event in a letter of 22 August 1919 to Siegfried Trebitsch (1869–1956), his German translator (CL 3, 632). A **tied** house is a pub owned by a brewery, and thus 'tied' to selling only its own alcoholic beverages; the opposite, a non-tied pub, is also called a free house. William **Archer** (1856–1924) was a prominent drama critic, translator of the plays of Henrik Ibsen (1828–1906), and close friend of both Ibsen and Shaw, though contentious to Shaw about dramatic and moral issues. His **brother Charles** (1861–1941) became his biographer in 1931. By February 1904 Shaw had become, as he put it, 'proprietor of the Fox & Pelican, **Grayshott**' (see Letter 20 below; by '**proprietor**' he means that he invested in the pub). **Tilford** is a scenic village near Farnham, not far from Haslemere. Of interest is a much later essay giving Shaw's reaction to America's prohibition of alcohol in January 1920, 'The Drink Question,' first published in *SHAW* 22 (2002): 185–92.

2 / To Gilbert Murray

Blackdown Cottage, near Haslemere, Surrey
28th July 1900

[ALS: CL 2]

Shaw had worked on Cæsar and Cleopatra *through much of 1898, with his idea of 'the classic actor,' Johnston Forbes-Robertson, in mind for his portrait of 'the greatest man that ever lived' (letter of 3 May 1899 to Richard Mansfield, CL 2, 90). On 11 February 1899, Charlotte wrote to Lady Mary Murray, 'Since "Cæsar & Cleopatra" was sent off to Mr. Forbes Robertson (about a fortnight ago) my husband has taken a real rest – the first since I have known him – ! & I really think it has made a difference' (Bod).*

The next year Shaw was readying the play for publication in the volume to be named Three Plays for Puritans. *He sent Gilbert Murray a copy and asked him – as Murray told Archer in late May – 'to see if there are any classical howlers.' His reply to Shaw's appeal apparently is not extant, but the manuscript of the play in the British Library contains a number of revisions, some of which are quite probably the result of Murray's critical perusal (Lathem Papers). Fortunately for us, in two letters to Archer he expressed his reaction to what Shaw had sent him. In one he noted that he had not found many 'howlers': 'There are very few that I can detect – except the obvious things – topical allusions to Cyprus & New Women &c – which he is proud of' (letter of 6 June 1900).*

In his second letter to Archer, Murray also summed up his opinion of the play: 'I think C & C rather a magnificent thing in its way, but of course desperately guyed and with its flashes of insight marred by somewhat pedantic details on the one hand and large historical misconceptions on the other.' (By 'desperately guyed' Murray may refer to striking instances of Caesar's self-debunking qualities that provoke laughter at his expense, such as his repeated inability to pronounce 'Ftatateeta'; the various platitudes of Britannus that cast ridicule upon his homeland; and the like.) Archer, in the Daily Chronicle *of 16 January 1900, will pronounce the play 'full of wit, whim, satire, penetration, flippancy, ingenuity, perversity, sophistry, sense and nonsense.' Such 'mixed' reviews, inviting 'as-you-like-it' responses, will remain typical of the already-famous critic. But he also told Murray that there was 'an amazing cleverness' in the play (Whitebrook, 207).*

Shaw had modelled his image of Caesar ([Caius] Julius, 102?–44 BC) from Theodor Mommsen's greatly respected History of Rome *(1854–6) rather than from ancient sources. On 13 April 1906 he wrote Siegfried Trebitsch, 'my Cæsar is Mommsen's Caesar dramatized' (CL 2, 616). Later he was even more explicit when he told Hesketh Pearson that Mommsen 'had conceived Caesar as I wished to present him'* (G.B.S., *208). Mommsen sums up Caesar's character and contributions as the finale to his book, 586–8.*

Shaw wrote the letter that follows from 'Blackdown Cottage,' near Haslemere, where he and Charlotte were spending part of the summer. He had become a member of the Vestry of the Parish of St Pancras, later the St Pancras Metropolitan Borough Council, in May 1897.

Dear Murray

Where are you at present? I shall soon submit to you a few notes which I propose to append to Cæsar & Cleopatra.

My vestry is in recess; and I shall have a clean run down here for a few weeks now, though I have to go up for a Housing Conference on Monday & Tuesday.

I have carefully considered your comments on my history, and have modified accordingly. I am not quite convinced that I have overdone Cleopatra's ferocity. If she had been an educated lady of the time I should have made her quite respectable & civilized; but what I was able to gather about her father, the convivial Flute Blower, and other members of the household, joined with considerations of the petulance of royalty, led me to draw her as I did. I submit to you that if a dramatist, 2000 years hence, were to portray George IV as an ideal First Gentleman of Europe, with all the culture of his age upon him, he would miss his mark very considerably.

I also demur to your dictum that we have enough information about the ancient Britons to shew that they were not like Britannicus. In every line that I have come across concerning them I see Mr Podsnap. Surely, if they are like Britannicus now, after such romantic adulterations as the Roman & Norman invasions & conquests, how much more like him must they have been then, when they were the pure products of the climate? I am quite serious.

Further, I suggest that in the Gallic Wars, the style is not the man – at least, not the whole man. As a writer, Caesar was an amateur, and could not have achieved complete self expression in letters even if he had lived now, when literature is no longer the game of style it was to Cicero's pals. If the dramatic stories about him are true, such as the burning of the letters after the final defeat of Cato, & the encounter with the mutinous legion – 'Comrades: what do you want?' 'Our discharge.' '*Citizens*: you have it. Sorry you will not be able to share my triumph &c' & so on, not to mention his personal address in getting round people of all sorts & sizes, he *must* have been an adroit comedian. Now the style-man of the Gallic Wars is not a comedian; but neither is he a dandy; and Caesar *was* a dandy. And I cannot conceive a great man as a grave man: to lack humor is to lack the universal solvent. If my Cæsar *can* be guyed, he is a failure. But I believe him to be authentic to the last comma.

yrs ever
G. Bernard Shaw

The **Housing Conference**, sponsored by the Sanitary Institute on 30–31 July, dealt with the housing of the working classes. As usual, Shaw took part in the discussion (*The Times*, 31 July, 2; 1 August, 6). **Cleopatra** (69–30 BC) became queen of Egypt at 19 with the help of Caesar, and later became his mistress before Mark Antony came along. The **Flute Blower** was Ptolemy XII, king of Egypt. He was dubbed 'Auletes' – Greek for flute-blower – because he neglected his duties by spending hours at that activity. **George IV**, King of England from 1820 to 1830, was derided for his extravagant and dissolute way of life. **Mr Podsnap** is a rich, pompous character in *Our Mutual Friend* by Charles Dickens (1812–70). **Cicero** (Marcus Tullius Cicero, or Tully, 106–41 BC) was a great Roman orator whose Latin prose is highly commended. **Cato** (Marcus Porcius Cato, known as Cato the Younger, 95–46 BC) was a Roman statesman with a reputation for incorruptibility who opposed Caesar and supported Pompey. When Caesar had clearly gained power, Cato committed suicide. Shaw's recollection of Caesar's **burning the letters** derives from Pliny: 'When Caesar had taken Pompey's files he did not read nor make copies of the pirate letters which showed their good will toward Pompey or their displeasure with Caesar. In a good deed, he soon burnt them all lest from the letters he should be compelled to act too severely against any man' (from http://swartzentrover.com / cotor / E-Books / christ / ussher / ussher_age61.htm).

The character nicknamed **Britannicus** is a slave from Britain who serves as Caesar's private secretary until he is freed at the finale. When the real Caesar was preparing to embark from Campania, Italy, on a demanding African expedition in 46 BC, he faced a **mutinous**

legion of exhausted trooops. Shaw's invented dramatic dialogue is based directly on a description in Mommsen's *History of Rome,* 466–7, including the humiliating substitution of 'citizens' for the expected 'comrades.' But nothing in Mommsen clearly suggests that Caesar could be characterized as a **dandy**. In the late eighteen nineties, the waning heyday of dandyism, a person described as such would evoke an overdressed and effeminate but self-possessed male who parades his nonchalance and artistic sensitivity.

3 / To G. Bernard Shaw

Churt
30th July 1900

[TLT: BL, SPA]

The play Murray was working on for Mrs Patrick Campbell (1865–1940), a notable actress whom Shaw romanced several years later, was a comedy entitled Mithia, *which was never performed. The chief character is a British journalist covering the Cretan revolt against the Turks in 1897. In a letter of September 1900 to Murray, Campbell commented that she found the journalist 'shadowy' and the play 'a little boneless' (Wilson, 83–4).*

My dear Shaw

I am here, and shall be for ever. I should like much to see the historical notes. You make a good defence at all points of my attack, especially about Caesar. I own I dont understand him, and your reading may be the right one. Still the impression he made on a very clever and sensitive man like Cicero goes for a good deal. Cicero, if I remember right, does not say anything about his wit, but is amazed at his 'inhuman' power of work and attention to business, and at the inferiority of his followers. He did not invent the sarcasm of calling the soldiers 'Citizens.' It was vieux jeu. If I thought great men were like your Caesar, I should like them better. I do not know if any Great Man has ever been generous or frank; Napoleon, Frederic, Cromwell & Co seem to me to be essentially mean and untruthful – like Chamberlain only vastly more so.

As to Cleopatra, do not you think you ought at any rate to represent a highly civilised court and society surrounding her, even if she personally was a savage? I dont think, however, that she could conceivably have thought that Romans had trunks and many arms. Roman merchants and sailors were very common in Alexandria and elsewhere in Egypt; her dancing masters and tutors and many of her slaves would probably have been in Rome. However …

As to Britannicus, he is a sweet creature, and I would not have him different.

I am doing a new play; a comedy for Mrs Pat, and working very hard. There is some Cretan business in it, I regret to say, which is rather like an imitation of Capt Brassbound; the people get imprisoned in a castle. However I hope it is not indecently like, and in any case it is only one incident in the first Act.

Yours very sincerely,
G G A M

I hope you can come over some time. I would come over to you only I am working all day till evening, and am then too tired for long cycling.

Churt, where Murray says he **shall be for ever**, is an ancient village in western Surrey, like Tilford close to Farnham. In January 1899 he and Lady Mary moved into an estate named 'Barford' in that town. **Vieux jeu** (French) means old-fashioned. Of the triad of 'mean and untruthful' great men that Murray mentions only **Frederic** might seem obscure, but almost certainly he means the extremely notable Frederick the Great (1712–86), king of Prussia, whose name is spelled 'Frederic' in some biographies (and of course 'Friedrich' in others). Joseph **Chamberlain** (1836–1914), colonial secretary at this time, was an avid imperialist skilled at Byzantine plots to claim land for England and for evasions of blame for some of his more questionable activities. '**Capt Brassbound**' is short for Shaw's play *Captain Brassbound's Conversion.* Murray often used the signature '**G G A M**' (George Gilbert Aimé Murray), though only four times in his extant letters to Shaw.

4 / To Gilbert Murray

Pitfold, Haslemere
5th October 1900

[ALS: CL 2]

Shaw had returned to work on Three Plays for Puritans, *and appealed to Murray for specific assistance on a passage in his 'Notes to Cæsar and Cleopatra.'*

Dear Murray

If you are at Barford, will you fill in on p 206 of the enclosed proof suitable names from the Ist book (I think it is) of Plato's Republic. Also, if you have Darwin's works, will you correct the title of the Beagle book on p 208 if I have got it inaccurately.

I am bookless here; and the neighbors have nothing but sermons & novels.

G.B.S.

The names that Murray evidently supplied appear in Shaw's statement that Shakespeare refrained from 'playing the literary man' and making Quince say, 'not "Is all our company here?" but "Bottom: was not that Socrates that passed us at the Piraeus with Glaucon and Polemarchus on his way to the house of Kephalus?"' ('Notes to *Cæsar and Cleopatra*,' CP 2, 299). The first paragraph of Socrates' narration in Book I of Plato's *Republic* begins, 'I went down to the Piraeus yesterday with Glaucon,' and later mentions that 'Polemarchus, the son of Cephalus, saw us from a distance.' Piraeus was a harbour near Athens; Glaucon was Plato's older brother and one of the chief interlocutors of Socrates. Cephalus (or Kephalus) was a wealthy Athenian; Polemarchus was one of his three sons. Murray did not correct the title that Shaw gave to the **Beagle book**, 'Voyage of a Naturalist Round the World' (301); the correct title is *A Naturalist's Voyage Round the World.*

5 / To G. Bernard Shaw

Churt
22nd December 1900

[TLT: BL, SPA]

The latest of Shaw's 'plays for Puritans,' Captain Brassbound's Conversion, *was performed by the Stage Society at the Strand Theatre on 16 December and the Criterion Theatre four days later, the day Murray attended. The 'producer' (equivalent of 'director' in America) was Charles Charrington (ca. 1860–1926); Lady Cicely Waynflete was played by his wife Janet Achurch (1864–1916, 'Mrs Ch' in the letter). The established actor Laurence Irving (1871–1914) played the male lead, Captain Brassbound; Harley Granville Barker (1877–1946; hereafter Barker), 23 at the time, took the lesser role of Captain Kearney.*

My dear Shaw

This is just a line to say that I saw Capt Brassbound on Thursday, and thought it even better than I had before. It struck me, by the way, as curiously like what I had thought it. Generally a play acted seems quite different from the same play read. This seemed just the same only rather stronger. Laurence Irving I do not praise (as St Paul puts it). But Barker was excellent, and so was Mrs Ch. She was so tactful and intelligent.

Why do you not write a volume of Sermons, perfectly straightforward and religious? They would sell, because if you wrote frankly everybody would think you were jesting; and they would be good metaphysical literature. Also, I have wished for a long time to read a volume of sermons, and have never been able to do so yet.

Yours sincerely,
G G A M

St Paul's admonition '**I do not praise** you' occurs in 1st Corinthians 11: 17–22. He applies it to permitting factions in churches and undisciplined eating habits. The passage begins, 'Now in giving these instructions I do not praise you, since you come together not for the better but for the worse.' Murray's use of the phrase is casual, but recalling its origin may have prompted the rather idle notion in the second paragraph.

6 / To G. Bernard Shaw

Churt
25th January 1901

[ALS: BL, SPA]

Murray had received the volume Three Plays for Puritans, *which was published on 15 January, and reviewed it in a popular magazine,* The Speaker. *By the end of 1897 he had completed his first modernized version of a drama by Euripides (480 or 485–406 BC),* Andromache, *but had so far failed to get it produced. The 'arrangements' progressed properly this time, however, and it would finally be performed by the Stage Society in late February. Meanwhile, he and Mary had acquired a new home in Churt called 'Barford.'*

Murray had been scheduled to lecture at Newnham College, Cambridge University, on 26 January, but Queen Victoria's death on the 22nd caused it to be postponed until 9 February. It was an introduction to and reading of excerpts from his translation of Euripides' Hippolytus, *soon to be published. Archer had written him on 12 November 1900, 'I am confirmed in my original impression that this is the best – most readable, comprehensible and delightful – rendering of a Greek play I ever came across' (C. Archer,* William Archer, *265). The mathematician/philosopher/activist Bertrand Russell (1872–1970) proclaimed the reading 'a wonderful experience, & one which I have found almost overwhelming' (letter of 26 February 1901, quoted in Morwood, 'Gilbert Murray's Translations of Greek Tragedy,' in Stray, 133). In his Autobiography, vol. 1, Russell declares that not only was he 'profoundly stirred by the beauty of the poetry,' but the reading led to a torrent of illuminations as soon as he reached home. 'Ever since my marriage, my emotional life had been content with flippant cleverness. Suddenly the ground seemed to give way beneath me, and I found myself in quite another region. Within five minutes I went through some such reflections as the following: the loneliness of the human soul is unendurable; nothing can penetrate it except the highest intensity of the sort of love that religious teachers have preached; whatever does not spring from this motive is harmful, or at best useless; it follows that war is wrong, … that the use of force is to be deprecated, and that in human relations one should penetrate to the core of loneliness in each person and speak to that.'*

After five minutes, he notes, 'I had become a completely different person' (219–20). Later he spoke of it as his 'first conversion' (letter to Ottoline Morrell, probably July 1911, quoted in Monk, Bertrand Russell, *135).*

My dear Shaw

I think The Devil's Disciple exceedingly good – It is the only one new to me. I have filled several columns of the *Speaker* with respectful objuration of you, in the style of Britannus. I think one of the things I say of you is unjust, but I agree with myself on the whole. – Thanks also for the soldier, which is fun.

I am lecturing in Cambridge on Feb 2, but hope to be here until then, unless by any chance the arrangements for Andromache should progress properly – of which there is not much likelihood.– Here I was interrupted & my pen taken away. Alas I find that the feelings of the University of Cambridge will be such that they could not bear to hear me so soon after the demise of the Crown, but they hope to be better by the 9th. So that I shall be here till then unless Andromache calls. Do come over if you get a chance.

Yours very sincerely,
G G A M

Shaw had evidently sent Murray a copy of his latest article, 'Civilization and **the Soldier**,' published in the *Humane Review* in January. The 'fun' that Murray extracted from it might have been in reaction to the frequent satirical flings at the conventional Englishman, such as 'We believe, every man of us, that we shall endure to the end, our Empire growing ever greater, until the Last Judgment shall be enacted – probably in Westminster Abbey – and the millennium inaugurated by the extension of British rule to the entire universe' (299). The article's serious point revolves around the unavoidable mindset of military leaders, especially in the ongoing second Boer War, and its support by 'public opinion' – e.g., 'What public opinion cannot create ... is the strength of mind that disdains its foolish fusses and self-conceits. Soldiering does not seem to encourage this quality. The general who will ride about under fire without – shall we say preoccupation? – will commit any atrocity to avoid being defeated, and will carry political cowardice – the only sort of cowardice that really matters in a general – to its uttermost extremity' (307). Devastating an enemy's country may bring a war to an end, 'but once you have begun it, *and if you are in the enemy's territories and do not intend to make them your own,*' which was not the case with South Africa, 'a better way is not to begin it' (309).

7 / To G. Bernard Shaw

Churt
3rd February 1901

[TLT: BL, SPA]

My dear Shaw

I see that I was 'too previous' in saying I had filled columns of the Speaker with denunciation of you. They have evidently hung up the review for a week or so. Perhaps it did not please their regular dramatic critic; or perhaps their printer has had one of his attacks of lunacy.

A propos of The Soldier, have you seen an article by Newbolt of the Monthly Review? It is like the sentimental howling of a very young and ignorant jackal. He seems to be still in Raina's frame of mind, or worse. His soldier is a blameless and benevolent St George, born in England and educated at an English public school, who kills dragons – after giving them all the possible odds – in such a manner that with the last pulses of their hearts they forgive and love him. Or at any rate he forgives them … so noble is he. I wonder why this sort of rubbish makes one angry? I fancy it must be because one sees in it one of those invincible illusions which will palliate and disguise any evil. That is to say, there is probably no conceivable abomination which, if committed by a British soldier of the proper personal appearance, could shock Newbolt out of his comfortable idealism. And I suppose most people, in every country, are more or less in the same state of mind.

Yours sincerely,
G G A M

The ***Monthly Review* article** written by H[enry] J[ohn] **Newbolt** (1862–1938), its editor from 1900 to 1905, was a long editorial entitled 'The Happy Warrior' (2, no. 5 [January 1901], 1–10). It heralded the British troops for their chivalrous behaviour during the second Boer War and called for the creation of a 'Universal Association for the Attainment of Peace,' to be effected by 'the elimination of Hatred from human affairs.' This approximates the heroic idealism of **Raina,** the leading female character in *Arms and the Man,* whose romantic delusions about Major Sergius Saranoff are punctured by the professional Swiss soldier Bluntschli. Appropriately, during the First World War Newbolt worked for Britain's War Propaganda Bureau.

8 / To G. Bernard Shaw Palace Green, Kensington W.
[10th February] 1901

[ALS: BL, SPA]

Well after Murray had alerted Shaw to his forthcoming review of Three Plays for Puritans, *it appeared in* The Speaker *on 9 February, entitled 'Mr. Bernard Shaw's New Plays.' Selections from its text follow: 'Let me confess at the outset that I always look forward to Mr. Shaw's writings with something like delight, that his views and doctrines are much more sympathetic to me than repellent, and that I have read this last volume of his plays three times through already. Let me add that it seems to me on the whole better than either of his preceding volumes … Now how far is Mr. Shaw a good portrayer of the past? … The convention has been thoroughly established; it makes play-writing very easy and mechanical; we know it and expect it … The man who is successfully to break through it will need a remarkable historical imagination, and perhaps, though that is not so certain, a remarkable amount of historical knowledge as well. Now Mr. Shaw has certainly some qualifications for this great task. He has imagination, insight into life, and some quality peculiarly his own which I can only describe as an ever-vigilant reflectiveness. There are many scenes full of brilliant gleams of historical imagination … If only Mr. Shaw would consent to do two or three things which he certainly will not do, his experiment in realistic historical drama might be wonderfully successful. As things are, it is not so. For one thing, he should not be so reckless in ignoring difficulties … Mr. Shaw makes the odds against him needlessly heavy by practically offering to show us in realistic detail, not a few of the best-known parts, but every single part that takes his fancy, of the life of ancient men and women. The fact is that Mr. Shaw … does not seem to me to realise how extremely good his work is – the good part of it. It would make any one angry to see such really great conceptions as those on which* Caesar and Cleopatra *is built treated with such frivolity. No artist can afford to be frivolous, least of all a thoughtful, keen-sighted and original artist. There is a delightful figure (which ought to be ruthlessly cut out!) in* Caesar and Cleopatra, *an ancient Briton … who on certain occasions observes, "Caesar, this is improper," and "O Caesar, great Caesar, if I could but persuade you to regard life seriously, as men do in my country!" I heartily echo his words.'*

My dear Shaw

My diatribe on you weighs on my mind, & I wish to make the general drift of it clearer than I was able to do in my article.

I start from the position that you do, as a matter of fact, produce the plays that I most enjoy reading of all modern writers except Ibsen. One might stop there: dwell on the wit, brilliance, variety of character &c. & say no more.

But I also feel in your plays other elements of a decidedly higher & greater sort; elements of philosophy or even religion, which I take absolutely seriously and believe that you do also. And somehow these do not seem to me to mix properly or in the right way in your plays with the first set of qualities. You can be a Sheridan with ease (a modified, 20th century Sheridan, of course): but I keep wishing all the time that you would be something else, something better in kind, which seems to be in your power if only you would choose to do something different or throw away some cartload or two of cargo (which wd make a good competence for many a playwright, but is inferior to your real best.)

Of course this may be all wrong and 'Brittanic.' But it is the point of view that I meant to express. – Nor do I want less wit; I want it 'duly subordinated.' Here again my view may be wrong as to the actual facts; but I suspect that your mind, through its own quickness very possibly, does not realize the disillusioning shock that some of your details produce – nor (I cd expand on this theme at length!) I really believe, how good the things are which you sacrifice to a burst of laughter.

I shall come to lunch one day, & you can slay me.

Yours very sincerely,
Gilbert Murray

Richard Brinsley **Sheridan** (1751–1816), like Shaw, was a Dublin-born comic dramatist who relocated to England. His most famous plays are *The Rivals*, *The School for Scandal*, and *The Critic*. Murray was wryly inviting himself to the Shaws' London residence at 10 Adelphi Terrace, which they had moved into in early November 1899. The two-floor flat, which overlooks the Victoria Embankment of the Thames, was situated over rooms occupied by the London School of Economics.

9 / To Gilbert Murray

London
12th February 1901

[ALS: Bod, SPA]

On the same day that Shaw replied to Murray, his wife Charlotte also sent him a letter. She first encouraged him to come to lunch, then expressed praise for his critical evaluation of her husband's work: 'I think your review of the plays was excellent, also your letter. You say just the things to G.B.S. that he ought to have said to him. But,' she cautioned, 'he is a hardened offender' (Bod). Shaw had finished an adaptation of his novel Cashel Byron's Profession *as* The Admirable Bashville, or

Constancy Unrewarded *on 2 February; in its preface he comments on why he wrote it in 'the primitive Elizabethan style,' blank verse (CP 2, 433).*

My dear Murray

The answer is that Nature puts jokes into my plays just as she puts bones into a fish – to interfere with your pleasure in eating them. The explanation and yourself, both, can be expanded simultaneously if you will come to lunch on Thursday (we lunch out tomorrow, worse luck).

Meanwhile I write to point out one quite extraordinary error in your Speaker article. Read Coriolanus again at once. You will find that with the single exception of the blank verse which Shakespear dropped into to save time (I have just dramatized Cashel Byron in that medium for the same reason) his method is that of 'C & C'. He assumes that Coriolanus & Co were exactly like the patricians & parish electors of his own day; and the greatest scene in the play is hardly over when Menenius remarks 'He no more remembers his mother now than an eight-year-old horse.' There is not a trace of the Tamburlainish rot in his attempt at Caesar. In haste – just off to lecture

G. Bernard Shaw

Tamburlainish rot refers to the protagonist of *Tamburlaine the Great* (first performed in 1587), the first drama that brought Christopher Marlowe (1564–93) enduring fame. Modelled on Timur, the tyrant king of the Persian Empire, Tamburlaine is an ambitious, ruthless conqueror whose emotional extremes are conveyed in impressive but often bombastic blank verse.

10 / To G. Bernard Shaw

Kensington W.
22nd February 1901

[APCS: BL]

I am so sorry. All *my* friends are coming on the Monday, so I hope the mortality will not be great. However all the cast have influenza, except Andromache who has bronchitis, & Alcimedon who is believed [by my wife] to have diphtheria. – But I hope your wife will not have it badly.

G G A M

Andromache was to be played by Edyth Olive (1872–1956), **Alcimedon** by Albert Gran (1862–1932).

11 / To Gilbert Murray

London
24th February 1901
11:15 p.m.

[ALS: Bod, SPA]

*The Stage Society was organized in London in July of 1898 'to secure the production of plays of obvious power and merit which lacked, under the conditions then prevalent on the stage, any opportunity for their presentation.' As originally projected, at least six performances were to be given spread out over a year; the actors and actresses were not to be paid for their services; and audiences were to be limited to members of the Society and their guests. (*The Incorporated Stage Society, Ten Years 1899–1909, *7–8; see also their* First Annual Report, *3–7.) Shaw quickly became involved with the affairs of the Stage Society; in the initial season* You Never Can Tell *was presented on 26 November 1899 and* Candida *on 1 July 1900;* Captain Brassbound's Conversion *was performed in its next season, on 16 December 1900.*

Gilbert Murray had joined but was largely inactive until Andromache *was produced by the Society on 24 February 1901 after having been rejected by several theatre managers. Charles Charrington directed and played the major role of Pyrrhus, son of Achilles. The other principals were Edyth Olive in the title role of Andromache and Janet Achurch as Hermione. The play had already been published by William Heinemann. The volume contains an interesting 'Prefatory Letter' addressed to Archer, who had worked at length on the play. Murray reminds Archer that in 1896 they had discussed 'how far it would be possible to treat a historical subject loyally and unconventionally on a modern stage … We talked of the extraordinary variety of plot that the Greek dramatist found in his historical tradition, the force, the fire, the depth and richness of character-play … We agreed that a simple historical play, with as little convention as possible, placed in the Greek Heroic Age, and dealing with one of the ordinary heroic stories, ought to be, well, an interesting experiment.' After the performances he wrote to Archer, 'As a book, Andromache, in prose, as it stands was worth writing, because it does give a picture of primitive Greece unlike any other that I know of, with a certain poetic and a certain "interpretative" value. I mean that it will actually help a small number of students and others to understand Homer and the tragedians' (letter of 5 March 1901; Lathem Papers).*

The play's reception was mixed; not surprisingly, it proved unfit for popular consumption, although more sophisticated viewers expressed pleasure. After reading it A.E. Housman (1859–1936) told Murray, 'It is very interesting, very unlike anything one could have anticipated, and the end of it is really moving' (letter of 23 April 1900 in Wilson, 86–7). Shaw tells him in his letter of 15 March 1901 that Charrington 'hadnt the least notion what a good play Andromache is & what a genius you are.' Below, he focuses on the quality of the performance.

I really did not believe that play could have drawn as much blood as it did with Andromache inarticulate and all the other drawbacks. Molossus was by far the best. Charrington made his part intelligible, and kept in the right key and died in it – died rather well ('nothing in his life became him' &c), though I do not approve of his falling down three or four flights of stairs instead of unaffectedly flopping. Tomorrow afternoon I should give Janet a dose of bromide in a tumbler of laudanum to get her down to French pitch. Andromache is hopeless – a mere aesthetic illusion, unintelligible and not really intelligent.

But the whole thing was impossibly ugly. One perceives the need of a noble form, a very highly bred convention, for art on that plane. And the altar scene was vile – altar in the wrong place too. They were not so paralysed by nervousness after the first act; consequently the thing began to move and seize as drama (in the theatrical sense); but it was a rottenly unworthy staging of a fine work. However, as you saw the rehearsals, you can probably conceive it worse done. Damn their souls!

G.B.S.

Molossus, child of Pyrrhus and Andromache, was played by Robert Bottomley (1885–?). **French pitch** is diapason normal pitch: 'a standard of pitch in which A above middle C is established at 435 vibrations per second' (Dictionary.com).

12 / To Gilbert Murray London

15th March 1901

[ALS: CL 2]

A side effect of the staging of Andromache *was discord within the Stage Society. Murray learned of it from Janet Achurch in a letter written in what she described as 'an excitable state.' She informed him that the Society's Managing Committee had decided it would 'look too clique-y' if she were, under her husband's direction, to take the leading role that season in Ibsen's* The Lady from the Sea. *Not only had Charrington and his wife had roles in* Andromache, *but each had played in one of the Society's other three productions. She told Murray that she considered the committee's decision 'ungrateful & mean' (letter of 26 Feb. 1901; Lathem Papers).*

Murray's response to Achurch on 29 February is extant in a typescript draft preserved among his papers (Bod). He wrote with his usual diplomatic firmness, citing as a possible ally a prominent member of the Managing Committee, Frederick Whelen (1867–1955). 'I am exceedingly sorry,' Murray told Achurch, 'that the fact of your taking the part of Hermione should make the Committee wish to exclude you from doing the Lady from the Sea. I am writing to Mr Whelen on the subject. Of course I cannot take a very strong tone; but I am reminding him (1) that so far from pushing yourself into the part of Hermione, you originally refused it, and only took it, with the author's full approval, at the last moment; and (2) that it may be [un]wise for the society after using you in a part which did not specially attract or suit you, to leave you aside in a part for which you are the obvious person.'

Dear Murray

Certain wars & rumors of wars at the Stage Society move me to warn you to waterproof yourself against all tales of intrigue & villainy which may reach you. The great object of the contending forces is to get an author as King's Evidence: the wise author preserves a bland neutrality. Do not allow yourself to be affected by the professional infamy, the treachery, the scoundrelism of Charrington, or the self-seeking intrigue, the hypocrisy, vanity, and mean envy of Whelen. It is all pure romance; but it always goes on, like schoolboy war & brigandage.

The fact is, the Stage Society is not a very eligible opening for professional ambition. It cant afford to pay its performers or to have scenic rehearsals. It begins rehearsing after a fortnight of applications & refusals, with an incomplete cast, and with performers of whom some, as the old hands pretty surely guess, wont go through with it when they find what a rough & tumble affair it is going to be. I rather suspect that Miss Collier was a case in point. In the end the manager calls in his wife or some of his old allies on whom he can depend; and then, for the first time, he gets to work on the assumption that the thing is really going to happen. Of course the Opposition immediately denounce this course of nature as an intrigue of the manager in the interests of his own gang & his own wife. Equally of course, the manager and his wife are stung by the infamous conspiracy to oust them. And so they wrangle & fight, occasionally changing the Government when the press pitches into a performance hard enough to give the Opposition a victory, but never changing the system, as the new manager finds himself exactly in the same fix. 'Andromache' has unseated Charrington & put in Foss; but the chances are about 10 to 1 that Foss will presently, after vainly trying to cast a play, fall back on Miss Winifred Fraser (Mrs Foss), and the recrimination will begin all over again. It may not happen the first time (Charrington got through The League of Youth, The Coming of Peace & Macaire without calling in Janet); but to that complexion it will come at last.

In the case of Brassbound I, anticipating all this, condescended to ask Mrs Kendal and Miss Lena Ashwell myself to play Lady Cicely. The committee tried; I tried; everybody tried, refusals coming in until there was no time left for anybody to rehearse, when I turned Janet on. But there was just the same faction afterwards: Charrington & Janet had intrigued to secure the part for her & so on. Every performance is followed by the same silly storm in a teacup & will be to the end of time. So sit tight; and dont believe a word that reaches you from either side. I am deep in the unwilling confidence of both parties.

'Andromache,' which I saw twice (an unprecedented honor) was necessarily a failure in point of execution – a failure that illustrated our difficulties very perspicuously. The play requires an artistic form for its representation – a convention of fastidious beauty & dignity delicately impressed with sincere & natural acting. You want people trained to speak & move handsomely, and to strike the chords of the human heart feelingly enough to touch Mr Guppy. Instead of which you get your milk & water in separate cans. You get two artist's models who look feebly graceful in the manner of a Leighton picture, and who are unintelligible & (in one case) inarticulate. And you get two realistic Ibsen people who drive the meaning of their parts home with instruments of torture. The boy was the sole success: his youth was classic, his feeling was touching.

I blame you to some extent for not forcing Janet to contract herself into the limits of her duty. I grant you it would have required either a serpent's tongue or a kitchen poker; but it could have been done. Two things you should have said & stuck to. 1. Miss Achurch: you will please be content to see the Furies, not to act them. 2. Miss Achurch: you will please avoid using that part of your voice (the upper register) which was intended by Nature for use in a saw mill. Janet is magnificent when she is bullied into reason & moderation; but when she is not brutally tamed she smashes everything to pieces. Even then there is something momentous in the fact that the audience *dares* not laugh – that line about her beauty would have evoked a titter if Mrs Pat or Cleopatra herself had played it; but Janet's unerring laugh-if-you-dare pause & the stroke after it that shoots the ship clear of the rock are really wonderful. Of course she should have played Andromache; and you should have hammered at her with an extra large poker until she was right; but she could have been made much less destructive as Hermione. An actress of genius is an incarnation of all the devils in hell: that is why it is such a fearful & perilous joy to have one to rehearse. Charrington couldnt have been made better: nothing could make him classically beautiful. He hates classicism and romance, and hadnt the least notion what a good play Andromache is & what a genius you are until I reviled him into waking up a little about it. – Here I am interrupted by a rehearsal of 'The Man of Destiny.'

yrs ever
G. Bernard Shaw

PS We return to Piccard's Cottage, St Catherine's, Guildford, this evening until Wednesday, bar a run up on Sunday afternoon to lecture at St George's Hall on the Problem Play or some such rot.

Shaw's comment on Frederick **Whelen** strongly implies that Whelen had not been sympathetic to Murray's appeal. **Miss** Constance **Collier** (1878–1955) and **Miss Winifred Fraser** (1868–1951) were actresses, the latter being the wife of George R. **Foss** (1859–1938), who 'unseated' Charrington as director and might have installed her in a major role just as Charrington (ultimately) installed Janet Achurch. Shaw cites a parallel case in regard to the Society's production of *Captain Brassbound's Conversion* in December 1900: his unsuccessful attempts to persuade both Margaret ('Madge') **Kendal** (1848–1935), wife of actor-manager William Hunter Kendal (1843–1917), and **Lena Ashwell** (1872–1957) to take the role of Lady Cicely Waynflete. **Mr Guppy** is a young clerk in Dickens's *Bleak House.* Frederick **Leighton** (1830–96) was a prestigious 'academic' painter whose works were frequently exhibited at the Royal Academy. Shaw's ***The Man of Destiny***, written in 1895 but still awaiting a London performance, was to be presented in a single '*Sunday Special* Matinée' at the Comedy Theatre on 29 March. The **lecture at St George's Hall** that Shaw was scheduled to give in two days was indeed entitled 'The Problem Play.' His audience was the Sunday Lecture Society, which gathered at the church's hall in Cannon Street Road (*The Era* 64 [23 March 1901]: 18).

13 / To G. Bernard Shaw Churt

16th March 1901

[TLT: BL, SPA]

The Stage Society imbroglio temporarily thwarted the Charringtons' ambitions to present The Lady from the Sea. *However, not only did it became part of the Society's program on 4 and 5 May 1902 with Charrington directing, but Janet, whom Murray had called 'the obvious person' to star as Ellida Wangel, played that role.*

Murray wrote his response to Shaw's description of the machinations of the Stage Society the very next day.

My dear Shaw

Thanks for your warnings. I think I have on the whole steered exactly the course you recommend. I wrote to Whelen soon after the performance to say that I had entirely approved of Ch doing Pyrrhus, and had originally asked Mrs Ch to do Hermione, and that I had no complaint whatever to make except my original complaint that Ch was unbusinesslike. I had heard the various theories of intrigues to get parts, and told Whelen I did not believe them. I also put in a tentative word in favour of their doing the Lady from the Sea with Miss Achurch as heroine. That is what I say 'in print,' as Aslaksen would put it.

My personal opinion is almost exactly the same. I thought Miss Achurch acted with perfect bona fides all through; Charrington told one rather startling falsehood, in sending the printed cast to Whelen with Graham Brown for Pyrrhus, when it was perfectly settled that he should do Pyrrhus himself, but I attribute this to instinctive cowardice – such as I would show myself under similar circumstances – rather than guileful deliberation. As to Ch's qualifications as Dramatic Manager, or as Manager of anything in the world, well, I would as soon have Mr Micawber. His arrangements about the cast and scenery &c would make a Five Act Labiche farce. At times I forgot the practical bearing of things and gazed in delighted amazement at his proceedings. But of course it may be that I am accustomed to much more businesslike people, and that most actors would be equally hap-hazard.

I am really very sorry, because I like both the Charringtons, and I have now put a spoke in their wheel. As to her acting, I fully agree with you. At times in rehearsal she was admirable; and one felt, even when she was bad, that she was an actress of genius. I doubt if I could have checked or improved her appreciably. – I thought, by the way, that Ch was not very useful in the actual stage-management; not as good as I should have expected.

My children, I regret to say, have found their ideal and are modelling themselves upon Drinkwater! They are reading Brassbound with me now. – I find that Drinkwater rather haunts me, as a kind of deplorably pathetic figure, and a real 'criticism of life.' In the acting he ended by bothering me, as too ugly and unpleasant; but I do not find that now.

Is it not odd how the public and the newspapers delight to insult Us, by ostentatiously wondering why it is that no one, absolutely no one, except the old stagers, ever attempts to write a play? Who is going to do The Man of Destiny?

Yours ever,
Gilbert Murray

I hope your wife's influenza is quite over.

Aslaksen is a printer in Ibsen's *The League of Youth* (1869), who reappears in *An Enemy of the People* (1882). W. **Graham Brown** (1870–1937) was an occasional actor and producer. He played Christy in the 7 September 1900 production of *The Devil's Disciple.* **Mr** [Wilkins] **Micawber** is the incurably optimistic fortune-seeker in Dickens's *David Copperfield.* The French dramatist Eugène **Labiche** (1815–88) wrote more than 150 farcical comedies, most of them highly popular. **Drinkwater** is the Cockney co-conspirator in *Captain Brassbound's Conversion* who induces Lady Cicely Waynflete and her brother-in-law to hire the Captain as their guide into the dangerous regions of Morocco. The producer of the 29 March staging of ***The Man of Destiny*** was Barker, who also played Napoleon.

With a nine-month hiatus in extant letters between Shaw and Murray, this note will bridge the span by bringing mutual activities and interests of the two up to date.

Murray's work on his play Mithia *had foundered, and the discouragement of its intended producer, Mrs Patrick Campbell, combined with his own dissatisfaction, prompted him to announce in a letter of 14 November 1900 to Archer that he had suspended the project. The relative failure of his attempts at original drama which were produced,* Carlyon Sahib *and* Andromache, *had caused both Archer and Shaw to urge him to focus on translating ancient Greek dramas in such a way that they would be attractive and moving on the modern stage. His first concerted efforts were the* Hippolytus *and* Bacchae *of Euripides and the* Frogs *of Aristophanes, which were published by George Allen & Sons late in November 1902. In the volume's 'Introductory Essay' Murray says of his method, 'My aim has been to build up something as like the original as I possibly could, in form and in what one calls "spirit."' He adds, 'I have in my own mind a fairly clear conception of what I take to be the "spirit" of Euripides, and I have kept my hands very free in trying to get near it' (vii, ix–x). In a passage that would resonate with his fellow agnostic Shaw when he was contemplating* Major Barbara, *Murray elucidates the main message of the* Bacchae *as: 'The kingdom of Heaven is within you – here and now. You have but to accept it and live with it – not obscure it by striving and hating and looking in the wrong place' (lxvi). Shaw would also have caught the Nietzschean echo in the statement that Dionysius 'gave to the Purified a mystic Joy, surpassing in intensity that of man, the joy of a god or a free wild animal' (lix). A recent scholarly study of Greek drama and the British theatre links Murray's first book of translations to* Major Barbara *quite explicitly: Shaw's play 'was in many ways a reworking of his version of [the* Bacchae*'s] first two acts. And with its clear allusions to Aristophanes'* Frogs *in its third act,* Major Barbara *can be considered a tribute to that 1902 volume of translations, which had so enthralled Shaw' (Hall and Macintosh, 499). Sidney P. Albert culminated his nearly life-long study of* Major Barbara *and the classics with his brilliant study* Shaw, Plato, and Euripides: Classical Currents in *Major Barbara (2012).*

The most significant political event that involved both Shaw and Murray at this time, the Boer War, is treated at some length in the 'Introduction.'

14 / To Gilbert Murray

10 Adelphi Terrace WC
22nd January 1902

[ALS: CL 2]

I have serious thoughts of beginning my lecture: 'Ladies & Gentlemen: I need hardly say that the English Drama to which the title of my lecture refers is the sensational tragedy now being enacted on the veldt &c &c.'

I have not had time to think about it, as I have been writing a terrific preface to Mrs Warren's Profession for its republication separately from the other plays.

On the whole, I am glad you are not coming, as I have nothing new to say; & you & Archer & Walkley have exhausted the interest of the series.

G.B.S.

Pithecanthropangelus was probably Tennyson.

Shaw's talk on 24 January, '**The English Drama**,' was reported in *Fabian News* 12 (February 1902): 5–6. After perfunctory comments on dramatists in preceding centuries, it ends as follows: 'The Fabian Society had produced only one dramatist, and his great advantage was that he had made a statistical study of actual life, a thing which had not occurred to the other modern dramatists. The drama was wallowing in erotic emotion, but it was a poor instrument for that purpose compared with the opera. Music had infinitely more emotional force than mere words. Dramatists had been for years trying to put on the stage opera without music. The attempt was a failure, and thus English drama would be forced back on its real work, the presentation of thought.' The **terrific preface** to *Mrs Warren's Profession* that Shaw was writing at this time, 'The Author's Apology,' accompanied a separate edition of the play which was printed on 12 March 1902. **Pithecanthropangelus was probably Tennyson**: lacking any context, this may be an allusion to the verse in 'In Memoriam' that plays with the idea of a missing link: 'men may rise on stepping-stones / Of their dead selves to higher things' (Oxford text, 39).

15 / To Gilbert Murray

Piccard's Cottage, Guildford
23rd March 1902

[TLS: Bod, SPA]

As far back as early 1894 Murray had speculated that a carefully edited collection of Euripides' plays might be rewarding for him and valuable for scholars and students. When, in mid-1896, Oxford University Press asked him to produce exactly that for their famous classical series, he jumped at the chance (see the headnote to the previous letter). Shaw had heard Murray read a selection of his translations before the Fabian Society late in 1901, and that was one factor that prompted him to prod his friend (in his usual exaggerated manner) to consider his efforts done before he worried about how they would be received. A perfectionist as both scholar and poet, Murray was subject to the charge of 'nursing to perfection,' but three days later he assured his habitual nagger that his caricature did not quite fit the man.

My dear Murray

I have for a long time been much concerned about those translations which you are nursing to perfection in the manner characteristic of university professors. Now let me tell you that every university professor is an ass, and that you, like any common man, are subject to this inexorable law. You think that because Gilbert Murray the poet is not an ass, Professor Murray cannot be one, just as no doubt the Colonial Secretary is convinced that he is a very decent sort of fellow because he is conscious that Joseph Chamberlain is incapable of compelling families to attend the executions of their breadwinners. The fallacy is the same in both cases. I have never known a university don who was not going to produce a great book (like the Churchman in Consuelo) as soon as he had brought his materials to completion, his judgment to absolute impartiality, and his style to perfection. The impression of underbred illiteracy I produce on such a person by telling him that the way to write one good book is to write nineteen bad ones first, cannot be conveyed by mere words. And when I go on to point out that the world would be better off during the period of gestation with a slightly imperfect book than with no book at all; when I cite the practice of the inventor who patents and puts on the market every successive step towards a better process, well knowing all the time that further improvements lie ahead of him, I seem to be bringing the coarsest commercial instincts into the Groves of Academe. Nevertheless to you I will go further still, and unfeelingly say that the Euripidean poesy is not the sort of thing that a man can alter for the better as he becomes more middleaged.

Further I have to observe that one Benjamin Bickley Rogers M.A., of Lincoln's Inn, Barrister-at-law, and sometime fellow of Wadham College Oxford, is publishing a translation of the Comedies of Aristophanes, much in the style of your respected uncle. Now Benjamin Bickley is thereby doing a public service. I daresay if he were to hatch his translation until a few days before his funeral, he might improve it by, say, .00001%, and impart a choice senile flavor to it which would otherwise be lacking. Would you advise him to take this course?

The moral is obvious, Send Euripides by next post to the printer. And then start something else. Mind, by the next post, I am *durchaus* serious.

Yours ever
G. Bernard Shaw

Shaw pits Murray the poet (**not an ass**) against Murray the professor (in Shaw's eyes always an ass), then supports the point by making an analogy to **the Colonial Secretary** Joseph Chamberlain (1836–1914), reviled as an unscrupulous imperialist during the Boer War – allegedly permitting the execution of breadwinners, but claiming a degree of virtue by saying that he did not compel their families to attend those executions. Shaw further likens Murray to an over-dutiful **churchman** in George Sand's novel ***Consuelo,*** who 'promised, and was to promise all his life, to make a book upon the rights, immunities and privileges of his chapter.' However, 'he was not writing it, he was never to write it.' Nevertheless, largely because he was in no haste to produce it, 'That book, which did not exist, had already made for its author a reputation of perseverence, of learning and of eloquence' (*Consuelo* [Boston: Ticknor, Reed, and Field's, 1850], vol. 3, 14–15). Finally, Shaw cites the case of classical scholar **Benjamin Bickley Rogers** (1828–1919), who had just published the first volume of *The Comedies of Aristophanes* rather than waiting for a 'senile flavor' to enhance it. (He errs in his allusion to W.S. Gilbert as Murray's **uncle**; he was merely a first cousin once removed.) As Shaw uses the German word '***durchaus***' ('thoroughly'), it would convey the semi-comic English amplification of 'absolutely.'

16 / To G. Bernard Shaw

Churt
25th March 1902

[TLT: BL, last part SPA]

My dear Shaw

Many thanks for your kindly advice, which I am in the spirit following. (I know that 'in the spirit' as a rule means 'practically' which means 'not.') I am writing as fast as I can a sort of desultory commentary, giving the minimum of information necessary to the general reader. It chiefly affects the Frogs, not the two Euripides plays. I have not really been nursing the translations; I had to lay them aside unfinished from pressure of other work.

As to the Lues Professoria, the mental disease which makes them aim at what they are pleased to call perfection, I entirely agree with you. It is largely due to timidity and largely to laziness. But as to my Middle Age, I must beg leave to differ entirely. I am vastly more sensitive, poetical, impressionable and emotional than when I was a young man, and am getting more so. I shall be a very Le Gallienne when I am sixty-five and begin to draw my pension. B.B. Rogers, by the way, must be near seventy – if he is the person I am thinking of. It is a nice old crusted scholarly translation – the main essence wrong, but the details excellently right. He is misled by the old error of supposing that because his College Tutor (probably a quiet old portwine-drinking materialist Tory Parson) taught him the Greek dramatists, therefore their minds were like that of his College Tutor ... except that now and again they seemed to talk nonsense.

What curious work it is, interpreting somebody else! I once heard the Warden of Merton, Brodrick, expounding Shelley ... rather like Jowett expounding Plato, by the way. As long as Shelley made remarks that, say, the Duke of Devonshire would agree with, and which were of no value or importance whatever, Brodrick expounded him with gusto. As soon as he said anything characteristic or important, anything that differentiated him from the Duke, Brodrick apologized and considered it mere verbosity.

When are you coming over here? Bertrand Russell is coming on Saturday.

Yours ever,
Gilbert Murray

Lues Professoria, loosely speaking, is professor's plague, but the term 'lues' is more strictly a synonym for syphilis. **I shall be a very Le Gallienne** implies that, like the English poet-critic Richard Le Gallienne (1866–1947), best known as the author of *The Quest of the Golden Girl* (1896), he will become more and more romantic and decadent in his tastes. At this time **B.B. Rogers** was seventy-four. George C. **Brodrick** (1831–1903) was warden of Merton College, Oxford, from 1881 until his death. Benjamin **Jowett** (1817–93) had been Regius Professor of Greek and Master of Balliol College, Oxford. Spencer Compton Cavendish, eighth **Duke of Devonshire** (1833–1908), was currently Lord President of the Council of the Marquess of Salisbury's government and the leader of the Liberal Unionists, anathema to Murray because of their opposition to Home Rule for Ireland.

17 / To Gilbert Murray

10 Adelphi Terrace WC
4th December 1902

[ALS: Bod, SPA]

On 10 April Shaw had assigned the rights to 'translate, publish or produce any of his published plays in Germany and Austria' to Siegfried Trebitsch (1869–1956), an Austrian novelist, critic, and playwright who had been introduced to Shaw by Archer (Gibbs, Chronology, *386). Trebitsch had asked Archer about new British dramatists; he replied, 'There was only one worth bothering about,' and that was Shaw, 'a dramatist to his fingertips' (Whitebrook, 214).*

In late November 1902 George Allen & Sons published Murray's book containing the Hippolytus *and* Bacchae *of Euripides and the* Frogs *of Aristophanes (but whose title page said merely, 'Euripides translated into English rhyming verse'). Murray stated in his preface: 'The object of this book is in the first place to put before the English reader a translation of some very beautiful poetry, and in the second place to give some description of a remarkable artist and thinker. This double purpose explains the somewhat unusual composition of the volume … I have taken first two plays of Euripides … chosen partly for their beauty, partly because they are very characteristic of their author … Next, I have selected the chief ancient criticism of Euripides, a satire penetrating, brilliant, and, though preposterously unfair, still exceedingly helpful to any student who does not choose to put himself at its mercy.' He did grant that to some 'there may appear to be something irrelevant in allowing two noble tragedies to be so closely followed by a hostile burlesque'* (Euripides, *v–vi.). Despite controversies about his choice of rhyme rather than prose or blank verse, the opinions of critics and friends were on the whole favourable. A review in* The *Speaker heralded the fulfilment of the author's clear purpose: 'he has ... made Euripides accessible to the English reader with a success that is astonishing.' J.H. Baddeley commended Murray for having managed to 'give to those who can never get it for themselves a vision of the beauty and power of Greek literature' (letter of 28 November 1902; Wilson, 90). And perhaps best of all, his lifelong friend John Maynard confided that in translating Greek poetry it was clear that he had at last found his ' true métier' (Herbert John Maynard, 1865–1943, later Sir John; letter of 27 June 1903; Wilson, 91). On 29 November 1904 Archer argued in the* Morning Leader *that if Murray had retained blank verse, the result would simply remind British audiences of Shakespeare. By using 'flowing rhymed pentameters' he had succeeded in preserving the spirit of the original while giving Greek tragedy a new and contemporary English voice (Whitebrook, 244).*

Thanks for Eurip. Our bookseller, however, got beforehand with Allen; so that I had two copies yesterday. I was going to send you the odd one, knowing by experience that nobody needs spare copies more than the author; but Chesterton came to lunch today, and it struck me that it would be a better investment to load it up on him, which I accordingly did.

Comparing your Frogs with the other fellow's I notice that what he translates as a bottle of oil you translate as an umbrella. No doubt you learnt Greek at different universities.

I should like to read you my new play, but for want of opportunity shall probably have to send you the TS.

G.B.S.

G[ilbert] K[eith] **Chesterton** (1874–1936) was a prolific, popular author of fiction, essays, and biographies with a conservative Catholic slant. His book on Shaw was published in 1909. The variant translations appear in a dialogue between Aeschylus and Euripides near the end of the **Frogs**: Rogers had written 'Nay then, by Zeus, no longer line by line / I'll maul your phrases: but with heaven to aid / I'll smash your prologues with a bottle of oil' (V, 183, ll. 10–12); Murray's rendition was: 'By Zeus, I won't go pecking word by word / At every phrase; I'd take the old umbrella, / God helping me, and smash your prologues whole!' (264, ll. 10–12). In his textual notes Murray explains that he chose to replace a common Athenian container with an object 'which both ancient Greeks and modern Englishmen would habitually use' (306). Shaw's **new play** was *Man and Superman*; **TS** stands for typescript.

18 / To Gilbert Murray

Overstrand Hotel. Cromer
12th January 1903

[ALS: Bod, SPA]

Shaw devised scenarios of the 'Don Juan in Hell' sequence of Man and Superman *in May 1900, began the rest of the play in July 1901, and finished it in June 1902. Considering it 'an immense play, but not for the stage of this generation' (CL 2, 174), he submitted it to what would become his perennial publisher, Constable. Issued in August 1903, it included not only the six-hour play but a long preface and longer 'Revolutionist's Handbook and Pocket Companion,' with its eminently quotable appendix, 'Maxims for Revolutionists.' Since his previous letter to Murray he had not sent him a typescript of the play (which he refers to here as 'D.J.'), but now he could send it in page-proof form.*

I have retreated to the seaside for a holiday. D.J. is here, being read to the Webbs & Graham Wallas; but it has taken a whole week to get through him, even with the preface omitted. I should like exceedingly to read it at Barford; but it takes five sittings; and the third (the interlude in Hades) exhausts the audience & whitens the locks of the author – Euripides would have made three whole plays of it. I must content myself with submitting it in proof, I fear.

The pince-ney incident simply paralyzed me. Every gentleman under that sort of cloud should be confined in a cell containing every possible facility for self destruction; and a strong public opinion should discourage any disposition to trouble the sheriff in the last resort.

G. Bernard Shaw

Shaw's audience is well described in Beatrice Webb's diary entry for 16 January: 'For the first time in many years the three old friends – Sidney, Bernard Shaw and Graham Wallas – spent a week together with their wives as chorus, the Shaws at the big hotel near by and the Wallases with us. Three delightful evenings we spent listening to GBS reading his new work – the *Superman*.' The diary continues: 'To me it seems a great work, quite the biggest thing he has done … He has found his *form*: a play which is not a play; but only a combination of essay, treatise, interlude, lyric – all the different forms illustrating the same central idea' (*The Diary of Beatrice Webb* 2, 267). **Wallas** (1858–1932), for years a prominent member of the Fabian Society, was currently on the faculty of the London School of Economics.

The **'pince-ney incident'** (pince-nez, pronounced as Shaw spells it) which Shaw comments on with grim wit refers to an article published four days before in *The Times* entitled 'The Leyton Murders.' On that day Edgar Edwards was charged with the murder of a couple and their baby daughter, whose bodies had been found in a garden in Leyton. In court, Edwards complained that the police had taken his 'gold-rimmed pince-nez,' 'specially made by an eminent London oculist,' and they were returned. On 29 January the jury found Edwards guilty of 'wilful murder.'

19 / To G. Bernard Shaw

Churt
30th September 1903

[TLT: BL, SPA]

Man and Superman *was the first of Shaw's books to be produced by Archibald Constable & Co. with a highly innovative contract: as he described it in a retrospective letter to the chairman of Macmillan, since by 1903 'I could command sufficient capital to finance my books and enter into direct friendly relations with the printers (Clarks of Edinburgh) ... I took matters into my own hands and ... manufactured my books myself, and induced Constables to take me "on commission"' (CL 3, 676–7).*

My dear Shaw

I should like to talk to you for an hour or so about The Superman. I think it is a most remarkable piece of work, and – like many of its brothers – the kind of thing that a reader may not like but does not forget. Of course I, like most of your friends, am anxious to point out to you just what is wrong with it; though I confess, I cannot at the moment quite see what it is. It makes on me, in general, the same kind of impression as Caesar and Cleopatra, of an extraordinarily good thing gone somehow wrong. I wonder when you will write the real thing that is in you – the thing that will not go wrong!

The mere comedy of this seems to me most brilliant – though the third Act worries me. But you have some delightful situations, and every character is real and interesting. Tanner quite delightful.

My main theory of what is wrong with you – for of course I keep several – is that you suffer from a lack of moral courage. This is borne out by the way you boast of your shamelessness; as a worldly man always boasts of his unworldliness. You express divers original or unpopular or odd opinions (always with a sense of your own courage, I think!) but do you ever stick to one and take the consequences? (In art, I mean; not in politics, which I do not know about.) Never. You lead your admirers on and on; and then, in a sudden panic, thinking that you may be laughed at, you laugh yourself and say it was a joke. Which it was not!

This damnable vice is intimately connected with another, which you share with Ruskin, Carlyle and, I think, Tolstoi: a fundamental preference for rhetoric to truth. There is a passage in your introduction (I cant find it, because my wife – who disapproves of the book strongly, has taken it away with her and wont give it up) where you observe that people let you say what you like; that the Times says 'another work by this brilliant writer' and does not wince. Well, that is the nemesis of going on as you and Ruskin and the rest have gone on. You sacrifice the accurate statement of fact to something that will make a proper effect on your audience – or, it may be, to something that gives you artistic pleasure. That leads to overstating things in order to get your effect. Then, at last, the ordinary Human Fool, whose instinct is after all a wonderfully fine organ, sees to his great comfort that you are saying more than you can possibly mean; therefore you do not mean what you say; therefore whatever he likes to believe is right, and the rest is 'brilliant' paradox.

However, I wont go on like this; partly because it is not exactly civil or called for, partly because my wife has just said to me meditatively, when I was holding forth at dinner with combined fluency and wisdom, 'I wonder if you have gout in the head!' I do not wish to produce the same impression on you.

Donna Ana's craving for the father of the Superman is very fine; haunting and tragic, and I dare say perfectly true. Also the conception of Hell and Heaven. Well, more power to your arm … or rather, since you have enough of that to satisfy any temperate person, more divine guidance to you!

I am writing a thing for the Independent Review about Euripides' Electra, in which there are points reminding me constantly of you. Chiefly a constant disappointment of the romantic expectation.

Yours very sincerely,
Gilbert Murray

Reading this over, I feel the proportions of it to be wrong. It is nearly all scolding. I do think Don Juan a most remarkable piece of thinking as well as a most original and irresistibly funny play. Perhaps I might as well have said that and left out the rest.

Murray refers to three prominent nineteenth-century men of letters: John **Ruskin** (1819–1900), art critic and economic theorist; Thomas **Carlyle** (1795–1881), author of the stylistically unique *Sartor Resartus*; and Leo **Tolstoy** (1828–1910), the great Russian novelist whose negative opinion of Shaw's undercutting seriousness with comedy closely resembles Murray's (CL 2, 900). Murray's article, 'The Meanest of Greek Tragedies,' appeared in the **Independent Review** (vol. 1) in January 1904. In it he takes issue with the opinion of August Wilhelm von Schlegel (1767–1845) that Euripides' *Electra* is 'the very worst of all his pieces' by giving 'a rather closer and fairer account of this very remarkable play' (590).

20 / To Gilbert Murray 10 Adelphi Terrace WC
undated; assigned to 23rd February 1904

[APCS: CL 2]

After serving as vestryman and borough councillor for over six years, Shaw resigned in November 1903. By early 1904, he had decided to stand as a Progressive Party candidate for membership on the London County Council in tandem with a Liberal baronet, Sir William Nevill Montgomerie Geary (1859–1944), who later gained prominence as the author of Nigeria Under British Rule *(1927). Shaw and Geary were unsuccessful in the contest; Conservative and Unionist candidates won majorities of four or five hundred votes over their Progressive opponents. Beatrice Webb recorded her judgment in her diary for 7 March: 'G.B.S. showed himself hopelessly intractable during the election: refused to adopt any orthodox devices … Insisted that he was an atheist, … laughed at the Nonconformist conscience; chaffed the Catholics about Transubstantiation; abused the Liberals, and contemptuously patronized the Conservatives – until nearly every section was equally disgruntled … He will never be selected again by any constituency that any wire-puller thinks can be won.'*

In the margins of the printed card that he sent to Murray, Shaw added the following handwritten note.

Geary contested Durham as a Liberal in 1900, a fact which entitles him clearly to the loan of all the motors the Stanley influence can command. The election will be won largely by brake horse power. He has incorrigible Radical leanings, I am sorry to say. I am running as an enthusiastic supporter of the London Education Act, and as the proprietor of the Fox & Pelican, Grayshott. There is a strong Nonconformist demand for atheist candidates just now, as a guarantee against Church influence; but my halo of high Anglican mysticism is proof against all such temptations.

G.B.S.

The **Stanley influence** refers to the family of Lady Mary Murray's mother, the Stanleys, who were prominent in Liberal Party circles. At the time this clan was led by Edward Lyulph Stanley, 4th Baron Stanley of Alderley (1839–1925). The **London Education Act**, which abolished the school boards established under the previous act (1870) and entrusted the administration of elementary, secondary, and technical schools to borough and urban district councils, had been enacted by Parliament during the previous summer. Candidates' positions on the law became a major political issue in the 1904 County Council elections. See Pearce and Stewart, 100–1. On **the Fox & Pelican, Grayshott**, see Letter 1.

21 / To Gilbert Murray

Harmer Green
6th January 1905

[ALS: Bod, Col]

Murray's Hippolytus *had been performed on 26 May 1904 at the Lyric Theatre, and then was given seven matinees at the Court from 11 to 28 April 1905. The actress [Agnes] Sybil Thorndike (1882–1976) acclaimed the first performance for the 'beauty and clarity of Murray's verse and its dramatic speakable-ness' (Wilson, 105), and an actor who understudied on that occasion, Lewis [Thomas] Casson (1881–1967), wrote: 'Verse should be spoken as simply, that is more simply, than prose. Its beauty lies in its structure, texture and substance; to add a tremolo to it is as if you played music with a tremolo obbligato' (Devlin, 42).*

Shaw developed a special interest in Barker's casting of the leading lady for The Trojan Women *– or* 'Troades,' *the Latin title that he chose to use.*

Dear Murray

I made a suggestion to Barker for the Troades – Gertrude Kingston for Helen – which, he tells me, shocked you. This was because it was a stroke of genius on my part. She is, superficially, a feather headed, artificial creature in French frocks, just as Helen would be if she were alive now, as she no doubt is. Perhaps Gertrude *is* Helen: what could she do but go on the stage & play heartless parts if she were reborn? My private acquaintance with her is limited to a single call which she paid me lately about a play of mine which she wanted. It was then that the great idea struck me. There is a certain inhuman self possession about her, a certain grace, a certain obvious power of crumpling up Menelauses & Parises & suchlike blighters, which seems to me to fit Helen better than anything else I can think of. And giving her such a part would have a tremendous moral effect on her; for she is never offered a part that is not an insult to her soul – and really the secret of dealing with these queer actor folk is to get at their souls. She would rise at it instead of stooping bitterly to it.

Of course I make the suggestion as a practical stage manager, comparing her, not with the ideal Helen of your imagination, but with the next best Helen you are likely to get. There is always the danger of shrinking from incongruous realities into nonentities. In Hippolytus, the impossibility of getting the Venus you wanted ended in a Venus whom nobody wanted – a lady with the qualifications of a horse for a quiet family: no vices. That is what I rather dread in these Greek plays of yours, which are to me so fine that every single stroke in their production ought to be an inspiration. I think it is quite possible that some god has actually suggested G. K. to me. For some reason you dont like superhuman people – I have often explained to you how totally you misunderstand the attitude of your convenient ghost Euripides, towards the gods – and therefore they naturally come to me instead of to you with their suggestions.

Of course you will get someone better if you can. But dont get someone worse because in your inmost heart you cannot bear to profane the part by giving it to anyone real at all.

Please assure Lady Mary that I have no corrupt interest in this matter. My relations with Miss Kingston are blameless. I say this because on a recent occasion I compromised myself for ever in your wife's eyes by betraying the fact that I had long come to take the adoration of her sex for my own person as a matter of course (a galling assumption for all really nice women).

Yrs ever
G.B.S.

Gertrude Kingston (1862–1937) did play Helen when the Court production opened on 11 April. She impressed Shaw so much that he chose her to play Lady Cicely in a 1912 production of *Captain Brassbound's Conversion*, and wrote two short plays with her in mind for the leads: *Great Catherine* and *The Inca of Perusalem*. *The Stage* called the production of *The Trojan Women* 'a genuine triumph' with an 'exceedingly strong company' (13 April, 10); *The Era* (15 April) commented, 'A good deal of the spirit of Greek art entered into this production ... and merits our warm gratitude and praise.' In his introductory note to the published edition, Murray grants that many find the play 'too harrowing,' but that the conquered women embody 'the first great expression of the spirit of pity for mankind exalted into a moving principle'; thus, 'like many of the greatest works of art,' the tragedy 'is also a prophecy, a bearing of witness' (6–7). In his book *Euripides and His Age* (revised in 1915), Murray says that the play tells the legendary conquest of Troy 'in a peculiar way. Slowly, reflectively, with little stir of the blood, we are made to look at the great glory, until we see not glory at all but shame and blindness and a world swallowed up in night' (65). He always regarded it as an anti-war play. The **Venus whom nobody wanted** was the actress Elinor Foster, who had played the Goddess Aphrodite in *Hippolytus* during its run of Court matinees.

22 / To Gilbert Murray

10 Adelphi Terrace WC
14th April 1905

[TLT: Bod, SPA]

By 1904 both Shaw and Murray had formed cordial friendships with Barker, who had already acted in several plays by Shaw and in Murray's Carlyon Sahib. *Starting on 26 May he had both directed and acted in Murray's verse translation of Euripides'* Hippolytus *at the Lyric Theatre. Its reception has been characterized as 'polite encouragement' (Kennedy, 23), but Archer praised it for 'illuminating antiquity and restoring beauty and deep poetic feeling' to the stage (Holroyd 2, 96), adding: 'In the harmony and equipoise of its parts, the play is constructed like a noble piece of architecture' (Purdom, 20). Half a century later Murray recalled the fortunes of the play in a radio broadcast: 'The first day there were about fifty people in the house. The second day perhaps a hundred. On the third day the house was full. On the fourth I found a crowd stretching down Shaftesbury Avenue and thought I must have come to the wrong theatre' (Thorndike, 153). Leon Hugo offered a neglected perspective in 1993, stating that* Hippolytus *'asserted a mood; it established a tone, reasserted by its Euripidean successors, that characterized the seasons throughout. The message was clear: dramatic excellence was to be the criterion' ('Shaw and the Twenty-Nine Percenters,' 54).*

The Vedrenne-Barker offerings at the Court in 1904 were inaugurated with a re-staging of Murray's Hippolytus, *with Barker in the demanding role of the Messenger, for six performances from 18 to 28 October, immediately followed by Shaw's newly written and as-yet unpublished* John Bull's Other Island *from 1 to 11 November. With Barker in the role of Keegan, Purdom says, 'the crowded theatre was amazed and delighted,' and, prodded by Beatrice Webb, prominent members of the Cabinet attended.* Candida *was repeated for ten performances later in the season (29). The following spring the second series of productions included five plays by Shaw:* John Bull's Other Island, How He Lied to Her Husband, You Never Can Tell, Candida, *and* Man and Superman *minus the Hell scene. Murray's version of Euripides'* The Trojan Women *was also performed eight times beginning on 11 April 1905. As something of a feminist as well as anti-war play, Murray's stake in it went beyond exposing people to the glories of Greek drama.*

Shaw's opinion of the presentation of The Trojan Women *at the Court was by no means as favourable as opinions expressed in laudatory reviews that appeared in the press. He wrote critically to Murray about several of the actors' performances, and also about stagecraft associated with the roles of Menelaus, king of Sparta, and young Astyanax, at the point in the play where the boy is about to be hurled to his death from the walls of the city.*

My dear Murray

I saw The Trojanesses this afternoon. It is good in parts, though Gertrude Kingston is the only one who is right. She has got the method of Athens: the others have the methods of Bayreuth and Bedford Park. Miss Wynne Mathison's playing is good straightforward sentimental acting: I thought her very good until the great passage about Hector coming from his grave and the closing line about death, where the part left her below on the emotional plane.

I am loth to reopen an old sore; but really the Spartan blighter ought to get a hint in deference to the fact that an English audience has never heard of Helen and is extraordinarily slow to believe just the contrary of what an actor says. Now as matters stand, three quarters of the house thinks that Menelaus is going to kill her after all because he says he will. To remedy this, there is the time honored aside 'I cannot do't' or 'I do but jest – ha ha!' Such interpolations would be quite as authentically Euripidean as many other passages in your version, probably; but they are not subtle enough for you. The thing can be done without any interpolation at all by simply making the blighter, after Helen goes off, force his threats to the blatant pitch of a man obviously trying to encourage himself by the sound of his own voice, with a corresponding accentuation of the collapses. A final effort to grip his sword in a bloodyminded manner, followed by an exit in the manner of a man following a perambulator, would do the trick.

I think Astyanax should be a rag doll. Nothing can get over the horrible fact that as he appears at the Court he is obviously old enough to understand Talthybius's announcement that he is going to be thrown from the wall – a sort of doom at once terrifying and eminently probable to the mind of a child. One expects him to yell like twenty thousand devils as soon as the words are out of Talthybius's mouth. And the legitimate horror of the broken arm is impossible with this flourishing kid.

I see nothing for it but the institution of an order of vestal virgins to play the higher drama. Miss Olive, who was quite right as Phedra, curdled my blood as Cassandra. Agamemnon, poor chump, with his notion that there was something rather appetizing in having a sacred vestal to ravish, became a highly comic figure when one saw him in imagination contemplating the reality of his dream – a warmblooded lady with an appallingly impure diction and a strikingly dramatic manner.

Miss Brema is not bad; but she's wrong. The conflagration chorus is badly set: if you want sensational music for it why not turn on Wagner's Feuerzauber from Die Walküre at once?

These reproaches are addressed to destiny, not to you. The more I see of these attempts to make young females from Maida Vale patuitate like goddesses the more I incline to an experiment with mask and cothurnus.

G.B.S.

For **Gertrude Kingston**, see the endnote to Letter 21. Murray wrote marginal comments on the letter above: Next to the comments on **methods** in paragraph 1: 'these geographical distinctions unconvincing.' He marked as 'true' the qualified judgment of the performance of Edith **Wynne Matthison** (1875–1955), an experienced Shakespearean actress who in 1906 was to play the starring role in Murray's translation of *Electra*. Opposite Shaw's suggestions in para. 2 to clarify the intentions of the '**Spartan blighter**' Menelaus with flamboyant gestures, he simply noted 'True?'; and what Shaw said of Astyanax in para. 3 he commented, 'perhaps true but too late to mend.' Finally, next to para. 4 he pronounced Shaw's opinion of Edyth Olive's portrayal of Cassandra 'rot.' The actress who displays the method of **Bayreuth** points to the mezzo-soprano Marie **Brema** (1856–1925), the first British-born singer to appear in Bayreuth's Wagner Festival (Sadie, 106). **Wagner's Feuerzauber** is Loki's magic fire in 'The Valkyrie.' Shaw's association of certain actresses with **Bedford Park** may be intended to evoke the arty character of 'London's first garden suburb' (Weinreb and Hibbert, 51); those identified as **young females from Maida Vale**, a ward in Paddington regarded as one of its 'pleasantest parts' (Hutchings, 2, 826–7), might suggest over-protected or unworldly women. The word '**patuitate**' does not appear in *Webster's New Universal Unabridged Dictionary*; however, its Latin derivative, '*patulus*,' means 'spreading widely from a center,' which can be strained to fit Shaw's context. Or it may be an error for 'parturiate,' which implies a desire to give birth (Webster).

23 / To Gilbert Murray The Old House. Harmer Green
17th June 1905

[ALS: CL 2]

The matinees of Murray's translation of The Trojan Women *were followed in the spring season of Court productions by a succession of Shaw plays: runs of three weeks' duration each for* John Bull's Other Island *(1 May on),* Candida *(22 May on), and* You Never Can Tell *(12 June on), interspersed with matinee offerings of* You Never Can Tell *from 2 to 19 May and* Man and Superman *from 23 May to 16 June (MacCarthy, 134–9). Notably divergent responses to the latter came from Archer – 'not a good play, or even a good play of Shaw's' – (Whitebrook, 250) and Max Beerbohm (1872–1956) – 'every phrase rings and flashes. Here ... is perfect art' (Holroyd 2, 70).*

While staying at Lord and Lady Carlisle's London residence in Kensington, Murray attended the play. He also visited the Shaws at their London flat, where he was introduced to a young Austrian who had in recent years become Shaw's German-language translator, Siegfried Trebitsch. He wrote to his wife on 23 May: 'Yesterday, I lunched with the Shaws, who were very nice. Met Trebitsch who is translating Shaw into German. T's English is fluent but odd ... [He] told us that he himself was not a vitty man, but he had once made a vit!' (Bod).

By mid-June, Shaw was helping Johnston Forbes-Robertson (1853–1937), in this case the producer rather than the actor, prepare the first English-language production of Cæsar and Cleopatra. *Its opening would be delayed until the end of October 1906, and then take place in New York's New Amsterdam Theater; it would finally be transferred to England – at the Grand Theatre in Leeds – on 16 September 1907 (Gibbs,* Chronology, *172, 178).*

Shaw found reason to consult Murray about a minuscule but vital issue, which led to another tiny one that was hardly vital.

Forbes Robertson is going to produce Cæsar & Cleopatra; and a dispute has arisen as to whether Britannus should be called 'Briton us' or 'Brit. Annus.' I do not ask you to dogmatize on the subject; but what would you call him if you met him? I mean, of course, apart from calling him an ensanguined fool or anything of that sort.

Also, can you give me an adjective to denote an author with several publishers? I have used publygamous; but this suggests the 'hippos a river & potamos a horse' style of derivation.

G.B.S.

Shaw needed an adjective for '**an author with several publishers**' because he was writing a review of Walter Hines Page's *A Publisher's Confession* (published as 'Confessions of a Benevolent and High-Minded Shark' in *The Author* 15 [July 1905], 305–7; Laurence, *Bibliography,* 2, 622).

24 / To G. Bernard Shaw

Oxford
18th June 1905

[TLT: BL, SPA]

Murray sent his response the following day. He and Lady Mary had recently purchased a house at 131 Banbury Road, Oxford, since he had accepted a teaching fellowship at New College, Oxford, to begin in October. This will be their home for the next four years. Unlike his postgraduate appointment to a similar post in 1888–9, this position offered Murray generous remuneration and freedom to choose not only the subjects of his lectures but also, presumably, his visitors.

Brit. Annus without doubt, though, if I met him, I should perhaps address him in the vocative, as 'Brit.Annie.' This is the sort of question that makes me feel the real superiority of a classical education over all others. Fancy the humiliating position you would be in, if you did meet him. No position for a creator.

The other question is difficult. A publisher is Ekdotês; so that 'monecdotous' and 'polyecdotous' would seem to be correct words. (The o short; the accent on the ec.) I should avoid 'publygamous'; it would be Graeco-latin for a prostitute, unless you could show by the context that it meant 'married to a poplar tree!'

I have relapsed into influenza, worse luck. – By the way, now that I am here, you must come down some time and talk to some undergraduates.

G.M.

Shaw chose to use '**polyecdotous**' in his review.

25 / To Gilbert Murray

Harmer Green, Welwyn
21st June 1905

[ALS: Bod, SPA]

A major problem arose for Murray and Shaw during the summer of 1905, the arrest of the Socialist activist and journalist H[enry] N[oel] Brailsford (1873–1958) for conspiring with Russian revolutionaries to undermine their government. Brailsford had been an impressive student of Murray's at Glasgow University and remained a close friend. Since then he had become associated with anti-Tsarist efforts being carried on in England by the Society of Friends of Russian Freedom. The episode of his trial and conviction, omitted from Duncan Wilson's biography, is recounted fully in Leventhal's study of Brailsford, The Last Dissenter, *51–5.*

My dear Murray

It is, Heaven forgive us, an awful waste of brass. However, You Never Can Tell brought me in £120 a week steadily from the beginning of the year until the last quarter of April: consequently my banker is in funds to an extent he has done nothing to deserve. I accept your assessment at £10; but I rather demur to the implication that the ideal appeals to you five times as much as to me. I have to the full as noble a heart as you or any man going; so let us halve the £50 + £10 = £60 ÷ 2 = £30, for which I enclose my cheque.

But when I think that by giving that detective £5 and a glass of port B. could have squared the whole business – ! Well, it's a poor heart that never rejoices.

Have you thought of a plea of insanity? Why should not B. leave the court in the custody of his friends? His protests would confirm the evidence. Quixotomania, eh?

Yrs ever
G. Bernard Shaw

Having completed their out-bound journey at Constantinople, Murray and Barker proceeded homeward by rail. While passing through Eastern Europe, Murray wrote his wife about a whimsical indulgence he and Barker were engaging in at the expense of Shaw: 'We are sending postcards to Shaw from the various Bulgarians in Arms & the Man … Rather fun' (letter of 27 July 1905). Murray's return to London coincided with the close of Brailsford's ordeal in what the press had styled the 'Passport Case.' At the trial on 26 July, the jury swiftly found that 'the defendants combined and conspired together to obtain … by false and fraudulent pretences and representations a passport in the name of the defendant McCulloch for his use in Russia with the intent that it should be used in Russia by some other person, and that in fact it was so used with their knowledge and consent.' On 4 August the conviction was upheld, and they were sentenced to prison until they could pay fines of £100 each, not £30 as previously stated. In a suspenseful but farcical finale, Murray desperately rounded up £200, fled back to court just in time, and saved both from prison.

26 / To Gilbert Murray

10 Adelphi Terrace WC
25th June 1905

[ALS: Bod, Col]

Murray and Barker were planning another trip abroad, having booked the steamship City of Cambridge *with the Papayanni Line. They embarked from Liverpool on 5 July and visited Gibraltar, Malta, Corfu, Patras, Syra, Smyrna, and Constantinople. (For details of their preparation, see Salmon,* Granville

Barker and His Correspondents, *210–20.) Shaw warned his on-and-off fellow vegetarian Murray about limitations of food available on luxury liners, probably drawing on his experience during the six-week Mediterranean cruise he and Charlotte had taken from 14 September to 30 October 1899 on an Orient steamer, the SS* Lusitania *(not the fated Cunard Line's* Lusitania, *launched in June 1906). Shaw's letter of 17 October to Sydney Cockerell is especially graphic on the problems that arose (CL 2, 111–12).*

Shaw had adopted vegetarianism from Shelley in the early 1880s. One of his most cogent explanations of his rationale is in an interview of 15 January 1898 in The Vegetarian, *reprinted in Gibbs,* Shaw: Interviews, *400–2. Typically, he began by challenging the question 'why': 'Oh, come, Mr Blathway! That boot is on the other leg. If I battened on the scorched corpses of animals, you might well ask me why I did that. Why should I be filthy and inhuman? Why should I be an accomplice in the wholesale horror and degradation of the slaughter-house?'*

I was in a Norient liner; and the cook, a large, grave blackbearded man, sent up the most amazing things every day, striped green, yellow, or pink. The whole table used to go for them until the stewards took adequate precautions. Perhaps it might be well to warn Pappayanni [*sic*] to lay in an extra bag of maccaroni [*sic*]; but you will probably be unable to eat anything (the reverse, in fact) until you reach your first port. I did not explain to anybody; but I have no doubt Charlotte did, exhaustively, to everyone on the ship from the Captain to the cabin boy.

G.B.S.

27 / To Gilbert Murray

10 Adelphi Terrace WC
1st October 1905

[ALĊS: CL 2]

The next chapter in the relationship of Shaw and Murray is a complicated one, and less harmonious than usual. It revolves around the next play that Shaw wrote for the Court, Major Barbara. *He had begun writing the play on 22 March, with 29 September scheduled as the first rehearsal and 28 November the first performance. The complicating issues that arose were the fact that he had modelled the* jeune premier *on his close friend, and at least one other character on a member of his family, and the nature of the ending that Shaw had devised, then revised partly at Murray's urging and partly because he himself was troubled about it. He never would succeed in resolving these issues to Murray's satisfaction, in spite of earnest gestures on the part of both men.*

The story begins with an incident that Murray recounted in 1947:

'I happened to meet G.B.S. in the Court Theatre … I suggested to him that a closely historical account of … the trial of Mary Queen of Scots would make an effective play of quite a new kind; but Shaw hardly listened; he said "I can't. I'm doing a play called Murray's Mother in Law*" … About a year later [1 October 1905] he turned up at my house at Oxford. "Were you a foundling?" he asked. "No!" "Do you mind my saying you were a foundling?" "Not in the least." Then he explained that he had brought the play, … which was now called* Major Barbara, *to read to us, to see if there was anything in it to hurt the feelings of my wife's family; "I don't mind about you." [Murray's memory of Shaw's reading was a degree faulty since his wife was away in Switzerland; Harley Granville Barker was present.] He read it in his own inimitable way, bubbling with laughter, like a boy, and also showing delicately the most varied shades of feeling … At the end of Act 2 my wife and I were thrilled with enthusiasm, especially at the Salvation Army scenes. Act 3, in which the idealists surrender to the armament industries, was a terrible disappointment to us and, I think, unsatisfying to Shaw himself. He tried to justify his general line of solution, but muttered: "I don't know how to end the thing."' ('The Early G.B.S.,' 128.)*

And indeed the next day Shaw wrote to Vedrenne, 'I now doubt whether Major B will be ready. I read it yesterday to Barker & Murray. The last act is a total failure: I must sit down and write it absolutely afresh' (CL 2, 565). He will not finish the play to his own relative satisfaction until 15 October.

Shaw's early nickname for the play, Murray's Mother-in-Law, *had made Murray aware that it would include characters based on himself and on his wife's mother, Lady Carlisle. Adolphus Cusins, like Murray an Australian by birth who had become a Professor of Greek, quotes, as his own, passages from Murray's translation of the* Bacchae. *(The passages [CP 3, 117–18] are taken – with minor deviations – from page 54 of Murray's translation of the play as published in 1904.) Lady Britomart Undershaft, like Lady Carlisle, is a domineering woman who is separated from her wealthy industrialist-husband Andrew just as Lady Carlisle was estranged from her husband, the Earl. A faithful teetotaler, Murray was irked by being likened to a character who willingly drinks too much one night and, as a person who had fashioned his own name, by being forced to endure 'Adolphus.' He told Barker, 'Tell GBS that I try to be a Christian and can stand a good deal, as such. But if people call me Adolphus, they do so at their peril. Moses, if you like, or even Ferdinand. But not Adolphus' (letter of 11 August 1905 in Salmon,* Granville Barker and His Correspondents, *223).*

One of the changes Shaw was to make in the text of the play was Lady Britomart haughtily telling her son Stephen, 'And dont call me mother.' Murray told Shaw that this statement might be embarrassing or painful to Lady Carlisle, since she had actually used those words in scolding one of her sons. Shaw did subsequently delete the line (holograph 185; courtesy of Bernard F. Dukore) and substituted 'dont forget that you have outgrown your mother' (CP 3, 157; a *slightly different version of this event is told by Lillah McCarthy in* Myself and My Friends, *166). On that same day Shaw, back in London, sent his friend the following postcard message.*

I find that the result of our conference is a most appallingly strong temptation, *not* to delete 'And dont call me mother' but to develop it to full tragic proportions with the utmost Euripidity. Fortunately there is not room in the play for this; so I hand the temptation on to you. Clearly there is a great dramatic theme here – a Woman Lear with three sons – just the sort of Aeschylean subject in modern life you want.

I am quite desperate about my last act: I think I must simply rewrite it. Merely cutting the cackle – and, cackle is just what it is – will be no use.

G.B.S.

28 / To G. Bernard Shaw

Oxford
2nd October 1905

[TLS: HRC via Guelph, SPA]

Lady Mary was currently abroad in Switzerland, and Murray wrote to her virtually every day whenever they were apart. On the day of the reading he sent her a postcard which began: 'No time to write a letter to-day ... GBS turned up this morning with HGB and we have spent the whole day reading Major Barbara ... It is all right, and the second act really most moving and finely conceived. Perhaps the best thing he has ever done.' The next day he sent her a note which said, in part, 'I have been really driven since breakfast yesterday. Yesterday you know of; to-day I began by writing a long letter to Shaw, re-writing his last Act for him and enclosing it! At least I thought I saw the way through his great difficulty, and I explained it by writing a stretch of dialogue. I wonder how he will take it. I had a most despondent postcard from him just after. He feels the second Act to be very fine, and also that the third is all wrong.' Then, on 3 October Murray gave his wife an extended commentary on the play's characters: 'As to Major Barbara; the caricature of me is rather tiresome. The man is not like me – more like the poet in Candida, unless Shaw adopts some proposals of mine to stiffen him ... But I am clear that, since duelling is out of fashion, there is no possible course except indifference. If I object, the incident will be more piquant. There is no harm in the character.

'My "Mother-in-law" is fortunately utterly unlike your mother! A little like your grandmother in some things; but no, merely a stage figure. Not a word to hurt sensitive feelings, I think, except one phrase, where she says to her son, as a final shaft, "And dont call me Mother!"! The context is merely harmless and funny, but he will alter the line ...

'Barbara is not in any way a caricature of you; except for her niceness, not like you a bit' (Murray to Lady Mary, Oct 1, 2, and 3, 1905; Bod and Lathem Papers).

If Lady Britomart is indeed what Murray told his wife, it was not what Shaw intended. In an undated letter of early 1913 to Henry Hyde Champion (1859–1928) Shaw declared with no qualification, 'The original of Cusins is Gilbert Murray ... Lady Britomart is Lady Carlisle, his mother-in-law. Both are lifelike portraits' (Champion, 165). The characteristics of Eugene Marchbanks, the shy, effeminate young poet in Candida, *match Cusins very little except when he overcomes his timidity and manifests what the stage direction describing him calls 'excessive nervous force' and a 'fiercely petulant wilfulness, as to the bent of which his brow, already lined with pity, is reassuring' (CP 1, 535).*

Murray's communication to Shaw is marked with several emendations and marginal comments.

My dear Shaw

In brooding over Act iii, the accompanying thoughts came to me. I put them down in the form of a dialogue merely for clearness' sake, on the chance of your finding them some use. What I am driving at, is to get the real dénouement of the play, after Act ii. And I think that something like what I suggest *is* the real dénouement of the play. It makes Cusens come out much stronger, but I think that rather an advantage. Otherwise you get a simple defeat of the Barbara principles by the Undershaft principles, which is neither what one wants, nor so interesting as the (as it seems to me) right way out: viz. that the Barbara principles should, after their first crushing defeat, turn upon the U. principles, and embrace them with a view of destroying or subduing them for the B.P.'s own ends. It is a gamble, and the issue uncertain.

Excuse the cheek of this interference. It is indeed 'a bit thick.' And it may be only a nuisance; but it seemed to me that this was your real meaning, and that you had not brought it out clearly. And I am so tremendously interested and moved by Act ii that the problem keeps working in my mind.

I expect that one error – perhaps the only one in the bones of the thing – is that you have made Undershaft too strong and both Barbara and Cusens too weak. You cant get any but an unhappy solution if they are really overpowered. (This looks as if it were all a plot to induce you not to represent me drunk like Prossie. And I am not sure that the incident is right. But it is perhaps the sin of all others which I least mind being associated with; and my motives are pure.) Also, I rather think, though I cant be sure, that there are a few lines here and there which definitely blur the right impression and give a false one .. I mean, as the 'meaning' of the last Act.

I must post this at once, lest I repent of rushing in between the author and his play.

Yours very sincerely,
G.M.

*Somewhere late in Act II, when it has become clear that the Army and society in general is run by Bodgers [*sic*] and Undershaft: that they hold the lever that works society.*

UND. Would nt you like to get your hand on the lever?

CUSENS. If I did, I would work it very differently from what you think.

UND. You would work it very differently from what y o u think!

In Act III, before and after the Armourer's Faith.

SOMEONE, PERHAPS LADY BRIT. 'I have no patience with all these fads. You can use your arms for philanthropy if you like!

UND. No, none of that. You must swear to the Armourer's Faith. &c &c. (*Gives it, as a present.*) You must swear to that.

CUS. Not a bit of it. I am not going to swear to anything. I want *(~~or Barbara and I want~~) to get the lever in ~~our~~ hands, and then I shall see what I want to do – or what Barbara wants to do. It may be all sorts of things.

UND. All right. Dont swear. You're all right, and in a year's time you'll be just like me! ~~You~~ (*Gasp from Barbara.*) You'll love the business, and run it for all it is worth, and come at six in the morning &c &c.

CUS. I shall probably love the business, because I always do like any work I am doing; and I shall come at six in the morning, because that sort of thing is ~~a habit~~ a second nature with me! But whether I shall be like you …

UND. You will; that's all right.

CUS. I venture to think I have got more will power than you.

UND. More will power than m e!

CUS. Yes; you're entirely in the power of the business. You dont work it, it works you. You say you're a lever to move society; but who works that lever? Society itself and all the rascality of society. You simply drift … I wonder whether I should drift too.

(Remark from Lomax or the like?)

CUS. Plato says that society cannot be saved until either the Professors of Greek take to making whiskey and gunpowder, or else the makers of whiskey and gunpowder become professors of Greek.

LADY B. NONSENSE. There werent any professors of Greek in Plato's time. ~~I suppose that is why he wrote it so well.~~

CUS. There was a Salvation Army, though … It is a frightful gamble, but I'ld like to try it.

LOMAX. There you're unjust. It's a sound business affair, no gambling. I'll say that for the old man.

CUS. Barbara's a born gambler, too.

BARB. Yes! (*This point could be explained, if necessary.*)

CUS. Then here goes. – Mephistopheles, give me the power, and I'll take it. But I'll make no pledge. I may use it for &c &c.

UND. That's all right, my boy. You'll use it just as I use it; You love power, with all your delicacy of intellect. You'll want more of it. It'll grow under your hand; and you'll live for it … for power and for ~~against~~ 'Andrew Undershaft'!

CUS. Well, all the powerful men in Euripides are bad. I have often wondered whether …

BARB. Dolly, have you no faith in anything? I know you hadnt in the Army?

CUS. Well, I have a kind of strong belief that if you and I really want to do a thing, we can do it.

BARB. (Some Salvation Army religious phrase? Something she said in Act ii, about God helping them, or faith in God.)

this depends,
of course, on
how far B is
with him, or
is keeping
aloof.
This cd be
Developed

Murray habitually misspelled 'Cusins' as '**Cusens**.' '**B.P.**'s are Barbara's Principles. **Prossie** is one of the nicknames of Proserpine Garnett, Pastor Morell's secretary in *Candida.* She gets somewhat intoxicated after attending one of his lectures.

29 / To Gilbert Murray

Edstaston. Wem. Shropshire
7th October 1905

[ALS: CL2]

On 5 October Shaw and Barker visited the Webbs, and Beatrice recorded in her diary that they 'spread out before us the difficulties, the hopes, the ridiculous aspects of their really arduous efforts to create an intellectual drama' (Purdom, 47). Shaw also confided to her the troubling truth about Major Barbara *in its present state: 'Though I thought I had finished my play, the result of my reading it to Gilbert Murray in Oxford on Sunday is that I am now writing the last scene over again – the first time I ever had to do such a thing' (*Bernard Shaw and the Webbs, *79). His response to Murray's letter was written while he and Charlotte were visiting 'Edstaston,' at Wem in Shropshire, the home of her brother-in-law and sister, Colonel and Mrs Hugh Cholmondeley (pronounced 'Chumley').*

On 6 October Murray had written a letter to Lady Carlisle, assuring her that the family resemblances to the females in the play were minimal: 'Barbara, though a charming character, is not in the least like Mary; nor is the Greek professor's mother-in-law the least bit like you … The caricature of me, however, is labelled quite clearly! He is a Professor of Greek, an Australian, is addressed as "Euripides" and quotes passages from my version of the Bacchae as his own.' His attempts to mollify Lady Mary and her mother failed, however: on 11 October he received a letter from his wife declaring, 'Mother is very angry with B. Shaw and so am I – furious – but if you say we are not to be furious what is the good!' (Bod)

Shaw's more or less final conclusions about Cusins and Barbara are stated below, but he reconsidered them to a certain degree in 1941 (see letter 131).

Dear Murray

Thanks for the Barbara stuff. If anything further occurs to you, send it along.

I want to get Cusins beyond the point of wanting power. I shall use your passage to bring out the point that Undershaft is a fly on the wheel; but Cusins would not make the mistake of imagining that he could be anything else. The fascination that draws him is the fascination of reality, or rather – for it is hardly a fascination – the impossibility of refusing to put his hand to Undershaft's plough, which is at all events doing something, when the alternative is to hold aloof in a superior attitude and beat the air with words. To use your metaphor of getting his hand on the lever, his choice lies, not between going with Undershaft or not going with him, but between standing on the footplate at work, and merely sitting in a first class carriage reading Ruskin & explaining what a low dog the driver is and how steam is ruining the country.

I am writing the whole scene over again. The moisture which serves for air in Ireland spoiled it hopelessly. I will send the new version to you when it is in shape.

I have taken rather special care to make Cusins the reverse in every point of the theatrical strong man. I want him to go on his quality wholly, and not to make the smallest show of physical robustness or brute determination. His selection by Undershaft should be a puzzle to the people who believe in the strong-silent-still-waters-run-deep hero of melodrama. The very name Adolphus Cusins is selected to that end.

As to the triumph of Undershaft, that is inevitable because I am in the mind that Undershaft is in the right, and that Barbara and Adolphus, with a great deal of his natural insight and cleverness, are very young, very romantic, very academic, very ignorant of the world. I think it would be unnatural if they were able to cope with him. Cusins averts discomfiture & scores off him by wit & humorous dexterity; but the facts are too much for him; and his strength lies in the fact that he, like Barbara, refuses the Impossibilist position (which their circumstances make particularly easy for them) even when the alternative is the most sensationally anti-moral department of commerce. The moral is drawn by Lomax 'There is a certain amount of tosh about this notion of wickedness.'

I have been writing this letter in scraps for three days – impossible to write letters here. I shall be back in London on Friday at latest.

Handsome of me not to make you a Rhodes scholar, by the way.

G.B.S.

The **passage** from Murray's dialogue that Shaw says he will use is the following: 'Cus. I venture to think I have got more will power than you. / Und. More will power than me! / Cus. Yes; you're entirely in the power of the business. You dont work it, it works you.' Shaw boils this down to: 'Cusins. I have more power than you, more will. You do not drive this place: it drives you' (CP 3, 169). **Lomax** ('Cholly') is engaged to Barbara's sister Sarah, and is comically addicted to conventional philosophizing. His observation in this case is unusually apt. Shaw's boast that he was not making Murray **a Rhodes scholar** was doubly ironic because, first, the Oxonian knew that the newly established Rhodes Scholarships program was not being assimilated smoothly within the University, and second, because Murray severely disapproved of the African policies of Cecil Rhodes (1853–1902). See Francis Wiley, 'The Scholarships Are Born,' 'First Arrivals,' and 'Settling Down,' in Elton, ed., *The First Fifty Years of the Rhodes Trust*, 59–102.

30 / To G. Bernard Shaw

131 Banbury Road, Oxford
7th October 1905

[TLT: HRC via Guelph, SPA]

Murray continues to reveal his sensitivity and scepticism about the portrayal of Cusins in the play by presenting an analogy between the way Shaw intends to have Barker mirror his appearance in the role and a hypothetical way he might have had Undershaft mirror Colonial Secretary Joseph Chamberlain, a member of a prominent manufacturing family from Birmingham who habitually wore an orchid on his coat lapel and a monocle. Murray even feels 'a sort of swear in it' (clash of tone), and likens specific details in the image of Cusins to 'tares' – undesirable elements sown by the Devil.

The letter is headed by the hand-lettered phrase 'πυκινὸν δόμον ἐλθεῖν,' the Greek equivalent of the term 'a bit thick.' Charles Lomax uses this colloquialism in reaction to the startling news that Undershaft will soon be visiting. It prompts Lady Britomart to ask Cusins to translate it 'into reputable English,' and he replies, 'If I may say so, Lady Brit, I think Charles has rather happily expressed what we all feel. Homer, speaking of Autolycus, uses the same phrase. πυκινὸν δόμον ἐλθεῖν means a bit thick' (CP 3, 81). Shaw had originally written that Euripides 'puts the same phrase into the mouth of Zeus,' but he adopted Murray's alternate suggestion.

Especially pertinent to the consideration of Shaw's revisions of Major Barbara *and of Murray's relationship to the play is Albert's article '"In More Ways than One": *Major Barbara*'s Debt to Gilbert Murray.' In this same connection, see also Dukore, 'Revising* Major Barbara.*'*

My dear Shaw

About 'a bit thick': Homer, speaking of Autolycus, the prince and archetype of robbers, uses the phrase 'pŭkĭnŏn dŏmŏn ĕltheĭn' meaning 'to come into a thick – i.e. a strong or fortified – house' but it would also construe 'It was thick (a bit thick) to come to the house.' Which fairly suits the Undershaft circumstances. Autolycus simply came as a burglar. On thinking it over, it seems to me that the *labelling* of Cusens as me is a flaw in the play! (I hesitate to say this, lest it should seem as if my feelings were hurt. They are not in the least hurt, there is nothing whatever to hurt them: but my judgment remains pretty firm.) I think you fall between two stools a little. If you made a study, or caricature, of me, it would no doubt be edifying and interesting and 'legitimate.' If you got Barker up like me, with spectacles and a moustache and a bald wig, & had all the Euripides business, as now, it would have a kind of music-hall funniness for the few people who knew about me, though I dont think it would be high art. But I feel now a sort of swear in it, something that leads one on a wrong scent ... As if, for instance, you gave Undershaft an orchid and an eyeglass, and said he made screws in Birmingham, without otherwise changing his character. It would seem pointless; a joke, but a joke not worth making.

Do not bother about this – I mean, dont treat this as a personal request. It is only a piece of advice. Has W A seen it, and, if so, what does he say? Of course I am rather in the habit of thinking that you dont know how good your best work is, and that consequently you allow the Devil to come and sow tares in it. But I think these labels – Australian, Greek Professor, translator of Euripides – are rather in the nature of tares.

My blessings on Act iii. I do hope it is shaping well.

Yours ever
G.M.

W A (William Archer) expressed his attitude toward the finished play in a review published in the *World* on 5 December ('The Theatre,' no. 1640: 914). Shaw, he wrote in part, 'has determined to prove … that he can make a mere discussion "as good as a play." And he has unquestionably succeeded; *Major Barbara* is a fascinating entertainment. Its plot is a negligible figment of unconditioned fantasy, which neither Mr. Shaw nor anyone else takes seriously for a moment. But we are pretty well accustomed nowadays to dispensing with plot: Mr. Shaw's real daring lies in dispensing with character. There are no human beings in *Major Barbara*: there are only animated points of view … It is evident from his description of *Major Barbara* as "a discussion in three acts" that Mr. Shaw deliberately intended the complete subordination of action to thought. But I do not think that he intended the unreality of the characters.' Shaw replied enigmatically in a letter of 1 January 1906 (CL 2, 599), which begins: 'Your article on "Major Barbara," the worst you ever wrote, delighted me. The complete success with which I wrecked your mind and left you footling – simply footling – was really the greatest proof of your fundamental sensibility to my magic.'

31 / To Gilbert Murray

10 Adelphi Terrace WC
29th November 1905

[ALS: CL 2]

Shaw proceeded with a substantial revision of Major Barbara*'s final act, then turned his attention to overseeing rehearsals at the Royal Court Theatre. The play's first performance of the six Vedrenne-Barker matinees that had been scheduled was given on 28 November. The cast included, in addition to Barker, Rosina Filippi (1866–1930) in the role of Lady Britomart, Louis Calvert (1859–1923) as Andrew Undershaft, Hubert Harsen as Stephen Undershaft, and Annie Russell (1864–1936) as Barbara (MacCarthy,* The Court Theatre, *145).*

In his letter to Murray on the day after the opening, Shaw tells him that at the last minute he made a crucial insertion in the text: new dialogue near the close of act 3, when he has Cusins say, 'My best pupil went out to fight for Hellas. My parting gift to him was not a copy of Plato's Republic, but a revolver' (CP 3, 182). This addition derived from his belief that Murray had, indeed, given a revolver rather than a classics text to his former student H.N. Brailsford in 1897 when he left England to side with Greece in the Greco-Turkish War.

A week after seeing the play performed, Murray wrote his daughter Rosalind on 7 December, 'I suppose somebody has told you about Major Barbara, and the caricature of me that Shaw had made? It is outrageously personal, but not a bit offensive or malicious. Mr Barker is got up rather like me, but not quite. (No moustache, and different baldness.) And he says he is a Greek Professor, an Australian, has translated Euripides, – he even quotes the Bacchae and says "My translation!" – and there are all kinds of little things that nobody would know about. E.G. that I gave Brailsford a revolver when he went to the Gk War' (Bod). (Leventhal in The Last Dissenter *notes that Murray's recollection of this may have been confused [32f.]). The fact that he let Barker use his spectacles shows a distinct touch of ambivalence.*

*Shaw's negative reaction to Calvert's portrayal of Undershaft partly underlies the unfavourable critique of the play by Beatrice Webb, who had argued about the third act with Shaw before she attended the performance and recorded her impressions (and those of Balfour) in her diary: 'GBS's play turned out to be a dance of devils – amazingly clever, grimly powerful in the second act, but ending, as all his plays end (or at any rate most of them) in an intellectual and moral morass. A.J.B[alfour] was taken aback by the force, the horrible force of the Salvation Army scene, the unrelieved tragedy of degradation, the disillusionment of the Greek professor and of Barbara – the triumph of the unmoral purpose, the anti-climax of evangelizing the Garden City! I doubt the popular success of the play. It is hell tossed on the stage, with no hope of heaven' (*Diary*, 29 November 1905, 13).*

My dear Murray

I have to congratulate you on a remarkable success. Your lines went immensely; and Barker surpassed himself in your spectacles.

I intended to send you the script of the last act; but I refrained, partly because I hadnt time to write, and partly because your reluctance to accept the Undershaft inheritance finally drove me to clinch the matter by a surpassingly mean reference to Brailsford, which I thought had better be exploded on you from the stage. I do not see how you can get out of it now. Barker suggested that if Stephen (the pious son) were to talk Murray-Margoliouth the effect would be irresistible; but we resisted the temptation as a breach of good taste.

Barker was at his best, even as a drum virtuoso: he came out magnificently after being sticklike beyond all belief at rehearsals. Calvert suddenly realized that his part was blasphemous, and that Balfour, glaring from a box, might order him to the stake at any moment. He collapsed hopelessly and said, in the last act, 'They have to find their own drains; but I look after their dreams.' The last act was consequently a hideous failure.

I hear you are all coming to next Friday's performance. For your presence I do not give a damn; but the prospect of Lady Carlisle, filled with idle rumors, contemplating Miss Filippi and drawing conclusions as to my conception of her, terrifies me. Miss Filippi, though genial and artistic, has not the grand manner. Her nose is seriously enlarged by a bad cold; and she doesnt know her part. She also thinks the play wicked. She is, on the whole, about as like the alleged original as I am like Gladstone.

Barker has been cultivating the closest resemblance to you in private life for a fortnight past. Everybody recognized it – Charlotte, Mrs Pat Campbell &c &c – instantly & spontaneously the moment the spectacles went on. On the stage he obliterated it by a careful make-up. Calvert, on the other hand, made up so exactly like a photograph of the Turkish ambassador I supplied him with, that he could get his dinner any day at the Embassy & give the real Turk to the police as an impostor. Yet nobody will find out Calvert; and everybody will find out Euripides.

I am urging Barker to take a music hall engagement for a turn entitled 'Bad Taste: or My Gallery of Eminent Men.'

yrs ever
G. Bernard Shaw

David **Margoliouth** (1858–1940) was a classical scholar at New College, Oxford, and a close friend of Murray's. Arthur J. **Balfour** (1848–1930) was prime minister 1902–5, a friend of Beatrice Webb, and a frequent member of the audience at the Court. The dialogue that Calvert had muffed was 'They find their own dreams, but I look after the drainage.' The **Turkish ambassador** to the Court of St James was Stefanaki Musurus Pasha.

32 / To G. Bernard Shaw

131 Banbury Road, Oxford
3rd December 1905

[TLS: HRC via Guelph, SPA]

Having attended the 1 December matinee of Major Barbara, *Murray briefly compares the play to a novel by Mrs Humphry Ward (1851–1920) entitled* Robert Elsmere *(1888), in which one of the characters was believed to have been based on R.L. Nettleship (1846–92), a distinguished and popular tutor at Balliol College, Oxford.*

Murray then mentions the rave review by Desmond MacCarthy (1877–1952) in the Speaker, *the second paragraph of which begins: 'We are bound to say that our impression of* Major Barbara *was that it is one of the most remarkable plays put upon the English stage.' The play is 'a noble story, real as life, of a woman who lives in her religion and loses it; who, after enduring the desolation of seeing her own and all the world's hope seem to hang torn before her eyes, finds at last a belief her passionate heart can live by. This account will seem ridiculous to those who heard only the crackle of wit, the rhetoric of theory, and brisk interchange of comment; yet it is the centre and significance of the play.' Near the end he proclaims:*

'Mr. Shaw has written the first play with religious passion for its theme and made it real. That is a triumph no criticisms can lessen' ('New Faiths for Old,' Speaker, *n.s. 13, no. 322 [2 December 1905]: 9).*

My dear Shaw

I dont think that Lady Carlisle minded a bit, though she was rather severe on Miss Filippi's acting. For my own part, though I do not think the personalities added to the value of the play, and on general grounds I rather regret to see you imitating Mrs Humphrey Ward, it strikes me as really remarkable that you can manage to be so exceedingly personal without being in the faintest degree disagreeable or offensive. When your Great Exemplar put Nettleship into a book, she made my blood boil by her unintentional offensiveness. Stupidity, I suppose it was.

As to the play, the criticism that I most agree with is that of Desmond Macarthey [*sic*] in the Speaker. The whole thing strikes me as: 1. a prologue, quite good but slight, and damaged by Miss F's bad acting: 2. a really magnificent religious tragedy, leading to an almost desperate situation: 3. a courageous and ingenious, but not successful, attempt to get out of that desperate situation by casuistry. I admit that Miss Russell gave you away at the end by not understanding or perhaps remembering her lines. But, even with a great deal of good will, I was not able to feel her speeches satisfactory. I suggest some thoughts that cross my mind as causes of this unsatisfactoriness ... though perhaps you, like Barker, deny that there is any unsatisfactoriness.

1. The emotional effect of Act 2 is so great, that mere intellect, without emotion, is not enough to set against it. Could you have got some *emotional* statement, so to speak, of the Nietzschian [*sic*] position, as well as the dialectical statement?

2. The rapidity of the change is too much for one. Barbara takes the shattering of her religion too lightly. She could scarcely have acted so promptly if it had merely been a question of transferring her affections from me to Lomax.

3. I suspect that you really wanted four acts, and some more 'story.' The audience tended to feel the end as merely a giving up of all religion, and morality, too, for that matter, instead of realising that it was a change from one system to another – equally strenuous and earnest. Hence the rage of the Heathen in the Morning Post and elsewhere.

It would, of course, be against your principles to re-write the end (again!) making it into four acts, and you are so dogmatically attached to your principles. I dont think I have seen anything on the stage so deeply ... I cannot get the word; so moving to emotions and intellect at once, as the second Act.

Yours ever
G.M.

I see that, donlike, I have written entirely about what I disapproved. I cd write – & have written – pages of admiration for the other parts.

The **Nietzschean position** Murray refers to is that man is primarily motivated by a 'will to power,' propounded by the German philosopher Friedrich Wilhelm Nietzsche (1844–1900). The anonymous review of the play in the *Morning Post* that Murray calls '**the rage of the Heathen**' had been published on 29 November (9). It had already occasioned a response from Shaw, an editorial rebuttal, another protest by Shaw, and several letters from other readers (one of them Vedrenne). The reviewer began by asserting that the 'ordinary playgoer' was puzzled and annoyed by the play – 'by its lack of straightforward intelligible purpose, its deliberate perversity, and its self-contradictory insincerity.' Focusing on act 2, the reviewer declares: 'For awhile it looks as though the triumph or at any rate the moral victory would ultimately rest with Major Barbara, who with her gentle firmness, her goodness, and her inexhaustible pity scores heavily in her dealings with ruffianism and imposture at the West Ham shelter, which she induces her father to visit. But unfortunately the playwright cannot make even this concession to what may be called an agreeable moral without a display of taste so distressingly bad that he merely pains those whom for a wonder he seems trying to please. It is bad enough when he makes one of the Major's sham converts refuse the offer of a piece of bread with the remark that he is satisfied with "the peace which passeth all understanding." It is worse – and it is so bad that we wonder at its escaping the notice of the censorship – when Major Barbara in her disappointment is allowed to exclaim: "My God! My God! why hast Thou forsaken me!" and to be answered by the ribald retort: "What price salvation now?"' The texts of Shaw's letters of 1 and 2 December are reprinted in CP 3, 191–3.

33 / To Gilbert Murray

10 Adelphi Terrace WC
16th January 1906

[TLS: BL, SPA]

An outstanding event that would affect Shaw directly and Murray indirectly occurred just before and after this letter. The general election brought Murray's Liberal Party into power, supplanting the Conservative Arthur Balfour, and the Labour Party gained enough seats to become a significant minority. However, only seven Fabians won seats. As Gibbs describes the reaction, 'These results leave the Fabian Society in disarray, their energies having been expended and apparently wasted on permeation tactics. Many Fabians, including Shaw, begin to feel that a harder, more coordinated party political approach would be more effective' (Gibbs, Chronology, *168).*

The next Murray translation to be offered at the Court after The Trojan Women *was Euripides'* Electra, *which was produced for six performances starting on 16 January 1906 and ending on 2 February. Murray's and Barker's choice for the role of the obsessed, bloodthirsty protagonist was Mrs Patrick Campbell, but when they did not want to meet her conditions it was played by Edith Wynne Matthison (Andromache in the previous play). E. Harcourt Williams (1880–1957) took the lead male role of Orestes, and Edyth Olive played Clytemnestra. In his introduction to the published version, Murray says that the play 'is a close-knit, powerful, well-constructed play, as realistic as the tragic conventions will allow, intellectual and rebellious. Its psychology reminds one of Browning, or even of Ibsen' (v).*

A unique collaboration, reminiscent of Shaw's with fellow Fabians, took place in deciding the music for the play. The conductor, Theodore Stier, explained that he wrote the music at the last moment: 'It was done by a committee of three seated side by side upon the piano bench: Gilbert Murray, Granville Barker, and myself, each phrase as I played it being subjected to the close analysis of the other two, and accepted, rejected, or modified according to the joint decision' (Purdom, 50).

Again Murray received extensive comments from Shaw.

My dear Murray

Just a line to point out a couple of passages where I think the stage business is wrong in the Electra.

It seems to me quite obvious that it was the habit of the Greek lady to bolt promptly on spying strangers, and that Euripides meant Orestes to spring out of ambush and seize Electra before she could get away. This explains why she urges the other women to escape, and why she at last says 'You are too strong for me,' meaning that she gives up struggling to get loose from him.

When Clytemnestra goes into the hut, the door has hardly closed on her when Electra, in stentorian tones, and within an inch of the keyhole, announces the fellest intentions concerning her. I see no reason why Electra should not come to the front of the tennis lawn stealthily, and speak in a terrible whisper. The very simplicity of the stage arrangements makes an improbability of this kind more obvious than it would be on a modern stage.

A minor point is the color of Clytemnestra's hair. The twinéd gold is all right; and the raven cloud is all right; but it ought to stay gold or stay black: a violent death does not act as a hair dye. The live Clytemnestra had brown hair: the dead had black, and had effected other changes in her appearance. Miss Olive might, I think, have sacrificed her comfort for five minutes and played her own corpse.

In my boyhood Aegisthus used to be Aegistheus – or so I recollect him. Why unsettle our minds like this?

I always saw Orestes in armor – a stern man in cold iron.

I found a certain element of incongruous comedy in the extreme gentility of the peasant. He began well; but towards the end every syllable was a claim to be a gentleman.

The play is immense: I feel that we must do that sort of thing again and now. But there are parts of it that go far beyond acting: acting is only possible half way up the mountain: at the top they should just efface themselves and utter the lines.

I am interrupted –

G.B.S.

Murray wrote a few brief marginal comments, parts of which are unintelligible (indicated here by [?]): Next to para. 2: 'Yes: something [?] might have, but I can't [see?] what.' First line of para. 3: 'I don't agree.' First line of para. 4: 'An accident.' Last line: 'Never!' para. 6: 'Yes: something in this.' para. 7: 'yes.' The **peasant**, whom Electra had been forced by Aegisthus to marry, was played by Stratton Rodney (d. 1932).

34 / To Gilbert Murray

10 Adelphi Terrace WC
10th July 1906

[ALS: CL 2]

Murray's Electra *and* Hippolytus *were revived starting on 12 March, but turned out to be financial failures, making Shaw talk openly about bankruptcy of the Court enterprise. Meanwhile, Shaw and Johnston Forbes-Robertson were rehearsing* Cæsar and Cleopatra *for its opening at the New Amsterdam Theater in New York on 20 October; it was received enthusiastically.*

At the rehearsals of Cæsar & Cleopatra there is much difference of opinion as to Mithridates of Pergamos. Mithriddities of Pergaymos sounds to me wrong: I incline towards Mithridaytes of Pergamos; but I have no settled convictions on the subject; and Robertson prefers Mithradytes of Pergaymos. How do you address the gentleman? Is P.Garmoss out of the question?

And is Clay O'Partrer admissible? Or Cleeopaytra. I say Cleeopattra, as she is usually called that in Ireland. Does Eupator rhyme with Equator or to Jupiter?

G.B.S.

Merriam-Webster's online dictionary sanctions Shaw's pronunciation of '**Mithri*da*ytes**' as well as that of '***Per*gamos**.' For **Cleopatra**, the same source gives 'Klē-ə-'*pa*-tra' and the variant 'Klē-ə-'*pä*-tra,' and for **Eupator** it confirms the rhyme with 'Equator.'

35 / To Gilbert Murray

10 Adelphi Terrace WC
22nd June 1907

[ALS: CL 2]

The volume John Bull's Other Island and Major Barbara *had been published by Constable on 19 June. In spite of a threatened boycott by the Society of Authors, Shaw arranged for the sale of a special, cheaper edition of 500 copies to the Times Book Club. Laurence discusses the controversy at length, along with Shaw's part in it, in CL 2, 677–8.*

At the time of this letter the first performances of the 'Don Juan in Hell' scene of Man and Superman *were being presented at the Court, with Robert Loraine (1876–1935) as Don Juan, Norman McKinnel (1870–1932) as the Devil, Michael Sherbrooke (1874–1957) as the Statue, and Lillah McCarthy (1875–1960) as Doña Ana. Charles Ricketts (1866–1931) designed the stunning costumes for the eight matinees that stretched from 4 to 28 June.*

My dear Murray

I am rather exercised in my mind by the proposed performances of Medea & The Trojan Women; and I have a quaint suggestion to make.

You will get no good out of The T.W. unless you have a strikingly beautiful and rather magical Hecuba. She ought to touch the imagination so as to make men see a past in her – not merely a personal or historical past, but *the* tragic past of all the destinies. The experienced actress in a strong part will shatter every such possibility. Therefore I, being of sound mind &c &c, do deliberately advise you to cast Lillah McCarthy for

Hecuba. She makes a curiously beautiful old woman; and her notion of conveying the dignity of age is to speak much better than she does in a young part. And her blitherings and lunacies will become Cassandrated in the Euripidean atmosphere.

I dont think she could touch Medea. Medea mustnt blither: there must be no holes in her; and Lillah is always tumbling from heights into holes and bouncing up again, like a pantomime demon with a star trap. There is only one woman on the stage who can do Medea, and that is Janet Achurch. In Little Eyolf she *was* Medea. I think we shall have to get her a new set of teeth; and she must not be left to the guidance of her own ear in delivering the verse, or she will decorate it with the most subversive caterwaulings; but Medea is a big thing that breaks through all mere prudences; and if any of her old strength remains (and I shouldnt hesitate to ask her to rehearse on approval to find that out) the next best within reach is a thousand miles behind.

I write this on the spur of the moment lest you should get committed to Lillah as Medea, and some too too solid chump of a Hecuba before you have heard me.

yrs ever
G.B.S.

Medea was performed on 22 October 1907 at the Savoy Theatre; Edyth Olive played Medea, not Janet Achurch or Lillah McCarthy. The performance of ***The Trojan Women*** which Shaw assumed was pending seems not to have materialized. **Janet Achurch** played Rita in Ibsen's ***Little Eyolf*** at the Avenue Theatre in 1896.

36 / To Gilbert Murray

10 Adelphi Terrace WC
30th June 1907

[ALS: CL 2]

Murray's introduction to the published version of Medea *calls it 'a study of oppression and revenge' with which few plays can vie for 'concentrated dramatic quality and sheer intensity of passion' (ix). Far from exonerating Jason (as Shaw seems to imply), he condemns him for trying to 'crush' Medea, who is thence 'transformed by her injuries from an individual human being into a sort of living Curse,' so that the judgment pronounced on Jason comes 'from his own victim transfigured into a devil' (xi).*

Historians of the period deduce that the play 'was deliberately performed against the upsurge of public interest in the movement for women's suffrage' (Hall and Mackintosh, 511). Murray had supported that movement since the late 1880s, and Sybil Thorndike recalled him admitting that Medea *'might have been written' for it (Thorndike, 74). In* Euripides and His Age, *Murray notes that Euripides now seems 'an aggressive champion of women,' and that 'Songs and speeches from the* Medea *are recited today at suffragist meetings' (32).*

My dear Murray

Now I have a subject for my next play – The Princess & The Professor. Excellent.

The only other Hecuba I can think of is Ada Rehan. If she could learn it and her doctors would let her play it, she would speak the verse beautifully. But I expect you will have to pull back on Lillah to save you from worse.

I should persist in recommending Janet for Medea but for your betrayal of the Court plot against Euripides to steal the sympathy from Jason. Have you ever read the life of Mary Wollestonecraft & poor Captain Imlay? Imlay is held up as a monster because Mary's habit of throwing herself into the Thames on the slightest provocation got on his nerves, and he ran away from her and took up with a more tranquil female. You want to trump up the same case against Jason. I protest in the name of my sex. Nothing struck me when Barker read Medea to me more than the curiously just effect produced by Jason – the superiority of Old Rip to the Serjeant Buzfuz point of view. I now gravely suspect you of an intention to Buzfuz. Janet would baffle that, at all events.

C.I. is no use for leading business on that scale. Remember Lady Inger. True, she might have done that better with better coaching; and when she was good in Phedra & Clytemnestra, she was quite good; but – well, she's possible, in spite of her lingo. Only, there will be no *hope*: we know exactly how far she will go; and I always like to have a sporting chance of getting to the limit.

G.B.S.

Shaw's speculation about his **next play** was idle or facetious. He began writing *Getting Married* in early August, a play with neither a princess nor a professor. The Irish-American actress **Ada Rehan** (1860–1916) was the leading lady of Augustin Daly's company for many years. Once again Murray wanted Mrs Patrick Campbell for the title role of *Medea*, but Barker and Vedrenne did not concur. Barker's wife, Lillah McCarthy, was their second choice, but Vedrenne had already promised the part to Edyth Olive. The play was not performed at the Royal Court but at the Savoy Theatre, in October 1907. This marked the end of Murray's partnership with Vedrenne and Barker (Wilson, 107–8). **Mary Wollstonecraft** (1759–97), best known for *A Vindication of the Rights of Woman* (1792), formed an alliance with the American businessman **Captain** Gilbert **Imlay** (1754–1828). They lived together as husband and wife for several years, but he took numerous trips alone, and in 1795 she discovered that he was being unfaithful to her in their own home. This drove her to despair and she tried to drown herself, but was rescued. Books about her had been published in 1885 and 1898. Within the context of the letter, it seems that **C. I.** must stand for Captain Imlay in spite of Shaw's ambiguous statement. **Serjeant Buzfuz** in Dickens's *Pickwick Papers* is the casuistic counsel for the plaintiff in the case of *Bardell v. Pickwick*. He 'proves' that Pickwick's note about 'chops and tomato sauce' is a declaration of love. **Old Rip** might bear the colloquial inference of 'old rake'; the alternative of Rip van Winkle does not seem to fit. **Remember Lady Inger** refers to the Incorporated Stage Society's final offering in January 1906, Ibsen's *Lady Inger of Ostrat*, in which Edyth Olive played Lady Inger. The comparison that Shaw implies between the play and the Wollstonecraft story may stem from the fact that Ibsen attributes its creation to 'a sudden love affair, violently broken off' (quoted in Meyer, 117).

37 / To Gilbert Murray

10 Adelphi Terrace WC
10th October 1907

[ALS: CL 2]

Early in 1907 William Archer corralled a large group of literary men to campaign for the abolition of play censorship. Shaw became the most active participant, although his efforts were finally spurned. See the 'Introduction,' xiii–xiv, and the headnote to Letter 41 for details on this development.

Dear Murray

Tell Barrie that he cannot disguise his thrifty Scotch desire to pay out the names in small instalments as statesmanship – at least not from me. He must pay in full, or we are lost.

We shall get in one blow, and one only; and it must be a smasher. The list of names will not be too long, unfortunately: it would not be that if we got all the decent playwrights in England. It is the length and completeness of the list that will make the impression. Nobody would read a second lot: in fact, no editor who was a good journalist would put them in except into a corner. Royal Academy – Second Notice – Third Notice – is a game now abandoned to provincial papers of special obsolescence.

It positively must not be. Stiffen your back; for I assure you your opinion is worth a round hundred of those of recluse-playwrights. They know nothing about public life, bless them.

The D's D. revolts Barker's soul: he strives earnestly to crush the cast and get a delicate galsworthy result. Then I sail in and turn the whole thing into a blatant Richardson's Show. Between us, we shall pull it through; but his loathing of the stage and of the vulgarity called acting is getting serious; so keep plenty of oxygen playing on Medea or he will mix it with hydrogen and apply it cold.

G.B.S.

J[ames] M[atthew] **Barrie** (1860–1937) was a popular novelist and playwright. '**The D's D.**' refers to the six-week revival of *The Devil's Disciple* at the Savoy Theatre which commenced on 14 October 1907. Barker directed and alternately played Dick Dudgeon and General Burgoyne. Shaw's phrase, '**a delicate galsworthy result**,' refers to the style of John Galsworthy (1867–1933), novelist and playwright. Laurence identifies '**Richardson's Show**' as 'a portable booth theatre in which plays and pantomimes were performed at fairs by John Richardson (c. 1763–1837)' (CL 2, 685). In an undated letter to Archer (ca. 20–24 May 1907), Shaw comments, 'When my Arms & the Man was produced in 1894, all its alleged novelties were as old as Richardson's Show' (686).

38 / To Gilbert Murray

10 Adelphi Terrace WC
18th November 1907

[ALS: CL 2]

Shaw's next letter to Murray addresses an issue of great importance to him: his anti-Darwinian, pro-Lamarckian 'theory of the inheritance of acquired habits.' Jean-Baptiste Lamarck (1744–1829) put forth the theory, now decisively discredited, 'that new traits in an organism develop because of a need created by the environment and that they are transmitted to its offspring' (Concise Columbia Encyclopedia, *448). In his 1921 preface to* Back to Methuselah, *Shaw applies this to account for miraculous cases of children exhibiting advanced capacities for their parents' patiently developed acquirements such as mechanical, mathematical, or musical comprehension (CP 5, 271–9). The following letter's cogent summary of the concept indicates that he had already worked out the theory.*

My dear Murray

I was sorry to miss you. I wanted to see you to ask you for a nice Greek word. You know my theory of the inheritance of acquired habits, which neo-Darwinians deny. First I say that since breathing, circulating the blood, and digesting food are beyond all question acquired habits – and rather late acquirements at that – the fact that they are inherited settles for ever the position of the neo-Darwinians as hopeless idiots.

But every man who has acquired the habit of bicycling knows that he relapses between each lesson & finally acquires the faculty in an instant, miraculously, as a fulfilled aspiration which has *created* the means of fulfilling it. Now, that relapse between the lessons is repeated in a still larger relapse between father & son; so that your son will not be born a bicyclist, but only an infinitesimal fraction of one; and many generations must elapse before little Murrays are born not only able to ride, but furnished with extensions of the skeleton into complete bicycles. Give me a good word for this phenomenon of relapse – something that will sound Weissmanic, like panmixia.

Dont send the book. Charlotte has already ordered it. Trade must be encouraged.

Arthur Ponsonby, one of C.B.'s secretarys, says that the Nation letter, which was expressly intended for him, fairly knocked him. In justice to Arthur I must add that this is not his own phrase; but I know no equally exquisite equivalent.

yrs ever
G.B.S.

Shaw addresses the same subject in a letter to Wells of 7 December 1916 (*Bernard Shaw and H.G. Wells*, 89–90), and in an *Observer* piece on 1 May 1932 reprinted in Shaw, *Agitations*, 281–6. [Friedrich Leopold] August **Weissmann** (1834–1914) was a German biologist known for the germ-plasm theory of heredity, which stresses the noninheritability of acquired characteristics (*Concise Columbia Encyclopedia*, 889). *Essays Upon Heredity*, a translation of his writings which includes the 1883 essay 'Life and Death' (Murray will refer to it as 'Origin of Death') was published in 1889 by Clarendon Press. One of his key terms was 'amphimixis'; thus to Shaw **'panmixia'** sounds **Weissmanic**. The **book** which Charlotte had already ordered was most likely Murray's Oxford edition of *Electra*, which was published in 1907. Arthur **Ponsonby** (1871–1946) was at this time private secretary to Prime Minister Henry Campbell-Bannerman (**C.B.**) (1836–1908). The only 1907 Shaw piece in the **Nation** which Laurence's bibliography lists is 'The Censorship of Plays,' *Nation* 2 (16 November 1907): 237–9.

39 / To G. Bernard Shaw 131 Banbury Road, Oxford
26th November 1907

[TLS: BL, SPA]

In full awareness of Shaw's views on women's rights, Murray ends the following letter by seconding his local women's suffrage society's invitation for Shaw to talk on the subject. From his Fabian Manifesto *no. 2 (1884), to 'The Womanly Woman' chapter in* The Quintessence of Ibsenism *(1891), through the 'New Woman' characters in* The Philanderer, Mrs Warren's Profession, *and* Captain Brassbound's Conversion, *up to his speech promoting women's suffrage at a meeting of the National Union of Women's Suffrage Societies in March 1907, Shaw had been a prominent spokesman for this reform. His 1908 play* Getting Married *will deal indirectly with the problem. The chapter 'Votes for Women' in Gibbs's* Bernard Shaw: A Life, *293–306, gives a full and cogent summary of the topic.*

As for Murray himself, his belief in women's suffrage even as an undergraduate had eased him into the good graces of Rosalind Frances Howard (1845–1921), soon to become Lady Carlisle, and was a factor in her support for his long-lasting suit to marry her daughter Mary. He voiced his specific views in a July 1909 inaugural address at University College, Aberystwyth. As paraphrased by Wilson (181), he 'regarded more freedom for women as a mark of advancing civilization. He spoke … in favour of change in the divorce laws – also for some restraint in the reporting of divorce cases. "We must accustom ourselves – and we must begin young – to regard women in all respects and in all relations of life as Fellow-citizens and not as property."'

Murray differed from Shaw in his disapproval of the more extreme actions of the suffragist campaign. Whereas Shaw, in a (self-edited and highly exaggerated) March 1906 interview had stated that women 'should have a revolution – they should shoot, kill, maim, destroy – until they are given a vote' (Gibbs, 294), Murray publicly deplored not only the hunger strike undertaken by jailed suffragettes in 1909, but also the protests that ensued against the policy of forcibly feeding them (Wilson, 181). Shaw disagreed on the latter issue; in a talk delivered at a meeting of the National Political League, he strongly berated the policy (printed as 'Torture by Forcible Feeding Is Illegal' in Weintraub, ed., Fabian Feminist, *228–35).*

My dear Shaw

I have discussed the intermittent relapse with Margoliouth, and we suggest two words: 1. *Metanesis,* accent on the second syllable (like 'I met Anna,

Ciss.'). *Anesis* is 'a letting go, a losing or slackening'; *Met-anesis* would be 'a doing so in between'; i.e. an intermittent loss of hold or of strength.

2. *Metasphalma* – 'a trip or fall in between.' The process of so tripping would be *Metasphalsis*, which is rather ugly.

3. You might make a plain intelligible Latin word 'interlapse,' but that is giving Weissmann an unfair advantage. I am strongly with you in the controversy. Weissmann's essay on the Origin of Death is very interesting and good, but I felt in the other essays that he was confusing two questions. He proved that for practical purposes acquired characteristics are not inherited right off, as wholes; and then argued that there was no faint modification which would need a hundred generations to be clearly visible – which does not follow at all. Your instances seem to me fair.

Yes: that was a good big play. I find two or three things in it that I dont quite like, but I think one has to criticize it on a high level, like a good novel of Hardy's, say. I was glad that Mrs Warren was such a success in Berlin.

By the way, the Woman Suffrage Society here are very anxious to have you to speak to their annual meeting some time next term, and asked me to reinforce their invitation. It is not a bad little society. In fact my wife and I are both on the executive. But all the future Highschool Teachers from the women's Halls would come to learn their duty. So do come if you can, and stay with us.

Yours ever
G.M.

'That was a good big play' refers to *The Devil's Disciple*, which was still in the midst of its revival. After Murray first read it, he called it 'exceedingly good' in a letter of 25 January 1901 (Letter 6), and when he reviewed *Three Plays for Puritans* for *The Speaker* in February (prefatory note to Letter 8), he said it was 'the best constructed and most uniformly strong' play in the volume. Thomas **Hardy** (1840–1928) was an English novelist who wrote *Far From the Madding Crowd* and other famous novels, plus an historical drama in verse, *The Dynasts*, which Barker adapted for the stage in 1914.

40 / To Gilbert Murray

Ayot St Lawrence
27th November 1907

[ALS: Bod, SPA]

Interlapse is so obviously right that I shall have to reserve the others merely to insult the Whiteboys.

I saw two acts of Waste again yesterday. Some of it was like listening a second time to a debate, but not much.

I am always refusing the W.S. people. The last thing they proposed was to take the Albert Hall & turn me on there. Except as an excuse for going to see you I shouldnt entertain it; *but* –

G.B.S.

The Shaws had moved to Ayot St Lawrence in November 1906. *Wikipedia* (confirmed in other sources) says that the term **Whiteboys** was used by eighteenth-century secret Irish agrarian organizations who used violent tactics to defend tenants' rights, and 'became a general term for rural violence connected to secret societies.' Thus, Shaw may imply rampaging roughnecks who might be intimidated by strange Greek sounds. Barker's *Waste* was performed by the Stage Society for two private performances on 24 and 26 November (CL 2, 720). The **W.S. people** must be members of the Woman Suffrage Society.

Once again there is a significant gap in extant letters. Murray was appointed to the élite position of Regius Professor of Greek at Oxford in October 1908. A significant Shaw-Murray connection occurred on 29 October when Shaw wrote to Margot Asquith, the prime minister's wife, urging her to use her influence to secure a knighthood for Arthur Wing Pinero (1855–1934). After that appeal (which was successful) he turned his attention to Murray: 'If a high-literary knight or baronet, or even baron is wanted, Gilbert Murray, now Regius Professor of Greek at Oxford and son-in-law to that extremely Liberal peer Lord Carlisle and his formidable and even more Liberal wife, is the very man. His translations of Euripides are magnificent' (Shaw, Theatrics, *93–4). Murray was eventually offered a knighthood, but he declined in early 1912 (Wilson, 193).*

At the time of the following letter, Shaw was in the process of writing what became an 11,000-word essay entitled Statement of the Evidence in Chief of Bernard Shaw before the Joint-Committee on Stage Plays. *Besides submitting it to the Committee, he sent copies to members of the Dramatists' Club, which he had joined when it was formed in March (CL 2, 851–3). Shaw likens the essay to John Milton's 1644 pamphlet* Areopagitica, *an argument addressed to Parliament against restricting freedom of the press. He will later print the full text in his preface to* The Shewing-up of Blanco Posnet. *Laurence explains why, in that context, it was entitled 'The Rejected Statement': 'Copies of Shaw's* Statement *were distributed to the members of the Joint Select Committee of the House of Lords and the House of Commons on the Stage Plays (Censorship) in advance of his appearance on 30th July … The Committee informed him, however, that it could not accept the printed statement as evidence since it would be going against precedent. To its chagrin Shaw was able to cite precedent in the 1892 parliamentary hearings on censorship in no fewer than three instances … all three statements being testimony in favour of censorship! The committee's acting chairman … abruptly closed the meeting until the committee could discuss the matter in secret session. When the committee reconvened, Shaw was informed – without explanation – that his statement would not be received' (CL 2, 853).*

One masterpiece of Greek drama was indeed being censored again: Sophocles' Oedipus Rex. *In the 1890s, both* Oedipus Rex *and Shelley's* The Cenci *were denied licences because both incorporated incest and parricide. The two were inextricably linked in discussions of censorship through 1909, but the Select Committee on Stage Plays was rethinking its rigid policies. When Murray submitted his translation of Sophocles' play in November 1910, G[eorge] A[lexander] Redford (1846–1916) refused to licence it. He even noted that the play's author and producer were enemies of the censorship bent on undermining the process through the prohibition of a classic familiar to most people (paraphrased letter from Redford to the Lord Chamberlain in his office's files as 'LCP Corr 1910/814 Oedipus Rex'; courtesy of Professor Brad Kent). However, the case was reviewed by the newly formed Advisory Board and their positive recommendation was heeded by the Lord Chamberlain's office, so that it was finally allowed to be performed at Covent Garden for two weeks beginning on 10 January 1912 (Hall and Mackintosh, 529–36). The director, John Martin-Harvey (1863–1944), starred as Oedipus; Lillah McCarthy played Jocasta (see CL 3, 72). Its reception was exceptional,* The Times *commenting, '*Oedipus Rex *undoubtedly held the audience last night spellbound.' From the first appearance of Harvey 'until two hours later, … you are taken far away from 1912, away from yourself, away from the fashionable dames and the eminent politicians, away to 425 B.C.' Murray told Lillah, 'Indeed I did not know that there was any actress in England capable of looking and speaking the part with that heroic strength and dignity' (Purdom, 129–32).*

41 / To Gilbert Murray

10 Adelphi Terrace WC
17th July 1909

[TLS: CL 2, minus the first two paragraphs, which SPA supplies]

My dear Murray

We are going out of town this afternoon and may not be back until you return to Oxford. Under these urgent circumstances, will you come to lunch today at half-past one? After lunch, Barker, Barrie and Galsworthy are coming in to be photographed here for an article by Archer. The photographer, Coburn, whose work you have no doubt seen at Barker's, will be of the party, and may possibly want to have a shot at your impressive head. Please, at this point, give the messenger your answer and send him back to say whether we may expect you or not – also whether you are a vegetarian. The rest of this letter was written before your card came, and can be read at your leisure.

I fear you will have to give evidence before this Select Committee on the Censorship. Send in your proof in Greek and let them examine you on it.

I am almost killed by the sudden addition to my work of the preparation of a huge proof that will supersede Milton. I will send you a copy of it as soon as I get it into print; for I think you are the man to back up my special line. I am hammering at the absolute necessity to the life of a nation of tolerance of immoral and heretical doctrines on the practical grounds that though the arguments used to justify the powers of the Censor are precisely those which justify the powers of any civil magistrate, there is a momentous difference between the two, founded, not on sentiment nor on any moral abstract theory of rights, but on the unquestionable historical fact that whereas nations prosper in direct proportion to their intolerance of theft and murder, they decay (witness Spain and the Inquisition) in direct proportion to their intolerance of immoral and heretical doctrines, the reason being, of course, that all doctrines are necessarily immoral and heretical at their first propounding (immorality and heresy being involved by novelty); but theft and murder are neither novel nor in any sense questionable, but are simply familiar and tried pieces of mischief.

Now it seems to me that if you would write one of your finest essays to shew that some of the masterpieces of Greek drama were censored in their time, and that they are actually being censored again now when after many centuries we are at last rising again to the point of being able to enjoy them, pointing out at the same time what a power they must have been in raising Greece from the Homeric level to the Euripidean, your scholarship would make a great impression; and your talent for making an essay on Greek civilization a vivid piece of contemporary social criticism, have a rare chance [*sic*].

The other fellows can do the drudgery of Old Baileying Redford and exposing the absurdity of the present system. Barker can deal with the loss and hardship to the author. Raleigh can deal with the music-hall side of the question. But you must ride the high horse. I want the Bluebook containing the evidence of the Select Committee to be a classic instead of the wretched piffling things the former bluebooks are.

yours ever
G. Bernard Shaw

Alvin Langdon **Coburn** (1882–1966) was an American photographer, resituated in England, whose growing reputation led to a sitting with Shaw in late July 1904. See Shaw's letter to Coburn in CL 2, 435–6. Unlike Shaw and Lady Carlisle, Murray was only a sporadic **vegetarian**, although he sometimes claimed to be a dedicated one (Wilson, 67). Cecil **Raleigh** (1856–1914) was a playwright specializing in Drury Lane melodramas. The production of *Oedipus Rex* was billed as that of Max Reinhardt (1873–1943), a prestigious figure in German theatre in this period whose principles of staging were anathema to Shaw, but it was actually done by Martin-Harvey.

42 / To G. Bernard Shaw

24 Upper Mall, Hammersmith
18th July 1909

[TLS: HRC via Guelph, SPA]

As part of his campaign against censorship, from 16 February to 8 March 1909 Shaw had written The Shewing-up of Blanco Posnet, *a long one-act subtitled* 'A Sermon in Crude Melodrama.' *It is a parable of the redeeming effect of the Life Force on an American cowhand proud of his disreputable behaviour. He has stolen a horse from his brother to pay him back for cheating him out of money, but he finds himself unable to resist giving the horse to a poor woman to take her child, sick with the croup, to a hospital. He is captured, and at his trial he preaches a sermon blaming his act of involuntary benevolence on pressure from God – whom he also holds responsible for making the croup that eventually killed the child. In the typical villain-conversion twist of timeworn melodrama, he ends by declaring 'theres a rotten game and theres a great game. I played the rotten game; but the great game was played on me; and now I'm for the great game every time' (CP 3, 798–9).*

Shaw knew the statement that God 'made the croup' would be singled out by the censor for blasphemy and prohibited, along with a conspicuous reference to a young woman's flagrant promiscuity. When Redford took this bait and censored the play in its present state, Shaw urged Lady Gregory (1852–1932) to have it produced at the Abbey Theatre, free of censorial control but subject to conditions dictated by Irish authorities. They permitted the performance with the stipulation that if it provoked a riot (a favourite reaction of Irish playgoers) the theatre would lose its licence. In the end the audience voiced its approval so strongly that Lady Gregory and Yeats sent Shaw a telegram saying: 'GLORIOUS RECEPTION SPLENDID VICTORY WHERE IS THE CENSOR NOW' (Gibbs, Bernard Shaw: A Life, *262).*

William Archer (WA below), had interested Murray in spelling reform in May 1907 and helped found the Committee of the Simplified Spelling Society in 1908, which elected Murray president three years later. Wilson comments: 'Curiously enough there is no trace in Murray's correspondence with Shaw that they ever discussed this subject, so dear to Shaw in his later years' (187). However, Shaw's interest in spelling reform had begun in the 1880s, and in the early 1900s he had published 'Spelling Reform v. Phonetic Spelling: A Plea for Speech Nationalisation' (plus a reply to criticisms) in the 16 and 22 August 1901 Morning Leader*; an article on simplified spelling for the Society of Authors bulletin,* The Author, *in April 1902; and 'The Simplified Spelling Proposals' in* The Times *on 25 September 1906 (all reprinted in* Shaw on Language*). Thus, it can be assumed that he had already exchanged his views on the subject with Murray. If he had not, Murray could not have missed his speech (or a report of it) on spelling reform at a Phonetics Conference in London on 28 January 1911 (Gibbs,* Chronology, *191).*

Shaw was not the only playwright who profited from Murray's critical acumen; Barker is a parallel case in point. In a mid-July 1909 letter to his friend, he bemoans his progress on The Madras House*: 'Oh, my poor new play!' A bit later he asks Murray if he may 'inflict' the draft upon him, mainly because 'I know that its philosophic flats are not joined. I seem to have said something quite different from what I had set out to say.' He added in still another letter: 'It is not what it should be and it certainly does want the light of your intellectual morality and moral intellectuality turned on it.' He conveyed the outcome exuberantly in a 1921 letter to Archer: '*The Madras House *is the best play I've written yet' (Salmon,* Granville Barker, *160–1).*

My dear Shaw

I ran round to your house in the afternoon yesterday, but you had already departed. I had to go to Sophocles' Electra at the Court. Shall I not endure what I have often inflicted on others?

I am sorry not to have seen you. I consider the censoring of Posnet to be the act of a man with no moral sense at all – and precious little intellect either. But somehow I can not get into the proper crusading spirit. Perhaps if I tried to write something it would come. Is the plan to send in written evidence – or a written statement of views – and then go and be vivaed on it? However WA will tell me; I am going to improve his Spelling to-morrow.

By the way, it might be a good thing if you gave my hostess, Mrs Wheeler, the chance of a talk about some of your heroines. She may be stricken dumb when she sees you, but she works at them and talks about them in a very interesting way. I think she has a way of rejecting bravura and getting right into the heart of a character which ought to be encouraged.

Do send me your Areopagitica. I fully see that the high and general line is the right one to take, if only I could rise to it.

Yours ever
G.M.

Sophocles' Electra, translated by Lewis Campbell, was performed at the Aldwych Theatre on 15 July 1909. Murray never did submit **a written statement of views**, but appeared before the Joint Commitee on 20 August 1909 (not 1908 as in Wilson) and argued that 'censorship was not based on any published law and was exercised according to no definite criteria; the Censor's decisions were bound to be arbitrary and it was thus impossible to argue logically or to lodge appeals against them' (Wilson, 173). He suggested that the Examiner of Plays should 'consider whether a play breaks any known law,' and, if necessary, 'put the Attorney-General or the Director of Public Prosecutions in motion' (Purdom, 94–5). **Vivaed**, as a verb, is a coined word; 'viva' can be short for 'viva voce,' as it is used in England to denote a demanding oral examination. Murray was staying at the home of his friends Christopher and Penelope **Wheeler**, the latter an accomplished actress who had starred in his Birmingham production of *Hippolytus* in 1908. On Lady Mary's suspicions of her husband's relationship with Mrs Wheeler during 1908, see Wilson, 143–4.

43 / To Gilbert Murray

The Ivy Bush Hotel, Carmarthen
15th August 1909

[ALS: Bod, SPA]

The day before Shaw appeared before the Joint Select Committee on 30 July the clamour raised against the Lord Chamberlain's powers of censorship had led to the formation of a committee of inquiry, which examined 51 witnesses – the first two, Archer and Shaw, designated as 'unofficial.' Meetings continued until 2 November, when it issued its Blue Book report. Further information on the controversy is available in Shaw's letters to Herbert Samuel, Lady Gregory, and Yeats in CL 2, 853–64.

The Lord Lieutenant of Ireland, John Campbell Gordon, Earl of Aberdeen (1847–1934), was in Scotland when the British government tried to influence him to ban Shaw's play. Laurence explains what happened as a result: 'In the absence of the Viceroy, his under-secretary Sir James Dougherty (1844–1934) reacted by sending a letter from Dublin Castle to the Abbey Theatre in which he committed, in the Viceroy's name, the impropriety of threatening to revoke the patent of the Abbey Theatre if Shaw's play were produced. Lady Gregory and William Butler Yeats, the theatre's directors, responded to the attempt at intimidation by issuing a public manifesto in which they obdurately refused to withdraw the play' (CL 2, 856). With the Lord Lieutenant back in control, Shaw agreed to a few cuts in the text (although none that Redford had demanded) and it was performed without further interference.

Shaw began writing Misalliance *on 8 September, while he was still in Ireland, and completed the play on 4 November.*

My dear Murray

I am running through here on my way to the west of Ireland for six weeks holiday (which means playwriting, I suppose). I passed through Oxford yesterday, & called at Woodstock Road after reading an inscription on Banbury Road, only to learn that you are at Castle Howard.

Dublin Castle is threatening to withdraw the patent of the Abbey Theatre if Blanco Posnet is produced. This is the work of understrappers, who assume that I am a notorious criminal; and they have committed the official indiscretion of ignoring the Lord Lieutenant, and demanding that the play be cut according to the requirements of Redford. I have of course jumped at this slip on their parts; and I shall make capital enough out of the row, no matter what the result is; but it has occurred to me that you may know the Lord Lieutenant through your Liberal connexion. What sort of person is he? I should rather like to get at him over the heads of the Castle people; but I have no idea whether he has any character to bite on.

Has Schloesser or Archer sent you a copy of my last circular to shew witnesses exactly where we have got to?

My next ascertainable address, which I shall probably not reach until Thursday, is the Southern Hotel, Parknasilla, Sneem, Co. Kerry.

Yours ever
G. Bernard Shaw

Dublin Castle was until 1922 the seat of British rule in Ireland. Henry H. **Schloesser** (1883–1979; name changed to Slesser in 1914) was a Fabian lawyer and author of several books on trade union law. Shaw refers to him again in a letter of 22 July 1912 to Sidney Webb, commenting that he 'and his reform committee *are* absolutely negligible' (*Bernard Shaw and the Webbs*, 120).

44 / To G. Bernard Shaw

Castle Howard, York
18th August 1909

[ALS: BL]

Implicitly acknowledging his 'Liberal connexion' with Shaw, Murray wrote a strongly persuasive letter on his behalf – to the wrong Irish official, Lord Crewe (Robert Offley Ashburton Crewe-Milnes, Marquess of Crewe, 1858–1945), a fellow Liberal but Colonial Secretary at the time. He argued: 'I do think, first, that the actual theme of the play is both grand and tragic, in spite of its ugly and grotesque setting; and secondly, that this is the play in which Shaw has quite directly and without any subterfuge or nervous laughter expressed his religious faith – or a fragment of it. The point is that there is something in a man's own heart which, at certain crises, compels him to act according to righteousness or some law of love, even if he lose everything by it … This internal moral law or impulse or whatever it is, Shaw calls God*; it comes over the man 'like a sneak' and has him in his power' (Letter of 17 August 1909 in Wilson, 174).*

My dear Shaw

I am so sorry we missed the chance of seeing you in Oxford. – This is perfectly monstrous about the Dublin Castle officials: flagrantly unjust to you and insulting to the intelligence of those who have any serious interest in Literature or Drama. I think, and my wife, whose tastes are severe, agrees with me, that the condemnation of Blanco Posnet is one of the most utterly unintelligent things in Redford's record.

The Earl of Crewe is by way of taking great interest in artistic things and, I believe, in literature. He is a friend of Walter Raleigh – and though Raleigh's ~~morals~~* are damnable his understanding of literature is beyond question. I have written a longish letter to Lord Crewe about Posnet – not that I have the faintest shadow of influence with him, but it may possibly be of use.

I go up to town to-day, to have a look at the Committee tomorrow and give my evidence on Friday.

*public morals

Yours ever,
G.M.

Walter Raleigh (1861–1922) was an eminent literary scholar who became the first holder of the new chair of English literature at Oxford in 1904. He was knighted in 1911.

45 / To Gilbert Murray Parknasilla Hotel, Sneem, Kerry
20th August 1909

[TEL: SPA]

Shaw sent the following enigmatic advice to Murray on the day he was to be interviewed by the Joint Committee.

SIMPLE TO LET MANAGER TAKE COUNSELS OPINION PLAN WOULD NOT WORK BECAUSE HONEST LAWYER MUST DECLARE ALL SERIOUS PLAYS AND MOST FRIVOLOUS ONES LIABLE TO PROSECUTION BEING THUS WORSE THAN TEN REDFORDS MOST HE COULD PROMISE WOULD BE NOT TO CALL PUBLIC PROSECUT[OR'S] ATTENTION TO PLAY THIS WOULD BE CONSPIRACY WITH AUTHOR AND MANAGER AGAINST LAW ONCE WE CONCEDE PRINCIPLE WE ARE LOST BECAUSE IMPROVED CONSPIRACY MEANS MORE EFFECTIVE SUPPRISION [SUPPRESSION] STAND FIRM FOR ABOLITION MANY THANKS FOR CREW[E] SHAW PARK[N]ASILLA HOTEL SNEEM SUBMISSION OF PLAYS SHOULD BE OPTIONAL SHAW

46 / To Gilbert Murray Southern Hotel, Parknasilla, Sneem, Co. Kerry
29th August 1909

[ALS: CL 2]

Lady Lyttelton (Katharine Sarah, 1860–1943) was the wife of General the Honourable Sir Neville Lyttelton (1845–1931), commander-in-chief of British forces in Ireland.

My dear Murray

You have contributed very materially to the Dublin victory.

The real point at issue was not the liberty of the stage or the merits of Blanco, but whether Lady Lyttelton, the wife of the Generalissimo, would come with her party. The fate of the Castle hung on that; and Lady L. at first said she could not possibly bring her young people to a wicked play or bring a blush to the cheek of the military. An unscrupulous use of your letter and Lady Mary's verdict [that the play was not immoral] decided the struggle. I sent the letter to Lady Gregory; Lady Gregory planked it down confidentially on Lady L's dressing table; and Lady L. took her Bible & hymnbook and brought her whole flock to the play with military honors. Down came the Castle flag; Charlotte was overwhelmed with invitations to the Vice Regal Lodge, and, on her regretting that her immediate return to her post by her palpitating husband would prevent &c &c &c, received through the Vice Regal telephone from the private secretary a long and agitated mixture of apology and hope that no further statements would be sent to the press in view of the good behaviour of the authorities. The rest you have seen in the papers, though I havnt, as this is within hail of the remotest tail-ends of Ireland. Really, it was Lady Mary who was the Woman of Destiny in the affair.

As to the mistake about Crewe, it is useless to deny that anybody except yourself enjoyed it most unworthily. I am really very sorry, because I know what it feels like. It is one of the terrors of the peerage that the difficulty of distinguishing one nobody from another becomes of enormous importance. Fortunately you mistook him for another possible L.L.; so there was no great harm done. If he had mistaken you for Lindley Murray, you could have forgiven him. He would probably have considered the error a flattering one.

I think the lid has been put on Redford finally by the wholehearted support of George Edwardes. It needed only that.

There is a case which interests me personally much more than any of our Monna Vannas & other stock grievances; and that is the case of Hall Caine's White Prophet. I think H.C. should be backed up. Egypt is a leading case on which we shall have to fight the whole question of coercive Imperialism versus federated commonwealths. The stock abuse of H.C. is nine tenths envy of a novelist who is supposed to make more money than anyone else except Marie Corelli, and one tenth superciliousness because H.C. goes in industriously for matter and doesnt practice style. I have read half through The White Prophet & seen some of the Aspects of the East articles in the Daily Telegraph; and I have no doubt that H.C. is in earnest and on the right tack. I hear Heinemann is getting up some sort of testimonial preface or manifesto as a counterblast to the Imperialist attacks on the book and to the snobbish shame that prevents the men who privately sympathize with H.C. from letting him use their names. I am quite game to contribute (much good will that do him, I fear!); and I also want him to go before the Select Committee & tell the story of how the censorship stopped The White Prophet at His Majestys – that is, if it really was the Censor, and not Tree, who stopped it.

yrs ever
G.B.S.

Lindley Murray (1745–1826) was a grammarian whose *English Grammar* was widely adopted in English and American schools. **George Edwardes** (1852–1915) was managing director of the Gaiety Theatre, which specialized in musical comedy and similar entertainments. Shaw singled him out in a letter to Lady Gregory written two days before this one as 'the single exception' among witnesses who defended the way the censorship was presently exercised (CL 2, 862). His support was therefore a welcome surprise. A play by Maurice Maeterlinck (1862–1949), ***Monna Vanna***, had been refused a license because a wife agrees to commit adultery in order to save her city. It became one of the '**stock grievances**.' Laurence clarifies the case of ***The White Prophet*** by [Thomas Henry] **Hall Caine** (1853–1931) as follows: the novel, 'published on 12th August, had been severely slated by the press. Shaw, in a reply written at Parknasilla on 6th September ..., argued that the savage reception was an emotional response to the home truths about Britain's policies in Egypt contained in the novel, and to the fact that its hero, an Arab, "has a 'creeping' resemblance to Jesus ..."' Caine's dramatic version of the novel had been announced for production several months earlier by [Beerbohm] Tree, but had been cancelled without public explanation' (CL 2, 865). **Marie Corelli** (1855–1925) was a popular novelist highly favoured by Queen Victoria. The eight '**Aspects of the East' articles** were published from 4 to 20 August.

47 / To G. Bernard Shaw

Castle Howard, York
3rd September 1909

[TLS: HRC via Guelph]

Murray had been reading Chesterton's George Bernard Shaw *(London: Bodley Head, 1909), along with Shaw's review of the book, 'Chesterton on Shaw,'* Nation *5 (28 August 1909), 787–8, reprinted in* Pen Portraits and Reviews*). In his review Shaw quotes Chesterton's opinion of Cusins: 'I do not know whether in Major Barbara the young Greek professor was supposed to be a fool. As popular tradition … declared that he is drawn from a real professor of my acquaintance, who is anything but a fool, I should imagine not. But in that case I am all the more mystified by the incredibly weak fight which he makes in the play in answer to the elephantine sophistries of Undershaft. It is really a disgraceful case, and almost the only case in Shaw, of there being no fair fight between the two sides.' Shaw replied in unflinching terms: 'As to the professor making no fight, he stands up to Undershaft all through so subtly and effectually that Undershaft takes him into partnership at the end of the play. That professor … is one of the most delightful characters in modern fiction; and that Mr Chesterton, who knows the original (evidently not so well as I do), has failed to appreciate him, is nothing less than a public calamity.' His jeering retort to Chesterton on the topic of Rationalism is an elaboration of ideas that Shaw had often expressed: 'I have tried to teach Mr Chesterton that the will that moves us is dogmatic; that our brain is only the very imperfect instrument by which we devise practical means for fulfilling that will; that logic is our attempt to understand it and to reconcile its apparent contradictions with some intelligible theory of its purpose; and that the man who gives to reason and logic the attributes and authority of the will – the Rationalist – is the most hopeless of fools; and all that I have got into his otherwise very wonderful brain, is that whatever is reasonable and logical is false, and whatever is nonsensical is true.'*

My dear Shaw

Posnet is certainly a triumph. Such a clear case of a condemned play proving to be perfectly 'unobjectionable' when acted. It must have some influence on the committee, though I am not pleased with the general trend of things there. I believe that the Speaker really represents the average public, and that if we once rouse them they will chastise us with scorpions. However, that would make a good clean fight …

As to Hall Caine, I have a vague sort of feeling that he is unjustly cavilled at by superior people, but I have not read anything of his since The Deemster, nor wanted to. But perhaps one should. It is a little ridiculous that we who profess to be interested in English literature should know nothing at all of the most popular writers. I have never read a word of the sainted Marie. – But as to the White Prophet, Archer says that Tree and the Censor say that the Censor had nothing to do with the stopping of it. One ought to find that out. I dont like the idea of Foreign Office control. It is perfectly absurd that no one should be able to speak slightingly of the false Mahound, though obviously undesirable that the Foreign or Colonial Secretary should do so. A foreigner is in every country recognised as a comic object, just as a drunken man is. And no harm is done, unless you deliberately go and make the government responsible.

I have been reading You on Chesterton on You. I agree vehemently with your exposition of your attitude towards Rationalism as against his … and indeed in itself. On the Cusens question I will only say that personally I like the young man.

As to Lords Crewe and Aberdeen, I have been rather consoled by a story of Fisher's. Birrell told him that when the King was travelling in the West of Ireland and having receptions at villages, at one village the peasants gathered under the head of an old man. The old man took off his hat and shouted: 'Three cheers for King … King …' then with a flash of remembrance 'King Henry the Fifth!'

Yours ever
G.M.

The Speaker was a monthly periodical. Caine published his fourth novel, **The Deemster**, in 1887. The **false Mahound** is a contemptuous epithet for Mohammed, the prophet of Islam. Anti-Muslim medieval and Renaissance Christians characterized him as a demon who inspired a false religion (*Wikipedia*, verified elsewhere). Murray's allusion to **Lords Crewe and Aberdeen** refers to his confusion in sending a persuasive letter about the Posnet affair to the wrong man. **Fisher** was Murray's friend, and soon-to-be co-editor of the Home University Library series, Herbert Albert Laurens Fisher (1865–1940). Augustine **Birrell** (1850–1933), was an English politician and chief secretary for Ireland 1907–16.

48 / To G. Bernard Shaw

82 Woodstock Road, Oxford
26th November [1909]

[TLT: BL, SPA]

The involvement of Shaw in committees focused on drama and theatre affairs was extensive. As a drama critic he strongly supported the Independent Theatre Society, the New Century Theatre, and the Stage Society. He joined the Society of Authors in 1897, was elected to its committee of management in February 1905, and joined its Dramatic Sub-Committee in 1906. (This seems to be what Murray means by 'the Drama Society.') In March 1909 a splinter group led by Pinero converted the sub-committee into an independent organization called the Dramatists' Club. Shaw joined and, on 28 July 1909, urged members to 'fight censorship in every form' (CL 2, 853). On 29 November he wrote to Pinero, strongly recommending Murray for membership even though by club standards he was not a 'dramatist of established reputation': 'Murray would be a very desirable member; and his position as Regius Professor of Greek at Oxford, and the social influence he has through his marriage with Lady Mary, a daughter of the Earl of Carlisle, would attach us to that big nerve system of the general social world from which our over-professionalized rank-and-file are a bit too much cut off … Murray is one of those very rare men who combine the genuine artistic anarchic character and sympathies with academic distinction and political and social attachments to the big outside world. The technical objection to him is that his great stage achievements have been his translations of Euripides … But I think we may accept really great translations – and his are jolly good – as enough for us' (CL 2, 885).

Shaw told Hesketh Pearson much later that the Dramatists' Club members 'were on the point of blackballing Gilbert Murray when Pinero, of whom they were mortally afraid, appeared and sternly ordered them to elect him' (Pearson, 265). But this simplifies the case to a significant degree; see Shaw's letters to Pinero on 2 December 1909 and 17 and 21 March 1910 (CL 2, 887–8, 909–11, 911–13).

Shaw was also a prime mover on an organizing committee for a Shakespeare Memorial National Theatre (SMNT), which began campaigning in late 1908, but took two decades to realize its goal. On 11 December 1921, in a Sunday Express *article on the reception of* Heartbreak House, *Shaw commented that 'the vain appeal of the Shakespeare Memorial National Theatre has shown that you can get money in England for sport, for religion, for party politics, for charity, … but not for art, least of all the art of the theatre' (CP 5, 196). He was finally enlisted to lay the foundation stone of the theatre in August 1929.*

My dear Shaw

I am so glad you are coming. The meeting is to be a combination of 1. the Annual Business Meeting of the Drama Society, at which the officers are impeached and the treasurer arrested, and 2. an Appeal for the SMNT. If I am in the Chair I can get the Drama Society business through in about ten minutes. If the Master of University is in the Chair it may take twenty.

I am afraid your last possible train is the 1 50 from Paddington, arriving 3 38 – not much better than the 1.45 arr. 3.3 The Meeting begins at 4 30, you will be called upon about 4 45.

Philip Carr said that a Bishop was coming with you, or a Conservative Peer. But we have heard no more of this. I will ask W Raleigh to come, in order to get a Conservative element. If he comes he will be pleasant and brief. Otherwise the whole meeting rests on you.

I think it base of you to have concealed the expedition from Mrs Shaw till it was too late for her to come.

Yours ever
G.M.

Philip Carr (1874–1958), London drama critic for the *Manchester Guardian*, had served as secretary to the Shakespeare Memorial National Theatre committee since 1908 (CL 2, 832).

49 / To Gilbert Murray

10 Adelphi Terrace WC
3rd December 1909

[TLS: Bod, SPA]

My dear Murray

I write to you on the spur of the moment, having just had a violent shock through the telephone. Said shock was caused by the voice of Lewis Waller asking me to make him a high-class translation of Cyrano de Bergerac for performance in the spring. Now from Euripides to Rostand is a long jump; but in a certain way the mere feat of translation is of the same character. There is a genuine vein of phantasy and grace of expression to be preserved – and more poetry, after all, than there is in Aristophanes.

Would you be disposed to take on the job? If so, although Waller has an unspeakable terror of you as the terrible translator of Euripides, and probably believes you to be personally exactly like Doctor Johnson, the thing might be managed.

There may even be money in it.

Yours ever,
G. Bernard Shaw

Lewis Waller (1860–1915) was an English actor-manager noted for romantic roles. ***Cyrano de Bergerac*** (1897) earned the French dramatist Edmond Rostand (1868–1918) enduring fame for its extravagant romanticism, theatricality, and fluid poetic speech. Murray was not disposed to take on the job, as he makes clear in the next letter through the persona of **Doctor** [Samuel] **Johnson** (1709–84).

50 / To G. Bernard Shaw

82 Woodstock Road, Oxford
5th December [1909]

[TL, postscript ALS; SPA]

Sir,

Deaf alike to the alluring call of Avarice and the seductive whisper of Vanity, I am bound to decline the tempting offer made by you on behalf of your friend, Mr Garrick, that I should translate a well-known French masterpiece for his use at Durury Lane this spring. Through the whole of that season and more I shall be absorbed in the preparation of the seven-hundredth edition of my immortal Dictionary.

Your most Obdt,
Humble Servant,
Saml Johnson.

It would have been rather fun all the same. – Do you remember Lady Bell's play 'The Way the Money Goes'? She tells me it is before the S.S. again. I think we ought to do it. It is very interesting & true.

Yours ever
G.M.

Durury is an intentional comic misspelling of Drury. **Lady Bell** (Florence Eveleen Eleanore Olliffe Bell, 1851–1930), writer and social reformer, had already collaborated with Elizabeth Robins on *Alan's Wife*, a play performed by the Independent Theatre in 1909. ***The Way the***

Money Goes did not attain a Stage Society (**S.S.**) production, but in *Play-Making: A Manual of Craftsmanship* (1912), Archer compares it to Elizabeth Baker's *Chains.*

During this time-gap Shaw wrote to August Strindberg, whom he had visited on 16 July 1909, replying to his query about possible translators of his works: 'We have only one English writer for the stage who can turn foreign poetry into English poetry; and that is Gilbert Murray' (letter of 29 March 1910, CL 2, 918). This was a period when Murray's translations of Greek plays began to be more widely criticized than they had been, a trend which at first focused on their infidelity to the text but culminated in a 1918 diatribe by the increasingly prominent man of letters T.S. Eliot (1888–1965). In a review of Medea *he issued such proclamations as 'Professor Murray has simply interposed between Euripides and ourselves a barrier more impenetrable than the Greek language,' and 'it is because Professor Murray has no creative instinct that he leaves Euripides quite dead' (Wilson, 196–7).*

The tangled history of the Academic Committee of English Letters is authoritatively described in Philip Waller's Writers, Readers, and Reputations: Literary Life in Britain 1870–1918. *After nearly two decades of failed proposals to form a British Academy of Letters analogous to the French Academy, in 1910 'the Royal Society of Literature invited the Society of Authors to collaborate in establishing an Academic Committee, each body to propose fourteen names, whereupon the twenty-eight would elect a further dozen to complete the fabulous forty [i.e., the French Academy's limit]. A list was compiled by a subcommittee of the Society of Authors' management committee then passed to the society's council, at which Mrs Humphry Ward objected to the absence of any woman's name and Bernard Shaw moved that the society should abstain from the enterprise ... The Royal Society of Literature proceeded alone, therefore. Its guiding hand was Edmund Gosse [1849–1928] ... He now outlined a constitution for "An Academic Committee of English Letters." Its main purposes were to incorporate a literary elite, representing literary criticism, the novel, poetry, and drama, and to uphold standards of language and style. [It] would start with some thirty members, who would progressively co-opt others, to a maximum of forty.' After a series of further objections, 'the Academic Committee sought to make amends by courting those excluded from its first intake. Bernard Shaw had been incorporated in June 1911, whereupon he championed the membership of Chesterton.' Also invited were Hilaire Belloc (1870–1953), Arnold Bennett (1867–1931), John Galsworthy, John Masefield*

(1878–1967), and H[erbert] G[eorge] Wells (1866–1946), but Bennett and Wells declined. A decade after the Academic Committee emerged, as 'a modest and partial experiment ... for the protection and encouragement of pure English style in prose and verse,' Gosse presented a sanguine assessment of its prospects: 'It was assailed, as was natural and right, by satire and by caricature, but it has survived the attacks ... and there can be little doubt that, with good luck, it may become a prominent feature of our intellectual and social system.' This optimism proved misplaced. The committee 'maintained a life of sorts until 1939, but it never attained the authority of the Académie française. Thus, literary men were compelled to cope as best they may with the existing system of random honour and informal influence' (459–63).

By the time of the following letter twenty-six members had been chosen, including a somewhat dubious Murray.

51 / To G. Bernard Shaw

Brackland, Hindhead
20th July 1910

[TLT: BL, SPA]

PRIVATE.

Dear Shaw

Have you had anything to do with the starting of this Academic Committee of Literature? I see that it emanated partly from the Soc. of Authors. I agreed to go on it and think, if well constituted, it may be some use in many ways. But why are you and Wells not on it? I believe Kipling and Barrie declined, tho' I dont know.

I think they were probably right to start with the sort of people they have got, old stagers and academic people, leaving them to choose the rest. You could not start with F M Hueffer and Sturge Moor [*sic*]. But I hope to goodness they will proceed as quickly as possible to get the people who really read literature. (I do not refer to FMH or SM under that head.)

I did not go to the only meeting there has been, chiefly from laziness, partly because my wife, as an Early Victorian Radical, became so abusive of this Committee, all Academies and all members of all Academies so far as she could remember their names, that I hardly dared to ask for lunch early, so as to catch the train.

By the way, I want badly to read Misalliance whenever it can be managed without inconvenience to you. At present I am engaged in splashing Ophelia's eyes all round the house. A great mess, but it is not our own house.

Yours ever
Gilbert Murray

H.G. **Wells** was a latecoming Fabian who disrupted the society with his radical proposals. Rudyard **Kipling** (1865–1936) was a romantic imperialist whose various writings often concentrated on India. Ford Madox **Hueffer** (1873–1938; changed last name to Ford in 1919) was a well-known novelist and editor whose best novel was *The Good Soldier* (1914). Thomas **Sturge Moore** (1870–1944) was a poet and artist who also wrote plays on Greek themes. **Misalliance** was first performed in 23 February 1910, but was not published (in English) until May 1914. **Ophelia** is usually played teary-eyed or crying, and she splashes into the water to drown herself. If Murray was reciting her most tragic lines and imitating her behavior while walking around the house, this speculation may not be far from the truth (courtesy of Albert H. Tricomi).

52 / To Gilbert Murray

The Giant's Causeway
24th July 1910

[TLS: CL 2]

Dear Gilbert Murray

Just this much: that I am a member of the Committee of the Society of Authors, and missed Hewlett's statement of the conspiracy to jump up an Academy by the Royal Society of Literature offering to elect a gang from the S. of A. if the S. of A. would return the compliment, and the nucleus thus secured electing anybody they were not too much afraid of.

I dont think it will do as it is. You are only on it because they little know your real character: they think you are only a Regius Professor. They have no right to form the thing yet. The final consent should take the form of 'I, Blank Blank, am willing to associate myself with the undermentioned 39 authors as an Academy of Letters.' There should be no *election*: the thing is ridiculous: we must boldly elect ourselves. The existing lot should consider themselves only the necessary organizing committee.

A list which omits Barker, Belloc, Chesterton, Herbert Trench, Barrie, Kipling, and myself, not to mention Galsworthy, and which includes a choice collection of old-age-pensioners, and recognizes the translations of classics into unreadable English by – you know who, whilst ignoring Archer's translations of Ibsen, is intolerable. I think Massingham should be on for his editorial services to literature. I think you could do a great deal by threatening to nominate Frank Harris. Margoliouth is worth six of some of the chaps they have put on. Two of them I positively never heard of.

Anyhow, I am not prepared to tackle Lady Mary without a better case than Les Quarant Gosses have supplied. (Gosse, by the way, is, I believe, rather sound on the subject.)

I have written to my secretary to send you a Misalliance if she can find one.

G.B.S.

Maurice **Hewlett** (1861–1923), novelist and poet, was currently chairman of the Society of Authors' Committee of Management. Hilaire **Belloc** (1870–1953) was a prolific Anglo-French writer with a Catholic slant. **Herbert Trench** (1865–1923) was an Oxford-educated Irish poet and, late in his career, a theatrical producer. H[enry] W[illiam] **Massingham** (1860–1924) was a prominent socialist editor of several periodicals. **Frank Harris** (1856–1931), owner-editor of the *Saturday Review* when Shaw became its drama critic, wrote a biography of Shaw published (with Shaw's revisions) after his death in 1931. Sir Edmund [William] **Gosse** was an English author and critic who collaborated with Archer in the first two English translations of Ibsen plays. Shaw puns on his name in his (mangled) French expression; **Les Quarant**[e] **Gosses** means, roughly, forty brats.

53 / To G. Bernard Shaw

Oxford
28th February 1911

[on stationery of The Home University Library]

[TLT: BL, SPA]

The Secondary Education Act, passed in 1902, aimed at providing a firmer basis of education for the general public, including the establishment of more secondary schools. It started a movement which, among other things, prompted the publishers Williams and Norgate to set in motion a project that became the Home University Library of Modern Knowledge. They envisioned a series of compact, simply written surveys which would appeal to a wide readership.

In August 1910 (not 1911 as Wilson's context implies) they asked Murray to act as chief selector of subjects and authors, and to serve as the literary editor who would evaluate every text. Three other editors were subsequently chosen: the Oxford historian H.A.L. Fisher, the Cambridge scientist J. Arthur Thomson (1861–1933), and the Columbia University humanist William T. Brewster. The first ten volumes appeared in the spring of 1911, and by October 1913 they had sold nearly a quarter of a million copies. Murray's own contribution, Euripides and His Age, *came out in 1913. The project was still alive after the Second World War, and Murray was still in his post. Shaw was sceptical of contributing to the enterprise. (See Glasgow, 'The Origins of the Home University Library,' 95–9; Wilson, 187–92; and West, 139–41)*

My dear Shaw

Does your conscience at all remind you of the existence of this Library? The first ten volumes will burst on the world in April, and Fisher and I hope, before we have done with it, to make it the vulgarest and most successful thing ever seen in the publishing trade. First edition of 20,000 of each book; on sale in all European capitals, as well as USA. And so on.

Fisher and I have written a severely restrained prospectus in order to save our faces, but no one will read it. It will be drowned in advertisements.

However, we really have got an extraordinary number of first rate savants and writers, and we want you to do a book on Music. You havent said anything about Music for a long time, and various musicians have told me that they pine for you. As to terms, the ordinary savant gets a penny on the shilling volume and £50 on account, but you could probably make Perris give you more. The books are 50,000 words.

It is good of you to come to the Martineau Club. I talked to them the other night and found them nice fellows and immensely pleased at the prospect of your coming. Stay with us, wont you? I havent seen you for such a time.

Yours ever
G.M.

[George] Herbert **Perris** (1866–1920) was a prominent journalist and peace campaigner who served as assistant editor for the Home University Library. He published *A Short History of War and Peace* in 1911. The **Martineau Club** met at one of the evangelical schools at Oxford, Manchester College, for lectures by notable speakers. It was named after James Martineau (1805–1900), a distinguished alumnus.

54 / To Gilbert Murray

10 Adelphi Terrace WC
4th March 1911

[TLS: Bod, SPA]

My dear Murray

I wrote a long and elaborate reply to your first letter about the Home University Library. To complete it I needed to refer to the documents you sent me. I could not find the documents; and so the letter was put aside until they turned up. They did not turn up. Your last letter replaces them; and now I cannot find the original reply, nor can I recapture that spirit of roused attention in which I wrote it.

In cold blood it seems to me that your plans are half a century out of date. Editions of 20,000 are no use. The next time you are in Edinburgh, go over Nelson's printing works and examine the machinery by which, from a roll of paper and a roll of red cloth, they turn out a cloth-bound book in about twenty minutes, eighteen of which are consumed in waiting for the paste to dry. The cheapest of these books are sold at 7d; and Nelsons have been known to pay the author an advance of £200; but the smallest remunerative edition is 40,000.

This is what you are up against.

The sort of machinery that Nelson uses would sweep everything before it if only the means of distribution were adequate. Unfortunately, there are virtually no bookshops in England; and if you want to sell books on anything like a heroic scale, you must put them on the market at prices suitable to the businesses of all sorts of little shops which mingle newspapers and cheap stationery with hairpins and herrings.

I am quite prepared to discuss with interest the notion of my doing a book on Shakespear or the musical glasses, especially the Musical Glasses; but the discussion must be carried on for its own sake, and not with a view to practical results. One of the economic anomalies of the situation is that although an enterprise such as you contemplate ought to be able to offer me enormously more for the job than I could possibly make by manufacturing and publishing for myself, it actually offers me so much less, even allowing for the screwing-up, that I should lose substantially by accepting it. However, when you come to deal with a playwright – even with one so exalted into precariousness as myself – it is hardly possible for him to write anything except plays without losing by it. I could write nearly three plays (the correct length for a play is 18,000 words) in less time than it would take me to write two books for your Library; and the tantièmes would take Perris's breath away. If you guarantee me a gigantic circulation and throw in some advertisements of my other works in each copy sold, then the thing might pay me as an advertisement, but not conceivably otherwise.

If you will order a copy of my new book from the Times Book Club, I will send you a nice private copy all to yourself. The prefaces are extremely stimulating. So much so, in fact, that not a soul has as yet taken the slightest notice of the plays.

Since we last corresponded I have been to Jamaica and back: thirty days on the rolling deep, though, as a matter of fact, it was the ship that rolled very damnably all the time. I did some writing and reading on the voyage. The reading included Houston Chamberlain's Foundations of the Nineteenth Century, which you simply must read. It is a magnificent manifesto of Protestantism, and of the soul of that old Liberalism which is now only a suit of rags on the backs of persons who have put it on by mistake. I also read a novel by Rosalind Murray. Rosalind has always filled me with awe. When I first saw her I divined a tragi-comic horror: a completely mature spirit and character imprisoned in the figure and person of a child, and thereby condemned to live in tutelage to two much younger children, Gilbert and Lady Mary, to wit. What Rosalind must have suffered from being ordered about and sent to bed and soaped and combed and short-frocked generally in an institution in which her natural place was that of matron, God only knows. Used you to have frightful rows with her, or did she bide her time patiently? At all events, she has made good her right to publish a book, which I am persuaded she could have written quite well at the age of four, not that the book is immature (Carlyon Sahib and Getting Married are crudely puerile in comparison) but that the infant was precocious.

When I read your allusion to the Martineau Club, my first impulse was to deny violently that I had ever heard of it. My secretary, however, assures me that I put it off with ambiguous civilities which may have left it under the impression that I am going down to talk to it. I have not the remotest intention of doing so; but going down to talk to you is another matter. That, clearly, will have to be managed some time or other.

Yours ever,
G. Bernard Shaw

Nelson's Printing Works in Hope Park Crescent, Edinburgh, employed some 600 people in 1870. The buildings are now under the aegis of the Royal Commission on the Ancient and Historical Monuments of Scotland. **Musical Glasses**, or the glass harmonica, consist of a set of glasses tuned to different notes by filling the glasses with liquid to the levels that create those notes. They are played by rubbing the rims or lightly striking them. Mozart worked with them, but it is still not conceivable that Shaw imagined writing a book about them. **Tantièmes** is the French word for royalties. The **new book** was Shaw's volume collecting *The Doctor's Dilemma, Getting Married,* and *The Shewing-up of Blanco Posnet,* with their prefaces. Shaw departed with Charlotte for **Jamaica** on 23 December 1910 and returned on 26 January 1911. ***Foundations of the Nineteenth Century*** by **Houston** [Stewart] **Chamberlain** (1855–1927), a transplant from England to Germany who wrote two books on Wagner, was a 1911 translation of an already famous German text published in 1899. It was at once impressively scholarly and sharply biased, extolling the Aryan-Teutonic races and deploring the influence of Jews. Shaw's review in *Fabian News* 22 (June 1911), 52–3, was unexpectedly favourable. **Rosalind Murray**, Gilbert's elder daughter, published her first novel, *The Leading Note,* in 1910. She followed it with *Moonseed* in 1911.

55 / To G. Bernard Shaw

82 Woodstock Road, Oxford
6th March [1911]

[TLT: BL, SPA]

Murray found a few hours to indulge himself during the spring of 1911 by turning an Egyptian story found in an ancient papyrus into a unique and elegantly produced book. Nefrekepta *is a poetic rendering of the tale which employs a meter he had never used before, that of Edward FitzGerald's* Omar Khayyam. *It was published in an expensive edition by Oxford's Clarendon Press at a price, as he says to Shaw, 'which none but the Truly Refined can afford to pay.' John Masefield was so impressed that he suggested dramatizing the story, and Thomas Hardy deemed it 'excellently weird and romantic,' especially citing the 'grotesque horror' of the climax (Wilson, 171). But it does not loom large in Murray's copious output; West's biography does not even mention it.*

Murray's comment in this letter, 'I dont like music myself,' is an understatement. He was drastically insensitive to music, as is evidenced when he said to Isobel Monro, 'I love ... trying to imagine what [music] is like to those who really know it ... I always feel as if there really was ἐν οὐρανίῳ τόπῳ a music which would send me into ecstasies ... but at a real concert I just get lost and sometimes want to howl like a dog' (letter of 3 November 1929 quoted in Wilson, 167). He was also ignorant of some musical classics, uproariously demonstrated in an anecote which Wilson reports: 'He once entered his own drawing-room where his wife and son were listening to a record of a Beethoven symphony. "Extraordinary," he said, "What stuff Americans dance to"' (168). Without referring directly to Murray, Shaw once proclaimed that 'a boy who knows the masterpieces of modern music [e.g., himself] is actually more highly educated than one who knows only the masterpieces of Greek and Latin literature' ('The Autobiographer's Apology,' reprinted from a 1939 limited edition in Sixteen Self Sketches, *then in CPr 3, 392).*

My dear Shaw

Of course 20,000 is a bagatelle. I believe that is what they *bind* straight off; the first edition – the total number printed off – is something tremendous. But these high questions are in the province of Perris rather than me. Of course there is not much money in it, at any rate for the authors. There is the chance of propaganda, which seems to attract most people; and, as you justly observe, there is the advertisement. It would give you a chance of emerging from that obscurity which weighs so heavily on meritorious writers. I fancy our machinery &c are quite capable of competing with Nelson; there is some dodge which has sprung armed from Demogorgon's mighty brain ... But for that I must again refer you to Demogorgon himself.

If there is something else that you would sooner instruct the farmers of the middle West about than Music, please say so. I dont like music myself, but I have occasionally begun to have glimmers of understanding what it is all about when I have read your writings on the subject.

I have not ordered your new book from the Times, but I have bought it and as soon as ever I can read anything that is not work (i.e. probably to-morrow) I am going to read it. But do give me a copy, and I will give mine to the Somerville Library. Also I will give you my great work NEFREKEPTA, just out and at a price which none but the Truly Refined can afford to pay. You cant think what a pleasure it is to be really foppish in a book after many years of conscientious cheapness – seventeenth century type, coloured pictures, vast margins, fat fat paper, and not too much beastly letter-press. It is the letter press that makes books so boring.

As to your engagement with the Martineau Club, you will find towards the end of Ashburner's Principles of Equity that it is no defence, in a case of breach of contract, for the defendant to plead that his intentions were fraudulent throughout. However, I will screen you to the best of my power.

The author of the Leading Note is away from home and so has not seen your letter. But she has shot a man in a duel for less than that.

Yours ever,
Gilbert Murray

Walter **Ashburner's** ***Principles of Equity*** was published in 1902.

56 / To Gilbert Murray Ayot St Lawrence, Welwyn, Herts.
14th March 1911

[ALS: CL 3; missing portion at start supplied by SPA]

Shaw's letter makes it clear that he had read the controversial psychoanalytical essay 'The Oedipus Complex as an Explanation of Hamlet's Mystery' by Dr Ernest Jones (1879–1958), which was published in the American Journal of Psychology *in January 1910. His theory, derived from Freud's concept of the Oedipus complex, is that Hamlet cannot bring himself to kill Claudius because the new king, having killed Hamlet's father and married his mother, has carried out what are actually Hamlet's own unconscious wishes. Shaw notes that in the play Jocasta says that 'men have often dreamt thus of their mothers.' The passage he recalls is a reply to Oedipus's 'But surely I must fear my mother's bed?' She says, 'As to your mother's marriage bed, – don't fear it. / Before this, in dreams too, as well as oracles, / many a man has lain with his own mother' (David Grene's translation). Shaw also says, 'Plutarch tells us that Caesar dreamt it, and was so encouraged that he crossed the Rubicon next day.' This is his half-accurate memory of a passage from Plutarch's* Lives*: 'It is said that the night before he passed [over] the river, he had an impious dream, that he was unnaturally familiar with his own mother.' Five years later, when Shaw was trying to convince Lady Gregory to stage plays by Ibsen rather than Sophocles, he called* Oedipus Rex *'that abominable play which leads up to nothing but a man tearing his eyes out because he discovers that his wife is also his mother: a really filthy insult to the human heart' (letter of 3 September 1916 at Cornell).*

In spite of Shaw's admonitions, Murray's translation of Sophocles' Oedipus Rex *would be published as* Oedipus, King of Thebes *in 1911, and performed on 15 January 1912.*

My dear Murray

Nefrekepta is very nice: so is Mrs Cockrell's picture. Also the cats at the end.

They tell me you have translated Edipus. I havnt seen your original; but the matter as between us is important. I beg your attention for a moment.

You once said you would like to write modern Medeas, Electras &c.

I once said I wished you would commit some disgraceful offence, and be extruded ignominiously from Oxford, like Shelley.

These two birds can be killed with one stone; and that stone is Edipus.

Let me lead up to this gradually.

If you have recently translated Edipus, you will agree with me that Sophocles was the sort of man the English like, just as Euripides was the sort of man they loathe. That is, he had the brains of a ram, the theatrical technique of an agricultural laborer, the reverence for tradition of a bee, and, as assets, what the English call 'immense character,' and (probably) brute artistic faculty for word music galore. The Sophoclean irony I take to have been a stupidity too dense to be credible as such: at all events, I never could discover it. Possibly I am prejudiced because I got into trouble at an early age by using his name as an appropriate rhyme to cockles. Roebuck Ramsden & John Tanner in Man & Superman are Sophocles & Euripides.

From Edipus you can learn the difference between spiritual construction and mechanical stage craft. The spiritual development – the gradual loading of a man's conscience bale by bale until his back breaks – is nearly as good as a bull fight, with its provocations and tortures ending with the matador. The stage craft is, as I said, crude to rusticity. Here it is in skeleton, as I remember it.

Edipus discovered with crowd (Chorus)

CROWD – We are unwell. What is the matter with me?

EDIPUS – I have sent to ask the oracle. My messenger ought to be back by this [*sic*]: he has been away a year. Ah! Here he is. (Enter Oracle Man).

ORACLE MAN – Somebody murdered old King Laius; and Apollo wont stand it.

EDIPUS – Damn his eyes – the somebody's, not Apollo's. Who is he?

ORACLE MAN – I dont know. I should ask the gentle hermit of the dale, who knows everything. Ha! Here he is. How opportune! (Enter Hermit).

EDIPUS – Who killed the king?

HERMIT – You did.

EDIPUS – Liar! Still, I certainly did kill somebody at a cross roads once. My wife Jocasta would know.

HERMIT – (enigmatically) Your wife! Ha! ha! Here she is, by the way. (Enter Jocasta).

EDIPUS – Look here, Jocasta. Do you think that man I killed could have been your first husband, the old king?

JOCASTA – Nonsense. A most respectable farmer saw the whole affair. Send for him and ask him.

EDIPUS – Why can't he turn up without being sent for, as the others do? (To the Call Boy) Go fetch him. (Exit Call Boy).

Enter a Corinthian Shepherd

C.S. – I seek Edipus, your king.

EDIPUS – By a happy coincidence, I am he.

C.S. – Allow me to congratulate you. Your father is dead.

EDIPUS – A corker for the oracle that said I should kill him! Hooray!

JOCASTA – I told you so.

EDIPUS – If only my mother were dead, my happiness would be complete. Unfortunately, I gather that she survives. They said I should end by marrying her. I shall never feel safe until she also is buried.

C.S. – Let me be frank with you. She is not your mother. The truth is, I got you when you were a baby from a most respectable farmer, and handed you over to your reputed parents.

JOCASTA – What next? Edipus, I shouldnt go on with this. Excuse me. (Exit).

EDIPUS – The respectable farmer must clear up this. Where can he be?

LEADER OF THE CHORUS – By one of those fortunate accidents which seldom occur more than six times even in a play by Sophocles, I recognize that most respectable man – whom I have not seen for forty years – in the gentleman who will now enter. (The Theban Shepherd does so).

EDIPUS – Who was the child you gave some years ago to this Corinthian?

THE THEBAN – If I were you, I wouldnt ask.

EDIPUS – Scourge him until he confesses.

THE THEBAN – Oh well, if you *will* have it, it was the child of Jocasta and Laius.

THE CORINTHIAN – The party he killed at the crossroads, probably.

THE THEBAN – That is so.

EDIPUS – Then – then – I – I – Oh Lord! (Exit)

CHORUS – Ah me, no chappy
Call I happy
Until –

The noise in the auditorium makes it impossible to hear anything more. The hitherto empty benches are filling up rapidly. A slave slides an ivory goad along the front bench and prods the Archon, who wakes up with a shriek, but collects himself with such majesty that nobody dares to laugh. Greetings of acquaintances, searchings for numbered seats, sales of programs & hirings of glasses & sunshades on all hands. At last the audience settles down; and the chorus is once more heard.

CHORUS – The life of Man
is but a span –

DERISIVE VOICE FROM THE GODS – Ten minutes for refreshments. (Ribald laughter).

VOICES – Messengerrrr. Messeng-e-e-e-rrrr. Cut the cackle. Dry up. Messengerrr.

THE ARCHON – Men of Athens: behave yourselves. Remember Marathon. Remember –

VOICES – The fifth of November. Messenger. Messenger. Mess-engerrrrrrr. (Tumult).

Enter Star Actor, as Messenger. Thunders of applause.

VOICES – Brayvo Icks! Give it mouth. Pile it on. Silence for the messenger. Silennnnce!

CHORUS – 'He who in quest of silence, Silennnnce hoots

SEMICHORUS – Is apt to make the hubbub he imputes.'

The Messenger proceeds to wallow at great length in the blood of Jocasta, who has butchered herself in a most sanguinary manner. The audience hangs on every drop. When he adds, in minute detail, how Edipus plucked his eyes out, the whole house is one ecstasy.

EDIPUS – (rushing in and scattering rose pink from his eyes all over the orchestra) Woe! woe! Pain! Ah me! Ai! ai! ai! Me miserable!

Stupendous applause. The Messenger & Edipus take six calls, and finally reappear with Sophocles between them. Immense enthusiasm.

CHORUS – Talk of bliss
After this! –

The house empties as if a hose had been turned on it. Nothing can be heard through the noise of the scramble for the doors.

CHORISTER (TO THE LEADER) Keep it up, old man. The second lot will be in for the satyr play before you are through. (In the hope of which the Leader slows down to 20 words a minute).

– And So Forth –

Give this apparently frivolous précis to your students, and they will at once understand what Euripides had to put up with, and what a curse this blood & thunder convention of the messenger was to the Athenian stage. Also what the stage craft of Sophocles came to, and the exact depth of the choruses.

The serious mischief of the convention was that it made it impossible for an Athenian to write a play. A drama was only a driving of somebody to death. For instance, here is a fascinating dramatic problem. Given a man who discovers himself to be the murderer of his father and the husband of his mother, how will he feel and what will he do? In Athens this was not a problem at all: it was only an excuse for a particularly sanguinary description by the inevitable messenger. Sophocles saw it that way too: he was too conventional even to wish to see anything more in it. He therefore left you what you desired: a Greek theme for a modern drama. This is your chance.

Let us consider the spiritual scenario. The modern play – yours – will not end by the completed disclosure: it will begin with it. How will Edipus feel about it?

Jocasta, if I recollect aright, says that men have often dreamt thus of their mothers (how did she know, by the way?); and she implies that they were none the worse for it. Plutarch tells us that Caesar dreamt it, and was so encouraged that he crossed the Rubicon next day. Evidently it did not shock *him.*

Let us get a little nearer home. I very seldom dream of my mother; but when I do, she is my wife as well as my mother. When this first occurred to me (well on in my life), what surprised me when I awoke was that the notion of incest had not entered into the dream: I had taken it as a matter of course that the maternal function included the wifely one; and so did she. What is more, the sexual relation acquired all the innocence of the filial one, and the filial one all the completeness of the sexual one. This surprised me the more, because my theory, as you may have noticed in my books here and there, is that blood relationship tends to create repugnance, and that family affection is factitious (I am now rather inclined to think that it is rather familiarity – that is, close domestic association – that creates sexual repugnance).

Suppose, now, I were to discover suddenly that my mother was not related to me at all, and that Charlotte was my mother. I have not the slightest doubt of what the effect would be. It would be that of the dream. My affection for Charlotte would be not only intensified but elevated. There would be the addition of the filial feeling and the redemption of the sexual feeling from 'sin' and strain. Although in my waking senses I could not possibly work up the slightest sexual feeling for my mother or filial feeling for Charlotte, yet if circumstances tricked me into marrying my mother before I knew she was my mother, I should be fonder of her than I could ever be of a mother who was not my wife, or a wife who was not my mother.

I now want to meet a woman who has dreamt she was her son's wife, so as to get Jocasta documented.

You see your drama. When Creon says to Edipus, 'Unhappy man: here are my razors. Give one of them to your wretched mother; and despatch,' Edipus replies 'Scandalous as it seems, I dont feel like that at all.' And a conflict with public opinion follows.

The messenger's speech would describe your expulsion from Oxford after the publication of your New Edipus.

I am not very appreciative of the psychiatrists; but there may be something in their theory that repressed instincts, though sub-conscious, play a considerable part in our lives, and that the first child's jealousy of the second, and even of its father, is the jealousy of Othello in a primitive stage of passion, before the specialization of a part of it takes place for reproductive purposes. The completeness with which that specialization is suppressed does not eradicate the passion; and in my case the suppression apparently vanishes in sleep, though it is perfectly effective when I wake. Dr Ernest Jones contends that Hamlet's inability to kill the king is produced by his subconsciousness that he was jealous of his father and would have done the same thing himself to get possession of his mother.

Has your interest in Edipus ever led you to collect any evidence on this subject?

Anyhow, even if you should conclude that the subject is too dangerous to be stirred up, especially in days when women remain attractive until they are past fifty, you may possibly see that there is a great poetic and psychological drama in it.

I mark this letter Private lest it should horrify your secretary, if you have one.

Is your translation of Sophocles published?

yrs ever
G.B.S.

PS I have said nothing about the parricide part of the problem, because, though I can perfectly understand Dr Johnson standing in the rain to expiate his unkindness to his father, I am quite unable to understand any man regretting having killed his father to deliver himself from tyranny. Despotism must be tempered by assassination.

16 March – Your letter has just come. We were writing to one another at the same time. The prefaces are as inartistic as dictionaries. The need to settle *everything* wrecked their architectoniky & made them exhausting to read. Pure self-sacrifice on my part – except that unless you make people suffer they dont remember or respect you.

Mrs Cockrell was [Florence] Kate Cockerell (1872–1949), a manuscript illuminator and artist who had married Sydney Carlyle Cockerell, a well-known businessman-turned-socialist, in 1907. The extremity of Shaw's '**apparently frivolous précis**' of *Oedipus Rex* can be graphically illustrated by a comparison of his opening lines with a paraphrase of the actual text. Shaw's start: '[*Edipus discovered with crowd (Chorus)*] Crowd – We are unwell. What is the matter with me? / Edipus – I have sent to ask the oracle. My messenger ought to be back by this: he has been away a year. Ah! Here he is. (Enter Oracle Man).' Sophocles's text begins with Oedipus assuring a crowd of children that he will hear their appeal from an old priest (the chorus does not speak until everyone else has left the stage). The priest explains the problem at some length, and Oedipus, after noting 'I know you are all sick,' tells them that he has sent, to the oracle of Apollo, Creon, Jocasta's brother, and that he has been gone 'far longer than he needed for his journey.' The arrival of the 'Oracle Man' is announced (David Grene's translation).

Shaw had probably read of **Dr** [Samuel] **Johnson**'s act of penitence long before, but his memory may have been prompted by a 1910 article in *Putnam's Magazine* 7, 33.

57 / To G. Bernard Shaw 82 Woodstock Road, Oxford
16th March 1911

[TLT: BL, SPA]

My dear Shaw

I am reading the prefaces – and the plays – with real delight. Your prose style is so wonderfully good, so direct and clean and free from every kind of weakness or affectation. A Greek writer on what they then called 'rhetoric' (almost the opposite of what the word now means) would have gone into raptures over you. One of their remarks is that it is a great virtue to use the 'proper word' for each thing you speak about and that most writers do not see this but like to use vague or metaphorical or ready-made conventional phrases.

I am not sure you do not slightly tire a subject out towards the end: or rather, that you find at the end that there are one or two odds and ends still to be mentioned, instead of ending with a climax or the like. But perhaps that is a necessary result of the naturalness of your whole method. It is jolly good, anyhow. Even if I did not generally agree with you as much as I do it would be an artistic pleasure.

Yours ever
G.M.

What classical Greeks **called 'rhetoric' (almost the opposite of what the word now means)**, derived from *rhētōr*, speaker or orator, and usually meant the art of persuasive speaking. The word evolved towards a wider application, often meaning the particular way of communicating, the language or even lingo of localities, businesses, newspapers, and other organizations.

58 / To G. Bernard Shaw 82 Woodstock Road, Oxford
19th March 1911

[TLT: BL, SPA]

Euripides' Phoenissae, *or* Phoenician Women, *begins with Jocasta recounting the story of Oedipus and its immediate aftermath; the focus then shifts to the strife between their two sons, who finally cause her to commit suicide. The plot of his lost play* Aeolus *is at least partially recounted by Ovid in* Heroides *11. Aeolus's son and daughter, Macareus and Canace, fall in love with each other (perhaps as the direct result of him raping her) and want to get married. The issue is debated at length, with no clear-cut decision. See Sergio Casali, 'Ovid's Canace and Euripides'* Aeolus*: Two Notes on* Heroides *11,'* Mnemosyne*, 4th ser., 51, fascicle 6 (December 1998), 700–10.*

My dear Shaw

Many thanks for your advice and your sketch of the plot of Oedipus. We all found it difficult to read without tears, and we admired the accuracy of your memory. A copy of my version shall go to you to-morrow. There does not seem to be one in the house just now.

I used to think almost exactly what you do about the play except I always thought the Sardou plot element more important and the sheer blugginess less. It is just used at one moment to send the audience, already shattered, right off into hysterics. But what strikes me now is the thorough-going blasphemousness and anti-theism of the whole thing. I suspect that S was not the old ram we take him for. Quite the reverse. He knew how to blaspheme and criticize without getting into trouble. He could steal a horse while they all yelled at Euripides for looking over the hedge. He deliberately makes Oedipus splendid – kind, generous, heroic – and Apollo and Tiresias beastly. Also, he stresses the affection of Oedipus and Jocasta, and her guiding and nursing of him.

I admit that he does not seem to care about the moral. He may have – he has – his private opinion about gods and superstition, but his immediate concern is to terrify the audience, so he does not run the risk of awakening their critical faculty.

As to the play you propose, I once thought of it. But I do not believe it would serve its purpose in getting me expelled. In Euripides Phoenissae (a rather longwinded play) Oedipus and Jocasta went on living together, she looking after him and managing the house and having great influence with her two revolting sons (revolting in both senses). She does observe, if I remember rightly, that she 'does not praise O's wisdom' … No. It is someone else. She eventually commits suicide because her sons murder each other, and Oedipus complains – very beautifully – that no one can ever care for him as she did. So the play has really been written. Also, I nearly quoted in the preface the remark of Zeno, the Stoic, who caused some sensation by saying that the act Oedipus performed to his mother was morally indifferent; of no more importance for good or ill than if he had massaged her forehead when she had a headache.

The difference of age is the chief difficulty in thinking out a modern parallel. In Gk heroic saga people have no exact ages. A man of thirty with a wife of fifty would do it. Certainly, for my own part, I cannot imagine having any emotion of horror at discovering that my wife was my mother or my sister. And so thought Euripides, who treats the sister point in his Aeolus. But lots of people would go into horrors over it, even now; much more in Oedipus's imaginary time.

I did a scenario of a play on the murder part of Oedipus once. Like this. Roughly speaking General Gordon was known to have escaped from Khartoum and be wandering in Africa. Winston Churchill volunteers to run incredible dangers to rescue him. Inquiries are made. It is found that G was killed by a white man. Winston pushes inquiries and it comes back to him that once in Africa somewhere, when young, he utterly lost his nerve, and seeing some one at night crawling towards his camp was too frightened to ask any questions but fired and ran away. (G crawled because he was too tired to walk.) Will you write it with me? Winston in love with G's daughter. Naturally.

It is true that I am rather overworked. It keeps one fairly happy, being always busy and never free to do real work, but it is bad for the soul.

What is all this I hear about your running over dogs? You oughtnt to do that. Or was your letter to the Car really written to Lady Selborne?

Yours ever,
G.M.

Victorien **Sardou** (1831–1908) was one of the most prominent of the French writers of 'well-made plays.' '**Blugginess**' is colloquial for bloodiness. Early Stoics such as **Zeno** (490–430 BC) were iconoclastic about superstitious beliefs – even the horror of incest. He once said, 'Why condemn incest, … when Oedipus had given Jocasta fine children?' (quoted in Louis Crompton, *Homosexuality & Civilization* [Cambridge, MA: Harvard University Press, 2003], 66, citing Sextus Empiricus, *Outlines of Pyrrhonism*, trans. R.G. Bury [Cambridge, MA: Harvard University Press, 1933], sect. 3, #246). General **Gordon**, often referred to as 'Gordon of Khartoum,' was Major-General Charles George Gordon (1833–85), who lost the battle of Khartoum to Sudanese rebels and was killed. When **Winston** [Leonard Spencer] **Churchill** (1874–1965) was 23, he went to Egypt attached to the 21st Lancers and took part in the re-conquest of the Sudan. Murray mentions Shaw's propensity for **running over dogs**. As a driver he was notoriously erratic, and in 'Dog v. Motor: Mr. G. Bernard Shaw's Views,' *The Car* 36 (22 February 1911): 37 (Laurence, *Bibliography*, 2, 643), he reported (or joked) that while driving he had killed thirteen dogs. Reported in 'Bernard Shaw Was a Serial Dog-Killer,' *Evening Standard*, 25 May 1993. **Lady Selborne** (Lady Beatrix Maud Cecil Selborne, 1858–1950) was the wife of the conservative second earl of Selborne who, along with his wife, became an ardent proponent for the rights of women in 1910.

59 / To Gilbert Murray 10 Adelphi Terrace WC
10th April 1911

[APCS: CL 3]

Shaw was elected to the Academic Committee of the Royal Society of Literature two months after writing this letter.

The project of asking me to join the Academic Committee was based on the rash assumption that I was sure to refuse. But whenever I have been sounded I have dispelled this hope so unequivocally that the invitation has never come. If I get half a chance I shall be on to that Committee like a tsetse fly.

As to the book on music, the time to write it is so far off that it is not worth pursuing the subject for the moment. I am full up for years.

G.B.S.

60 / To Gilbert Murray Cardiff
23rd November 1911

[TEL: SPA]

WE REACH OXFORD ABOUT TEATIME HOPE TO SEE YOU BERNARD SHAW GRANVILLE BARKER

61 / To Gilbert Murray 10 Adelphi Terrace WC
3rd February 1912

[TLS: CL 3]

Shaw had begun Androcles and the Lion: A Fable Play *on 2 January 1912 and finished three days after he wrote this letter. The premiere would take place on 1 September 1913.*

My dear Murray

A young man named Bridges Adams who is up at Oxford rehearsing the Julius Caesar mob called on me the other day; and as he has a very presentable figure, a good voice, and all the less offensive marks of a University education, it struck me that he might be useful for Greek plays. I asked him did he know you; and he said he did only as one who knows the Monument, and was therefore afraid to call on you unless he has some sort of introduction. I thought – with an eye to Iphigenia – that you might as well have a look at him; so I have encouraged him to write to you for an appointment, and promised to break the ice for him. He will be up until the 20th.

I thought your letter to The Times about Oedipus very excellent. It would be very nice to do another production with Apollo as the villain of the piece. When I was looking at it I had an odd mixture of the spectator's illusion and the stage manager's eye to business. I was sitting just over the central entrance to the stalls; and when Harvey was coming along making his final exit I began wondering what signal they would give him to warn him that he was approaching the flight of steps so that he might not tumble down them in his blindness. When they took the lime off him I said to myself 'That's the signal'; and it was not until quite half a second after that I realized that he could see the steps as well as I could. Calvert is the best of them technically. He pitches his voice properly (one newspaper called it baying) and I did not miss the meaning of a single sentence that he uttered. The others were, in comparison, only so many phases of clergyman's sore throat. One or two more injurious personal criticisms I shall reserve until we meet. Lillah was good; but I have abused her for slurring every accent in the line except the caesura in the middle.

On Thursday a nice criticism by me on the Censor's official statement appeared in the Pall Mall Gazette. Did you by any chance see it?

Yours ever,
G. Bernard Shaw

PS The Christian Martyr sketch is now very nearly finished. I have got your St Augustine variety in very effectively. But I want you to go over it and correct any howlers, also to give me in charity some Roman names that are not hackneyed to death: I can think of nothing but Metellus &c &c; and I dont know which emperor my Caesar should be – not Nero if I can possibly help it. I think I'll call him the Emperor Nemo.

William **Bridges-Adams** (1889–1965) was at the time an Oxford student performing with the Dramatic Society. A month after this letter he took the role of Pylades in Murray's translation of Euripides' *Iphigenia in Taurus*. After a wide range of experience acting and directing, in 1919 he was appointed director of the Shakespeare Memorial Theatre in Stratford-upon-Avon. Murray's **letter** on a production of *Oedipus* appeared in *The Times* on 23 January. John Martin-**Harvey** (1863–1944) was a distinguished actor-manager whose performance as Oedipus was lauded for its 'stark horror and relentless, heart-moving … sorrow and grief' (Hartnoll, ed., *Oxford Companion to the Theatre,* 3rd ed. [1967], 432). Louis **Calvert**, a leading actor in the Court during the Vedrenne-Barker years, played Creon in *Oedipus Rex.* Shaw's letter to the *Pall Mall Gazette* (1 February), 'The Doom of the Play Censor,' pointed up the incongruity of the appointment of Charles Brookfield (1857–1913) as Joint-Examiner of Plays. In 1908 his play *Dear Old Charlie* was attacked as unsuitable for the stage, but escaped censorship. The play caricatured Barker as 'Mr. Bleater,' and *Waste* as *Sewage* (Purdom, 127). In announcing the event *The Times* writer noted that Brookfield had recently stated that 'the palmy days of English drama began to decline with the introduction of the work of Ibsen,' and he added that 'the action of the Lord Chamberlain is but further proof, if further proof were needed, that he is hopelessly out of touch with the theatre over which he exercises despotic control, and that the continuance of his legalized tyranny is inimical to the drama's welfare and its good name' (Salmon, *Granville Barker and His Correspondents,* 572). On the **St Augustine variety**, see the next letter.

62 / To G. Bernard Shaw

82 Woodstock Road, Oxford
17th February 1912

[TLT: BL, SPA]

Following are the passages from Augustine's Confessions *that Murray not-too-accurately recalls as 'facts,' then interprets in his own way for Shaw's possible application in his play. The events take place during the process of Augustine's conversion to Christianity with a group of likeminded men:*

Book 8, chapter 5, 117: 'Verecundus, a citizen and grammarian of Milan, and a very intimate friend of us all[,] … vehemently desired, and by the right of friendship demanded from our company, the faithful aid he greatly stood in need of.'

Book 9, chapter 3, 131: 'Verecundus was wasted with anxiety at our happiness, since he, being most firmly held by his bonds, saw that he would lose our fellowship. For he was not yet a Christian, though his wife was one of the faithful; and yet hereby, being more firmly enchained than by anything else, was he held back from that journey which we had commenced. Nor, he declared, did he wish to be a Christian on any other terms than those that were impossible. However, he invited us most courteously to make use of his country house so long as we should stay there … Thou, O Lord, wilt recompense him for this at the resurrection of the just, seeing that Thou hast already given him the lot of the righteous. For although, when we were absent at Rome, he, overtaken with bodily sickness, and therein being made a Christian, and one of the faithful, departed this life, yet hadst Thou mercy on him … Thy exhortations, consolations, and faithful promises assure us that Thou now repayest Verecundus for that country house at Cassiciacum where from fever of the world we found rest in Thee, with the perpetual freshness of Thy Paradise, in that Thou hast forgiven him his earthly sins' (Basic Writings of Saint Augustine, vol. 1).

Shaw gets the 'St Augustine variety' in edgewise: Androcles and his wife Megaera (Mag at this stage) have been expelled from their home because of what she calls his 'addiction' to Christianity.

My dear Shaw

A friend of St. Augustine called Verecundus was a well-to-do, well-mannered, and respectable pagan. He had inclinations towards Christianity, and would have become a Christian had it not been for his wife. She was a very saintly and amiable Christian, and according to the ideas current at the time if he had become a Christian he would have had to repudiate her and spend his life in celibacy, which he could not bear to do. It was all right for her to live with her husband, because that was just her cross, and the sin was compulsory. Also it was her duty to remain with him in the hope of converting him; so long as he did not become a Christian all was well. She wept and prayed every day, and they lived happily.

All the members of Augustine's circle who became Christians seem to have repudiated their wives and driven them into convents. You perhaps may remember that his mother owing to her saintly tact was one of the few ladies (I think, *the only* lady) in Augustine's circle who did not go about with a black eye as a mark of her husband's displeasure; but that of course is another story.

I lay these facts before you as a philosopher and a playwright.

Yours,
G.M.

63 / To G. Bernard Shaw Beckhythe Manor, Overstrand
12th July 1912

[TLT: BL, SPA]

Murray's facetious handling of the concept of God in this letter exposes his agnosticism, which he usually concealed within his liberal humanism, but on occasion allowed to break out at an extreme. In a letter of 10 February 1931 to Lionel Curtis, for example, he attacks the beliefs of Arnold Toynbee, his daughter Rosalind's husband: 'He considers that the liberal principles of justice, co-operation, the brotherhood of man, etc., are worthless unless they are combined with a belief in the divinity of Jesus, the Virgin birth, and Lord knows what other bizarre and speculative beliefs. This seems to me pernicious rubbish, leading straight to a revival of the wars of religion and the persecution of heretics' (quoted in Madariaga, 'Gilbert Murray and the League,' 181).

My dear Shaw

Repeated attacks of hay fever have ended by reducing me to a condition of mild melancholia for which I believe the only cure would be a careful study of your Androcles and the Lion. Is there a MS of it disengaged?

I dont know what I could send in return. If I were at home I might send three pamphlets: one, by a clergyman of the established Church, to prove that Jehovah *was* a small red snake, very venomous; the second, by a mad German, to show that he was not a snake but a fish; the third, by a methodist professor, to explain that he was not either, he was only a widower.

Yours ever,
G.M.

64 / To G. Bernard Shaw

Beckhythe Manor, Overstrand
23rd July [1912]

[TLT: BL, SPA]

My dear Shaw

Androcles is a joy, though I dont see how you are going to get it on the stage. But perhaps stage lions have improved since my time. What amazes me is the bubbling high spirits in which you write, making an atmosphere as if we were all twenty years old and slightly drunk at that.

The names seem to me quite good, except that it ought to [be] Megaera, not Mag. I like the way she vanishes. Of course she settled down to respectable paganism and was always ready to tell how badly she had been treated by her first husband.

There are one or two sacred phrases – 'This day thou shalt be with me ...' and the like, that I should cut if I were you. What is the Diderot story?

To please 'un ou deux impies' you shock des douzaines d''honnetes gens,' or something to that effect. But your Christians are delightful, and Androcles one of the most completely charming people I have ever met.

I have just heard from Archer in Japan, where they believe him to be 'the celebrated music hall artist.' However more accurate beliefs were also current.

I want to keep Androcles, if I may, till my daughter Rosalind turns up, which will be in a day or two. Many thanks for sending him. – He did, by the way, cure my hay fever. It went the day after his arrival.

Yours ever,
G.M.

Shaw did take Murray's advice and change Meg's name to **Megaera. I like the way she vanishes**: While Androcles is waltzing with the lion, Megaera revives from her faint and rants, 'Oh, you coward, you havnt danced with me for years; and now you go off dancing with a great brute beast ... that wants to eat your own wife. Coward. Coward! Coward! [*She rushes off after them into the jungle*].' The sentence **'This day thou shalt be with me'** in Luke 23:43 ends with 'in Paradise.' **To please 'un ou deux impies' you shock des douzaines d''honnetes gens'** translates as 'To please one or two impious people, you shock dozens of honest ones.' Denis **Diderot** (1713–84) was a French novelist, playwright, and philosopher, but Murray may have guessed the wrong author: the probable source is François Arnaud (1721–84), as a passage in Boswell's life of Dr Johnson (3, 235) suggests: 'Boileau wrote some such thing, and Arnaud struck it out, saying, "*Vous gagnerez deux ou trois impies, et perdrez je ne sais combien des honnêtes gens.*"' William **Archer**, on his second trip around the world, reached **Japan** on 27 April 1912. While visiting his sister's residence, the local missionary's wife who had read several articles about him 'concluded that he must either be a comic actor or a music-hall singer' (Whitebrook, 293).

65 / To G. Bernard Shaw

Beckhythe Manor, Overstrand
30th July [1912]

[TLT: SPA (not in BL)]

Murray's comment in the following brief letter about Androcles being 'very like my private conception of the ideal man' might be diagnosed by a statement he made at this time in Three Stages of Greek Religion *(the cover-title of three lectures separately issued in 1912, then revised as* Four Stages, *then as* Five*), in which he contrasts Hellenic beliefs and values with early Christian ones. Androcles, although a Christian, clearly manifests the former rather than the latter: 'Any one who turns from the great writers of classical Athens ... to those of the Christian era must be conscious of a great difference in tone. There is a change in the whole relation of* *the writer to the world about him. The new quality is not specifically Christian … It is a rise of asceticism, of mysticism, in a sense, of pessimism; a loss of self-confidence, of hope in this life and of faith in normal human effort; a despair of patient inquiry, a cry for infallible revelation; an indifference to the welfare of the state, a conversion of the soul to God. It is an atmosphere in which the aim of the good man is not so much to live justly, to help the society to which he belongs and enjoy the esteem of his fellow creatures; but rather, by means of a burning faith, by contempt for the world and its standards … to be granted pardon for his unspeakable unworthiness, his immeasurable sins' (*Five Stages of Greek Religion, *155).*

My dear Shaw

Here is Androcles at last. Rosalind has been duly edified by him and her laughter has been ringing through the house.

On repeated reading it strikes me that you have got Lavinia rather priggish and preachy here and there. Like the didactic heroine of our Ibsenite youth. It is very slight, but I think it is there. Androcles himself is very like my private conception of the ideal Man.

Do you like the introduction of flogging for these beastly White Slavers? I dont.

Yours ever
G.M.

Parliament was deliberating the proposed 'Criminal Law Amendment (**White Slavery** Traffic) Act,' enacted in December 1912, which re-introduced **flogging** into British penal law after weeks of public controversy over the issue. In 1904 and 1906 Shaw had written three letters of protest to *The Times* about flogging in the Navy and one about the Denshawi floggings (Ford, *Letters*, 38–44, 53–6). He applied his Fabian / *Mrs Warren's Profession* viewpoint to the topic in the November 1912 issue of the *Awakener*, declaring that until society ensures 'every respectable woman a sufficient wage for a decent life with reasonable hours of labor, you will never get rid of the White Slave traffic.'

66 / To G. Bernard Shaw

82 Woodstock Road, Oxford
2nd October 1912

[TLT: BL, SPA]

My dear Shaw

I saw a book parcel lying in the hall three days ago, and from sheer disgust did not open it till this morning, when a peripeteia of emotion at once occurred. Many thanks for it. I sat down at once to read and almost leapt with joy over Shakespeare and Bunyan. It is quite amazingly good, just what one was longing to have said, but had not the courage even to think.

By the way, my daughter Rosalind has gone to live in London just to feel her feet and see if she can earn a living, and would, I am sure, at any moment be grateful for food or advice. Address, 4 Wellington Square, SW

Yours,
G.M.

The **book parcel** was *Selected Passages from the Works of Bernard Shaw, Chosen by Charlotte F. Shaw,* which was published on 23 September. A reprint of the 'true joy in life' section of the 'Epistle Dedicatory' to *Man and Superman* includes a comparison between **Shakespeare and Bunyan** which greatly favours the latter's view of life (27); the extended section on Shakespeare is largely devoted to his 'word music' and other virtues (242–54). Murray soon realized that Charlotte had sent the book and thanked her, adding: 'It must have been interesting work, making the selection. I think he shines particularly in extracts' (letter of the same date; Bod).

67 / To G. Bernard Shaw Beckhythe Manor, Overstrand
17th December 1912

[TLT: BL, SPA]

Murray's reference to 'the Crusader,' which he is 'immensely interested to hear about,' is almost surely an understandable error for the journal which the Webbs and other Fabians were actively planning, The New Statesman, *first published four months later. The chosen editor, Clifford Dyce Sharp (1888–1935), was currently editing* The Crusade, *a publication with a Fabian slant, and Beatrice Webb first favoured that title for the new journal. Its provisional title then became* The Fabian, *and then* The Statesman, *before the final decision was made. See Adrian Smith,* The New Statesman, *38.*

My dear Shaw

Just a line to say (1) all good luck to the Crusader. I am immensely interested to hear about it. (2) I have just refrained – through sympathy and respect – from sending you a copy of my Four Stages of Greek Religion. When one is busy a friend's book, unless it happens to be on exactly the right subject, is such a nuisance.

I like the way the Horniman people do the Devil's Disciple: they play for emotion, quite simply, and by Jove they get it.

Yours ever,
Gilbert Murray

I wish you would come to Oxford to address the Fabians again.

The **Horniman People** were the repertory group in the Gaiety Theatre, Manchester, which Annie [Elizabeth Fredericka] Horniman (1860–1937) had bought in 1908 and refurbished. They had performed *The Devil's Disciple* on 14 October and 2 December 1912.

68 / To G. Bernard Shaw Beckhythe Manor, Overstrand
9th July [1913]

[TLT: BL, SPA]

My dear Shaw

You have, as usual, laid your finger on the one possible flaw in our projected marriage. Arnold is a little old; seventy-seven, to be exact. But he shaves clean and his wig is so extraordinarily good that he has no difficulty in passing as his own nephew on the rare occasions when he ventures near Toynbee Hall. The thing that has influenced Rosalind and me is the reflection that, if the dates on the Parian Marble are right, Euripides was seventy-nine when he wrote the Bacchae. Further, many ancient authorities say that his wife ran away from him the year before. So there is just time to bring about the same conditions and see what happens. It is very exciting.

Why dont you ever come to see us? You must sometimes be tired of the people you do see, and we should at least be a change. We always have a bed and vegetarian food.

Yours ever
G.M.

In some unrecorded form, Shaw had responded to the news that Murray's daughter Rosalind was about to marry **Arnold** Toynbee by pretending to think that it was the famous nineteenth-century economic historian Arnold Toynbee (1852–1883), not his nephew, Arnold [Joseph] Toynbee (1889–1975). Murray goes along with the joke, even making the groom sixteen years older than he would be in order to work in the amusing Euripidean foreshadowings that have even **influenced Rosalind.** In a letter of January 1914 congratulating Murray for the marriage, Barker will inform Murray that Shaw had told him 'but Good Lord what age is the man – he founded Toynbee Hall before I was born' (Salmon, *Granville Barker and His Correspondents*, 282–3). The nephew became the world-renowned author of the twelve-volume *A Study of History* (1934–61).

69 / To Gilbert Murray

10 Adelphi Terrace WC
6th August 1913

[TLS; postscript ALS: Bod, SPA]

The main added features of Shaw's expansion and revision of The Quintessence of Ibsenism, *first published in 1891, were a new six-page preface, analyses of the last four plays, and two essays which are considered seminal in Shaw studies: 'What Is the New Element in the Norwegian School?' and 'The Technical Novelty in Ibsen's Plays.'*

Without mentioning it in his new section on When We Dead Awaken, *Shaw counteracts Archer's negative view of the play (Archer had told his brother Charles that it was 'a mere hash-up of fifty-year-old ideas' and Murray that it was 'a sacrilegious outrage' [Whitebrook, 209, 219]) by arguing that 'it shews no decay of Ibsen's highest qualities: his magic is nowhere more potent.'*

Shaw's 'new volume of plays' was Misalliance, The Dark Lady of the Sonnets, *and* Fanny's First Play, *published by Constable on 18 May 1914.*

My dear Murray

As my long delayed second edition and final completion of The Quintessence of Ibsenism is to be published on the 26th of this month, The New Statesman has asked me whether I cant let you have a set of proofs on the chance of your being moved to review it for them at the moment of its appearance. As I should like you to read it anyhow, I make myself a party to this corvée by enclosing you a set of the sheets as passed for press. Later on I will send you a properly bound copy. The new part begins on page 119; but pp 159–172 are part of the old edition. Of course there is the inevitable new preface. I am growing old and I dare say the new stuff is slushy here and there and possibly sentimental; but it is the best I can do, and must now stand as it is. If it is not finished, I am, as far as Ibsen is concerned. At all events I have made an end, I hope, of Archer's view that When We Dead Awaken is a deplorable bit of senile drivel.

What I would really like you to read in proof for me is something that I cant finish. It is the preface to my new volume of plays. I intend it to be the last of my prefaces. It is on Parents and Children, and in it I launch my solemn pontifical curse on the whole imposture of our school system. But I keep cursing and repeating myself and cant get on to any constructive suggestion. I have come to the belief that there is no constructive side to it possible until we are out of the present horror. A child is in prison: it cries to be let out; and I am expected to ask it whether it has any constructive suggestions to offer before I unlock the door. Perhaps if I throw it at your head I may get something back that will pull me through. May I?

On the whole I think you are well out of Rosalind's youthful romance. There was an obvious danger of her turning up some day with a large blond moustached captain from the Guards, and inviting you to make conversation for your son-in-law. When I last saw her she was leading her terrified Grandmother up a flight of stairs, very goodlooking, very determined, and visibly capable of anything except doing or not doing anything she had made up her mind not to do or to do. I hope Toynbee likes her (fortunately she is very attractive); for I will not pretend to believe that he had any choice in the matter. She is very like Cusins.

Charlotte is going to France on the 8th leaving me behind until September, when I will take the car to the Auvergne to fetch her back, possibly by way of the Pyrenees. During August I shall wander a little. Barrie wants me to go to [obliterated text] (I am losing the power of writing) KILLIECRANKIE; and I have refuges in Northumberland & Shropshire. If you are at Overstrand and intend to stay there during August I might look in on you some day; for, like you, I have taken to motor cycling – Lea & Francis, twin cylinder, 3¼ h.p. My first exploit with the machine was brilliant: 77 miles in 3¼ hours; but this was on the open road from Coventry to St Albans. When I tried next in the Hertfordshire lanes, narrow places like the ground plan of a corkscrew, with fearful corners & steep pitches, I entered on a period of extreme terror, in the agonies of which I oscillated between launching the accursed thing like a thunderbolt when I wanted to stop it and stopping the engine when I wanted to accelerate it. But by dint of haunting all the most difficult places I could think of I have at last acquired a fitful control over the brute; and I now propose to go about the United Kingdom on it; so why not Overstrand on my way north? I shall be here or hereabouts until the middle of next week; but then I can take the road.

Yours ever
G. Bernard Shaw

Corvée (French) in this context means labour by compulsion. **KILLIKRANKIE** is a scenic village in Perth and Kinross, Scotland, on the River Garry.

70 / To G. Bernard Shaw

Beckhythe Manor, Overstrand
1st September 1913

[TLT: BL, SPA]

My dear Shaw

What about the Preface on Education? I should like immensely to see it, both for its own sake and because I am composing a lecture on Sandford and Merton, a book which always delights me.

Rosalind is in a state of enthusiasm over the Quintessence, and spends all the time left over from getting married and finishing her new novel in repudiating her duties.

Yours ever
G.M.

Sandford and Merton was a serial collection of children's stories published in the 1780s by Thomas Day (1748–89). It became extremely well known, especially for its lessons, and remained popular through the nineteenth century. Shaw, whose next letter mentions it, would have been attracted to its persistent stress on the wrongs of wealth. Murray's observation that his daughter spends her leftover time in **repudiating her duties** is a direct echo of Shaw's statement in 'The Womanly Woman' chapter of *The Quintessence of Ibsenism* that 'Woman has to repudiate duty altogether. In that repudiation lies her freedom' (40).

71 / To Gilbert Murray

Folkestone en route for the Auvergne
6th September 1913

[ALS: Bod, SPA]

On 2 September 1913 Charlotte had thanked Murray for his 'splendid review in the New Statesman, including the delightful little allusion to my Selected Passages' (Bod).

My dear Murray

If you can find time within the next 10 days to look through the enclosed, send it, with your comments, to me at the

Palace Hotel Sararon
Mont Dore
Puy de Dome, France

whither I am going to join Charlotte. Later on you had better address to 10 Adelphi Terrace W.C., as all letters will be forwarded more or less promptly.

Sandford & Merton is an admirable book, much more revolutionary than Marx's Kapital; and its present disuse is really a suppression. By the way, Cæsar & Cleopatra was a success in Moscow; and the Tsar stopped it!

Your letter was very interesting. I sent it on to Charlotte, who was greatly pleased by it – I dont quite know why.

I am utterly dead beat & need this holiday frightfully.

G.B.S.

Cæsar & Cleopatra was presented in Moscow in 1910, but the only authoritative source I have found does not mention it being **stopped** by the **Tsar**. See Laurence Senelick, '"More Looked at than Listened to": Shaw on the Prerevolutionary Russian Stage,' *SHAW* 27 (2007): 87–104.

72 / To G. Bernard Shaw Beckhythe Manor, Overstrand
13th September 1913

[TLT: BL, SPA]

Shaw had asked Murray to give his provisional preface to Misalliance, *'Parents and Children,' a critical reading, and Murray complied at length. After granting that his occupation as an educator differs greatly from Shaw's 'business' of 'destructive criticism,' he states an array of objections in his firm but inoffensive manner. Not surprisingly, the final version of the preface reveals that Shaw did not honour most of those objections.*

My dear Shaw

I have just been marrying Rosalind to her Toynbee. We did it at a jolly little Registry in the orchard of an old farm at Northrepps, as quietly as could be, and they have gone off to Castle Howard for a honeymoon.

And I am left feeling shattered and sentimental, like a mid-Victorian mother. Which has delayed my return of the Preface.

I append a lot of disjointed remarks on it. In a way I am vaguely disappointed – probably because I am too much in the machine of education to see it from the outside. I think I cannot help reading it with a view to positive suggestions, whereas your business is destructive criticism. But a great deal of it seems to me important and true. I am horrified continually at the rude and overbearing way in which adults treat children, simply because they are too small to retaliate. I agree that they ought to be treated – until a state of war breaks out – with as much courtesy as adults, and rather more because they are sensitive.

I cant quite agree about the 'experiment.' First of all, I think the metaphor an exaggeration. An experiment implies a fully conscious and deliberate agent who arranges all the conditions. But, apart from that, if your Life Force makes a child as an experiment and puts it into certain definite surroundings, surely those surroundings are part of the experiment. If I made the experiment of dropping a female infant into a Chinese house I should not afterwards complain if the people of the house deformed its feet. Nor should the Life Force, if she drops a child into the arms of a drunkard or a confirmed lover of virtue, complain that they try to make the child drink or love virtue. And, on the same line, I think you overstate your very valuable point about the tendency of parents to confuse troublesomeness with wickedness. Of course they do make the confusion; they do behave hypocritically and selfishly in trying to make out that a child is morally bad just because it angers or humiliates or dislikes them. But there still remains the enormous difficulty that you must – unless you are to mess your whole business – look after the child's or young person's character. And there is a quite special anxiety, entirely different from annoyance, which you feel when a boy or girl is apparently 'getting into bad ways.' And constantly the convenient course would be to ignore the danger and shirk the trouble, and reflect that after all before anything serious happens the young beggar will be over twenty-one and you can wash your hands of him.

'Children as Nuisances' is very good and full of true points. Feeling the continued society of the child a nuisance is quite compatible with considerable affection for it. I incline, tentatively, to think that the anthropological division of society into age-groups, rather than family groups, is a good one. Twenty years difference in age makes a huge barrier, even when there is affection to bridge it over. This is partly a justification of schools.

Another justification is that children are usually easy and pleasant to manage if you give them your whole attention, they are maddening if you are trying to do something else, or listening to them with half your mind. Hence the 'child fancier' does his work better than the parent, who has, or ought to have, other things to do.

P xx. I cannot quite think schools 'horrible.' I find that at both Basil's and Agnes's and Rosalind's school the pupils who were going to leave at the end of term used to weep and pity themselves. Denis and Agnes get angry if a single word is said in criticism of their schools. Nor do I pity the masters – at any rate in the rich public schools. I am constantly surprised at the brilliant men who take schoolmasterships in preference to the Civil Service.

School-books. Yes. How rum they are! Are they utterly vile and wrong, or are they the right kind of literature for the unformed mind? Remember that the average boy or girl finds all serious grown-up books equally loathsome. They will enjoy adventure and romance – if very easy to read – but they hate Macbeth and Stevenson's essays and the Quintessence of Ibsenism just as much as Brown on the XXXIX Articles. They cant see any difference between Macaulay's History and the stodgiest textbook except that Macaulay is worse because longer. I dont believe that we literary people have any conception of the mind of the stupid man, and the stupid average boy is fathoms below the stupid man.

xxviii. A very interesting question. You want a strictly limited minimum of compulsory education. My old tutor, Snow, says that no intellectual work is any good whatever unless it is done in the spirit of a poet or discoverer and the aim must always be infinite. I dare say both are right. So far one justifies the main feature of the Oxford system, the sharp division between Pass and Honours. On the one hand a bare minimum (which happens to be badly chosen at present) of stuff which *must all* be known; on the other a great vista of knowledge which you cannot possibly cover, and honours awarded according to the quality of the work done in – practically – any part of the field. I sometimes think that this division is what saves Oxford and Cambridge from the ruin which seems inevitably demanded by their vices in other respects. It implies, your compulsory minimum for all followed by an attempt at the infinite on the part of an intellectual few.

Pp xxxiii ff are very important. And I vehemently agree with the first few lines of xli – both parts of the sentence. Also the top line of xlii

P xlv surprises me. I am so dismayed at the inability of my younger friends, and my worst pupils (for of course my pupils are nearly all exceptionally clever at their subject or they would not come to me) to read five pages of matter that does not interest them instantly – or to listen for five minutes to a consecutive argument. I dont see how any one is to get through the ordinary routine of life, to earn his livelihood or keep out of jail, without a considerable power of enduring boredom – i.e. of doing something which he does not much like tolerably well.

Pp xlvi ff bring up a point that always puzzles me. In the circles in which I have moved, all my life through, Art is always inculcated, gassed about, glorified, whitewashed, with the utmost hypocrisy. No girls school now but has its walls covered with Italian pictures which not one in twenty of the girls cares about, in order to impart culture to their conversation. And even the public schools are falling. Winchester is a perfect Art Gallery. Again one of the advantages of the old-fashioned classical training was that when a young man felt lecherous he honestly looked up obscene passages in Latin writers or in Aristophanes and revelled in them, knowing what he was doing. The modern young man and woman do the same with Aubrey Beardsley or Anatole France or devil knows whom and say it is Art. I suppose there *are* circles in which 'story books &c &c are forbidden' (p xlvii) but I wish I could catch a glimpse of one for an hour or two. The young people whom I know go about very nervous lest they should fail to admire something that very likely seems to them simply beastly because it is the correct thing. The Creator is 'implicitly convicted of indecency.' Of course He is. Guilty on every count. Just as He is convicted of cruelty and injustice and anything else you like. You will not improve your case by associating persons of that character with your defence. I would sooner fall back on Redford and George Edward[e]s than on Him.

How frightfully verbose I have become. And abusive, too. Anyhow I love reading anything you write. Écrasons l'infame.

Yours ever
G.M.

Murray's critique of Shaw's **experiment** in 'Parents and Children' pertains to the section which begins: 'WHAT IS A CHILD? An experiment. A fresh attempt to produce the just man made perfect: that is, to make humanity divine' (CP 4, 20). His comment on parents confusing **troublesomeness with wickedness** refers to Shaw's statement that parents tend to substitute 'Don't be naughty' for 'Stop that noise,' implying that the child, 'instead of annoying you by a perfectly healthy and natural infantile procedure, is offending God' (22). Murray's insistence that parents must look after the child's **character** directly opposes Shaw's remonstrance that 'you had much better let the child's character alone' lest you defeat 'the experiment of the Life Force' (25). Murray's idea that a **'child fancier'** will do his work better than the parent is not congruous with Shaw's narrow use of the term to encompass 'flogging schoolmasters and orphanage fiends and baby farmers' whose love of children is 'obviously unnatural' (32–3). Finally, he attempts correctives to Shaw's extreme comments on schools ('there is ... nothing on earth intended for innocent people so **horrible** as a school') and textbooks ('you are forced to read a hideous imposture called a **school book**'). Here as before, Shaw does not seem to have altered a word (35). Robert Louis **Stevenson** (1850–94) wrote many essays, some of them collected in *Memories and Portraits* (1887). **Brown on the XXXIX Articles** was E[dward] Harold Browne (1811–91), author of *An Exposition of the Thirty-Nine Articles, Historical and Doctrinal* (London: J.W. Parker, 1887; 13th ed. 1950). It must have been used as a textbook, since a volume of examination questions on its contents was published. Browne, a Cambridge doctor of divinity and professor, became bishop of Ely and then of Winchester. Thomas Babington **Macaulay** (1800–59), English historian and diplomat, is best known for his five-volume *History of England.* T[homas] C[ollins] **Snow** (1852–?) was a classicist who published widely before the turn of the century. **Aubrey** [Vincent] **Beardsley** (1872–98) was a writer and illustrator who often employed erotic themes. **Anatole France** (1844–1924) was a prominent French writer best known for the novels *Thaïs* and *Penguin Island.* **Écrasons l'infâme** was the signature cry of the French philosopher François-Marie Arouet, known as Voltaire (1694–1778), usually directed at various forms of intolerance: 'Let us crush the infamous one!'

73 / To Gilbert Murray

Hotel Croix d'Or. Valence sur Rhone, France
22nd September 1913

[ALS: Bod, SPA]

This letter is distinctive for Shaw's detailed exposition of the basics of his theory of the Life Force. Its escalating importance in his mind since 1900 serves him by justifying his views on parents and children, as it does on 'the battle of the sexes' in Man and Superman, *the delusions of doctors in* The Doctor's Dilemma, *Blanco's conversion in* The Shewing-up of Blanco Posnet, *and the thematic thrust in many other plays – as well as most of the prefaces that he wrote* after *having told Murray that this one would surely be his last.*

Shaw had fallen 'violently and exquisitely' in love with Mrs Patrick (Stella) Campbell on 26 June 1912 while reading Pygmalion *to her. The affair had flourished for over a year – with Shaw keeping his wife informed of its progress – when*

Charlotte engineered a separation by insisting on a six-week auto tour through France and Germany to begin with her leaving on 8 August and Shaw joining her later that month. Somewhat ironically, the affair was brought to an abrupt halt three days after Charlotte left for Marseilles, with Stella rejecting his attempted rendezvous at a hotel on the coast of Kent.

Typical of his and Charlotte's fortunes on pleasure trips – although this time the chauffeur, not Shaw, was at fault – accidents interfered with their enjoyment.

My dear Murray

Here I am, with Charlotte laid up with a cold, and the car broken. Some bump on the mountains was too much for her: her steel frame tore like a piece of paper. An artificer here with what looks like a very dirty old garden fire engine says he can vulcanize the frame – put a patch of steel on the wound and melt the whole into homogeneity – in two days for 40 francs or thereabouts. Such are the marvels of modern wayside repairing now that every tinker can achieve the temperature of hell with the aid of some bottled oxygen.

Rosalind being disposed of, let us consider the education of her children. First, you have the XIX century conception of an experiment as manufactured evidence. This is really illustration, not experiment; and even at that the illustrations are always faked: the piece of cotton wool which ought to burst into flame in the focus of the heat rays when the light rays are picturesquely cut off never does so unless the lecturer dips it in phosphoric oil and keeps talking until spontaneous combustion takes place. My theory is that the Life Force proceeds by the method of Trial & Error (mostly Error) and that everything it produces is a real experiment: that is to say, a Try On. But it cannot create anything except by organizing itself into the thing it creates (the Word made Flesh); and as it cannot commit suicide, and the thing it organizes itself into is often a horrible mistake, it can remove the mistake only by creating something else that will murder the mistake. Hence the strained relations of Man and Flea. Hence also the fuss about the Problem of Evil, the reconciliation of the God of Love with the God of Cancer & Toothache, & so forth. The moment you see that the Life Force is feeling its way by Trial & Error, all these problems and difficulties disappear. You pray with sincerity 'Our Blunderer which art not in heaven, blessed be thy excellent intentions, hurry up with thy kingdom which is so long coming, get thy job done on earth which will then be heaven. Give us this day our daily vitality; and forgive us our trespasses as we forgive yours, knowing that you mean well. Lead us into all sorts of temptations, and never say die; for thine is the impulse and the gumption and the glory, world without end, Amen.' The late Colonel Cody, who made more aeroplanes and had more accidents with them than any other high flier, was the most godlike man of our times.

Incidentally, of course, the Life Force *is* convicted of indecency; and I must make that point clear; but there is a frightful lot of manufactured subjective indecency, which was what I was thinking of when I wrote that sentence. Still, I wonder whether the Superman, when he walks out of a bush someday and proceeds to wipe us out as we have wiped out the megatherium, will retain our digestive and reproductive processes, or whether he will simply not be ashamed of them and enslaved by them. The longer I live the more I doubt whether Man can get much further than he has. If the Life Force cannot supersede the Yahoo, then the L.F. is played out. But I dont believe the L.F. *is* played out. Slightly paraphrasing Blake, I contemplate Man and say 'Can he who superseded the Mastadon [*sic*] not supersede *thee*?'

But to the point, which is, that the child is a Try On, not a Put Up Job, like the experiments at the Royal Institution Christmas lectures for children. I think that if you get it that way, I come right. If you dropped a child into a Chinese house it wouldnt be an experiment at all. If you were a professor of physics you would drop the child into a Chinese house, and then hold it up with its feet deformed to prove that the house was a Chinese house, which is rot. Someday, when the Chinese were giving up foot binding (as they are) you would find the child with its feet all right. If you were a daring original genius, you would then convulse the scientific world by declaring that the house was not a Chinese house. If you were an ordinary man, but very honest, you would simply say to your class, 'Well, the experiment hasnt come off; but you must take my word for it that when you drop a child into a Chinese house its feet, if female, come out deformed.' But if you were a smart pushing fellow you would always take care to deform the child's feet yourself before you dropped it in; and then your experiments would always be applauded and described as 'brilliant.' That is the sort of science that chucked out poor Jehovah, who had at least moments of poetry about him.

The honors system would be excellent if the knowledge of the examiners were infinite. As it is, the science of passing examinations is the science of telling the examiners what they think they know and what they know they think. I doubt if I should have come out very high. But the system works perfectly in athletics. There is no mistake about the High Jump, because the greatest fool among the judges can see higher than the most accomplished kangaroo can jump.

Why should you be dismayed because your pupils will not allow you to bore them? Probably you set too high a standard of interest in your inspired moments; but anyhow the view that endurance is a thing to be cultivated for its own sake is a survival of the Australian in you. There they initiate a boy into manhood by hammering his head with sharp stones and otherwise shewing him how much he can stand if he makes up his mind to it. But that view would justify anything, from making children learn the book of Numbers by heart to wearing a shirt of spiky mail. As a matter of fact I dont believe that people ever learn anything they dont want to learn, or retain any knowledge that they dont frequently use. They may want knowledge for its own sake because it interests them, or they may want it as a means to an end though its acquisition is drudgery to them. But they must want it or it is waste of time to teach them. Very few people want to know arithmetic, but everybody wants to have money and spend it without being cheated or miscalculating how far it will go. And they pick up enough for that. Lots of people who dont care for mathematics do care enough for being ship captains or land surveyors to use logarithms and ascertain the difference between a crumpet and a cosine. I shouldnt worry about want of application, though it is a simple fact that not one per cent of our routineers has any understanding of his business, or does it really well.

The difficulty about my age groups is that age is an illusory thing, except physically. Roughly speaking all persons have fixed ages at which they remain all their lives, though they alter in size, and their hairs and teeth and eyesights incommode them by conventional changes. Consequently there are always people to whom the society of people of their own *years* is unbearable except at one point in their lives. An Oxford eight of all ages from a cox of ten to a bow of ninety would probably be defeated by a Cambridge eight of the usual ages; but it is possible that if the two crews stopped half way for rest & conversation, the Cambridge eight might bore one another more than the Oxford owing to a greater disparity of evolutionary age. Then you have to consider that the society of the young is part of the education of the old, and vice versa. Therefore there must be opportunities of intercourse between young & old. The fearful fact that you note, that the young demand all one's attention and never know when to go should be met by simply informing the young that they must never stay more than 15 minutes. Herbert Spenser [*sic*] used to put plugs of cotton wool into his ears when he had had enough of conversation, which, after all, was nicer than yawning or looking at his watch. This should be tolerated exactly as a baby's going to sleep (not that it ever does) is tolerated.

As to Basil & Agnes, they may be unnatural young vipers in reaction against their parents' insurrectionary tendencies. Or, again, the homes of their schoolfellows may have been horribly unhappy. But do not forget my old Man & Superman view that hell is a place where the damned are happy, or at least where they have the greatest dread of heaven. The death of the worst parent is seldom hailed with shouts of joy by the children – often rather with tears. When the Bastille fell, and the revolutionists after a long search succeeded in saving their faces by discovering a few prisoners, the prisoners who had been there longest wept at the destruction of their home. Liberation is a terrible thing to those who have never been free.

As to books, we morbid people with literary tastes must frankly admit that literature is idiosyncratic, and that people who can learn only with their eyes (patrons of the cinema) and ears (of the phonograph, church, theatre &c), often know more than those who can take in nothing except by reading about it. One of the curses of the world is that it is conscious, not of itself, but of a literary version of itself, made nine tenths by men who were never in contact with real life.

Finally – for I mustnt begin another page – I am quite sure that the Uranian Venus can alone keep youth out of the arms of the other lady. The boy who took his sexual impulses as obscenities was surely more disastrously wrong about them than the boy who takes them as Art. Pictures and operas make young people fastidious as to beauty & charm & give a great deal of pleasure. The alternative is obscenity & harlotry. Can you hesitate?

G.B.S.

Colonel Cody (Samuel Franklin Cowdery, then Cody, 1867–1913), a transplanted American aviator and showman, became the first Englishman to sustain powered flight. A **routineer** is a rarely used term for one who adheres to a routine. **Herbert Spencer** (1820–1903) was an influential English philosopher and advocate of Darwin's theory of evolution. **Basil and Agnes** were two of Murray's children. On Shaw's concept of **the Uranian Venus** as a prompter of 'imaginary amours on the plains of heaven' which can make one 'inhuman through a surfeit of beauty and an excess of voluptuousness,' see his original holograph letter to Frank Harris of 24 June 1930, printed in CL 4, 190–3.

74 / To Gilbert Murray

Pau
1st October 1913

[APCS: CL 3]

Have just made my pilgrimage. I cannot deny that my car was healed of a rather troublesome knock. But still Lourdes, for an Irish Protestant, is a bit thick. What looks like wickerwork on the left of the grotto in the picture is really discarded crutches – the lame man leaps like a hart. Crowds of English, ministered to by priests with elaborate Oxford accents, who slur over the references to the Virgin's womb in a truly gentlemanly manner, flavor the place.

On the whole I should like to bring a huge procession of atheists, and unite myself to Jane Harrison by civil registration in front of the Basilica. Tomorrow I shall (N.D.L.V.) reach the Grand Hotel, Biarritz, and stay there, probably, until it is time to return. I must be in London on the 20th.

G.B.S.

One miracle of the advent of Jesus was that **the lame man leaps like a hart** (Isaiah 35: 6). **Jane Harrison** (1850–1928) was an English classical scholar who wrote on mythology and the social origins of Greek religion. **N.D.L.V.** is the abbreviation for 'Notre Dame Le Veuille!' ('Our Lady Grant It!').

75 / To G. Bernard Shaw

82 Woodstock Road, Oxford
11th October 1913

[TLT: BL, SPA]

My dear Shaw

Glad to get your Lourdes postcard. I always knew that in religious matters, in spite of occasional wanderings, you were sound at heart. It is very provoking of people to go and get cured at Lourdes. I dont mind it so much at Hindu and Buddhist shrines. There one expects it. But at Lourdes it sets a bad example to young men.

We have just been giving a real party. I believe you were invited to it and will find the documents on your return. Three hundred people in New College Hall, to meet the Toynbees. Mary and I stood at the door to ask all comers who they were and whether they were really invited. If they got past us they had a right to cakes and ices to the value of 1s 6. It is wonderfully easy when once you try, like such a lot of things. And now we have to marry Lady Dorothy from this house on Tuesday. I am not sure I shall not have to show people to their pews.

J S Haldane, our physiologist here, younger brother of the baron, has just written a book on what he calls the Mechanist view of the world. It is like Lodge, though shorter and stronger in thinking power. But it is awful how these scientific men wallow in orthodoxy when they get the chance. I believe that Benn is right in saying that Free Thought really depends on the men of letters – and progressive thought, too. Haldane is a very good man. By the way, I rather liked Sir Almroth's Unexpurgated Case against W.S. I thought it very serious and honest, and most of the things he said really true, though I should draw different conclusions from them.

I must prepare a lecture on the Agamemnon.

Yours ever,
G.M.

Lady Dorothy was the Countess of Carlisle's third daughter, Dorothy [Giorgiana] Howard (1881–1968). She married Francis Eden, 6th Baron Henley, on 14 October 1913, thus becoming Lady Henley. **J**[ohn] **S**[cott] **Haldane** (1860–1936) was an eminent scholar in the history of physiology, best known for experimenting (often dangerously) on himself. In 1913 he published *Mechanism, Life and Personality: An Examination of the Mechanistic Theory of Life and Mind*. **Lodge** is probably Oliver Lodge (1851–1940), a friend of Murray devoted to psychical research, and **Benn** may be Alfred William Benn (1843–1915), an agnostic and positivist who wrote *The History of Ancient and Modern Philosophy* (1912). **Sir Almroth** Wright (1861–1947), the model for Sir Colenso Ridgeon in *The Doctor's Dilemma* and a personal friend of Shaw, published *The Unexpurgated Case against Woman Suffrage* in 1913. A passage from its introduction conveys his judicial but dogmatic tone: 'The task which I undertake here is to show that the Woman's Suffrage Movement has no real intellectual or moral sanction, and that there are very weighty reasons why the suffrage should not be conceded to woman.' Shaw replied negatively to the book five days after Murray's letter in 'Sir Almroth Wright's Polemic,' *New Statesman*, 18 October; reprinted in *Fabian Feminist*, ed. Rodelle Weintraub, as 'Sir Almroth Wright's Case against Woman Suffrage,' 243–7. The heart of his rebuttal is that what Wright describes as 'Woman's mind' is 'exactly like Man's mind.' Michael Holroyd quotes a key part of this letter in his biography but attributes it to Shaw (2, 161).

76 / To Gilbert Murray

Adelphi Terrace WC
2nd February 1914

[APCS: Cornell, SPA]

Sheafs of invitations, mostly from people who make downstrokes like this (the only really infallible symptom of lunacy) remind me that I have not yet embraced your offer of hospitality, which reached me just in time to prevent me inviting myself. I shall probably have to rush away again on Sunday morning. Many thanks.

G.B.S.

77 / To Gilbert Murray or Lady Mary

10 Adelphi Terrace WC
23rd February 1914

[APCS: ECL]

Shaw had begun Pygmalion *on 7 March 1912 and completed it on 16 June of that year.*

Rehearsals for the English premiere, scheduled for 11 April 1914, had begun on 19 February, with Shaw reading the play. Neither Mrs Patrick Campbell nor the popular actor-manager Beerbohm Tree (1852–1917) satisfied him in their roles as Eliza Doolittle and Henry Higgins; at the rehearsal mentioned below he stormed out, 'driven to distraction by the antics of his two stars,' and at the premier on 11 April he would leave before the final curtain, 'furious at Tree's performance' (Gibbs, Chronology, *208–9).*

Charlotte would very much like to come, but daren't in cold weather. She gets attacks of bronchitis whenever she leaves London; and they are asthmatic and very troublesome.

As for me, I am rehearsing a play with Mrs Campbell & Tree in the principal parts: an experience not to be described on a postcard. I can guarantee the 8·30 breakfast; but I may be forced – very unwillingly – to start at ten. Possibly, however, I may murder the company and burn down the theatre before Saturday, in which event I shall be free and happy.

G. Bernard Shaw

In his biography of Murray, Duncan Wilson fills in the following half-year gap in correspondence by concisely describing his subject's complicated political

involvements at the time: 'In summer 1914 it would have been difficult to forecast Murray's attitude to the outbreak of a war between Britain and Germany; everything would depend on the circumstances in which war broke out. Murray was by this time a favourite intellectual of middle-of-the-road Liberals, ... and he enjoyed his position as part-time member of the political establishment. On the other hand, the Radical in him was by no means dead; he was still committed to the cause of Votes for Women and progress towards Home Rule for Ireland ... He had been associated with the Webbs and the Fabians in their efforts to reform the Poor Law, and with Christian Socialists at Oxford on local social issues ... He was in touch with the Independent Labour Party through Ramsay MacDonald, and with other groups on the left through G. D. H. Cole [1889–1959]' (217).

War had seemed both unlikely and ill advised during the spring and summer of 1914, and Murray was certainly opposed to it. But on the first of August Germany declared war on Russia, which was in the midst of a vast rearmament program; and two days later they declared war on France, partly because the Franco-Russian alliance of 1894 was still in effect. The very next day they began sending troops through Belgium to gain access to France. Murray was swayed to favour the war by a single speech of Sir Edward Grey (1st Viscount Grey of Fallodon [1862–1933]), British foreign secretary 1905–16, in the House of Commons on 3 August. After learning that Belgium had been invaded he responded wholeheartedly to Grey's declaration, which explained his country's present situation and declared that war was now the only alternative. Murray came away convinced that Britain 'had no choice' but to go to war, since an 'absolute duty ... lies upon us to save Europe and humanity' (letter to Lady Mary quoted in Wilson, 218). He saw fit to support 'The Writer's Manifesto,' an appeal to eminent writers to support Britain going to war against Germany.

78 / To Gilbert Murray

The Hydro, Torquay
12th September 1914

[TLS: SPA]

Shaw's response to Murray's direct appeal for him to sign the Manifesto was at first scathingly ironic, then bluntly negative as well as impossibilist.

My dear Murray

I have signed the Manifesto with the greatest pleasure. I have made a few trifling corrections; but I feel sure you will all accept them gratefully, especially Owen Seaman, as they bring the document into harmony with the recent numbers of Punch since his startled *volte-face* from Non-Intervention.

But at worst you and I can sign *contra mundum.*

yours ever
G. Bernard Shaw

PS Seriously, I shouldnt issue that Manifesto. What it says is not true and not new; and it gives Grey a testimonial just when the war gives us a chance of discrediting all this Cromer-Milner-Grey diplomacy & reviving what is valuable in the Liberal tradition. I am struggling laboriously through a Manifesto of my own on the subject.

Owen Seaman (1861–1936) was a professor of literature with a gift for political parody which had led to the editorship of *Punch* at the time. He was serving as chairman of the committee that drafted the Manifesto. Shaw notes in *Common Sense about the War* that 'an amusing and witty No-Intervention poem' by Seaman had appeared in *Punch* shortly after Grey had persuaded Germany that he did not intend to go to war (29). ***Contra mundum*** means 'against the world,' which Shaw, tongue in cheek, seems to imply that if no one else signs he and Murray will. By **Cromer-Milner-Grey diplomacy** Shaw is probably lumping the newly converted Grey with the strongly imperialist Liberal Evelyn Baring, first earl of Cromer (1841–1917), who was the virtual ruler of Egypt from 1883–1907, and the colonialist / businessman Alfred Milner, first Viscount Milner (1854–1925), who was chosen a member of Lloyd George's war cabinet in 1916. [James] Ramsay MacDonald (1866–1937), who resigned as leader of the Labour Party on 5 August 1914 when the party's executive committee reversed its opposition to the ruling Liberal government, was one of the few prominent voices to side with Shaw; he went as far as to say that Sir Edward Grey had been 'a menace to the peace of Europe for the last eight years' (Shaw, *Agitations*, 164).

79 / To G. Bernard Shaw

Westminster House, Buckingham Gate, SW
27th October 1914

[TLS: Bod, Guelph]

Murray had written an open letter 'To our colleagues in Russia' (signed by himself and H.G. Wells), which he circulated to various British men of letters inviting them to sign as a gesture of good will to their Russian counterparts. It begins: 'At this moment, when your countrymen and ours are alike facing death for the deliverance of Europe, we English men of letters take the opportunity of uttering to you feelings which have been in our hearts for many years. You yourselves perhaps hardly realize what an inspiration we English writers the last two generations have found in your literature. Many a writer among us can still call back, from ten or twenty or thirty years ago, the thrill of delight and almost of bewilderment with which he read his first Russian novel. Perhaps it was Virgin Soil *or* Fathers and Sons, *perhaps*

War and Peace *or* Anna Karenina, *perhaps* Crime and Punishment *or* The Idiot*; perhaps again, it was the work of some writer still living. But many of us then felt, as our poet Keats did on first recalling Homer, "like some watcher of the skies / When a new planet swims into his ken"' ('On Looking into Chapman's Homer').*

The letter, lacking Shaw's signature (as well as Barker's), was published in the Manchester Guardian *on 23 December 1914. On 12 September Barker had quipped to Murray that he 'would sign it with my blood if anything were to be gained by shedding it, ... But my principal admirers are alien enemies' (Salmon,* Granville Barker and His Correspondents, *287).*

Dear Sir,

We hope that you may feel disposed to add your signature to the enclosed letter, which will shortly be sent for publication to the Russian press. It is not meant for a general manifesto, but for a more personal expression of feeling from men to letters to men of letters, to be signed by a small number of English writers who care particularly for Russian literature and whose names are likely to be known in Russia. We have reason to believe that some such statement would be surely welcomed by our Russian colleagues.

Yours sincerely,
GILBERT MURRAY
H.G. WELLS

80 / To Gilbert Murray

10 Adelphi Terrace WC
5th November 1914

[ALS: CL 3]

In Common Sense about the War, *Shaw does not launch a concerted attack on what he calls 'Prussian Tsardom,' and he even grants 'Gilbert Murray's plea that the recent rate of democratic advance has been greater in Russia than anywhere else in Europe,' and follows by mocking the actual quantity of that rate (61–2). But he does go so far as to generalize that Russia's government 'is the open enemy of every liberty we boast of,' citing 'the Tsar's successful attempt to arrest thirty members of the Duma [congress] and to punish them as dangerous criminals,' and adding that under that government 'people whose worst crime is to find The Daily News a congenial newspaper are hanged, flogged, or sent to Siberia as a matter of daily routine' (62–3). He says nothing about the prohibition of vodka.*

Shaw regularly uses the term 'Potsdam' to mean the seat of German militarism and its effects. The city is on the outskirts of Berlin, where important government functions were often held. On 11 August Shaw had published 'The Peril of Potsdam: Our Business Now' in the Daily News, *charging that England's unreasonable fear of what Potsdam stood for had plunged her into an 'unholy alliance' that led to the war (CL 3, 244). In a letter of 22 August 1919 to Trebitsch he terms it 'Potsdamnation.'*

My dear Murray

On the 14th my War Manifesto will appear. In it I explain my attitude towards the Prussian Tsardom and the occasionally inspired idiots whom it hangs, flogs, & sends to Siberia. I am curious to see how far Russian genius will be extinguished by the prohibition of vodka.

Some of the circular is so good that I conclude that you drafted it. But I will not put my name to any document that deals with Russia unless it expressly and emphatically damns the Tsardom uphill, down dale, and all the way to hell. It is our business, not to help this abomination to hide itself under the mantle of Tolstoy, but to take care that neither at home nor abroad shall the enemies of mankind steal the sacred fire that will, we hope, destroy Potsdam. I shall be as explicit as Anatole France's peasant, who, having prayed in vain for rain to the child in the arms of the statue of the Virgin, burnt a candle to her instead, with the explanatory remark, 'It is not to you, you son of a whore, that I offer this candle, but to your sainted mother.'

Also, I have a strong feeling that if we start making international assurances of good feeling, we should begin with the Germans, to shew that in the republic of Art & Literature, & the Humanities generally, there are no frontiers and no wars. Only, the war seems to prove that this is a lie, and that the professors, saving your chair, are the worst of the lot.

I have a little move in The Nation for next Saturday to prevent America coming down on the wrong side of the fence in mere irritation at our hypocrisies & rancors.

yrs ever
G.B.S.

PS The telegram reached me, as it happened, too late to use the reply form.

The episode involving **Anatole France's peasant** occurs near the beginning of his novel *Sur la pierre blanche* (*On the White Stone,* 1905). French tourists at the Forum in Rome are discussing how contemporary Italian religious beliefs and attitudes parallel those of ancient Romans. Both are pragmatic and demand immediate results from their array of gods and genies, or now the Madonna and saints, showering them with invectives if the miracle is slow in coming. A peasant who had solicited a favour from the bambino returns to the chapel and berates him, 'Ce n'est pas à toi, fils de putain, que je parle, c'est à ta sainte mère' (courtesy of Michel Pharand). The '**little move in The Nation**' was Shaw's 'Open Letter to the President of the United States,' *Nation* 16 (7 November 1914), 166–8. He asked Wilson, Weintraub says in *Journey to Heartbreak,* 'to use his impartial good offices to ask all belligerents to get out of Belgium, "for the effect of our shells on Belgium is precisely the same as that of the German shells ... In London and Paris and Berlin ... nobody at present dares say 'Sirs: ye are brethren: why do ye wrong to one another?'; for the slightest disposition toward a Christian view of things is regarded as a shooting matter in these capitals; but Washington is still privileged to talk common humanity to the nations"' (51).

In early July 1915 Murray published The Foreign Policy of Sir Edward Grey, *a 140-page paperback. He received some assistance from Archer, Arnold Toynbee, and the Foreign Office, which supplied him with some official documents. His chief argument, as Wilson decribes it, was that Grey 'knew of German aggressive designs, and had to build up a system of alliances to counter them, without openly denouncing Germany and thereby closing the door to peaceful accommodation with her. At the same time he must do so without deceiving his cabinet colleagues' (222–3). Murray asserted that during the highly controversial twelve days before the war Grey's policy was 'exactly right,' and exhibited no signs of the 'secret diplomacy' of which he was accused by his detractors (34, 40).*

Shaw took a radically different perspective on the role played by the German intrusion into Belgium. He elaborates upon the 'secret diplomacy' underlying the British response that he had described briefly in Common Sense about the War *in 'The Great War and the Aftermath' (1925), reprinted in* Table-Talk of G.B.S. *Historically, Britain had declared that no military power should invade the continental shores of the North Sea. 'This was perfectly straightforward balance-of-power diplomacy; and when the German Empire invaded Belgium, the British expeditionary force, with all its alliances ready in its pocket, including an arrangement with the ostensibly neutral Belgians, flew at it. Therefore it is true that the invasion of Belgium by Germany was the provocation on which England declared war, having prepared for this contingency since 1906.' However, as this kind of diplomacy 'was neither popular nor comprehensible by the man in the street ..., it was camouflaged with a mass of nonsense about our disinterestedness, our unpreparedness, the sacredness of neutrality and of a long-extinct treaty, and all the rest of it. This went down .... until the Germans occupied Brussels and found all the records of our secret military arrangements with the Belgians' (140–1).*

Even more uncompromising was the elaborate attack on Murray's book by his sometime neighbour Bertrand Russell: Justice in War-Time: A Reply to Professor Gilbert Murray, *a 243-page rebuttal. He had told a friend that he made 'a terrible piece of invective in the book,' since he could not 'discover any infamy in the whole wide world which the Foreign Office had not done its best to support – it is beyond belief. I think every word the Germans say against us is justified' (Russell,* Prophecy and Dissent, 1914–16, *202).*

A recent judgment on Murray's reaction to Sir Edward's speech, 'the defining moment of his political career,' occurs in Ceadel's essay 'Gilbert Murray and International Politics': 'Grey's ill-prepared performance proved unexpectedly persuasive, for a reason which the historian Cameron Hazlehurst [in Politicians at War, *46] neatly put his finger on: "The one massive virtue of Grey's speech was the stumbling manner, mistaken this time, as so often before, for honesty. Here was a man, it seemed, who had struggled for peace" ... Murray was one of those taken in: he evidently felt sympathy for a fastidious Oxonian statesman from an old Whig family struggling to do the right thing. What thus separated Murray from those radicals who maintained their neutralism and suspicion of secret diplomacy ... was as much a difference of temperament as an alternative reading of international politics. Murray was temperamentally disposed to trust certain members of the Liberal establishment, whereas the likes of E. D. Morel, Arthur Ponsonby, and Bertrand Russell were not' (223–4)*

On 2 September 1914 the minister responsible for information (and/or propaganda), Charles F.G. Masterman (1873–1927), convened a meeting of well-known writers, including Murray, 'to discuss how best to counteract German propaganda among the neutral countries ... It was unanimously resolved that a Bureau of Information should be set up, with sections devoted to various groups of neutral countries; and that a manifesto should be prepared for signature by the greatest possible number of eminent writers, in support of the war ... This was the beginning of Murray's connection with what he himself sometimes referred to as the "Mendacity Bureau"' (Wilson, 219). He became a sporadic but valuable propagandist for the Liberal government. His tract How Can War Ever Be Right? *(Oxford University Press, 1914) was the eighteenth of 87 Oxford Pamphlets, one of more than 1600 pamphlets issued between late summer 1914 and September 1918 sponsored by what was renamed the War Propaganda Bureau (William Bruneau, "Gilbert Murray, Bertrand Russell, and the Theory and Practice of Politics," in Stray, 209f.).*

By October Murray's focus had shifted to the nature of a peace settlement. He published a pamphlet, Thoughts on the *War, which argued that another Germany than the militarist one existed, and (in Wilson's paraphrase) that the peace 'must solve more than Anglo-German problems. War must be extinguished, as leprosy and typhus had been extirpated. There must be a drastic resettlement of all problems, especially territorial ones, which carried the seeds of future war. There should be a permanent Conference of Europe, and perhaps a permanent Council' (245–6). For a balanced account of these events see Pearce and Stewart, 287–9.*

In spite of the refusal of Shaw to sign the manifesto, it was duly published in The Times *on 18 September 1914. Shaw's own war 'Manifesto' was* Common Sense about the War, *originally published as a Special War Supplement to* The New Statesman *4, no. 84 (14 Nov. 1914): 3–29; repr. in Shaw,* Major Critical Essays, *21: 'What I Really Wrote about the War,' 23–115. The essay has also been reprinted in a scholarly edition,* What Shaw Really Wrote about the War, *16–84, from which I will quote.* Common Sense *documents the Byzantine political manoeuvres of diplomats in several countries, focusing especially upon Grey (28–31), whom, he says, an autocratic foreign policy permitted to make war 'without consulting the nation, or confiding in it,' leading 'inevitably to a disastrous combination of war and unpreparedness for war' (43). For a detailed, authoritative account of the background, content, reception, and consequences for Shaw of this publication, see Weintraub, 25–139, esp. 53–82: 'The Storm over* Common Sense*').*

In mid-1915 Murray's The Trojan Women *was touring the United States in the cause of peace, sponsored by the radical Woman's Peace Party headed by Jane Addams (1860–1935). It was enthusiastically received by drama critics as well as activists. The Chicago critic's response was typical: 'Here is a play of the most exquisite beauty bringing, through Gilbert Murray's magic translation, Greek and modern together in the realization of what life may hold … That the aroused imagination of the nation which is brought into such close contact with war again should have this means of crystallizing itself is a boon for which we cannot be too grateful to the Woman's Peace Party'* (Chicago Evening Post, *12 April 1915, quoted in Degen, 60). Murray drafted a 'Note by the Translator,' but it was not included. The text: 'While I am heart and soul with the Woman's Peace Party in their abomination of War and Militarism and their pursuit of Peace, and while*

I feel the continuance of the present war a daily and nightly horror, taking the ease and joy out of life, I do not wish my co-operation in this National Tour to be interpreted as meaning that I am in favour of making peace with Germany on whatever terms the German Government may propose. To "crush Germany" is fortunately a sheer impossibility, deliberately to "hate Germany" is a sin against civilization. But I believe that in order to secure the rule of Peace and Public Rights in Europe certain safeguards must be obtained and certain reparations must be made. And therefore, as I believe it was the duty of my country to declare war on August 4, 1914, so I believe that it will be her duty, both to herself and to humanity, to scrutinize earnestly, though I hope generously, the proposed terms of Peace' (Thorndike, 163f.).

*Britain had issued war loans (the equivalent of American war bonds) in November 1914 and June 1915. As Laurence reports it, 'Shaw contributed £20,000 (a staggering sum) to the second loan' (*Theatrics, *119).*

81 / To G. Bernard Shaw Beckhythe Manor, Overstrand
11th July 1915

[TLT: BL, SPA]

As early as 1894 Murray had developed an interest in extrasensory perception and psychic phenomena. His good friend and fellow classicist Arthur W. Verrall (1851–1912) heightened his interest through the 1890s. Ever the rational sceptic, Murray nevertheless acknowledged 'the enormous dominion of those forces in man of which he is normally unconscious ... the blind powers beneath the threshold.' In Five Stages of Greek Religion *he speaks of the 'Uncharted,' which 'surrounds us on every side,' and urges following the guidance of reason in dealing with it, but when this fails, using our 'fainter powers of apprehension and surmise and sensitiveness' (206). In 'Gilbert Murray and Psychic Research,' N.J. Lowe declares, 'Murray was the most significant telepath of his age, amateur or professional, and his fifty years of so-called "experiments" were still being cited into the 1970s as the most important and compelling existing evidence for extra-sensory powers' (349–50). Interest in the possibility of many cases of psychic apprehension and thought transference escalated during the war; such books as Hereward Carrington's* Psychical Phenomena and the War *(1918) were widely read. The atheist Archer turned desperately to 'psychics' after his son Tom was reported missing in action late in the war.*

Murray did indeed seem to possess these faculties. The main issue at stake, Wilson notes, was whether the results could be classed as evidence of genuine thought transference or simply hyperaesthesia – in this case, abnormally acute hearing (277). In an address in 1952 he opts for telepathy: 'I do feel that there is one almost universal quality in these guesses of mine which does suit telepathy and does not suit any other explanation. They always begin with a vague emotional quality of atmosphere: "This is horrible, this is grotesque, this is full of anxiety"; or rarely, "This is something delightful"; or sometimes, "This is out of a book," "This is a Russian novel," or the like. That seems like a direct impression of a human mind' (quoted in Stevenson, 150). Several members with great experience in the field (Verrall's wife Helen and Aldous Huxley, for example) did not think that hyperaesthesia could account for all of the results, and, as Wilson avers, 'they seem to have convinced him that they were right' (277–8). However, a prominent scholar on the subject notes that Murray 'made no attempt to display his abilities under reasonable test conditions' (Hansel, 37).

In any event, Murray's participation in the Society had grown until, in 1915, he was elected president (an annual honour; he was elected again in 1952). With the Shaws in the audience, he delivered the presidential address two days before he played the prankster for them in the following letter (Gibbs, Chronology, *214; CL 3, 300).*

My dear Shaw

I feel I ought to warn you that on Friday July 9, shortly after 5, I saw a distinct apparition of you and your wife at a meeting of the Psychical Research Society. I looked repeatedly at the phantoms and once went so far as winking at them, but had no opportunity of seeing whether the hallucination was auditory as well as visual, since towards the end of the meeting they rose in the air and floated away – whether through the door or the ceiling I cannot be sure.

Now there is no great harm in frequenting SPR meetings in this life, but after death it becomes a perfect vice. There are some spirits who spend their whole eternity in going from one rather shabby seance to another, with barely room for tea at an ABC in between. So I hope you will not form the habit here.

I thought of coming round and trying to see you, but I had only time to rush through some engagements and catch my train.

If you want a medium, experts recommend Mrs Handcock, 1 Egerton Gardens or Terrace, Brompton Rd. She told Rosalind (who had removed her wedding ring) that it was a long time before she would be married but she was oppressed at home and needed a freer life.

Yours ever,
G.M.

The chain of **A.B.C.** tea shops started with a single shop in London in 1864 owned by the Aerated Bread Company, and grew in popularity.

The Denshawi (or Dinshawai) incident took place on 13 June 1906 in that Egyptian town when five British officers visited it to go pigeon shooting and started firing. The farmers, for whom the pigeons were the main source of revenue, were enraged and sought redress, but failed. This led to calamities on both sides, and British tribunals sentenced the delinquent villagers to awful punishments, including four hangings and many floggings. An Egyptian police officer who had accompanied the hunters testified that their stories were false, and he was sentenced to fifty lashes and two years' imprisonment. Shaw discusses it at length in the last section of his preface to John Bull's Other Island, *'The Denshawai Horror' (CP 2, 853–72). For a detailed, authoritative account of the event, see Luke, 'Order or Justice,' who makes a convincing case for the ultimate impact of the incident: 'As a result of Denshawai, British imperialism in Egypt was painted in stark relief and found wanting' (278). The chief culprits among the administrators, in her view, were Lord Cromer, consul-general of Egypt, who sanctioned the extraordinary penal measures (281), and Grey, who supported Cromer's policies 'vigorously' in Parliament while – as he later admitted – feeling that the actions taken were excessive and 'open to question' (279).*

Murray's book on Grey's foreign policy, while alienating him from some allies during his radical days, solidified his position as a force to reckon with among the Liberal establishment. As Wilson perceives, it 'marked a turning point in Murray's political development,' and gained him recognition as 'a most effective propagandist.' (Today he might be called 'an imbedded intellectual.') This talent would carry him through the loss from the government near the end of 1916 of his 'two Liberal heroes,' Asquith and Grey, when the former was forced to resign as prime minister in favour of Lloyd George and the latter retired (224–5).

In his 666-page memoir Twenty-Five Years, 1892–1916, *Grey does not mention Murray's controversial efforts on his behalf, although he had told him on the date of the following letter that 'the terms in which you write are a very real pleasure and encouragement' (Wilson, 223). Grey also doesn't mention his most relentless attacker, Shaw. At least one authoritative historian of the war, Peter Clarke, has summed up Murray's book as 'the classic defence of Grey's foreign policy … It tapped a rich vein of Liberal self-righteousness, which, stage by stage, helped to invest war-making and peace-making with high moral objectives' (*Hope and Glory, *72).*

82 / To Gilbert Murray Ayot St Lawrence, Welwyn, Herts.
14th July 1915

[TLT: CL 3]

In the enigmatic letter that follows, Shaw warns his friend about his coming public response: 'Professor Gilbert Murray's Defence of Sir Edward Grey,' about to appear in The New Statesman *(5, 17 July, 349–51). Excerpts: 'I approach the actual contents of the book with reluctance. I ask myself will Murray ever forgive me if I turn on my own share of the Euripidean irony, and, so to speak, seethe [boil] the kid in its mother's milk. I have marked passage after passage that seem to be the work of the sub-conscious translator of The Trojan Women rather than of the champion of the Foreign Office. The italics might have been underscored here and there by Mephistopheles …*

> *What annoyed the Democrats was their suspicion that Sir Edward really did like the Russian view because it was the autocratic and antinationalist: in short, the country house view. Professor Murray shews, I think successfully, that Sir Edward simply took the course dictated by circumstances. He always does. But Sir Edward forgets that England is a circumstance, and should do some of the dictation. And that is the whole case against Grey: the case that Murray, with the friendliest intentions, has proved up to the hilt (349, 351).*

My dear Murray

We saw you being mobbed and knew that some of your mob would mob us when they were through with you. So we fled.

I have done you in (the Grey book) for this week's New Statesman. I thought it better to slaughter you myself than leave you to some young butcher with no respect for his elders. And you have done Grey in. What ironic fiend possessed you? The horrid cruelty with which you put all his footle in italics would revolt Euripides. Even that damning passage in which he says that he is not quite sure whether the neutrality of Belgium is a fighting matter is there. Poor Edward, with the vials of wrath slowly turning upside down over his head in the hands of the avenging angel of Denshawai, fluttering about and saying to the Germans, 'If you can only suggest something – I assure you I'm quite reasonable.'

Dont you KNOW that youve destroyed him? Your dramatic faculty has enabled you to get into his skin in the most wonderful way: you defend him exactly as he would have defended the King of the Belgians if he had accepted the German offer (as Grey would have accepted it); but there come bits where the laughter of the sub-conscious Murray breaks through and gives the show away. Those Persians sawn in two with the dear delightful Russians marching between them – the Caudine forks up to date – and Grey taking it like a mixed biscuit at afternoon tea, though shocked to his soul by Shuster's bad form in not paying his calls: did you really see that with Grey's eyes as you wrote?

The knock-out is perfection. He was always guided by circumstances. Not like Napoleon, who said 'I make circumstances' or like me, who, going one better than Nap, say '*I* am a circumstance.' Youve really handled the man barbarously in your dramatic delirium.

It is funny; but I feel a certain remorse about it. Ever since that Egyptian horror I have raged against the folly of leaving Grey at the Foreign Office after such a sensational revelation of his utter want of character. But that is not quite the truth. It is not that he has no character, but that he has the wrong character for the job. There is the fear that if he found himself out he would have character enough in another direction to shoot himself, and that would be quite horrible – like a child doing it. Will he ever realize that he could have stopped the war, probably, by a shake of his fist, and that he was too nice and cautious to do it. Do the ghosts of the million slain never come to his bed and point to their mangled entrails and Edipusted eyes and say 'Thus didest thou'? I hope not. The only consolation one has in thinking of him is that he will never know. He will say, to the end, 'I asked them to come and confer. They *wouldnt.*

Simply wouldnt. And I'd have given them such nice tea. And we could have talked about Servia. What more could I do? I may as well think about something nice and go to sleep.'

Have you noticed the latest military discovery? When the Germans turned on the gas, the French and British armies instantaneously bunked from a front of FOUR MILES, which were left as open as your garden gate to the victorious chlorineers; and it was not the slightest use to them. The road to Calais was opened; and we coughed 'Walk in and be damned to you,' and they might as well have been the gassed as the gassers for all the effect it had on their fortunes or ours.

I am to meet Rosalind at the Webbs on Friday, fortunately before my review appears. The worst is, I havnt read Toynbee's book. Ought I?

My More Common Sense About the War is mouldering on my desk. The New Statesman says it is drivel, and is regurgitating it in Notes of the Week.

Barker has chucked the theatre. Fact. He has devoted himself to poverty and playwriting. As I have been urging him to do this for years, I cant object; but I did not intend him to select the exact moment when he was £5000 to the bad and on the brink of getting it all back by exploiting the big reputation his extravagance in trying for the perfect thing regardless had won him. However, it is something to have got him out of this producing business at any cost. £2000 of the five is fortunately due to me, which means, of course, that it [is] not due at all (half of it was only royalties); and he may be able to get the remaining three by squashing his marriage settlement (made recently enough to be vulnerable to creditors); but liquidation will leave him without a rap. He has a lecturing engagement on in the States; and the tour of Androcles may bring him in something; but he may be face to face with a relapse into heroic poverty, and you are clearly one of the people who ought to know this, and who can judge as to what other people ought to know it.

I hadnt been at a meeting of the [heavily type-scored deletion] (bother this typewriter!) S.P.R. since Hodgson exposed Madame Blavatsky there thirty years ago. I have made infamous use of your speech in the review. I dont think you are a good man for that job. It needs a hardy liar: nobody else is of any use.

Charlotte, who has just gone up to town, sends her devoted love.

G.B.S.

The current **King of the Belgians** was Albert I (Albert Leopold Clemens Marie Meinrad, 1875–1934), who ruled from 1909 until his death. **Those Persians sawn in two** refers to the treaty of 1907 between Britain and Russia, who agreed to divide their 'interventions' evenly in the chaotic country of Persia. The **Caudine forks** is a narrow mountain pass in ancient Samnium in southern Italy where the Samnites under Gavius Pontius defeated and captured a Roman army in 321 BC. William Morgan **Shuster** (1877–1960), an American lawyer, was treasurer general and financial adviser to Persia in 1911–12. According to Gilbert's history of the war, **Germans turned on the gas** for the first time on 22 April 1915, discharging 168 tons of chlorine against French, Algerian, and Canadian divisions over a four-mile front. The effect of the gas was 'devastating'; hundreds of men became comatose or died. 'The Algerian troops fled, leaving an 800-yard gap in the Allied line. Wearing respirators, the Germans advanced cautiously, taking 2,000 prisoners and capturing fifty-one guns. But no reserves had been brought forward to exploit the success by driving through the gap' (144). **Bunked**: departed hurriedly. **Toynbee's book** – that is, Rosalind's husband Arnold Joseph's – was most likely *The New Europe: Some Essays in Reconstruction*, an essay of 85 pages. **Barker** was depressed because of the war, the inability of the Kingsway Theatre to draw enough spectators to support advanced drama, and his current attempts at writing plays. His last production was Thomas Hardy's *The Dynasts* on 25 November 1914. In 1917 he divorced his wife, Lillah McCarthy, after a long and painful separation. He turned his attention to Shakespeare criticism, at which he excelled. Richard **Hodgson** (1855–1905) **exposed Madame Blavatsky** in an 1885 report to the Society for Psychical Research, a meeting which Shaw apparently attended. Hodgson concluded that Madame Helena Petrovna Blavatsky (1831–91), the most famous promoter of theosophy and, in practice, séances conducted by self-styled mediums, was a fraud. (In CL 2, 497, Laurence misidentifies Hodgson as W. Earl Hodgson, author of *Trout Fishing* and other books, but he corrects the error in 3, 300.) Shaw himself was challenged about his views of psychic phenomena during an interview when he was in his nineties: a self-styled expert from the tabloid *Psychic News* pressed him (unsuccessfully) to grant that consciousness after death is possible and opens the door for psychic communication ('Bernard Shaw: Exclusive Talk with *Psychic News*,' no. 773 [29 March 1947]; Cornell, box 35, folder 58).

83 / To Gilbert Murray

10 Adelphi Terrace WC
30th October 1915

[ALS: Bod, SPA]

On 26 October Shaw had supplemented his inflammatory analysis in Common Sense about the War *with a public lecture widely quoted in the press, 'The Illusions of War.' Drawing upon Shaw's notes as well as the press reports, Gordon Bergquist in* The Pen and the Sword *notes the most scathing assertions in the speech about specific illusions: 'the destruction of Germany is an illusion; the notion that we can never again be friends with the Germans is an illusion; the conclusive peace is an illusion; the inviolability of neutralized buffer states is an illusion; the sacredness of treaties is an illusion; the war to end war is an illusion.' The lecture concludes with a moral: 'Let your romanticists and rhetoricians make your speeches; but let your realists, however unpopular and disagreeable, conduct your wars' (136).*

Shaw had received the following letter, dated 27 October, from the officers of the Dramatists' Club, President R.C. Carton and Honorary Secretary H.M. Paull: 'My dear Shaw: I regret to say that at today's meeting of the Club I was instructed (as the secretary) to write to you to inform you that several members of the Club have intimated that they refrain from attending the meetings as they do not wish to meet you, owing to your attitude in regard to the war. In these circumstances the members present presumed that you will prefer that the usual notice of the meetings shall not be sent to you for the present' (Col, SPA).

Two of Shaw's intimate friends, Henry Arthur Jones and William Archer, registered their objections to Common Sense *in contrasting ways. Jones topped the attackers, calling Shaw in 'A Manual for the Haters of England' a 'freakish homunculus, germinated outside of lawful procreation,' and ending their friendship forever. Archer, whose patriotic son had been sent to Flanders and was missing in action, decried Shaw's capacity for 'seeing, and believing, the opposite of what other people saw and believed,' but did not break with Shaw (Holroyd 2, 355). For a publisher of war propaganda Archer wrote a pamphlet called* Fighting a Philosophy, *which does not mention Shaw, but the philosophy he singled out was the same he believed underlay many of Shaw's writings: 'It is the philosophy of Nietzsche that we are fighting' (Whitebrook, 310). He had told Murray in 1905 that* Man and Superman, *in Whitebrook's paraphrase, was 'neither comedy nor philosophy but an exasperating exhibition of the old Shawpenhauerism mixed up with a dose of Nietzsche' (250). Robert Blatchford (1851–1943), one of the most notable advocates of socialism and enemies of capitalism in that era, but a 'patriot' highly critical of Germany, published a long, sensationalist diatribe against* Common Sense about the War *in the* Weekly Dispatch *of 22 November 1914. It was entitled (by the editors, one assumes) 'The New Enemy in Our Midst: Bernard Shaw's "Insensate Malice and Dirty Innuendo": Anti-British Case Exposed.' An array of similar subtitles were sprayed throughout (Cornell, box 40, folder 19).*

Members of the Society of Authors signalled that they did not want Shaw to attend their meetings (one of his few supporters was the Irish playwright James Bernard Fagan, 1873–1933), and The New Statesman *rejected his 'More Common Sense about the War' and a few other submissions. Shaw resigned from all three of these organizations, to which he had dedicated so much valuable time and support (Holroyd 2, 354–9). In a letter of 7 December 1916 to Wells, he explained why he resigned from* The New Statesman: *'Nobody trusts me. [It] took my money greedily* *enough, and then turned into a suburban Tory-Democratic rag and forced me to kick myself out ... The paper has its uses, but not for me' (*Bernard Shaw and H.G. Wells, *88). However, he made significant use of it during the Second World War, after the editorship had changed.*

Shaw wrote a retrospective sum-up of his inflammatory missive's reception in 1919 (which did not appear in print until 1995, when it was printed in CPr 2, 367–72): 'I could and did distinguish between war on the cinema film and war in the trenches. I knew the diplomatic history of the war ..., and knew it, as it proved, accurately and essentially. All this, added to my Irish detachment from the sentimentalities of British patriotism, was so revolting to Englishmen in the delirium of the war fever, and so contradictory to the current legends of melodramatic patriotism, that my Common Sense About the War, launched in November 1914, when the war fever was at its height, produced furious demands for my immediate execution as a pro-German, a Pacifist, a traitor, ... and what not.'

Shaw sent the following note to Murray below the secretary's letter, which he enclosed.

My dear Murray

This latest development of patriotism may interest you as a refraining member. I received no notice of the move, and presume you didnt either.

ever
G.B.S.

It is curious that a twenty-seven-month gap occurs here in the extant correspondence of Shaw and Murray. No evidence appears in their biographies that they were estranged during this period or that they destroyed the letters they wrote. By 4 June 1917 the two were at least communicating indirectly and risking contact: Murray had told Charlotte that he would like to attend a scheduled reading of Heartbreak House, *and she replied by inviting him – certainly after obtaining her husband's agreement (unpublished letter quoted by permission of the Sidney P. Albert estate). Also, Murray's note that follows clearly indicates that Shaw had written to him before 8 February 1918. The ensuing correspondence printed here reads as if nothing had happened that would create enough friction to alienate them from one another.*

The two were allied – though in different ways – in attacking Asquith's First Conscription Act of 3 January 1916, aimed at unmarried men from eighteen to forty-one. This had passed the Cabinet despite the proud fact that Britain had been 'the only nation in Europe to depend upon voluntary enlistment for its armed forces' (Shaw: Interviews, *237, headnote). As one would expect, Shaw took a unique and startling slant on the issue. In a* New York American *interview of 28 November 1915 he contended that 'an unlimited supply of soldiers to either side might quite conceivably lead to its defeat' since 'military general staffs will not invent or think as long as they can snow enemies under with piles of corpses' (ibid., 238). Even more singular were his comments in a 14 July 1916 interview on 'what we think of the foreigner': asked if the English public adopted a sensible attitude what effect would it have, he replied: 'It would drop down dead, slain by the novelty of the sensation'; to the question if he could predict what the public would especially crave after the war is over, he quipped: 'Yes, beer' (243). One cannot imagine Murray hailing these realistic impertinences as effective ammunition for the cause.*

In March and April of 1917, two events that affected the war decisively occurred: Russia's revolution unseated the tsar, and America declared war on Germany. These were turnabouts in Shaw's eyes, Weintraub states, since 'he had, almost alone, rejected Imperial Russia as an ally to nations claiming democratic ideals, and he looked on America's neutrality as a good thing, enabling her to be the eventual mediator in a hopeless stalemate' (Journey to Heartbreak, *238–9).*

Murray visited the United States in 1916, partly at the behest of Grey (now Viscount Grey) to test America's feelings about a League of Nations. He described his impressions in a pamphlet, The United States and the War, *recording enthusiasm for a 'League of Powers' which must be 'bound to settle their differences by Conference or arbitration, and equally bound to make joint war' on any power that refuses arbitration (Wilson, 247). Another pamphlet,* The Way Forward *(1917), recommended policies for Britain to follow after the war, including 'much less government interference in private affairs' and 'much more industrial democracy' (248).*

Murray became deeply involved in the controversy over the treatment of conscientious objectors, finally managing to improve the harsh type of imprisonment inflicted upon the crusty pacifist Bertrand Russell. When the son of an old Oxford friend, L.T. Hobhouse (1864–1929), joined the Society of Quakers and received a series of penalties because he refused to go to war, the young man's mother published a pamphlet, I Appeal unto Caesar. *Murray supplied an angry preface, which concluded: 'However wrong-headed, conceited, self-centred and self-righteous ... the objectors may originally have been, the long and pointless persecution of those few hundred men leaves on the coldest observer the impression of sheer moral heroism on the part of the culprits and sheer moral and intellectual vileness on the side of the Government' (Wilson, 241–3). 'On the first day of 1919,' Whitebrook reports, Archer 'joined Murray, Wells and the novelist John Buchan in signing a letter to Lloyd George asking for the immediate release of the remaining 1500 conscientious objectors still held in British prisons' (333).*

During this two-year hiatus Shaw continued to unleash a battery of highly critical analyses of various facets of the European situation, all involving British foreign policy to one degree or another. The most relevant pieces are reprinted in What I Really Wrote about the War. *In March 1917 Shaw 'finished the draft of a manifesto declaring for a republican solution of the territorial problems raised by the war, and calling for the establishment of a republican party'* (Diaries 2*: 'The 1917 Diary Fragments,' 1174); Weintraub's editorial note adds that the manifesto 'called for republics to replace the discredited European monarchies.' It was presented at a Fabian Society meeting (see* Fabian News*, 28 [March 1917], 13). In* Journey to Heartbreak*, Weintraub revealed the little-known fact that in 1920 Shaw had written a playlet entitled* The War Indemnities *'to underline the economic and political stupidity of the Allied insistence upon German reparations' (328). It was subsequently published in* Pearson's Magazine *in June 1921.*

On 1 October 1916 Shaw also had the memorable experience of seeing a German Zeppelin pass over his house. Four days later he wrote Beatrice Webb that the pilot's audacity, the spectacle, and the sound were so enchanting that he 'caught himself hoping next night that there would be another raid' (Shaw and the Webbs*, 161). The germ of the finale of* Heartbreak House *was born. But a later experience, recalled in a* New York Evening Post *interview on 13 March 1920, occurred when a Zeppelin dropped three bombs too close for comfort: 'I was reading one night when I heard the warning signals. First the maroons – "Boom! Boom! Boom!" Twenty minutes later came heavier reports – the anti-aircraft guns. I was horribly frightened.' Then three more bombs fell in succession about a hundred yards away, completing 'the triangle with me in the centre' (Rattray, 214).*

84 / To G. Bernard Shaw Board of Education, South Kensington
8th February 1918

[TLT: BL, SPA]

The new prime minister, Lloyd George, had persuaded Murray's fellow editor for the Home University Library, H.A.L. Fisher, to become minister of education, and Fisher convinced a reluctant Murray to work for him part-time. He thus became assistant secretary to the University Branch of Education and dealt with a variety of proposals, including several from the Workers' Educational Association and the Anglo-Russian Commission (Wilson, 321).

Most of the following two notes defy explanation.

My dear Shaw

Your letter and autograph for the Glasgow bazaar are splendid. We are gumming it into a copy of the Christian Year and pricing it at 20 guineas. You misread and undervalued the sensitiveness of my nature. I was already laughing when I got to the passage about your accident and your battered head, when I became grave and full of tender concern.

Yours ever,
Gilbert Murray

85 / To Gilbert Murray Ayot St Lawrence, Welwyn, Herts.
13th February 1918

[ALS: Bod, SPA]

Good Gracious! the man can have intimate personal letters addressed to himself for £1000 a dozen – or say postcards. And I'll give you 10% commission.

G.B.S.

86 / To Gilbert Murray 10 Adelphi Terrace WC
9th October 1918

[ALS: Bod, SPA]

Potentially worse than bomb threats for anyone but Shaw was a double assault on his health, as he reported to Lady Mary Murray on 6 February 1918: 'Last week a woman poisoned me with a war substitute for cocoa, as a result of which I not only suffered internal convulsions … but pitched head foremost down a flight of

17 stairs and landed on my valuable head, which now looks like a composite of Michael Angelo's Moses and Shakspear' (Bod).

Did I mention any names in the letter? I accused Mrs Patrick Campbell of having given me the dope in a cup of some stuff called Ovaltine, into which she put about half a canister. If I mentioned this in my letter, Ovaltine would get £20,000 damages out of us; and Mrs Campbell would be held up as Mrs Lucretia Borgia. Just look through it and censor it if necessary. I can copy it out again if it comes to that.

But I shall be surprised if it fetches twenty pence.

Until Thursday I shall be at Ayot St Lawrence, Welwyn, Herts.

G.B.S.

87 / To Gilbert Murray Ayot St Lawrence, Welwyn, Herts.
24th October 1919

[APCS: CL 3]

Shaw had begun writing Heartbreak House *on 3 April 1916; he finished it on 12 May 1917. The first reading took place on 8 June 1917, an occasion that Murray attended. According to Weintraub, the play shows the direct influence of Murray's translation of Euripides'* Trojan Women*; see his 'Shaw's Troy:* Heartbreak House *and Euripides'* Trojan Women.*'*

Meanwhile, Shaw had published Peace Conference Hints *on 12 March 1919. In Holroyd's words, it is partly 'an admonition to Britain against exploiting her self-righteousness at the Versailles Peace Conference,' and partly an exhortation to make the treaty 'a nucleus for the League of Nations' (3, 5). He asserts that 'the moral cleaning-up after the war is far more important than the material restoration'; those moral flaws are 'the poisoning of the human soul by hatred, the darkening of the human mind by lies, and the hardening of the human heart by slaughter and destruction and starvation' (*What I Really Wrote about the War, *347–8).*

In May 1919 the terms of the Treaty, composed over six months, were made public: it required Germany to accept sole responsibility for causing the war and – under what came to be called 'the War-Guilt clauses' – to disarm, make substantial territorial concessions, and pay reparations of what today would be $400 billion. Murray became one of forty scholars and men of letters who signed a letter of protest, which appeared in the Daily News *on 24 May.*

An attempt has been made to locate Heartbreak House. My neighbor here, Cherry Garrard (naturalist with Scott's last Antarctic expedition) said 'It's what Shaw's house would be like if his wife would let it.'

I was relieved by your approval of the preface which Mrs Buxton extorted from me; for I knocked it off in such a hurry, being cornered at a frantically busy moment, that I concluded it must be rather a scamped job.

G.B.S.

Apsley George Benet **Cherry-Garrard** (1886–1959) accompanied Robert Falcon Scott (1868–1912) on the ill-fated Terra Nova Expedition (1910–13), which he described in *The Worst Journey in the World* (1922). The founder of the Save-the-Children Fund, **Mrs** Charles **Buxton**, had written a book, *Family Life in Germany under the Blockade*, published the previous July.

88 / To Gilbert Murray Parknasilla Hotel. Kenmare. Co. Kerry
22nd July 1920

[APCS: Bod, SPA]

The Shaws stayed in Parknasilla from 19 July to 23 September (Gibbs, Chronology, *238).*

I have just had a letter from Vienna asking for money for the actor Moissi, who played Dubedat in The Doctor's Dilemma so realistically that he has now got tuberculosis in earnest. I have sent some; but the letter, which is perfectly legible at all its inessential points, is perfectly illegible at the crucial ones. The writer's Christian names are Agnes Elizabeth: the surname might be anything. Her street is unmistakeably Singerstrasse; the number may be 11, 16, or 66. I have chanced Murray and 16, because her style is a reaction against yours. Have you by any chance a daughter in Vienna?

G.B.S.

The actor Moissi was one of the best-known Austrian / German actors, Alexander Moissi (1880–1935), who played Dubedat in the 21 November 1908 production at the Kammerspiele des Deutschen Theaters in Berlin. He survived tuberculosis, only to die of pneumonia at age 55. Shaw has fun pretending he is not sure that **Agnes Elizabeth** is Murray's daughter, who had accompanied Lady Mary to Vienna and who wrote Shaw requesting money for Moissi. In his letter sent on the day of the above he replied that the actor's 'most direct claim' on him was 'his playing of Dubedat in The Doctor's Dilemma and the resultant success of that play in Germany' (Bod, SPA).

89 / To Gilbert Murray Ayot St Lawrence, Welwyn, Herts.
7th November 1920

[ALS: Bod, SPA]

Shaw began writing Back to Methuselah: A Metabiological Pentateuch *on 19 March 1918, finished the first draft on 27 May 1920, and sent the revised version, complete with the huge preface, to the printer on 15 September 1920 (Gibbs,* Chronology, *238).*

Murray had been invited by the Liberals of Glasgow University to compete for the rectorship in 1919 but lost in a fairly close contest (West, 176).

My dear Murray

I have been waiting for the enclosed proof to write to you. If you have time, will you look through it and expose to me any howlers that may betray the enormity of my ignorance.

Parts of the five plays will amuse you. I will send you the book when it is ready; so do not buy a copy.

I knew your chances at Edinburgh would vanish at a touch from me, but could not resist meddling. At the last general election I made 13 star speeches lasting 90 minutes each. The platform success was immense; but not one of the 13 candidates got in.

The young Countess in Vienna sent me back the money she had demanded for the starving and moribund Moissi (the actor), having ascertained that he was acting vigorously every night and in opulent circumstances. Can you explain how it is that you, being the sanest man I know, married to Lady Mary, the sanest woman I know, have produced a large batch of children who are all as mad as hatters?

ever
G. Bernard Shaw

90 / To G. Bernard Shaw Yatscombe, Boar's Hill, Oxford
13th November 1920

[TLT: BL, SPA]

Compare Shaw's views on Darwin, materialism, vivisection, etc., as he expressed them to Archibald Henderson in 1905: 'I am not a materialist ... I am in the line of descent from the German philosophers & composers (Schopenhauer & Wagner, for instance) rather than from the materialist-natural selectionists ... My part in *the humanitarian campaign against vivisection, "education," flogging &c &c are all part of my attitude as a "mystic"' (letter of 11 September 1905, CL 2, 556). He argued his views on vivisection to a highly unreceptive Wells in a letter of 7 July 1921 (*Bernard Shaw and H.G. Wells*, 104–7), and, as a counter to Wells's article 'For Vivisection' in the* Sunday Express, *24 July 1927, in 'Against Vivisection' on 7 August in that newspaper (Laurence,* Bibliography, *1, 168). His most sweeping statement in the latter was: 'We cling to it dishonorably because we are repeatedly assured that it has led to the discovery of cures for our diseases and we are prepared to snatch at any dirty receipt for immortality rather than face death like ladies and gentlemen ... They must not seek knowledge by criminal methods, just as they must not make money by criminal methods' (quoted in Rattray, 231).*

Discussing what he calls 'official liberality,' Richard A. Chapman begins his study of this concept by focusing on Murray's apolitical humanism: 'Gilbert Murray preferred the word Liberality, rather than Liberalism, as a term connected with Liberals. He used it instead of Liberalism partly because he wished to keep clear of mere party politics ... "Liberality," he said on one occasion, "is not a doctrine; it is a spirit or attitude of mind, constantly changing in its outer manifestation according to the circumstances it has to meet, but always essentially the same in itself, an effort to get rid of prejudice so as to see the truth, to get rid of selfish passions so as to do the right"' ('Official Liberality,' 123; quoting from Murray's Liberality and Civilization *[1938], 37).*

My dear Shaw

Many thanks for the Preface. I think I have never agreed so warmly with any of your prefaces. Of course I love old Darwin himself, with his gentleness and modesty and his charming style, and I like his descendants, all I know of them. But you safeguard yourself sufficiently, in distinguishing the Neo-Darwinians from the old man himself. And I am inclined to think that it is true, what we thought was parsonic rubbish when people said to us twenty years ago, that this age has gone to the Devil, or rather near him, by laying all the emphasis of its beliefs and emotions on material and mechanical things, circumstantial selection, and the economic interpretation of history &c &c. We really have gone near to forgetting the importance of will and spiritual effort and duty. And the men of science have been, and are, simply awful leaders for a nation. (They are boasting loudly here that no man of science signed Bridges' love-letter to the German professors!) I am not at all sure that vivisection is not a touchstone. Whether a man, or a group, will or will not torture perfectly innocent sentient beings for his own convenience, is a jolly good way of deciding whether he is a good or a bad man.

I dare say some philosophers get on perfectly well without any religious belief (subject to definition, that statement). But if you take phenomena like Lloyd George, or the average daily paper in England or America, one thing that is clearly wrong with them is their godlessness. They have no sense of true or false, and no sense of high or low, but welcome indiscriminately eveything that suits their convenience at the moment and reject indiscriminately what doesn't. I sometimes suspect that in most previous ages it was only wicked men who did that, but now it is average men and popular and influential men. Of course one may be wrong.

I am glad you appreciate the astonishing nature of my children. A certain New Guinea chief, who was brought down to the coast by my brother and saw a horse for the first time, stared at it for a moment and then laughed till he fell on the ground. The parallel is obvious.

I am told that my votes in Edinburgh would have been more had not the enemy taken possession of the voting booths and kept my admirers out. But only a pretty large majority can do that. I did not have to go there or make an address or anything.

Yours ever,
G.M.

I am eager to see the whole play.

Robert [Seymour] **Bridges** (1844–1930), literary scholar and poet laureate 1913–30, was trying to induce literary and educational luminaries to sign a letter addressed to German professors 'which should bring together the generous minded on both sides' (letter of 20 December 1920, *Selected Letters*, 2, 766). Three days later he records that Austrian universities have been 'enthusiastic' (773). Murray's **brother**, John Hubert Plunkett Murray (1861–1940, known as Hubert), was governor of Papua from 1908 until his death and author of *Papua or British New Guinea* (1912).

91 / To Gilbert Murray

10 Adelphi Terrace WC
3rd December 1920

[ALS: Bod, SPA]

Shaw had become closely involved with the Royal Academy of Dramatic Art (RADA) after being chosen for its managing council on the death of W.S. Gilbert in 1911. RADA was founded in 1904 by Herbert Beerbohm Tree to promote theatre as a fine art; in 1920 it was granted a royal charter. Its director from 1909 to 1955, Kenneth [Ralph] Barnes (1878–1957; knighted in 1938), is credited with making it one of the leading schools for theatrical achievement in the world. Shaw was more generous than he could have known when he donated the royalties from Pygmalion *in 1912 to the school, which carried over into the bountiful royalties for* My Fair Lady *starting in 1956. In 1927 he donated £5000 for reconstruction costs. In 1941 he contributed a long unsigned preface to* The R.A.D.A. Graduates' Keepsake & Counsellor *('printed by R. & R. Clark at Shaw's expense' [headnote in CL 4, 594]; preface reprinted in Shaw, CPr 3, 396–407). See Barnes, 'GBS and the RADA' in Winsten, 177–9.*

My dear Murray

On Monday at 4:30 Sir John Simon will try to persuade the London County Council that acting is a fine art, and that therefore the Royal Academy of Dramatic Art (founded by Tree: I am on the Council) should be exempted from rates under the Prince Consort's Act. The Registrar refused the application on the ground that it means pictures and nothing else; and the appeal lies to the Council. Simon would like to call witnesses – not too obviously interested in the theatre.

Could you come, or send somebody, or bring Bridges, or suggest any classical passages recognizing acting as a fine art, or give us a lift in any direction. The notice is absurdly short: Simon apparently thought of calling witnesses at the last moment. Do you know Raleigh?

The man to communicate with is Kenneth Barnes, the director of the R.A.D.A. 62 Gower St W.C. 1.

As a member of the Council I had to promise to do something; and as they mentioned you with awe (very properly) I seize on you as the nearest victim.

I shall try Q. at Cambridge too.

When I report those operations I shall acquire merit as a person of influence at the Universities. Dont bother to acknowledge.

ever

G. Bernard Shaw

PS The sum at stake is £500 a year; and our people are underpaid: hence our anxiety to dodge our municipal burden.

Sir John Allsebrook **Simon** (1873–1954) held prominent legal positions in the government, ultimately becoming Lord Chancellor of Great Britain in 1940. Whatever Shaw means by the **Prince Consort's Act**, the term probably derives from the fact that Queen Victoria's consort, Prince Albert (1819–1861), was chosen in 1841 to chair the Royal Commission on the Promotion of Fine Arts in Britain. In any event, Sir John Simon's appeal to the London County Council was denied, probably because in 1903 the distribution of funds to art schools had been taken over by its Technical Education Board in order to bring them into 'close relation with industrial needs' (Saint, 80). The question of what constituted 'fine art' had become irrelevant. It was not until February 1924 that a grant of **£500** from the government was finally recommended by the Financial Secretary to the Treasury, partly because of Shaw's urging. See his letter in CL 3, 864–5. **Bridges**: see Letter 90. **Raleigh**: possibly Cecil Raleigh (see Letter 41), but more probably Sir Walter Raleigh (see Letter 44), Murray's Oxford colleague. **Q** was the pen name of Sir Arthur [Thomas] Quiller-Couch (1863–1944), literary critic and Cambridge professor, best known for the *Oxford Book of English Verse 1250–1900,* later extended to 1918.

92 / To G. Bernard Shaw

Yatscombe, Boar's Hill, Oxford
25th July 1921

[TLT: BL, SPA]

Shaw had completed Back to Methuselah *in September 1920; it was published on 1 June 1921. Murray had read and commented on the preface (see Letter 89). The following letter reflects his first look at the five parts of the play. In part 2, two caricatured politicians visit the brothers Barnabas: Joyce Burge, modelled on Lloyd George, and Henry Hopkins Lubin, modelled on Asquith. It would not have surprised Shaw that Murray would have voted for Lubin, since Lloyd George was anathema to him (if anyone was).*

My dear Shaw

I read Methuselah with eagerness as soon as I returned home. (I had a motor-cycle accident, and went to the Norway Fjords to recover in the company of W.A.) and I find I have never written to you.

Of course I enjoyed it enormously. I do not know whether you will take it as a compliment, but you carry me back to the bad old world which I enjoyed so much more than this one, when we were not all on the point of starving and fighting, and still took an interest in ideas. I loved the first part, especially Eve's speeches. And the Brothers Barnabas did not make me as indignant as it might, because I thought that even on your showing I would have voted for Lubin rather than for anyone else.

The Newly Born at the end delighted me. She takes one out of the circle of ideas on which the Play depends, like a suddenly opened window or a hole in the roof. But it is all great fun, and I shall get refreshment from re-reading it.

By the way, are you apt to be in London on Thursdays? I am generally there on Thursday and often hungry about lunch time.

Yours ever,
Gilbert Murray

Murray began what Wilson calls 'his long and quite dangerous career' on a **motor-cycle** in the pre-war years. He often visited friends on it – 'not without occasional spills' (Wilson, 214–15). **W.A.** is William Archer. **The Newly Born**, in part 5, emerges as an articulate seventeen-year-old; her two-year incubation has passed her through the earlier stages of development.

93 / To Gilbert Murray

Atholl Palace, Pitlochry
16th July 1924

[TLS: CL 3]

Shaw had begun writing Saint Joan: A Chronicle Play in Six Scenes and an Epilogue *on 29 April 1923, and finished it on 24 August. The Theatre Guild gave it its first performance at the Garrick Theatre in New York on 28 December 1923; the British premiere took place at the New Theatre in London on 26 March 1924. In spite of critics complaining about Shaw taking liberties with historical facts and leaving realism far behind in the Epilogue, the play's reception was in general favourable to an extreme, with reactionary critics praising Shaw for writing a real play at last, and religiously inclined spectators stunned into approval despite the subtle undercutting of Joan's 'voices' and 'miracles.' As Shaw puts it, 'I am being sainted for Joan's sake.' The play was almost surely the principal reason why he was awarded the Nobel Prize in literature for 1925.*

The Holy Mother is so pleased at getting any sort of fair play that she feels like the American Vigilance Committee that hanged the wrong man, and owned up to his widow that the laugh was on her side. The Vatican does not think that the book need go on the Index for English Catholics. But there is nothing so damning to a guilty party as fair play. The persecuted, however in the wrong, can always play for sympathy; but when not only justice, but even gross flattery is conceded, the demerits of the case are left staring.

My Irish Protestant nose does not forget the dead men's bones; but the Protestant cellar smells just as vilely. I am being sainted for Joan's sake, and am contemplating some feat that will force all the Churches to excommunicate me. – We are touring, and will take steps to see you when we return in Sept. or thereabouts.

G.B.S.

The incident that Shaw recalls in the first sentence eludes verification. But on 10 May 1905 the *Times of India* received a statement from Shaw which uses the same fiercely ironic thought: 'As the **American Vigilance Committee** said to the widow, when they had lynched her husband for a horse stolen by somebody else, the laugh is with you.' What Shaw calls the **Index for English Catholics** is the *Index Librorum Prohibitorum*, a list of publications prohibited by the Catholic Church. Shaw subtly implies that if their judges had fully understood the play, they would surely have prohibited it. He is thus being **sainted for Joan's sake**, not really for his own. The Shaws had started **touring** Scotland on 13 July.

The preceding letter is dated three years after the previous one, and nearly four years before the one that follows. In this seven-year period, Murray was actively involved in politics, especially the League of Nations and similar organizations provoked by the terrible events of the world war. Shaw was largely preoccupied with writing and rehearsing Heartbreak House, Back to Methuselah, *and* Saint Joan, *but still managed to follow what Holroyd calls 'a dashing public life, giving some thirty lectures a year to local Labour parties, groups of feminists, gatherings of chief constables. He pitched into debates at the Smoke Abatement Society, the Art Workers' Guild, the British Drama Guild, and the London School of Economics; and he would turn up for meetings at the Royal Academy of Dramatic Art, Stage Society Council, British Music Society, and latterly the British Broadcasting Corporation's Spoken English Committee' (3, 97–8).*

Shaw also worked on The Intelligent Woman's Guide to Socialism and Capitalism *from late 1925 to late March 1927. Prompted by a request from Charlotte's younger sister, Mary Stewart Cholmondeley (1858–1929), for a 'leaflet' on socialism, it was published on 1 June 1928 (Gibbs,* Chronology, *269). Nearly a quarter of a million words and 470 pages long, its thesis, as Shaw told Wells, 'is that a really fundamental consideration of the problem of Distribution will entirely dissociate it from payments for work or rewards of virtue, and will lead to equality of distribution by the reduction to absurdity or impossibility of every alternative' (letter of 19 March 1932,* Shaw and Wells, *170). The foreword states the negative side of this thesis as 'the hopelessness of our attempts to build up a stable civilization with units of unequal income' (ix). Earlier he had proudly told Beatrice Webb, 'I firmly believe that our literature is the really revolutionary literature ... Our motto is, Be as clever as you like, but keep on the ground. In the I.W.G. I have kept hard on the ground all through: that is the real virtue of the Webbshaw school' (letter of 5 July 1928,* Shaw and the Webbs, *216–17). It is interesting to note that the editor of the most recent edition (expanded by Shaw as* The Intelligent Woman's Guide to Socialism, Capitalism, Sovietism and Fascism*), Susan Moller Okin, heralds it as 'an important piece of feminist political theory, in both form and content ... His refusal to use he as a generic pronoun, his constant use of women as examples in his argument, his particular attention to the ways in which capitalism exploits women, his reference to at least as many issues of concern to a woman reader of his time as to those generally regarded as "male concerns" – all these make his arguments for socialism refreshing to the female reader' (xix–xx). Ramsay MacDonald went as far as to proclaim that 'after the Bible, this, in my estimation, is humanity's most important book' (Ervine, 506).*

*During the war two similar organizations, the League of Nations Society and the League of Free Nations Association, emerged with somewhat conflicting agendas. They were united as the League of Nations Union on 9 November 1918. Murray had chaired the second of these, and became a prominent figure in the LNU. In alliance with Lord Robert Cecil (1864–1958) and Sir Edward Grey, the group not only helped spawn the League of Nations but endured as an independent entity until 1945, when it was succeeded by the United Nations Association of Great Britain and Northern Ireland. According to Donald S. Birn, the LNU 'became the largest and most influential society in the British peace movement' and 'played an important role in inter-war politics' (*The League of Nations Union, *1–11). In 1921 Murray published* Problems of Foreign Policy, *a general statement of the LNU's positions in favour of arbitration, conciliation, and disarmament (Wilson, 299). When in January 1924 Ramsay MacDonald became the leader of the first Labour government in England, Murray experienced one of his few setbacks when the new PM refused his invitation to be one of the LNU's Honorary Presidents.*

Birn sums up Murray's contributions during this period succinctly: 'After the war, Murray plunged into work in support of the League. He followed in Cecil's footsteps by accepting an appointment to represent South Africa as a delegate to Geneva from 1921 to 1923. He also became active in the League-sponsored Committee on Intellectual Co-operation in 1922 and followed Henri Bergson as President of that body for eight years. And he took on the demanding post of LNU Chairman, coming down twice weekly from Oxford to London to attend meetings and supervise the work at headquarters ... He skillfully played the role of moderator and arbiter, ... answering countless letters and resolving staffing and financial problems' (21–2).

*A later League of Nations event in which Murray became deeply involved was the proposal in the spring of 1928 referred to as the Kellogg-Briand Pact, or 'General Treaty for the Renunciation of War.' Named after United States secretary of state Frank B[illings] Kellogg (1856–1937) and French minister of foreign affairs Aristide Briand (1862–1932), the pact renounced war, prohibiting it as 'an instrument of national policy' except in matters of self-defence, but making no provisions for sanctions. The attempts of the British and French governments to attach conditions pertaining to security delayed the signing, but efforts to counteract this objection by Murray and other LNU members resulted in the pact being signed by all countries on 27 August (*Wikipedia *and Wilson, 308). Kellogg was awarded the Nobel Peace Prize for the treaty in 1929.*

94 / To Gilbert Murray

4 Whitehall Court, London SW1
23rd May 1928

[ALS: Bod, SPA]

My dear Murray

It's an extraordinarily good article. I should call it Atheism Without Tears. I made Charlotte read it; and she is delighted with it beyond measure, and thinks it ought to be available 'as a book.'

If Nietzsche had known anything (and in spite of – or perhaps because of – his university training I have never been able to believe that he ever in his life consulted a real document) he might have anticipated your masterly handling of his Slave Morality stunt. You have straightened out his job magnificently.

I have made a correction on 33, to make it clear that the adventures narrated were those of old EP., and not of his innocent father.

On page 60 your humane impulse to offer a glass of water to the creed which is dying of your exemplary kicking leads you to use the word 'unique.' Is that defensible? Islam did the same thing more thoroughly. Of course it was not really done at all by Church teaching; but if you have visited the church of St Anthony of Padua, with its wealth of worshipped relics and its chapel to the minor deities (the saints), and afterwards inspected St Sophia's in Stamboul, it must have struck you that the mosque was far clearer from polytheism and 'objects of superstitious worship' than the church.

As my reputation as an expert in early Christianity (founded on Androcles) is entirely due to your secret instructions, we are naturally at one as to the questions of learning involved.

ever
G.B.S.

Repeated efforts at uncovering the article that Shaw would rename '**Atheism Without Tears**' unfortunately proved futile. A section in Nietzsche's *On the Genealogy of Morals* treats 'Master-**Slave Morality**.' The initials **EP** fit too many 'old' individuals that Shaw and Murray surely knew (Edward Pease and Esmé Percy come to mind), but the inference in 'innocent father' suggests 'guilty son,' and, combined with the term 'adventures,' points to a daring man whom Shaw championed in 1889, Ernest Parke. Murray might have used him as an example in his article. As proprietor of the *North London Press* when a scandal exploded about a minister involved in a high-class house of male prostitution, many of whose clients were aristocrats, newspapers refrained from reporting the incident until the editor of *Truth*, followed by Parke, broke the story. Parke was prosecuted by one of the named aristocrats and given a one-year sentence. Shaw not only wrote a letter to *Truth* (which was rejected) exposing the irony and attacking the violation of human rights in the case, but wrote the leading articles of Parke's newspaper while he was imprisoned. (Expanded from the headnote to the letter, CL 1, 230. Laurence cites one of these articles in his bibliography [2, 565, item 682], where he misspells the name Parkes.) **The church of St Anthony of Padua** is the most famous church in Padua, Italy; **St Sophia's in Stamboul** was the largest church in Istanbul (called 'the Hagia Sophia') until it was converted into a **mosque** in 1453 and later into a museum.

95 / To Gilbert Murray

Grand Hotel Bellerue, Geneva
13th September 1928

[ALS: Bod, SPA]

The Shaws had completed a seven-week visit to the French Riviera that had begun on 20 July, and moved to Geneva on 2 September for two weeks. On 5 September Shaw attended a League of Nations meeting, which Murray surely had to attend, and the headquarters of the International Labour Organisation.

My dear Murray

Nanson, Zilliacos, & Mrs Z. are dining with us at 7·45 this evening at the Hotel la Residence, a shebeen on the other side of the lake.

If by happy chance you have no other engagement, will you join us?

I don't know whether Lady Mary is with you; but of course the invitation includes your party.

It will be pot luck at the hotel; so do not bother about us if you cannot come; and come if you can.

ever
G. Bernard Shaw

Shaw's distinguished visitors at the Hotel de la Residence were: **'Nanson'**: Fridtjof [Wedel-Jarlsberg] Nansen (1861–1930), a Norwegian scientist / explorer and diplomat. After moving to London in 1906, he was appointed the League of Nations' High Commissioner for Refugees in 1921, which led to winning the Nobel Peace Prize in 1922. (Murray mentions him in Letter114.) **'Zilliacos'**: Konni Zilliacus (1894–1967), Finnish citizen who settled in England in 1909. He became a highly prominent leftist politician, joining the Labour Party in 1918 and advocating its foreign policy while working for the League of Nations. He served as private secretary to Norman Angell and, like H.N. Brailsford, attempted to undermine Britain's counter-revolutionary activities aimed at Russia.

96 / To Gilbert Murray

4 Whitehall Court, London SW1
28th October 1928

[ALS: Bod, SPA]

The article that Shaw mentions, first excerpted in several newspapers under various titles from 18 to 21 October, was published in full in November 1928 as 'The League of Nations: A First Visit Impression' (Laurence, Bibliography, *2, 721). M. Albert Thomas (1878–1932) was a dynamic Frenchman appointed as the first director-general of the International Labour Organisation, founded in 1919. The agency became an autonomous part of the league dedicated to establishing standards in the fields of labour law, social welfare, and human rights. In the article Shaw singles out Thomas as 'a first-rate administrator and a devastating debater' who 'wiped the floor' with those French militarists who tried to cripple the Labour Office by following their sentiment, 'How could a gentleman and a Conservative tolerate a Labour Office?'*

Shaw perceives a dramatic opposition in the league's procedural structure between assembly meetings at the Victoria Hotel, 'daily foisted on the public as the real thing,' and the committee debates at the National Hotel 'on the upshot of which the very existence of the league as an effective international organ depended.' At the assembly meetings, 'nothing happens but pious speeches which might have been delivered fifty years ago,' with 'occasional sensations' such as 'M. Briand intervening and shaking the League to its foundations by getting his feet on the ground with an allusion to real things as they really are.' Through the debates among the league's various governing bodies, 'the really great thing' happening is the 'growth of a genuinely international public service,' largely because of the efforts of the Secretary General, Sir [James] Eric Drummond (1876–1951), to build up 'his staff of Internationalists from the ground.' Shaw sums up: 'In short, the League is a school for the new international statesmanship as against the old Foreign Office diplomacy' – the 'Palace of the Nations' versus 'The Assembly or Hot Air Exchange.'

My dear Murray

Name not that importunate Union to me. The effect of my article has been to convince it that I intend to devote the rest of my life to lecturing to it. Whereas, in fact, I regard my debt to the League paid and my bolt shot, so that, thank Heaven, I need never mention it again.

As to lecturing in general I enclose a postcard which I recommend you to adopt for your own use, mutatis mutandis.

I have just had a very appreciative letter from Albert Thomas, who rather sees himself in the rôle of Pope.

We are in the country on Tuesdays; and our next two Thursdays are bespoke. What about the 15th? It and the later Thursdays are still free. Is there anyone you'd like to meet whom we know well enough to ask? Or anyone you'd like to fetch along? The young sometimes like to see this animal as well as the ones at the Zoo. We are assuming that you and Lady Mary take a holiday from one another when you come up to London; but we should be delighted to find ourselves mistaken.

I was sorely tempted to say that the Government's choice of Genevan delegates was making Intellectual Co-operation impossible through lack of the indispensable qualification, but forebore. There is something subtly funny about the title that makes me afraid to mention it or joke about it. Why not change it to Innovation Commission to deal with the Application of Brains and some Elementary Historical Knowledge to European Politics?

ever,
G.B.S.

Albert Thomas (1878–1932) was a French socialist.

One of Murray's most notable and least noted books was published in 1929 as The Ordeal of This Generation: The War, the League, and the Future. *These were his Halley Stewart lectures except for the last essay, a 1928 Basil Hicks lecture entitled 'The Special Problems of the British Empire in Relation to the League of Nations.' Essays three through five are critical discussions of the Covenant of the League, and the sixth deals with the need for intellectual cooperation. The first lecture in the book, 'Peace and Strife as Elements in Life: The Ideal of "Unhindered Activity,"' will serve as a sample of his thought: he accepts the inevitability of the law 'Kill-to-live' but not the necessity for war, and urges following the law 'Co-operate-to-live,' which necessarily involves strife: 'the moral equivalent of war in the formation and strengthening of character.' To prepare for his finale he paraphases Aristotle: 'Happiness in the highest sense, or the true end of human life, is first activity, next unimpeded activity, and lastly unimpeded activity "according to virtue"' (38, 40).*

Peter Wilson, in 'Retrieving Cosmos: Gilbert Murray's Thoughts on International Relations' (Stray, 239–60), seconding E.H. Carr's The Twenty Years' Crisis *(1939), makes ample use of Murray's declarations in this book to demonstrate exactly what he stood for in international relations: 'In broad terms he stood for honesty, sincerity, good faith, honourable dealings, openness, fairness, reason, the rule of law, mutual trust, discussion, moderation, cooperation, concern for the welfare of others, and commitment to the "high and remote" motive of the general good over the "low and immediate" … motive of national self-interest. It might be said that he wanted to inject into international affairs the values, manners, and code of conduct of the nineteenth-century English gentleman.' However, he continues, this aspiration was 'not a good strategy in the age of Lenin, Stalin, Mussolini, and Hitler … It was not that [his] ideas and values were wrong, but that they had become inappropriate, dangerously so, in a world that had moved on to new forms of economic, social, and political organization. The nineteenth-century order policed by Britain's benign hegemony was dead. Attempts to recreate it were doomed to failure' (241–2).*

One important constituent of the League of Nations was its Intellectual Cooperation Organisation, founded in 1922, part of which was the International Committee on Intellectual Cooperation. This group not only directed the organization's work, but promoted fruitful international relationships between scientists, researchers, teachers, artists, and members of intellectual professions, which even embraced improving the working conditions of these workers. The ICIC formed committees of experts in various fields as the needs arose; one was the Permanent Committee on Arts and Letters.

In response to the Five Power Conference in January 1930, held in London, disarmament was discussed with the United Kingdom, United States, France, Italy, and Japan participating. The world economic recession largely caused by the Depression would make it seem that zeal in pursuing disarmament would be read as an indication of Britain's increasing economic difficulties. Murray, speaking for the LNU in May, 'wanted to make international economic co-operation the main aim of the LNU, rather than launch another campaign for disarmament' (Wilson, 309). Shaw agreed with Murray's opinion. His strongest expression emerged in an interview of 19 March 1935, shortly after Prime Minister Ramsay MacDonald had stated that some British rearmament was needed in response to Germany's. He declared: 'The Prime Minister's position is perfectly correct. If we are to have armament at all ... it must be up to the very latest mark.' He even stated that he would not try to impede Germany's attempts to rearm. Asked 'when the Powers are all armed to the teeth, what then?' he replied, 'Then they will be strong enough to impose peace on the world' ('That Silly Game – Disarmament,' 358–9).

97 / To G. Bernard Shaw

Yatscombe, Boar's Hill, Oxford
17th November 1930

[TLT: BL]

My dear Shaw

There is an International Committee of Arts and Letters being founded on the invitation of the C.I.C. (Committee of Intellectual Co-operation). They are getting as far as possible the leading people in the different countries – Maeterlinck for Belgium, Paul Valery for France, Thomas Mann for Germany, etc. Would anything induce you to be the British representative? We want two – a senior and a junior. You would be far and above the best representative of English letters – both for obvious reasons and because of your familiarity with committee work – and it would give a great lift to the Committee if you would join.

The general idea of the Committee of Arts and Letters is to get some sort of bond of union between different countries through the contact of their leading writers or artists. Bergson says that this is what he always meant the C.I.C. to do, but the C.I.C. has devoted itself chiefly to scientific and educational work and this more general effort at linking up has so far come to nothing. There will probably be about two meetings a year – one at Geneva and one somewhere else.

I know it would be rather a bother, but you would find it interesting too and I need not say it would be a great pleasure to me. You might also suggest a suitable junior.

Yours ever,
[no signature on copy]

Maurice Maeterlinck (see Letter 46) was a playwright noted for 'the drama of stasis'; **Paul Valéry** (1871–1945) was a symbolist poet; **Thomas Mann** (1875–1955) was a prolific novelist. Henri-Louis **Bergson** (1859–1941) was a French philosopher whose *L'Évolution créatrice* (1907) partly parallels Shaw's theory of the Life Force.

98 / To Gilbert Murray

4 Whitehall Court (130), London SW1
20th November 1930

[TLS: Bod, SPA]

The Malvern Festival was founded in 1929 by Barry [Vincent] Jackson (1879–1961), who had founded and maintained the Birmingham Repertory Theatre, and Roy Limbert (1893–1954), lessee of the Malvern Theatre in Worcestershire. Jackson's long association with Shaw led him to devote the first year's program entirely to his plays: the first English production of The Apple Cart *(19 August 1929) and revivals of* Back to Methuselah, Cæsar and Cleopatra, *and* Heartbreak House. *At first the summer festival was held for two weeks, but it soon stretched to four, with twenty Shaw plays in all being presented. Shaw attended as patron-in-chief every year until Jackson's final season in 1937 (CL 4, 128, and Hartnoll,* Oxford Companion to the Theatre, *4th ed., 520).*

St John Ervine, who was to write a biography of Shaw, took the occasion of the first Malvern performance to rehash an old critical saw about his plays in terms that are almost self-parodic: The Apple Cart *'is not, of course, a play … Mr. Shaw has spent a long life in writing plays which are not plays, and has persuaded people all over the world to prefer them to plays which are plays' (*Observer *[25 August]: 11); C.B. Purdom tried to counter such criticisms by declaring the play 'a gem of dramatic writing, smooth, witty, and charming' (*Everyman, *2 [5 October]: 133; both reviews in Cornell, box 37, folder 5).*

My dear Murray

This invitation of yours troubles my conscience a little; but I think I must refuse. I am much too old (75); and the obligation to make two journeys a year to Geneva is one that daunts me, especially now that this confounded institution of a Malvern Festival in August has upset our domestic holiday plans very inconveniently.

Experience has convinced me that what I call Figmentary Committees: that is, committees with no definite object or reference, like committee rooms in Castles in the Air, are valuable as well as humorous. But they are no good except to people who make a hobby of them and practically devote their lives to exploit them at every opportunity. The C.I.C. is certainly the most important such committee at present in the world (which, by the way, makes you one of the most important persons in the world); and this Committee of Words and Letters might possibly become important as its satellite. But whether the establishment of contact between leading writers and artists will contribute to the peace of Europe is very doubtful. It will certainly not contribute to the peace of the particular apartment in which they meet; for these eminent creatures, not always amiable in private life, are in committee simple hogs. No doubt I could manage them to the extent of tricking them into allowing me to impose on the stormy chaos of their temperaments the law that Nature, abhorring a vacuum, will fill it with resolutions supported by a minority of one if that one can *planer au dessus de la melée* and draft resolutions instead of quarrelling. And if I had a plan of campaign – if I could see anything definite that the committee could do, I might be tempted to shatter the peace of my senility by joining up. But I can see nothing of the kind. The sole subject which presents itself to me with any sort of tangibility is spelling reform in France and Britain, and the abolition of classical grammar and its replacement by Pidgin.

Just compare the number of words in this letter with its simple and more eloquent equivalent NO CAN.

As to Charlotte, she would be most indignant if I told her that you had belittled her accident to the extent of calling it a hurt wrist. Man alive, she cracked both her arm and her pelvis. Today, three weeks after her tumble, she is exulting in having walked from her bedroom to the drawingroom with a nurse at each elbow. She is mending satisfactorily.

Ever
G.B.S.

PS I forgot to suggest a suitable junior. If you really want a junior why not Noel Coward? But if what is really needed is somebody under 70, Galsworthy seems to like games of this kind; and Granville Barker has nothing else to do and can afford his fare to Geneva. Inge still looks almost youthful in his gaiters. But I doubt if the vacancy created by the death of Gosse can ever be filled.

PPS Give my love to Lady Murray if you dare.

In reference to meetings, ***planer au dessus de la mêlée*** means 'glide above the fray.' The expression, which recurs at least three times in Shaw's letters, became widespread with the publication of *Au-dessus de la mêlée*, a collection of polemical letters and essays published in 1915 by Romain Rolland (1866–1944). The French novelist, essayist, art historian, and lifelong pacifist won the Nobel Prize for Literature in that year. **Noël Coward** (1899–1973) was an English playwright whose witty, sophisticated comedies were extremely popular. William Ralph **Inge** (1860–1954) was an Anglican priest and philosopher who became known as Dean Inge after being chosen in 1911 as Dean of St Paul's Cathedral. Murray might have shown Shaw a letter of 7 July 1931 later printed in his *Unfinished Autobiography* to suggest the term '**Figmentary Committee**,' in this case the Committee on Arts and Letters: 'Yesterday … a really interesting and exciting discussion … Old Destrée [the Belgian delegate] thought he ought to make an eloquent speech. Looking like a bloated crocodile, with eyes half shut, he held forth on … "*le spectacle de la jeunesse moderne dévouée aux jouissances matérielles*" ("the spectacle of modern youth devoted to material pleasures") – just as Margaret Wilson, my secretary, looking very Quakerly and clean, came in … Destrée's secretary had been explaining to her with admiration what a dog Destrée was, how "*il aime toutes les bonnes choses, les vins, les femmes …, les bonnes viandes*" ("he loves all good things, wines, women, fine meats") … It was rather like a Shaw play' (191).

99 / To Gilbert Murray G. Soulas, Paris
[date from postmark] 4th May 1931

[ALCS: Bod, SPA]

No luck in Paris. Charlotte immediately developed congestion of the right lung, and has spent her time in bed. We hope to be able to cross on Thursday, as I MUST be in London on Friday even if I have to fly with a return ticket.

This (I hope) concludes the usual cycle of three misfortunes. 1 Scarlet fever at Buxton. 2 Crash & bone fractures in London. 3 Congestion as aforesaid. I am becoming insensible to catastrophe.

Au revoir G.B.S.

100 / To G. Bernard Shaw Yatscombe, Boar's Hill, Oxford
3th March 1932

[TLT: BL]

Shaw had visited Russia in July and met Josef Stalin (1878–1953). See the 'Introduction' for the context of his reactions; a gloss on them can be gleaned from an unpublished address to the Fabian Society on 11 November 1931 entitled 'What Indeed?' (Cornell, box 7, folder 54). He advocates a change in terms from 'Fabianism, Social Democracy, Collectivism, Socialism and so on. All that is gone. There is now nothing but Communism.' Then he argues that Russia's communism has evolved into Fabianism. This development had been predicted as far back as 1921 by Morgan Phillips Price (1885–1973), a Labour Party member of Parliament who published his reminiscences of the Russian Revolution in that year and showed sympathy for Lenin and the Bolsheviks. Shaw also credits Lenin for profiting from Sidney Webb's writings.

In his letter to Shaw of 17 November 1930 (Letter 97), Murray explains that the 'general idea of the Committee of Arts and Letters is to get some sort of bond of union between different countries through the contact of their leading writers or artists.' In the summer of 1931 a meeting of distinguished artists was held which featured speeches by Murray, John Masefield, Paul Valéry, Thomas Mann, and the composer Béla Bártok (1881–1945). The 'symposium' that Murray brings to Shaw's attention may well be one of a series of entretiens *(talks) he hoped to arrange. One of these was held two months later in Frankfurt, Germany, to celebrate the centennial of Goethe's birth (Wilson, 360).*

My dear Shaw

Does the enclosed plan at all smile upon you? Pirandello is anxious to address a letter to you on some subject or other if you will consent to receive it and answer it, but it might be even better if you took the initiative and addressed a letter on any subject you liked to some foreign writer or philosopher. It seems to me that the plan has a chance of producing something really interesting. It might bring into public currency the real ideas of the comparatively few individuals who both think and have the power of making people listen, but of course I realise that you have every possible pulpit open to you for saying anything that you may wish to say. Still, the symposium would be terribly maimed if you were out of it.

I was so sorry to hear of your accident – but I dare say you are tired of hearing of it by now. Charlotte has certainly had bad luck recently.

Yours ever,
[no signature on copy]

The novelist/dramatist Luigi **Pirandello** (1867–1936) was the author of several noted plays, chief among them *Six Characters in Search of an Author* (1921) and *Henry IV* (1922). He would be awarded the Nobel Prize for Literature in 1934. His review of the American premiere of *Saint Joan* in 1924 (repr. in Weintraub, ed., *Saint Joan Fifty Years After*, 23–8) was memorable for its judgment that 'there is a truly great poet in Shaw.' In 8 August 1950 Shaw stated that he had 'never come across a play so *original* as Six Characters' (CL 4, 873).

101 / To Gilbert Murray 4 Whitehall Court, London SW1
13th April 1932

[TLS: Bod, SPA]

The Wells book that Shaw looked into on shipboard was Work, Wealth, and Happiness of Mankind, *which bears the publication date 1931 but was actually issued in early 1932. Shaw wrote to Wells from 'R.M.S. [Royal Mail Ship] Warwick Castle one day out of Capetown' on 19 March 1932 that he had 'sampled' the book, a gift of the Cape Fabian Society (*Bernard Shaw and H.G. Wells, *168–70). However, he refrains from mentioning the 'onslaught' that he rails against below. Wells begins his critique by citing a book called* Scientific Disarmament *(1931) by Victor Lefebure (1891–1947), a specialist in chemical warfare. Lefebure is disturbed by 'irresponsible and mischievous experts' who produced gas warfare, and calls for 'a real pacifist organization' and 'a new scientific morale in regard to war.' Wells asserts, 'This would be an obvious objective for a committee of intellectual cooperation throughout the world, but I find no evidence of any such attempt on the part of the existing organization.'*

More telepathy! When I read H.G. Wells's onslaught on the Int. Cop. and the League generally on the ship returning from the Cape it came into my head that I might start something by addressing a letter to the Committee calling on it to organize an Intellectual Terror for the defence of Europe against the Philistines, and to urge the chemists and radio physicists to devise effective methods by which we intellectuals will be enabled to liquidate numskulls and political scoundrels duly sentenced by the committee.

I am for the moment too full of arrears of work to do more than assure you of my only-too-receptivity; but I will return to the project presently – especially if you stir me up.

G.B.S.

102 / To G. Bernard Shaw Yatscombe, Boar's Hill, Oxford
15th April 1932

[TLT: BL]

My dear Shaw

Splendid. I should love to have a letter calling on the C.I.C. to organise an Intellectual Terror. Would you prefer to initiate the correspondence or shall I get someone to provoke you? Our method is always 'faciliter et provoquer' and I am ready to do either. In any case I will remind you of the business in three weeks' time.

Why do you call me SIR Gilbert? I never call you Sir Bernard – not even behind your back.

I read the DAILY EXPRESS for the second time in my life the other day and much enjoyed your interview. The first time was when my son Basil joined Beaverbrook's staff.

Yours ever,
G.M.

The **interview** was 'Am I Unpopular?' with Winifred Loraine and the literary editor, ***Daily Express***, 12 (11 April 1932), 3–6 (Laurence, *Bibliography*, 2, 738). William Maxwell ('Max') Aitken, first Baron **Beaverbrook** (1879–1964), was a Canadian businessman who moved to London in 1910 and founded the *Daily Express.*

103 / To G. Bernard Shaw Yatscombe, Boar's Hill, Oxford
28th April 1932

[TLT: BL]

The letter that Murray prompts Shaw to write may be the one that he wrote on 4 May 1932 to Henri Barbusse (1873–1935), who had asked him to be a member of the organizing committee of a Congress against War and Fascism along with other international luminaries (see CL 4, 291–2). Parts of the letter have direct relevance to Murray's and Shaw's concerns about the Committee of Intellectual Co-operation, which Murray had chaired since 1928: 'You may use my name for what it is worth in convening your Congress provided the Committee for Intellectual Co-operation of the League of Nations be invited to organise the Congress, and that we take independent action only in the event of its refusal … I do not know whether you have noticed that we treat the League of Nations just as the bellicose Powers do. Whenever a serious international difficulty arises the Powers act precisely as if the League of Nations did not exist. We do the same. The League of Nations has a Committee for Intellectual Co-operation. It is impotent and almost useless because nobody takes any notice of it … Barbusse-Rolland et Cie convene their Congresses as if the League's Committee for Intellectual Co-operation did not exist. And we are repeating the slight at the moment when Gilbert Murray, on behalf of the Committee, is appealing to us to make use of it to conventulate [create a conventicle or assembly] our views by writing open letters to oneanother which it can publish as complete correspondences on definite subjects.'

My dear Shaw

Have you thought about your great international letter? There is no need, of course, to address it to any particular foreigner. Keeble, whom I met in the train, said that the idea occurred to you of writing to Wells, which I think would be excellent from every point of view; but if not Wells, Einstein or Lounatcharsky, or even the Pope, would be quite at your service.

Yours ever,
[no signature in copy]

Sir Frederick **Keeble** (1870–1952) was an Oxford University botany specialist who married Lillah McCarthy, Barker's former wife, in 1920. Anatoly Vasilyevich **Lunacharsky** (1875–1933) was a Russian Marxist who became commissioner of enlightenment after the October Revolution of 1917. In 1930 he represented the Soviet Union at the League of Nations until his death; in 1932 he met Shaw in Moscow. Albert **Einstein** (1879–1955) was a German theoretical physicist whose special theory of relativity made him world famous. His citizenship was revoked because he was a Jew, and he moved to America.

104 / To Gilbert Murray

Ayot St Lawrence, Welwyn, Herts.
20th July 1932

[ALS: Bod, SPA]

Shaw's explanation of his comment that he is 'a thoroughly unsound pacifist' may be supplemented by Alfred Turco's cogent summary of the topic in his 'On War and Peace' in SHAW *16 (1996), 165: Shaw believes that 'the best outcome that can be hoped for from the "colossal stupidity of modern war" is a concluding peace conference capable of creating structures of international cooperation banning war as an instrument of future policy. Pacifism, while admirable in theory, is not practical because "we must face the fact that pugnacity is still a part of human nature, and that civilization is still in its infancy."' For Murray's partial agreement with this last statement see his next letter.*

I think I mustnt take this on: I am a thoroughly unsound pacifist. I really dont see how the world is to be saved unless the Communists are as conscientiously resolved to kill the Capitalists (if it comes to that) as the Capitalists undoubtedly are to kill the Communists. And the notion that the change can be made as a development of bourgeois democracy, with its 'liberties' and safeguards against any sort of real government, is chimerical. The Russian experiment is conclusive on that point. We must accept its results and throw 'the putrefying corpse of Liberty' overboard.

Have you read Maurice Dobb's Soviet Russia and The World? It is an excellent cheap summary by a man who has really got his feet on the new ground.

G.B.S.

I saw somewhere that you had been knighted. You must have forgotten.

In 1924, the Fascist party of Benito Mussolini (1883–1945) had won a majority in parliament. He won wide acclaim for his exhortations to build military strength at the expense of '**the putrefying corpse of liberty**.' Shaw had used the phrase before in a preface to a 1931 reprint of *Fabian Essays in Socialism*, in which he declares that Mussolini believed that the people 'wanted not liberty ... but hard work, hard discipline, and positive and rapid State activity: in short, real government' ('Forty Years Later,' CPr 3, 91–2). **Maurice** [Hubert] **Dobb** (1900–76) was a British Marxist and Cambridge University lecturer who published many books, among them *Soviet Russia and the World* (1932). Murray had never been **knighted** (as Shaw undoubtedly knew) and never would be, partly due to pressure from Lady Mary. He had turned down the offer in 1912.

105 / To G. Bernard Shaw

Yatscombe, Boar's Hill, Oxford
2nd August 1932

[TLT: BL]

My dear Shaw

I trust your refusal only refers to the public meeting, not to your letter for the C.I.C. in which you can utter all your most murderous sentiments with freedom. I find that my feelings swing between two poles: the virtuous, philanthropic, Christian, pacifist pole, and that of the disinterested anthropologist, looking on with interest at the behaviour of this rather beastly species of animal and quite recognizing that they like killing and torturing one another and that on the whole perhaps that suits them. Why shouldn't they go on perishing by wars and pestilences and then breeding again up to the limit till the earth grows cold?

Have you seen an interview with Sybil Thorndike in which she says that you are more interesting than me but that I am a better Christian than you, though we are both of us very much both? I am pleased to think that though you may score in this world I shall have the better of you in the next.

Yours ever

After playing the part of Joan in *Saint Joan*, **Sybil Thorndike** tossed off a casual comment about both Shaw and Murray: 'I loved him – almost as much as I loved Gilbert Murray' (*Evening Standard* interview of March 1924; Gibbs, *Interviews*, 310–11). But Murray must have read the specific comment somewhere else.

106 / To G. Bernard Shaw

Yatscombe, Boar's Hill, Oxford
3rd September 1932

[TLS: BL, SPA]

My dear Shaw

I have been writing a little book on Aristophanes and should rather like to dedicate it to you, if I may. I have carefully avoided saying that you are the modern Aristophanes or that he was the ancient Shaw, but you have been greatly in my mind while the book was writing and it would be a pleasure to have you associated with it.

Have you thought about your public letter for the C.I.C.? A learned Chinaman, Tsai-Yuan-Pei, President of the Chinese Academy, fortunately responded to our bait and wrote a delightfully Chinese letter to the Secretary of the Institute, which has given me a peg for my first letter. I think we shall get Paul Valéry and probably Einstein, but people seem rather afraid of plunging.

Yours ever,
G.M.

Tsai-Yuan-Pei (Ts'ai Yüan-p'ei or Cai Yuanpei, 1863–1940) became the first president of the **Chinese Academy** (Academia Sinica) in 1928. A prominent educator notable for progressive measures, he became minister of education of the new Chinese republic in 1912 and chancellor of Beijing University in 1917. Murray describes the slant of his communication in Letter 108.

107 / To Gilbert Murray

The Malvern Hotel, Malvern
9th September 1932

[ALS: BL, SPA]

By all means dedicate a book to me: it will be something to be remembered for. Aristophanes was an early attempt at Shaw. Almost all of the Greeks were early attempts at modern men, except when the modern men are late failures at Athenian philosophers.

Can you let me have the correspondence as far as it has gone (if it is published)? It would be much easier to pick up a fresh scent than to start a fresh hare.

I return to London on Tuesday next, the 13th.

G. Bernard Shaw

Shaw was attending the annual **Malvern** Festival, which was presenting the first English performance of *Too True to be Good.* The ensuing London production was unfavourably reviewed by St John Ervine (1883–1971), drama critic for the *Observer* and, in 1956, biographer of Shaw. Charlotte wrote an angry letter to him: 'I, who am G.B.S.'s severest critic, specially like this play. To my mind it is not pessimistic, not despondent, & not a recantation of any of his beliefs. It is a play of *revolt.* One character after another declares that this is "not enough": that they are getting glimpses of the "reality that was hidden": that "their way is the way of death, & the preacher must preach the way of life" – "Oh, if I could find it!" ... Honestly, St John, I do think that in the future, when things straighten out, it will be understood that this is among G.B.S.'s *big* plays ... However! One amusing thing about Too True is that nearly all the women like it & nearly all the men loathe it!' (quoted in Dunbar, *Mrs. G.B.S,* 281).

108 / To G. Bernard Shaw

Ganthorpe, Terrington
13th September 1932

[TLT: BL, SPA]

My dear Shaw

Thanks. That is capital. – As to the correspondence, I will ask Bonnet to send you any specimens he has of the correspondence. I have seen nothing except the letter from Don Yuan, in which he shows on Confucian principles that the members of the CIC ought to surpass other men in wisdom and virtue – and, with true politeness, does not go on to ask why they dont. My answer to him is an inquiry why there is danger of civilization coming to an end, considering that on the face of it we are progressing in control over nature, riches, science & c. Not finished yet.

Yours ever,
G.M.

Henri **Bonnet** (1888–1978) had been director of the Paris Institute since 1930. On **Don Yuan**, see Letter 106.

109 / To G. Bernard Shaw Yatscombe, Boar's Hill, Oxford
2nd June 1933

[TLT: BL, SPA]

My dear Shaw

It has just dawned upon me that I never sent you a copy of the 'Aristophanes,' which was dedicated to you! The explanation is, of course, that when the book came out you were inspecting the government of Manchu-Kuo in an aeroplane and had no more definite address. I am so sorry that the book was not in time to pay its respects to you on your return home. I took much pleasure in the dedication and think it has the advantage of being strictly true.

Yours ever

The Shaws had visited Hong Kong and Shanghai from 11 to 17 February.

110 / To Gilbert Murray Whitehall Court, London SW1
7th February 1934

[TLS: ECL]

Murray's dedication in his book, Aristophanes: A Study *is 'To my old friend G. B. S. / lover of ideas and hater of cruelty / who has filled many lands with laughter and whose courage has never failed.' The conclusion of his 'Preface' throws light on his own convictions: he perceives Aristophanes as 'devoted to three great subjects, Peace, Poetry, and the philosophic criticism of life. He laughs, and cannot help laughing, about all of them, except indeed sometimes about the first; for the loss of Peace means ultimately the subjection of all life to the reign of brute force, and that, even to the Prince of Comedy, is too ghastly a thing for laughter' (x).*

My dear Murray

Ever since you sent me the Aristophanes with its noble dedication I have begun innumerable letters to you, and at least half a dozen to Lady Mary. You will find most of them in these prefaces.

The rest boil down into a proposal that we make the Intellectual Co-operation apply to the International Court at the Hague for a warrant to arrest on a charge of assault and false imprisonment. Fill in the name of any Beggar on Horseback you please.

Think it over. I am quite serious.

ever
G.B.S.

The **prefaces** Shaw sent to Murray are most likely proofsheets or a preliminary edition of *Too True to be Good, Village Wooing, & On the Rocks* (London: Constable, 1934), which was published on 15 February. Both full-length plays include prefaces, the one for *On the Rocks* nearly ninety pages long. But it may also have been a draft of his volume *Prefaces by Bernard Shaw,* which was published on 12 June. 'Set a **beggar on horseback** and he will ride to the Devil' is a proverb dating from the sixteenth century. Marc Connelly and George S. Kaufman popularized the key phrase when they staged their *Beggar on Horseback* in 1925.

111 / To G. Bernard Shaw Yatscombe, Boar's Hill, Oxford
15th February 1934

[TLS: BL, SPA]

In Autumn 1933, Wilson reports, Murray composed 'a special article for The Times *on the work of the CIC, describing the vision which inspired him. Had an average man been able to attend the whole series of CIC meetings that year, he wrote, 'he would at least have realised that he was listening to a record – fragmentary indeed and imperfect – of the unseen process which creates and maintains human progress; a process which seldom gets into the front page of any popular newspaper, because it does not consist of explosions or spectacular triumphs; only of the steady growth, and amid much discouragement, of the activity that will save civilisation, if civilisation is to be saved' (Wilson, 364).*

My dear Shaw

It is a great pleasure to have your new book. My wife was indignant that you did not acknowledge the Aristophanes but I told her that if I had a dedication like that I should have found it frightfully hard to know exactly what to say, and I thought it very likely that you felt the same. It is rather like receiving a fullsome vote of thanks after a meeting, to which one feels disposed to respond by saying, 'All that the proposer and seconder say is of course perfectly true, but I think they might have pitched it a little stronger.'

I have a conspiracy against you in my mind. There is a possibility of the Commission des Lettres et de Arts, a branch of Intellectual Co-operation, coming for a meeting in Oxford in June. If they come I want you very much to attend and tell them something about 'L'Avenir de la Culture' or some similar subject. However, the plan hangs fire because the poor Committee, like most of its betters, is stony-broke at present and does not quite see how it can pay its railway fares.

Well, it will be a great delight to read some more evidences of your inexhaustible youth.

Yours ever,
G.M.

The **new book** must have been an advance copy of *Too True to be Good, Village Wooing, & On the Rocks* (London: Constable, published the same day as this letter). **'L'Avenir de la Culture'** is simply 'the future of culture.'

Here a fifteen-month hiatus in their available correspondence occurs. In his capacity as executive chairman of the League of Nations Union, in March 1934 Murray had an illuminating interview with the Soviet ambassador, Ivan [Mikhailovich] Maisky (1884–1975), on the subject of the USSR's revolutionary activities. Maisky smiled while replying, 'At the beginning, we were all excited. We thought your capitalist system of society would be overthrown in a few months. You thought our government would not last even that long – we have both learned that we must put up with each other, and see which system lasts best' (Wilson, 377).

Murray became deeply involved in the world reaction to Adolf Hitler's seizure of power in Germany in early 1933. Hitler (1889–1945), who headed the National

Socialist German Workers' (Nazi) Party since 1921, had been appointed chancellor, and by the end of the year had become dictator. The LNU itself was split, roughly according to their emphasis on Germany's recovery from its disastrous treatment by the Versailles peace treaty and aggressive takeover of the government and behaviour towards the Jewish population since. Murray's attitude (like Shaw's) reflected that of the benevolent camp until he had an interview with the German ambassador, Joachim von Ribbentrop (1893–1946), on 11 November 1934. Wilson recounts that Murray reminded him of his stand towards more equitable terms after the armistice, then commented that 'he had been forced reluctantly to an unhappy conclusion: Germany had abandoned the path of international co-operation and was following that of revanche *[revenge]. Ribbentrop replied by accusing Murray of furthering Marxist principles (Murray's gloss was that this apparently meant ... international co-operation in general). These had brought Germany to ruin, and it was due to Hitler that Eastern Europe as a whole had not been overwhelmed by Communism. As it was, the Führer, who loved peace, had effected a moral revolution in Germany' (376–7). On another LNU issue in which Murray was closely involved but Shaw was not, see chapter 9, 'The Peace Ballot,' in Birn's study of the organization.*

Shaw had felt the sting of German prejudice against Jews when a performance early in 1933 of Too True to be Good *in Mannheim was met with Nazi taunts of 'Jew Shaw!' (Holroyd 3, 418). His first public statement on this issue is in an interview of 4 June with Hayden Church, entitled 'Halt, Hitler! by Bernard Shaw,' which sums up his reactions: 'The Nazi movement is in many respects one which has my warm sympathy; in fact, I might fairly claim that Herr Hitler has repudiated Karl Marx to enlist under the banner of Bernard Shaw. You can therefore imagine my dismay when at the most critical moment Herr Hitler and the Nazis went mad on the Jewish question' (*Sunday Dispatch, *12 [4 June 1933], 3–4; 13, 3–4; Laurence,* Bibliography, *2, 742).*

His private reactions appear in a letter to Trebitsch dated 12–15 May 1933, commenting on 'Hitler's stupid mistake in trying to make political capital out of Judenhetze [Jew-hunting or -harassing], and on the attempt to cover up the essentially Communist character of his proclamation of compulsory labor and his nationalization of the Trade Unions (the first being pure Bernard Shawism and the second borrowed from Russia) by a senseless denunciation of Marxism' (CL 4, 336). But a month later he confided to Trebitsch (accurately), 'Tell Colonel [Hermann Wilhelm] Goering with my compliments that I have backed his regime in England to the point of making myself unpopular' (CL 4, 413). And as late as 1938 he stated in a newspaper article that the Treaty of Versailles had put Germany at a severe disadvantage, and (as Holroyd states it) 'that Hitler had been hoisted to power by the force of national resentment… He had urged the Allies to dismantle the military frontiers imposed by the Treaty, and when they failed to take this initiative he applauded Hitler for "the political sagacity and courage with which he has rescued Germany from the gutter and placed her once more at the head of Central Europe"' (Holroyd 3, 421; 'Bernard Shaw Answers Eight Questions,' Daily Express, *26 March 1938, 12, 3–6; Laurence,* Bibliography, *2, 761).*

On 8 February 1934, the Shaws embarked from Tilbury for a voyage to New Zealand via Kingston, Jamaica, the Panama Canal, and Pitcairn Island. On 12 April Shaw delivered a 24-minute broadcast from Wellington, New Zealand, entitled 'Shaw Speaks to the Universe.' The broadcast reached Australia and was thus considered the most notable ever transmitted in the Southern Hemisphere. On their five-week return voyage starting on 14 April and ending 17 May, Shaw completed The Simpleton of the Unexpected Isles *and* The Six of Calais, *and began* His Tragic Clients, *later renamed* The Millionairess *(Gibbs,* Chronology, *297).*

On 24 November, Shaw collapsed in a faint due to a minor heart attack. He told his friend Henry Salt (1851–1939): 'I just dropped down dead in the middle of a telephone conversation; and it is the greatest pity on earth that I revived like Lazarus. I was literally tired to death: hadnt even a Sunday off for months and months; and I slept for three days on end' (CL 4, 391–2). Due to a bout of blood poisoning that Charlotte suffered in January 1935, a planned eight-week trip to South America had to be cancelled, but on 21 March the Shaws sailed from Tilbury for a 'voyage around Africa, taking in Gibraltar, Palma, Marseilles, Genoa, Port Said and Suez, before sailing south to Mombasa, Zanzibar, Beira and Lourenço Marques.' On 28 April they landed at Durban, South Africa, for a three-week stay. They would begin their return voyage on 24 May via Cape Town and Madeira, arriving at Southampton on 10 June (Gibbs, Chronology, *300).*

Shaw wrote Mrs Patrick Campbell on 17 March 1935 that he intended to 'spend the voyage finishing a play I began a year ago, The Millionairess*' (CL 4, 407). He revised the play in time for a planned production at the Malvern Festival in July, but it had to be postponed. That annual event, now extended from two weeks to four (22 July to 16 September), featured the English premiere of* The Simpleton of the Unexpected Isles.

In March, Shaw had busied himself with reading and revising the proofsheets of one of Sidney and Beatrice Webb's most noteworthy books, Soviet Communism: A New Civilization? *(CL 4, 407). The product of their radical conversion to the*

Soviet development of a socialist state under Stalin followed by a long visit to Leningrad and Moscow, it filled two large volumes with detailed description, arduous documentation, and earnest propaganda. Fabians greeted it with awe, and despite inevitable criticism it remained an impressive argument to be reckoned with for years. Shaw had despaired of Beatrice's early disapproval of the Russian experiment, but praised her contribution to the book by telling John Maynard Keynes that, 'to her great credit,' she was 'a selfmade ethical Socialist, and not a convert by Marx or Mill or any other economist' (CL 4, 669).

112 / To Gilbert Murray

Durban
18th May 1935

[ALS: SPA]

I was tempted to say that nothing less than a dukedom could properly be offered to Lady Mary's husband, but forebore. Still, it's a real difficulty.

We expect to be back in the middle of June.

G.B.S.

Another international issue that drew the attention of both Murray and Shaw was Italy's invasion of Ethiopia on 3 October 1935. The ambivalent attempts of the LNU, and ultimately the League of Nations, to decide on a policy of sanctions is well described in Birn's chapter on the Ethiopian crisis (155–67); see also Wilson, 382–3. Shaw recorded his highly distinctive reactions to their decision in 'Shaw Argues for Hands Off Italy; Holds Gain for Hitler Is Only Peril,' New York Times *(30 August 1935), 6. Bergquist paraphrases his statement as follows: 'The blow to the League of Nations by the ignoring or circumventing of sanctions was considerable, and Shaw, long a League supporter, was distressed. But Shaw said that it was only the result of the League's having ignored his earlier advice to admit only psychologically homogeneous nations to the League. Ethiopia was clearly not a civilized nation and had no business in the League ... It was, further, Shaw's view that Mussolini should have a free hand in Ethiopia. Applying the principle of the "higher civilization," as he had so often before, Shaw concluded that it would be for the benefit of civilization as represented by the administration of the Italian government.'*

In fact, eight years earlier Shaw had shocked fellow socialists with a 24 January 1927 letter to the Daily News *strongly backing Mussolini's regime over existing political democracies; the editor entitled it 'Bernard Shaw on Mussolini: A Defence' (Laurence,* Bibliography, *2, C2632). In her diary Beatrice Webb deplored his statement as 'a crude and flippant attempt at reconstruction, bred of conceit, impatience and ignorance'* (Shaw: Interviews, *354).*

In the summer of 1936, the Spanish Civil War broke out. Its international ramifications drew Shaw's direct and Murray's indirect attention: the Nationalists, embracing the landed aristocracy, Roman Catholic Church, military leaders, and the fascist Falange party, were pitted against the Loyalists, consisting of liberals, anarchists, socialists, and Communists, including volunteers from many countries. The conservative forces, led by General Francisco Franco (1892–1975), defeated their opponents, overthrowing the second Spanish Republic. (Concise Columbia Encyclopedia, *778). Shaw expressed his opinion in 'Shaw Sees Drift to War,'* New York Times *(3 November 1937, 4). Bergquist comments: Shaw 'regarded it primarily as only a civil war,' but feared 'danger to the general peace of Europe' if the conflict got out of hand. 'The actual civil war itself Shaw viewed as a war between Capitalism and Communism, and Shaw naturally supported the Communist or Loyalist side' (195). He elaborated upon this a half-year later in an article that Holroyd paraphrases: the war was 'an internal class war with Franco standing for property, privilege and "everything we are all taught to consider respectable," and though his sympathies were generally on the left, he distanced himself from other British intellectuals. "Spain must choose for itself," he wrote: "it is really not our business"' (Holroyd 3, 422;* Daily Express, *26 March 1938, 12). See also Weintraub's discussion in* The Last Great Cause, *145–6.*

This event triggered Murray's involvement with the International Peace Campaign, which was provoked largely by the war. The LNU's president, Lord Robert Cecil, saw the advantage of following the popular Peace Ballot with a strong link to the British Committee of this campaign, and accepted the chairmanship partly as a means of reviving the LNU after the Ethiopian debacle. Murray was sceptical about this link, and (as Wilson notes) relationships between the two organizations were 'bad from the start.' Cecil, 'on the rampage,' induced Murray to resign as executive chairman and become (nominal) co-president. A letter to Lady Mary conveyed his reaction: he was 'glad to be rid of it' (384–5).

113 / To Gilbert Murray

4 Whitehall Court SW1
8th July 1938

[ALS: CL 4]

The following note (related to Letter 100) was inscribed on a proof copy of Geneva, *to which Shaw refers. Over three years had passed between the previous extant letter and this one. In the interim, on 22 January 1936, the Shaws embarked on a cruise to the Pacific with stops in Miami, Honolulu, the Grand Canyon, and Mexico, returning home on 6 April. On the trip Shaw wrote* Geneva *and began* The World Betterer, *which he abandoned for several years until it became* Buoyant Billions *(Gibbs,* Chronology, *302).*

In December 1937 Gabriel Pascal (1894–1954) visited Shaw and introduced him to Leslie Howard (1893–1943), slated for the role of Henry Higgins in the 1938 film version of Pygmalion. *Shaw had granted Pascal the film rights to the play on 13 December 1935, but he would deplore the demeanour of Howard ('he thinks he's Romeo!' [Holroyd 3, 390]) and the romantic twist given to the play's final scene.*

Dear Gilbert Murray

You may remember our correspondence about the Intellectual Co-operation Committee. It ended in my being invited to write letters to the Committee about nothing in particular, for burial, apparently, in the Committee's pigeon holes. I made one or two efforts to induce Barbusse, Romain Rolland & Co, to make use of the Committee instead of firing off manifestoes of which nobody took any notice. They repudiated the suggestion as 'bourgeois.'

Finally I produced THIS [*Geneva*].

I was driven to the conclusion that the Hague court, *not* the Geneva Assembly, is the possibly operative organ, and its weapon (or 'sanction') so far, Excommunication.

What do you think?

G. Bernard Shaw

PS I am recovering from 'pernicious anaemia,' and may possibly be pronounced well if I keep very quiet for the next three weeks.

On the **manifestoes** of Rolland, see the endnote to Letter 98; on those of Henri Barbusse, one of whose books was entitled *Manifeste aux intellectuels,* see Letter 103. The **Hague court**, or Permanent Court of Arbitration (popularly the Hague Tribunal), had since 1900 provided a variety of dispute resolution services to the international community, especially those involving disagreements between countries. Its ultimate goal was to prevent wars. On 4 June Shaw collapsed and was diagnosed with **pernicious anaemia**, necessitating several injections of liver hormone into the strict vegetarian's body (with Charlotte's consent but not his) and confining him to his home for six weeks (Dunbar, *Mrs. G.B.S.*, 282–3).

114 / To G. Bernard Shaw

Yatscombe, Boar's Hill, Oxford
13th August 1938

[TLS: BL, SPA]

Wilson comments (365), 'Curiously enough, it was Bernard Shaw who, in his play Geneva *(1938), expressed what were perhaps Murray's unspoken and final ambitions for the work of the CIC. Writing to Bonnet, the Secretary of the [French] Institute, Murray remarked that it was by no means one of Shaw's best plays, but it did show the CIC in the centre of the picture, and the complete neglect of it by the British government. "He makes the C.I.C. summon the Dictators before the International Court," and they comply with the summons in order to gain the good opinion of the world' [letter of 16 August]. In the* Spectator *[28 August] Murray wrote that Shaw's moral was correct. World public opinion was still important, though as a tribunal it was 'weak and slow and helpless and confused, and would not always test the evidence before it.'*

The original version of Geneva *(radically different later versions exist) begins in Geneva at the office of the International Committee for Intellectual Co-operation, where a 'cheerful person with absolutely no mind,' the typist Begonia Brown, takes complaints about various world leaders. After she sends letters recording them to the Court of International Justice at The Hague, the senior judge orders a trial of three dictators: Bombardone (Mussolini), Battler (Hitler), and General Flanco (Franco). The British foreign secretary, Sir Orpheus Midlander (Sir Austen Chamberlain), thinks the gesture will be futile, but – attracted by the spotlight – all agree to come. The three argue fiercely, displaying their hopelessly militant attitudes, so that nothing is accomplished. The secretary of the League of Nations calls it a farce, but the judge diagrees: 'Not a farce, my friend. They came, these fellows. They blustered: they defied us. But they came. They came.' Meanwhile, ambitious Begonia runs for Parliament, wins, and becomes Dame Begonia. Shaw's letter of 23 October 1940 (Letter 141) to Murray describes the play from his point of view, largely focusing on Begonia.*

An illuminating article on the play from the political point of view is H.J. Fyrth's 'In the Devil's Decade: Geneva *and International Politics,'* SHAW *11*

(1991): 239–55. For the complicated evolution of the play's text, see Pilecki, Shaw's *Geneva.*

My dear Shaw

Many thanks for 'Geneva.' I have just returned from the town of that name, and have read the play with the same bubbling delight as most of its predecessors. I read a rather stupid Times notice in Geneva, & suspected at once that the reviewer had missed most of the points. He seemed to want you to take sides, and did not see that you were flinging your satire impartially all round.

As to the C.I.C., I will not say that all your statements of fact are strictly accurate, but you don't exaggerate the neglect of it by the British Government and indeed by all the politicians. If they had had enough sense to take it seriously they might, of course, have altered the whole current of world affairs. This was what Bergson and Leon Bourgeois hoped when they proposed the foundation of the C.I.C., and Balfour I will not say shared their enthusiasm, but did seem to see what they meant.

Begonia Brown is a very good symbol of British democracy, and Sir Orpheus of the F.O., though I should say that of late years it has rather lost its traditional grace of manner. I think also that your climax is essentially true: the dictators and other scoundrels do have to come to judgment. The enormous pains they take to shut out public opinion are a proof of how much they fear it, and it can never be entirely stifled. In happier days I used always to maintain that publicity was the real weapon of the League. It is practically impossible for a Foreign Minister, when questioned in the Assembly, to stand up before fifty-two nations and a hundred journalists and confess that his Government has been lying or behaving like a cad. In the early days Nansen and Cecil and I used to use that instrument, but Sir Orpheus and his friends have managed to get back to methods of diplomatic privacy.

I was very sorry to hear of your pernicious anaemia. The vulgar cure it now by swallowing pounds of raw liver, but I think perhaps death is preferable to that, and you evidently have a superior way of your own.

Yours ever,

G.M.

PS I may as well send you my last words of wisdom: there is no necessity to read them.

Léon Bourgeois (1851–1925) was president of the Council of the League of Nations. Murray's '**last words of wisdom**' (here 'last' means 'latest,' not 'final'; he published several more books) may have been in the two Hibbert Trustee lectures he published in 1938, *Liberality and Civilization.* A review by John Laird in *Philosophy* 51 (July 1938), 372, states its main points: 'The loss of liberality ... is the legacy of the insecurity of the Peace ... Liberality and humanity go together and require a comity of nations' (i.e., the League of Nations).

115 / To G. Bernard Shaw Yatscombe, Boar's Hill, Oxford
28th March 1939

[TLT: BL, SPA]

On 14 March 1938 Hitler annexed Austria to 'protect' the ten million Germans living there. This drew protests from Britain and France, but British prime minister Neville Chamberlain (1869–1940) and French premier Edward Daladier (1884–1970), in the Munich Agreement, adopted a policy of appeasement which permitted Germany to take the Sudetanland, with a third of Czechoslovakia's inhabitants, most of whom were German. In Chamberlain's immortal words, this would insure 'peace with honour ... peace for our time.'

It is interesting to note that Geneva, *which Shaw revised again and again, nevertheless drew enough negative criticism to become his 'most frequently disparaged play.' Prophetically, as long ago as the end of 1938 he had commented to H.K. Ayliff (1872–1949): 'What a horrible horrible play! Why had I to write it? To hear those poor devils spouting the most exalted sentiments they were capable of, and not one of them fit to manage a coffee stall, sent me home ready to die' (letter of 11 December,* Bernard Shaw: Theatrics, *206). Still, when the play was transferred to the West End in January, it enjoyed a run of 237 performances (*Bernard Shaw and Barry Jackson, *98).*

*By 17 September 1939, in letters to Roy Limbert and Beatrice Webb, Shaw exulted that he had found a reason to welcome the Second World War. He told Limbert: 'The declaration of war is the making of Geneva, which has always lacked a substantial climax ... I have written a new scene – the arrival of the news of Battler's attack – which will just do the trick' (*Theatrics, *208). He described the new scene in more detail to Beatrice: it not only involved Hitler's declaration of war but also 'his betrayal by Mussolini and Franco, so far idiotically unnoticed by press and Cabinet' (CL 4, 538).*

My dear Shaw

Many thanks for the box. I had meant to take the two Toynbee boys and Rosalind, but in the mean time, as no doubt you saw, Tony shot himself. A sad thing: he was a charming fellow, gentle, ironical and exceedingly clever: he spoke Russian Serbian and Chinese as well as the more ordinary languages. I always found him a pleasant companion.

Yes, Geneva is in its way a 'horror.' There is the real horror underneath, felt from the first entrance of the Jew, though boldly filmed over. But Begonia Brown and Sir Orpheus are among your immortal creations, and I know people very like the Judge, though not so handsome.

I picked up by chance a volume of the articles written by Dr Bridges, the Positivist not the poet, for the Positivist Review from 1890 to 1904. They are not particularly striking in themselves but they do seem to come from [a] wiser and serener world. And what small things people complained about then, such as the payments to Church schools and the absence of Arbitration Boards for dealing with African tribes, compared with the things that trouble us now!

Yours ever,
G.M.

Tony Toynbee (1914–39) was the eldest son of Murray's daughter Rosalind. **Dr Bridges** (John Henry Bridges, 1832–1906) was a devotee of Auguste Comte (1798–1857), the founder of Positivism. The book that Murray mentions was *Illustrations of Positivism: A Selection of Articles from the 'Positivist'* (1915).

116 / To Gilbert Murray

4 Whitehall Court, London SW1
30th March 1939

[ALS: Bod, SPA]

My dear Murray

Never heard a word of it until your letter arrived.

It felt as if you had calmly shot me – for nothing.

If only he had waited to hear the play! And how wise of you to go!

And Rosalind! Was he a favorite? It is impossible to imagine the effect of these catastrophic surprises. I have no children, and greatly doubt whether I should like them if I had. I certainly should not like them all.

I am guessing in the dark. Tony was your grandson, was he not?

Talk of Greek tragedy!
What can I say?

G. Bernard Shaw

PS Wasted badly in Europe: an iconoclastic reaction.

117 / To G. Bernard Shaw

Yatscombe, Boar's Hill, Oxford
31st March 1939

[TLU: BL]

My dear Shaw

Thanks for your kind note; I thought probably you would have seen the notice of Tony's death in the papers – there was a good deal about it. The coroner's jury returned an open verdict.

He was the eldest of my grandchildren, and as I think I told you, a very handsome and attractive creature, gentle and clever and absent-minded, and always rather a prey to melancholy. He spoke Russian German and Serbian quite well and Chinese imperfectly as well as the ordinary languages, but never seemed to get really interested in any job, or indeed in life at all. He was quite well-conducted and never got into bad scrapes, but just did not care much to be alive, and for some queer reason, firearms fascinated him, and he knew all about their invention and history.

Rosalind takes it with her usual commonsense and stoicism, made perhaps more easy to her now that she has become a devout Catholic. Very rum, these alternations among the generations: my father a Catholic, her two eldest boys rather more free-thinking than me in religious matters. I suppose their children will be monks or Yogis.

I should like to come to lunch sometime if I may, but after Easter. I go to Paris to co-operate intellectually next week.

Yours ever,

118 / To Gilbert Murray

4 Whitehall Court (130), London SW1
29th April 1939

[APCS: Bod, SPA]

On Friday Charlotte had to undergo a minor operation. A cyst between her shoulders had to be cut out. It has left a cavity in her person which is filling up quite satisfactorily, but may take ten days or so to be rid of finally. Until then we cannot be sure of our movements, though Charlotte expects to return to normal activity in the course of the week.

Still, she thinks you had better know.

What jolly good speeches Battler makes! But so, being an intelligent being, he is now almost as much frightened as we are – more, possibly, being more intelligent – we may sleep in peace for a while. Douglas Reed's sketch of him in the Sunday Graphic is worth reading.

G.B.S.

Douglas Reed (1895–1976), London *Times* journalist until 1938, had published a book about the megalomania of Hitler, *Insanity Fair*, in 1938. He came to believe that a long-term Zionist conspiracy exists to impose a world government on an enslaved humanity (*Wikipedia*).

119 / To G. Bernard Shaw Yatscombe, Boar's Hill, Oxford
2nd May 1939

[TLT: BL]

My dear Shaw

So sorry to hear of Mrs. Shaw's operation, though I gather it ought not to give trouble for long. The only serious operation I ever had made me feel just like broken china mended with seccotine, for about a year.

Yes, Hitler makes clever debating speeches; I am told they are written by Rosenberg. But I agree with you that he is at last beginning to be frightened, and to suspect that in spite of Ribbentrop 'the Lion of least resistance' may at last do something more than growl. I have lectures on Hitler's character from time to time in the train when I happen to travel with William Brown.

Yours,
G.M.

In early May 1897 Murray had had a **serious operation** to remove a cyst on an eye (Wilson, 65). Alfred **Rosenberg** (1893–1946) was the Nazi Party's chief racial theorist. He was executed after his trial in Nuremberg. **William Brown** has not been identified.

The Second World War began one week after Germany and Soviet Russia signed a mutual nonaggression pact on 23 August 1939. On 1 September German troops and aircraft attacked Poland, and, partly in response to a U-boat sinking a British ship two days later, Britain and France declared war on Germany. Soviet troops invaded Poland on 17 September, Warsaw surrendered to the Germans ten days later, and the next day the country was partitioned between the two attackers. Five months previously Shaw had declared to Trebitsch, 'I am very sceptical as to the likelihood of war' (letter of 25 March in Shaw's Letters to Siegfreid Trebitsch, *386). Then, on 18 October, he told him, 'All my writing energy is expended on the war controversy' (389). Holroyd confirms this: 'As in the First World War, he poured forth journalism – over 250 broadsides, obituaries, contributions to symposiums, answers to questionnaires, reacting to almost every aspect of the war and examining how best to secure the peace afterwards' (3, 430).*

Shortly after the war started, Shaw published an article in The New Statesman and Nation, *'Uncommon Sense about the War' (n.s. 18 [7 October 1939]: 483–4) in which he urged a conference between Great Britain, Russia, and Germany so that the demands of each could be presented and mutually adjusted. He advocated pursuing peace with Hitler since he believed that Stalin would pressure him to agree (headnote by L.W. Conolly in* Bernard Shaw and Barry Jackson, *109). Bergquist also cites an unpublished article Shaw wrote in 1940, 'How to Talk Intelligently about the War,' which continues to present his cold, rational view. 'Aggression was a word to be cautiously used,' he said; 'the British should not accuse Hitler of aggression since it was the British who attacked him by declaring war on Germany after the invasion of Poland' (197). Then, in a cancelled B.B.C. broadcast of June 1940, reprinted in* Platform and Pulpit, *286–92, Shaw said he regarded the attack a 'reconquest.' Moreover, 'he also urged listeners to stop talking nonsense about dictators; dictators are absolutely necessary in a modern civilized country, both in industry and in politics. The problem is not to get rid of dictators because they are automatically evil, but to impose on them "a code of social obligations that remind them continually that their authority is given them for the benefit of the commonwealth and not for their private gain"' (197–8).*

Holroyd states that these war years 'were to witness an extraordinary refuelling of Shaw's popularity in the theatre ... But the topmost year was 1944 when no fewer than nine of Shaw's plays were put on in London' (3, 429). Immersed in public controversy, he wrote no new plays during the war.

Meanwhile, in letters to the Times *of 8 July 1940 and later, Murray had protested the conditions of internment and lack of discrimination applied to refugees, some of whom were being deported against their will to Canada and Australia. As a consequence of the resulting agitation, an advisory committee addressed the problem and determined that no more internees would be sent abroad without their consent (Wilson, 400).*

120 / To G. Bernard Shaw

Yatscombe, Boar's Hill, Oxford
16th October 1940

[TLS: Bod via Guelph]

My dear Shaw

I was wondering how you were getting on, but your Encyclical to the School of Dramatic Art is delightful; as full as ever of life and commonsense.

We have a comparatively peaceful time here and I have just translated the *Antigone*. We have various London workers staying with us for a week or a few days at a time to make up for arrears of sleep. Rosalind and Stephen are both in London, she working for 'The Sword of the Spirit' in the Cardinal's house at Westminster, getting Catholics from East London into sound Catholic homes in the country, without any danger of contact with Black Prots. She seems serene and entirely fearless. Stephen has an air pilot's certificate and is first-rate at navigation, consequently they will not have him in any post connected with the Air Force or Navy, but he does what little law work and defence work he can, and tries to keep the extreme Left Wing of the Hampstead Labour Party from being misled into moderatism by its perjured leaders. You once observed that all my children were mad.

It seems odd that at our age we should mind being killed by enemy action at once rather than by natural causes in a year or two, but I suppose it is a natural instinct rather than any reasoning process. I confess I should greatly like to see how the war ends, though of course there will be still more exciting problems then waiting solution. In real life, the curtain never comes down.

Our kindest remembrances to Charlotte.

Ever yours sincerely,
Gilbert Murray

Shaw's **Encyclical to the School of Dramatic Art** was probably another periodic 'keepsake' for RADA, though none is listed in Laurence's bibliography, and the current RADA office was unaware of it. See the headnote for Letter 91.

From 5 to 17 September **Charlotte** was 'bedridden with lumbago, an early sign of the osteitis deformans' which would worsen steadily until her death in 1943 (Gibbs, *Chronology*, 312).

121 / To Gilbert Murray Ayot St Lawrence, Welwyn

23rd October 1940

[TLS: CL 4]

My dear Murray

We are here in a village where there are no shelters, no fire brigade, no guns, nothing warlike except a searchlight and little siren which explodes every ten minutes or so. As the raiders are highly scientific, and fly blindly by their instruments, they begin every night by bombarding us in the firm conviction that they are making direct hits on Churchill's hat when as a matter of fact they are missing mine by a mile or two and shaking the house to remind us that there is a war on and that we are all in the front line.

I began by being pigheaded and refusing to let them disturb my routine of 3½ days in the country and 3½ in town every week. This alarmed Providence for my safety. The day before the Blitz, as we were starting for town as usual, Charlotte fell and hurt her knees so badly that she had to be helped upstairs, and the journey to London was out of the question. She is well now; but the pigheadedness has been bombed out of us; and we havnt been up to Whitehall Court for seven weeks. We can see fireworks there from our windows, which is quite enough for us. Two of our windows and a door panel have been smashed by one of the 12 hits in the Whitehall district; but here we only get shaken. We console ourselves with the mathematical chances against our being hit; but the facts, as usual, ignore mathematics and strongly support the theory of a mystical human polarization by which some people attract bombs and torpedoes, and others repel them.

The village people all call the war senseless; but as they are as helpless as you and I there is nothing for it but fatalism, which the wireless calls our heroism, and a strong objection to allow Ittler to control our destinies. The childishness of the politicians is appalling. Churchill occasionally tells as much of the truth as he safely can over the wireless. Then he takes an audible gulp of his favorite stimulant and, with a preliminary yell, gives the gallery a peroration and denounces Nazi scoundrels who actually bomb civilians, women and children. He is immediately followed by the news announcer, who begins by describing how the R.A.F. has rained bombs on the railway stations of Berlin etc. etc. In a sardonic mood one can turn on the Rome Radio, or Haw Haw, and listen to the news over again, with the names reversed, but the moral indignation an exact echo. But this poor amusement does not bear its daily repetition.

The clamor for a statement of war aims (as if anybody had any aims except with guns) does not interest me. What it comes to is a statement of the conditions on which we will stop fighting; and what we can demand with any hope of success depends on the odds for or against our winning the fight. When the odds are ten to one in our favor we can clearly demand much more than when they are merely even. When they are against us we cannot demand anything: we can only beg for mercy. At present the odds seem even or thereabouts; consequently I think Churchill is right when he decides that the position is not yet good enough to demand as much as will be on the cards if we get the odds on our side.

But why does not the League of Nations take the initiative? It is true that the Assembly does not exist, and cannot be resuscitated until the Powers consent to assemble. It would be no use if they did, as from the first it has been reduced to absurdity by the rule that its decisions must be unanimous. The fact is that when Chamberlain declared war it never even occurred to him that he should have referred the case to the League. So much for the Assembly.

But Begonia Brown still exists, and is indestructible as long as the Committee exists. What is to prevent her pointing out that it is not for the belligerents to declare their aims, which are necessarily selfish. It is for the intellectual élite to demand in the name of civilization why they are disturbing the peace of the world, and what they hope to gain by the senseless and horrible bombing match which they are at present carrying on. In England Hitler is exterminating the natives at the rate of 233 a day. There are 40 millions to be exterminated. Begonia can do arithmetic enough to demonstrate that at this rate it will take 470 years to finish the job, or, since the extermination of the women would be sufficient, say 235 years. Similar figures confront the R.A.F. The Committee can ask whether ministers entering on such programs can be regarded as sane. Then the Committee can state the minimum requirements of civilization as impartially as it can.

During the Four Years War Barbusse, Romain Rolland and Co, kept asking me to sign some such manifesto. I told them that as they were nobodies the thing should be done through the Committee, of which they had never heard. Rolland wanted us to *planer au dessus de la melée*, and though I made fun of this it is what the Committee should try to do.

In 'Geneva' I made fun of the Committee; but in such a way as to make this the first step to its publicity and popularity.

Roughly, do you think anything can be done in this direction. Are its members young enough? You are 74. I am 84. And we both know too much.

I am trying to write a Penguin sixpenny stating the facts that persons ought to know before they are allowed to vote or present themselves for election. They may have any opinions they like as to how to deal with the facts; but they must know the facts. Any person using abstract terms should be disqualified at once: measures not mouthings should be the rule. At present we are governed by people who do not know the world they are living in: the Old School Ties have the mentality of Edward III, and the Merchant Taylors that of Henry VII, whilst adult suffrage enables them to get elected by irresistible majorities with no political mentality, but with a strong snobbery which loves the Old School Tie and its associations.

This letter is too long: I must stop.

My love to Lady Mary.

Oh, I forgot. The filming of Major Barbara, now just completed, convinced me that the old beginning would not work, as nobody with the punch of Lady Britomart was available. So I had to begin with the first meeting of Cusins and Barbara, including his courting and proposal, all in ten minutes or thereabouts!!! It seemed impossible; but it came off quite well. I had to add dozens of new scenes. I wonder what you will think of them. It is so new to have a production-cost-limit of £200,000 instead of £200.

I await the Antigone. It is something to think about – and I often do think about it that though I have lived in the thick of a revolutionary burst of playwriting activity in London, the only plays that seem to me likely to survive it are the old Greek ones in your translations.

Do you ever see Granville-Barker now? He is not allowed to have any communication with me, as his Helen sticks pins into wax images of me; but we are – on my side certainly, as I suspect on his also – as good friends as ever.

enough
G. Bernard Shaw

PS I contributed a string of Notes by The Way to the last number but two of Time & Tide. It might interest Stephen, as it explains the policy of the Labor Party, which is not mere Moderation, but Trade Unionism, otherwise Labor Plutocracy.

There goes the wretched siren.

Lord **Haw Haw** was the nickname for broadcasters on Nazi German radio (most often William Joyce) whose propaganda reached both Great Britain and the United States throughout the war. Shaw's article in the '**Notes by the Way**' series of ***Time & Tide*** appeared in the 12 October issue; a condensed version in the *English Digest* (5, January 1941, 20) was entitled 'Einstein, Hitler, and Me.' The **Penguin sixpenny** that Shaw visualized 'became the Constable ten-shilling *Everybody's Political What's What?*' on 15 September 1944 (headnote in CL 4, 583).

122 / To G. Bernard Shaw Yatscombe, Boar's Hill, Oxford
28th October 1940

[TLS: Bod via Guelph]

My dear Shaw

It was a great pleasure to hear from you, especially in these days of isolation. I was particularly interested, as you might expect, in what you said about the 'revolutionary burst of play-writing.' I doubt if much of it will survive. *You* will, of course, not merely as a precious historical document about the social and intellectual movements of the nineteenth century, but particularly because of your style. You are always easy and pleasant to read, and I am sure posterity hates reading the great writers of the past when they are heavy and difficult. Lillo's George Barnwell was a much bolder advance in British drama, both technical and intellectual, than The Rivals, but it is rather a bore to read, and it is therefore forgotten, while The Rivals still holds the stage. Voltaire again is still read because it is fun to read him, though his science, philosophy, and the controversies he was engaged in, all belong to the past, except in so far as there is a certain eternal element in all fighting against oppression. I think Greek plays will also have a continuous intermittent life – people will have to reinterpret them from time to time.

As to the war, I feel as if civilization had been caught in a trap. We couldn't in the circumstances avoid making the war: we can't stop it now: but the state of the world at the end will be worse than at the beginning. Of course I still think that if Americans two or three years ago had been willing to say the sort of things they are saying now, we could have avoided it; but that is past history. One way in which the trap works is that nations get governed by stupid or bad people; we by stupid people – witness the internment policy, the work of people who could not tell the difference between Nazis and Anti-nazis, Fascists and Anti-fascists; Germany by sheer gangsters of a peculiarly cruel kind; France by politicians and soldiers with all sorts of brilliant qualities, but peculiarly unfitted for politics, both morally and intellectually.

I will think about Begonia; we had one meeting of the Committee in Geneva since the war, but it was poorly attended, and the Swiss Government was terrified lest we should compromise them. I am hoping that the thing will be reconstituted in America. There is a good National Committee of Intellectual Cooperation there. They will get the South American, Indian, and Chinese members, and pretty good representatives of England, France, Holland etc., but whether they can make any pronouncement of value is very doubtful. Of course we are mostly too old, but apart from that no one would listen.

I am glad about your Penguin Book. The longer I live, the more I feel my ignorance of the world. All we intellectuals are dreadfully shut off from understanding the average man, and the average man doesn't know enough. I remember at the beginning of the century you were asked to say something and you said that problems were getting bigger and the stature of man remaining fixed. I have often thought of that. It is practically what Liddell Hart said about the mismanagement of the Great War. It was just too difficult and too large for any general staff to manage.

Major Barbara will be fun to see; it is astonishing how well Pygmalion went as a film. I remember your reading the play to us in Woodstock Road, and Mary rolled off her chair with laughing – which she now firmly denies. I hope Charlotte is better, and that Hitler will continue to miss you.

Yours ever,
G.M.

The English dramatist George **Lillo** (1693–1739) is remembered only for *The London Merchant; or, the History of George Barnwell* (1731), with its innovative focus on social concerns. Sheridan's ***The Rivals*** was first staged in 1775. B.H. **Liddell Hart** (1895–1970) was a military historian who derived basic principles of effective warfare from studying past conflicts and proclaimed that both sides in the First World War violated them: *Wikipedia* states that he reduced this set of principles to 'two fundamentals: direct attacks against an enemy firmly in position almost never work and should never be attempted, and to defeat the enemy one must first upset his equilibrium, which is not accomplished by the main attack, but must be done before the main attack can succeed.'

123 / To G. Bernard Shaw Yatscombe, Boar's Hill, Oxford
27th January 1941

[TLT: BL, SPA]

My dear Shaw

Thanks for your letter. Of course I quite agree with you about the come down from the great Fifth Century people to Menander. I find in an old essay of mine in a book called English Literature & the Classics, a description of the way in which the New Comedy got rid of all the things that a modern playwright would object to, drew its material from real life, invented its plots &c, 'And, as often happens, Fate was ironical. Every single change seemed an obvious improvement and the total result was an incomparable loss. It led from the AGAMEMNON to the EPITREPONTES.' (The best preserved of Menander's plays.)

It is always a comfort to me that you are a supporter of my Greek Plays. The young, instructed partly by T S Eliot, think them wrong and almost wicked. One donkey has written lately to say that it is grossly Victorian of me to imagine that the tragedians were at all interested in women's characters; all their 'romantic interest' was homosexual. In reality there is no homosexuality at all in tragedy except as one of the unpleasant or ridiculous tastes of the Cyclops; and, if they were not interested in women, why did they give Clytemnestra, Antigone, Electra, Medea, Hecuba &c the centre of the stage and much the longest parts?

The BBC are going to do the CROPPED HAIR on Feb 28, though I dont quite see how they will get it across. Nearly half will have to be cut. I shall also have a shot at Tyrone Guthrie or Nugent Monck, but I doubt if I shall make £29000.

We ruin ourselves – or rather Mary ruins us – on Refugees, a rather less irritating way. Nice people mostly, and greatly to be pitied, but they do swarm. I dont find them pushing or greedy, but when M finds herself in the midst of a crowd of unfortunates there is no holding her. Lady Cecil's last message to her was: 'Tell Mary to avoid the unfortunate as she would the plague.'

Dont tell the censor I asked, but is Winston really a great War Minister or only a magnificent actor of the part? Speeches, fire, manner, attitude are all just what is wanted, and certainly inspiring to the nation and to USA; he also has great diplomatic tact and generosity; but is he a good strategist or administrator or judge of men? I dont say he isnt, but I wonder.

I am so glad Charlotte is conquering her lumbago. Electric shocks do wonders for mine when it comes, but are [a] little less effective each fresh time. Mary has been sent to bed for some days with non-descript exhaustion and sickness, but is up again.

Yours ever,
G.M.

The **old essay of mine** that Murray recalls is 'Greek and English Tragedy,' in Gordon, ed., *English Literature and the Classics*, 7–24. He paraphrases and quotes from the last two pages. **Menander** (ca. 342–293 B.C.) was a Greek poet and dramatist whose plays made him the finest exponent of the 'new comedy,' a comedy of manners with stock characters and conventional turns of plot. Until 1905 Menander was known only through fragments, but in 1905 a papyrus was uncovered which contained large parts of four of his plays. Murray would complete and translate the *Perikeiromene* as *The Rape of the Locks* (a title that Shaw suggested) in 1941 and the *Epitrepontes* as *The Arbitration* in 1945 (*Oxford Companion to the Theatre* [1983], 591, 541).

On **T S Eliot**'s response to Murray's plays see the headnote for Letter 51. **The BBC are going to do the CROPPED HAIR** (elsewhere referred to as *The Rape of the Locks*): in '"That Living Voice": Gilbert Murray at the BBC,' Morris documents that fifteen of his plays were broadcast between 1925 and 1956 and several of them were repeated, among them his two completed Menander fragments (310–11). It was estimated that audiences of 300,000 listened to *Hippolytus* in 1936 and 450,000 to *The Trojan Women* in 1946 (303–4). As late as 1953 Murray gave a series of talks entitled 'Hellenism and the Modern World,' published the following year by Beacon Press. **Tyrone Guthrie** (1900–71) was a respected English actor and director, especially noteworthy for his Shakespearean productions. **Nugent Monck** (1877–1958) was a professional actor who worked with the amateur Norwich Players from 1911 on, then founded the Maddermarket Theatre in 1921 to house the group. His specialties were Shakespearean and non-conventional plays. **Lady Cecil** was the wife of Sir Robert Cecil, Murray's diplomatic associate and good friend.

124 / To G. Bernard Shaw

Yatscombe, Boar's Hill, Oxford
16th April 1941

[TLS: Bucknell via Guelph]

Murray was awarded the Order of Merit on 1 January 1941.

Shaw's article on the alphabet was 'A King's Spelling: Letters and Sounds,' The Times *(15 April): 6: 1 (repr. in* Shaw on Language, *65–71, and in* The Letters of Bernard Shaw to *The Times, 227–9). His main argument is that an economical alphabet would save tons of time, space, and paper, e.g.: 'By shortening a single common word instead of lengthening it, we could save the cost of destroyers enough to make an impregnably guarded avenue across the Atlantic for our trade with America ... My surname has two sounds; but I have to spell it with four letters: another 100 per cent. loss of time, labour, ink, and paper' (68–9).* Shaw on Language *reprints several other articles on alphabet and spelling reform, including phonetic spelling.*

My dear Shaw

I was delighted with your letter in the Times about the alphabet, but your case is actually stronger than you stated.

Our alphabet was not made for Latin, but for a Semitic language with no vowels and several queer gutterals and sibilants which we have lost. Our 'e' was an aspirate, and our 'o' a 'gh.' I think one could show that the alphabet never suited Greek, for the different cities made various experiments with new characters; and never really suited Latin. In the time of Augustus there were proposals for dropping 'q' and 'x' and for adding at least two other letters, a vowel half way between 'u' and 'i' and a semi-consonant for the final 'm' that gets elided. ˧ and μ respectively

I always think the invention of the alphabet an extraordinary stroke of genius. Picture writing is so much more obvious and leads to such a mess. Syllabaries again seem simple and get so fearfully complicated.

I think there are three possible reforms for English.

(i) A modification of the alphabet, in which I see two difficulties
 (a) It rather breaks up the unity of Europe.
 (b) The vowels will go on changing while the signs remain fixed.
(ii) Simplifies spelling with the present alphabet – an interesting job, though the result is hideous to the eye.
(iii) Some possible compromise which I have never worked out. I should base it roughly on keeping words derived from the Latin, the termination 'tion,' etc., for the sake of European unity, while knocking out the 'gh's and other Anglo-Saxon eccentricities.

I am ready for anything, but fully expect that we shall get nothing.

By the way, you may be amused at an article I am sending to you, in which, as you will see, I had supernatural help, or rather acted merely as an amanuensis to lower powers.

I hope all goes well with you. Our kindest regards to you both.

Yours ever,
G.M.

Syllabaries are sets of symbols that represent syllables, usually an optional consonant sound followed by a vowel sound. Murray would have known that Mycenaean Greek used them (*Wikipedia*). I was unable to trace the article that Murray sent to Shaw.

125 / To Gilbert Murray Ayot St Lawrence, Welwyn, Herts.
20th April 1941

[ALS: Bod, SPA]

On 18 April, the German government had broadcast a warning that both Athens and Cairo might soon be bombed as a reprisal against the British bombing raid on Berlin the night before. Churchill at once issued a statement for publication which began: 'In view of the German threats to bomb Athens and Cairo, His Majesty's Government wish it to be understood that if either of these two cities is molested, they will commence a systematic bombing of Rome. Once this has begun, it will continue as convenient till the end of the war.' At the last minute a 'minor' amendment was added at Churchill's insistence: 'The greatest care will be taken not to bomb the Vatican City' (Gilbert, Winston S. Churchill, *1065).* Time *magazine reported on 29 September: 'Last week Axis planes raided Cairo, cultural center of the Moslem world.' Berlin announced that 'an airfield near Cairo was raided, hangars and munitions dumps destroyed. But from Cairo it was reported that bombs had spread wider over the city, killing 39, wounding 93.' This act 'brought Great Britain face to face with a crucial decision: to bomb Rome or not to bomb Rome.' Negotiations followed, Churchill reneged on his threat, and staffers announced that 'only suburbs of Cairo had been bombed.' See Shaw's letter of 24 April below on the futility of bombing cities.*

My dear Murray

How would it do to send the enclosed to the Press from the three of us? Churchill has lost his temper (his most dangerous weakness); and the papers I have read are all utterly demoralized. It is a complete rout, and a triumph for Hitler.

Somebody must say something *cool*, no matter what it is. Besides, I think we are bound to come to the rescue of the Bishop of Chichester.

We three can make an impression that no other combination could, and that we could not make singly.

So far, duplicated to Wells.

On the other affair (orthographical) I will write further and send you a book with a Shaw preface which is in hand. Meanwhile do not suggest as possible a phonetic use of the Sheeny alphabet. Sweet did so, with the result that AGE (3 letters for 2 sounds) became EIDZH (5 letters for 2 sounds). My point is that the cost of even one superfluous letter is colossal.

G. Bernard Shaw

The **Bishop of Chichester** at the time was George Bell (1883–1958); see the following headnote. The **Sheeny alphabet** is the Sheen variety of classical Arabic associated with the Shiites. Henry **Sweet** (1845–1912) was a pioneer in English phonetics. His *History of English Sounds* (1874) was a landmark.

126 / To G. Bernard Shaw Yatscombe, Boar's Hill, Oxford
21st April 1941

[TLS: HRC, SPA]

Pope Pius XII, who reigned from 1939 to 1958, denounced the atrocities of the war in early 1941. The Bishop of Chichester wrote to The Times *on 17 April in support and proposed that the British government pledge to refrain from night bombing 'provided that the German Government will give the same undertaking.*

*If this single limitation were achieved it would at least make a halt in the world's rushing down to ever deeper baseness and confusion' (*Bernard Shaw and H.G. Wells, *192).*

My dear Shaw

I fully agree with you about the bombing of Rome, and I should quite like to back up the Bishop of Chichester about the general wholesale destruction of cities. But, though it is cheek to ask for alterations in your letter, there are some three passages that I should not like to sign. You have a privilege which would not be extended to respectable classical professors.

My objections to the three passages are that they seem to me to raise issues which are not strictly relevant and on which various answers and scored [*sic*] might be made. But would it not be better for you to write a thoroughly Shavian letter to the TIMES and I would gladly back it up? However I should rejoice to sign the letter without those passages, either with you and H G or with you alone, if you thought the omission did not spoil the letter.

I really think that fifty continuous blitzes on London like that of last Wednesday would have a real military effect in breaking people's spirit, but the total result would be, like the bombing of Rome, merely to leave the world poorer and more miserable at the end of the war.

About the alphabet: it would be rather fun to make a statement of the obviously desirable reforms which might be made if men were rational animals: a new alphabet, a duodecimal system, a thirteen month year, &c. The more the merrier.

Yours ever,
G.M.

I have been finding solace in re-reading a lot of your plays.

127 / To Gilbert Murray Ayot St Lawrence, Welwyn, Herts.
24th April 1941

[ALS: Bod, SPA]

Shaw wrote to Murray and Wells urging them to join him in signing a statement to be sent to the press. He vainly 'bullied' Wells on 23 and 24 April. The editor of their correspondence notes that at the bottom of the second letter the word NO is printed and circled, presumably by Wells' (196–7).

The Times *published the statement on 28 April after pruning it severely and replacing the title, 'Cui Bono?,' with 'Bombing of Cities: Military and Non-Military Objectives.' It was signed simply 'Gilbert Murray and G. Bernard Shaw' (Shaw,* Agitations, *321–2). A selection of the text follows.*

'Sir,

'First, we must make clear that though we are about to propose an arrangment with the Axis, it is not in the nature of an armistice or a statement of war aims or anything else that could be interpreted as a symptom of weakening on the part of the Allies. Nor is it a new departure. As a precedent we cite the dealings between our postal authorities and those of the enemy by which at last prisoners of war on both sides are receiving letters from home with certainty and regularity in three weeks after their date. This enormous improvement on the pre-existing state of things could not have been effected without negotiations which, if not precisely cordial, were governed by a reciprocal disposition to listen to reason and make a bargain benefiting the belligerents equally.

'There are methods of warfare which not only cannot produce a decision but are positively beneficial to the side against which they are directed. The bombardment of cities from the air may be one of them. Its conditions are quite unprecedented. Both victory and defeat are impossible, because the vanquished cannot surrender, and the victor must run for home at 300 miles an hour, pursued by fighters at 400 miles an hour. The recent bombardments of Berlin and London, though quite successful as such, have not produced any military result beyond infuriating the unfortunate inhabitants. Some of them have been killed …

'As to one specific course which the War Cabinet has been provoked into taking: to wit, the threat to demolish Rome if Athens or Cairo be attacked from the air, it forces us to ask whether Rome does not belong to the culture of the whole world far more than to the little Italian-speaking group of Benitos and Beppos who at present are its loyal custodians. By destroying it we should be spiting the noses to vex the faces of every educated person in the British Commonwealth and in America, to say nothing of the European mainland. We may smash it for the Italians; but who is to give it back to us? In Rome no one is a stranger and a foreigner: we all feel when we first go there that we are revisiting the scene of a former existence …

'That we should in the same breath indignantly deny that our last raid on Berlin was a reprisal, and announce a major reprisal which must have staggered the historical conscience of the world, shows that our heads are not as clear as they might be on this subject. The more we endeavor to think it out the more we find ourselves driven to the conclusion that whatever may be said from the military

point of view for our treatment of Bremen, Hamburg, and Kiel, there is nothing to be said for the demolition of metropolitan cities as such, and that the Bishop of Chichester's plea for a reconsideration on that policy is entirely justified.'

Right you are. I quite intended those Shavianisms to be cut out, except the warning against the rush to the Vatican, which seems to me a practical point. However, it doesn't matter: out with it.

I am now bullying Wells, who is troublesome as usual, and hope to extort his signature. If not, the letter will go to The Times from us twain.

Admiral of the Fleet, Lord Chatfield, calmly lifted all the part of your Le Neve Foster lecture that dealt with the effect of insularity on the British character when he broadcasted the other night. The Navy is becoming literate and intelligent. Fancy Nelson doing such a thing!

G.B.S.

The original version of the statement is printed in *Bernard Shaw and H.G. Wells*, 193–5. A sample of one of **those Shavianisms** that was deleted: 'If the Germans, instead of dropping tens of thousands of bombs on us, had parachuted thousand of live babies, they would have embarrassed us and reduced our food supplies much more effectively. But as we should retaliate in kind, we should solve our evacuation problem at Germany's expense.' Ernle Chatfield, **Lord Chatfield** (1873–1967) was **Admiral of the Fleet** from 1935–9, then minister for coordination of defence until the position was abolished in April 1940. Sir Clement **Le Neve Foster** (1841–1904) was a distinguished geologist and mineralogist. From 1890 to his death he was professor of mining at the Royal College of Science (*Wikipedia*). **Nelson,** of course, was Admiral Horatio Nelson (1758–1805), hero of the French revolutionary wars and the battle of Trafalgar.

128 / To G. Bernard Shaw

Yatscombe, Boar's Hill, Oxford
28th April 1941

[TLT: BL, SPA]

As usual, Shaw's opinion of a prominent politician, in this case Winston Churchill, differs sharply from that of Murray. In an interview later this year, he said abruptly: 'Mr Churchill and Mr Anthony Eden are for private property and oligarchy. Stalin is for public property and democracy. So am I' ('G.B.S. – If I Were Churchill! Shaw Discusses War Strategy,' Cavalcade *n.s. 3 [1 November]: 1). During the First World War he had shown a grudging admiration for Churchill; in fact, Holroyd found evidence enough to speculate that 'Shaw kept his eye on Churchill as someone who might emerge in Europe as a Shavian-permeated superman' (2, 350; see also 3, 226–8). But by 1924 Shaw diagnosed him as a sad case of 'Russophobia,' picturing Bolshevism as a devouring cancer. 'What does Mr Churchill mean by it? He is not a brainless parasite like many politicians of his class: on the contrary, he is a conspicuously clever man, justly proud of being able to live by his wits … Why then, does he, the moment Socialism or Russia is mentioned, lose his head, see scarlet, and become the most ridiculous tosh-merchant of his class in Europe?' With a Labour Party government in power for the first time, and Churchill in its Cabinet, Shaw was responding to Churchill's attack on socialism as a 'fraud,' unable to accept that utopian dreams of a socialist state were impossible because of man's 'selfishness, self-seeking, self-interest,' whereas capitalism rewards free enterprise, 'the right of the individual to make the best for himself, or, within limits, the worst of himself, if he chooses' ('The Socialist Fraud: Bernard Shaw Replies to Winston Churchill,'* Sunday Chronicle, *13 April 1924, 1: 5–6, 2: 4–5; repr. as 'A Debate on the Principles of Socialism: Winston Churchill vs. George Bernard Shaw' in the* New York Herald Tribune, *11 May, 2, 1: 3–6, 5: 2–7; Laurence,* Bibliography, *2, 699; partly quoted in Weintraub,* Shaw's People, *222–3)*.

My dear Shaw

Good. I was pleased to see the letter over two names, tho' the Roman alphabet added to its other faults that of putting first the signatory who did not write the letter. I imagine that now, with the Germans established in Athens, the Parthenon will be safe from bombing. As to Rome, Hitler would not care but Musso would, I suspect, actually like to see Rome destroyed if he was destroyed. It would do something to satisfy his pride. In the Abyssinian crisis he said 'If I fall Europe shall fall with me' or something like.

Winston is a very remarkable man. He always leaves the impression of saying just what he wants to say, and not what the Whips and his private secretaries have said was suitable. Most politicians put up a sort of veil between themselves and the ordinary man, but Winston with all his eloquence and large vocabulary talks so that anyone can understand, and never pretends to be too good for this world. I am continuing my dramatic studies with much enjoyment and profit.

Yours ever,
G.M.

German troops had invaded Greece on 6 April.

129 / To G. Bernard Shaw Yatscombe, Boar's Hill, Oxford
16th May 1941

[TLS: BL, SPA]

The Shaw / Gabriel Pascal film version of Major Barbara *had premiered on 7 April after delays caused by wrangling about the text and coping with the results of German bombing. Shooting was scheduled for ten weeks, but lasted for six months; running time should have been 137 minutes, but was reduced to 121 for the British premiere and 115 for the American. In both countries it was a success, although minimally so in contrast to the film of* Pygmalion.

*Shaw sensed the need for a new opening sequence, and it bears directly on the play's relation to Murray: he introduces Cusins as a lecturer for a 'University Extension Open Air Meeting' sponsored by the Workers' Education Association. The placard reads 'Five Stages of Greek Religion' by the 'Regius Professor of Greek in the University of Oxford.' His address is interrupted by a Salvation Army band, which is building up to the main event: a speech by 'Major Barbara,' after which Cusins confronts her with the revelation that he is 'hopelessly and for ever' in love with her (*Collected Screenplays, *281–2).*

My dear Shaw

I have had one or two sympathetic letters and only one abusive. However, none seems particularly original excepting the enclosed. I like the idea of a solidly mined atmosphere which will explode when anyone travels through it. Do you remember Wilkes' remark, 'I hope to God, Sir, you don't take me for a Wilkesite.'?

I have been surprised, however, at the number of people who confided in rather a low voice their agreement with our letter. I suspect at the end of the war there will be a tremendous demand from the ordinary civil population of Europe for the abolition of bombing. Bob Cecil thinks it will be so strong as to be decisive, but I rather expect it will be baffled by the intense desire of the victorious nations to be secure against another attack.

I have not had a chance of seeing 'Major Barbara' as a film yet, but Rose Macauley told me it was splendid. I am trying to write a thing on the historical influence of Greek drama. I think the Classical stuff, both tragedy and comedy, passed through Menander and the New Comedy. It was they who really invented the modern play.

Yours ever,
G.M.

John **Wilkes** (1725–97) was an English radical politician and, in the 1780s, the power behind the Supporters of the Bill of Rights, or 'Wilkesite movement.' A notorious rake as well as activist, he bounced in and out of Parliament and prison, then suddenly became conservative, even ordering London soldiers to fire on protesting mobs during the 'Gordon Riots' in 1780. Whether he said it or not, he was indeed no longer a Wilkesite (Cash, *John Wilkes*, 362–3). [Emilie] **Rose Macauley** (1881–1958) was a prolific writer of fiction and non-fiction. She had worked in the British Propaganda Bureau during the First World War, so that she undoubtedly had known Murray for a long time. Wilson notes that from the mid-1930s on they exchanged many letters.

130 / To G. Bernard Shaw Yatscombe, Boar's Hill, Oxford
26th July 1941

[TLS: HRC via Guelph, SPA]

Pascal's transformation of the last act of Major Barbara *was the focus of Shaw's criticism of the film. In a letter written some time in July to the playwright Ronald Gow (1897–1993), husband of the actress who portrayed Barbara, Wendy Hiller, he inadvertently railed at him for doing things that Pascal had actually done: he 'quite disregarded building up the interest to the climaxes of the play, cutting it up into little pieces like a jig saw puzzle, but assuming that it did not matter in what order you put them together again' (CL 4, 567). Dukore's perceptive introduction to the* Collected Screenplays *generalizes: 'Pascal's rearrangement of the scenes in Undershaft's factory is dramatically illogical and prevents* Major Barbara *from being the superior film it could have been' (116). He offers a number of substantiating points, among them: 'Bill [Walker's] return at the end – happy, clean-shaven, and well employed – is contrived, trite, and unconvincing' (114); Undershaft's speech on why poverty is a crime is omitted (116); and Cusins 'does not tell Barbara why he will join her father's firm or that he intends to give the people power … to work for the common good' (117). A review in* The New Statesman *stated bluntly that Pascal made 'drastic cuts in Mr. Shaw's argument,' which 'rather make hay of the play's last act' (117). See also Shaw's response to the following letter.*

On 31 May and 7 June Shaw had published a two-part article in The New Statesman *entitled 'What Price Stalin?,' the primary contention of which was that Hitler would never dare to attack Russia. But the attack came on 22 June against minimal resistance. He admitted his error in a follow-up of 5 July: 'Two Views on Russia and the War: My Mistake.' In a letter from Blanche Patch which conveyed this news to Barry Jackson, she noted that Shaw says 'he never makes mistakes and has now lost prestige. I ventured to say that I could recall other mistakes, but he wouldnt have it.' In the article itself Shaw casually comments: 'I was wrong. I am always making mistakes by imagining that other people are as clever as I am myself'* (Bernard Shaw and Barry Jackson, *123).*

My dear Shaw

I took Mary to the film of 'Major Barbara' yesterday and was completely bowled over by the beauty and magnificence of all the main part. Mary rebelled violently against the end, and I think it is probably true that in the film you do not succeed in making clear what has happened to the young people or what is meant by 'the faith of an armourer.' But it is years since I have been so moved and thrilled by anything, up to that tragic scene on the wharf with the sign of Bodger's Whiskey, where Barbara throws her hat into the water. The new Cusens is not as like me as Barker was, but you seem to have the gift of prophecy in one incident. Once when lunching with Maisky I saw a decanter full of what I took to be water, and poured out some and began to drink, and found it was vodka. However, I stopped before it had the fatal effect that it had on Cusens.

I have been re-reading the fragmentary papyri of Menander and trying to think out the stage directions and tones of voices. It is extraordinary how mouvementé and full of little theatrical tricks he is compared with the tragedians.

Our warmest remembrances to Charlotte.

Yours ever,
G.M.

On **Maisky**, see Letter 112.

131 / To Gilbert Murray Ayot St Lawrence, Welwyn, Herts.
5th September 1941

[TLS: CL 4 (Guelph has a copy of the original shorthand)]

In 1937 Professor Richard Albert Wilson (1874–1949) of the University of Saskatchewan had published a small book with a ponderous title: The Birth of Language: Its Place in World Evolution and Its Structure in Relation to Space and Time. *With the simplified title that Shaw mentions – and with his own preface – it became a classroom classic, selling more than 100,000 copies. Shaw had described the book in a letter of 17 February to Beatrice Webb as 'up to date and emancipated from the damnably post-Darwinian Materialism cum Determinism'* (Bernard Shaw and the Webbs, *254). Shaw's long preface (repr. in CPr, 3, 408–28) reviews the evolution controversy, then embarks on a detailed argument for spelling reform based on the costs that would be reduced by using a phonetic alphabet.*

My dear Murray

Your letter of the 26th July moved me to go to St Albans at the sacrifice of some scarce petrol to see the Barbara film. These provincial picture houses believe that they must have at every performance two films and the news reel. To make room for this they cut the last third of the film all to pieces, and left Barbara's and Undershaft's position so hopelessly confused that I am inundated with letters accusing me of making Barbara sell out, and glorifying a scoundrelly war profiteer. You may have seen the film uncut. If so, there was nothing else in the program except the news reel. If there was another film then Barbara was cut.

As I write plays as they come to me, by inspiration and not by conscious logic, I am as likely as anyone else to be mistaken about their morals. It seems to me that what Barbara finds out is that the ancient Greek (whoever he was) who said 'First make sure of an income and then practise virtue' was rightly preaching natural morality. Clearly the conversions of Snobby Price and Rummy Mitchens by 'the bribe of bread' were not worth the few pence they cost. It was Barbara's business to get rich with Cusins while he fed the poor with honestly earned wages, and then, when their bellies were full, see what she could do with their souls, if she still thought herself qualified for that impertinence.

Thatt (as Bridges spells it), and the rule that until you have abolished poverty you have done and can do nothing but tinker with the wreckage, is what comes out of the play for me.

The enclosed book, originally called The Birth of Language, seemed to me worth boosting with a preface and a revised title to secure a cheap edition here. I grow more and more intolerant of official religion as I grow older, and also more convinced that a negative attitude towards it is no use. People rightly object to having their minds just emptied, no matter how poisonous the contents are. Better die of drinking brandy than of thirst. The only thing we have to fill up with is Creative Evolution; and Professor Wilson is strong and positive on that point.

The preface is nothing but an expansion of my Spelling Reform letter to The Times. I calculate that I have lost four years of my productive life writing superfluous letters. I could have written at least three good plays in four years.

Old Tito Pagliardini converted me many years ago to duodecimals. That also has an overwhelming economic side that has never been urged. The defeat of the French is probably due to their counting their money in three ha'penny francs and writing the results in decimals. An American named Terry has published a table of duodecimal logarithms. He ought to get a Nobel Prize for it.

G. Bernard Shaw

Almroth Wright said the other day that translations are contemptible, as nobody could possibly quote them. I cited the English Bible and your version of Euripides to confute him. He said you were the original poet masquerading as Euripides. He declared that he could quote you by pages, but that he had compared some of the finest of those pages with the alleged originals without discovering the faintest resemblance. Not being a Greek scholar I could not contradict him. I did not want to, in fact.

It was Barbara's business to get rich with Cusins while he fed the poor with honestly earned wages seems to imply a crucial factor that the text of the play does not. The text strongly implies that Cusins, having been locked into the Undershaft mould, will feed only his employees, poor or not, but not 'the poor' in general. **Thatt**: In Robert **Bridges**'s popular poem 'The Testament of Beauty' (1929), the deliberate misspelling occurs twice in a passage following a statement which would have alerted Shaw: 'This Individualism is man's true Socialism.' 'This is thatt excelent way whereon if we wil walk / all things shall be added unto us – thatt Love which inspired / the wayward Visionary in his doctrinal ode / to the three christian Graces.'

The oft-quoted Greek proverb that Shaw recalls is usually stated as 'First secure an independent income, then practise virtue.' In his preface to *Pygmalion*, Shaw refers to **Tito Pagliardini** (1817–1895) as a notable 'phonetic veteran' (CP 4, 659). The '**duodecimals**' which he introduced to Shaw is a system for simplifying numbers, thus saving time, space, and cost. George Skelton **Terry** published *Duodecimal Arithmetic* in 1938. In 'Decimal Systems Early and Late' (*Osiris* 9 [1950]: 581–601), George Sarton says that 'In recent years ... Terry has been the main protagonist of the duodecimal system,' but he adds: 'one wonders what [his book's] use could possibly be' (596). For **Almroth Wright** see the headnote to Letter 75.

132 / To G. Bernard Shaw Yatscombe, Boar's Hill, Oxford
1st October 1941

[TLS: BL, SPA]

Sir Isaac Pitman (1813–1897) published Stenographic Soundhand *(later entitled* Pitman's Shorthand Instructor*) for the first time in 1837. A system of phonetic shorthand for the English language based upon Samuel Taylor's, it was for a century the most widely used handbook of its kind. His grandson, James Pitman (1901–85), chaired his family's businesses and invented the* Initial Teaching Alphabet *for use in secondary schools. Shaw had begun using Pitman's shorthand in his teens, and in 1882 decided it was the most practical alternative among the options he had tried, all unsatisfactory to some degree. But in a letter of 3 January 1905 to Archibald Henderson he called Pitman's 'probably the worst system of shorthand ever invented' (Holroyd 1, 97). In contrast, Murray declares a 'romantic attachment' to it below.*

My dear Shaw

Many thanks for sending me 'The Miraculous Birth of Language.' I think he really makes his point about the enormous jump involved, and the book set me thinking on lines suggested by Sherrington's Gifford Lectures called 'Man as he appears to himself' or something of that sort – a really remarkable and original book. A great deal of human conduct, both social and individual, goes on simple biological lines, but there is no doubt, I think, that in what some call 'higher' and what some call 'ideal' or 'religious,' efforts, we seem to get outside the proper biological motives. On the one hand, we become absurd and talk nonsense; on the other, we feel that something in the nonsense is immensely valuable to us. What I would suggest is a question whether this does not mean the groping out of the genus homo towards some higher species which he may attain in a million years or so, if he hurries up. Probably before then he will have a duodecimal system and a handsome alphabet actually representing his pronunciation or a standard form of it.

I am sorry you do not like Pitman. I have a romantic attachment for it. It forms such pretty shapes. Think of the word 'mormon' for instance, or 'merman' for that matter. Of course the difference between light and heavy strokes is very awkward. But old Pitman himself was everything that a man should be – teetotaller, vegetarian, capitalist, radical, key man of business with whiskers. Tears of admiration come to my eyes when

I think of him. And I like his grandson, who is now an ardent spelling reformer and a governor of the Bank of England.

Something will have to be done about English spelling, but certainly the S.S.S. system is not likely to be adopted. I think sometimes that one could make a compromise by reforming the Anglo-Saxon words (through, bough, rough and light, etc.) and leaving the Latin terminations, such as 'tion,' on the ground that they are so widespread over Europe.

Does a man called Foley write to you about bombing? I think clearly the time has passed when one could check it, though I wonder whether we are not taking on a form of warfare in which the Germans have an overwhelming advantage, viz. that they can get at London in about forty miles, whereas it takes us three or four hundred to get at their vital points.

Did I tell you I was reading the Fragments of Menander a good deal? He seems to me to have been immensely important in the history of drama.

Yours ever,
Gilbert Murray

Sir Charles Scott **Sherrington** (1857–1952) published *Man on His Nature* in 1940, developed from his series of **Gifford Lectures** in 1937–8. That prestigious series, delivered at four British universities, was instituted in 1888 by the Scottish judge Adam, Lord Gifford (1820–87) to 'promote and diffuse the study of Natural Theology' – i.e., theology supported by science and not dependent on the miraculous (*Wikipedia*).

133 / To G. Bernard Shaw Yatscombe, Boar's Hill, Oxford
13th January 1942

[TLT: ECL (not in BL)]

My dear Shaw

I wonder if you have the time to read a play half by Menander and half by me, and tell me whether it's at all interesting. The job of filling in the gaps has certainly been amusing, but it's difficult to judge of the result. If you think it's any good, I might see whether the Old Vic was inclined to act it.

I like your argument about the people who pay 39 / 6d. in the £.

Yours ever

The **Menander** play would be his translation of *Epitrepontes* as *The Arbitration*, which he published in 1945.

134 / To Gilbert Murray

Ayot St Lawrence, Welwyn, Herts.
23rd January 1942

[TLS: Bod, SPA]

My dear Murray

It is such an appalling come-down from Aristophanes to Menander, and so impossible to put him in the same street with Euripides and the two other great Greeks that his admission to your collection revolts me. Cropped Hair (Rape of the Locks) might very well be placed on record in a magazine article or a volume of Learned Society Transactions. It might even be printed as an appendix in your First Folio; but except in some such casual way it is an intruder to be kicked out from the glorious company of the apostles and the goodly fellowship of the prophets.

I believe that when the drama of this time fades into the distance and only the peaks are seen, your resurrection of the great four will stand out alone in a waste of dust and ashes. Already they are quite outside and above everything that the Vic-Georgic age has produced. Menander, even with your help, is not presentable among them.

Molière was enormously better at the same job.

However, a performance is another matter. It would be quite lively on the stage. One of the repertories might be tempted if the old Vic failed. Nugent Monck in Norwich will do anything that nobody else will do. The Birmingham Rep. may take a fancy to anything unexpected.

Half way down the last page I have made an obvious suggestion. The proverb runs 'Nothing for nothing; and damned little for a halfpenny.' Why not use it?

Is Lady Mary well and vigorous? Charlotte isnt; but is recovering marvellously from two bad years of lumbago. We have not been in London since 1940.

I got £29,000 without lifting a finger from the Pygmalion film, and have consequently had to pay the Government £50,000 in two years. Happily Barbara has flopped in America and must be boosted into solvency there. It owes me enough to ruin me utterly; so I heroically refuse all royalties until it has repaid its monstrous cost. I hope you are poor enough to be able to live on your income. Thirtynine shillings in the pound has done for me.

But there is hope. Have you noticed that war always begins when capital falls to 2½% and stops when it rises again to 5?

Always yours,
G. Bernard Shaw

Jean-Baptiste Poquelin **Molière** (1622–73) was an early master of comedy. I have found no origin for the **proverb** Shaw cites, and Eric Partridge's *A Dictionary of Catch Phrases* states 'orig. by George Bernard Shaw,' but adds possible earlier sources. A 1947 article in an Irish journal repeats it, using 'damn' rather than 'damned.' For the **Birmingham Rep**ertory Theatre, see Letter 98; it was still being directed by Barry Jackson.

135 / To G. Bernard Shaw Yatscombe, Boar's Hill, Oxford
13th October 1942

[TLT: BL, SPA]

My dear Shaw

I was so pleased to meet you in the columns of The Times. As a matter of fact I nearly telegraphed to you to propose a joint letter, and then thought that might cause delays and it was best to get something off to The Times at once.

How are you and Charlotte keeping? The process of getting old is rather pleasant in its early stages, but later on one begins to feel the truth of Wordsworth's remarks about 'the prodigal's favourite' ending up as a 'miser's pensioner,' and the perpetual burden of the war does not make it easier. But you have a fine life to look back upon.

Unwin has been a preposterous time in producing 'The Rape of the Locks', but tells me it will be out on the 22nd.

Yours ever,
G.M.

On this day Shaw had published a brief letter to the editor in ***The Times*** 5:5, 'Reprisals: German and British Methods.' The first and last sentences sum it up: 'The Führer's resort to the Mosaic law and our announcement of reprisals in kind raises several questions … As the retaliatory process is self-perpetuating how is it to be stopped before the human race is exterminated?' (*Letters of Bernard Shaw to* The Times, 236). On 5 September Shaw had reported to Jackson: '**Charlotte** has visions like St Joan, and is gravely ill' (*Bernard Shaw and Barry Jackson*, 135). The quotations from William **Wordsworth** (1770–1850) are from 'The Small Celandine: There Is a Flower'; the lines are 'To be a **Prodigal's favourite**, – then, worse truth, / A **Miser's Pensioner,** – behold our lot!'

136 / To G. Bernard Shaw Yatscombe, Boar's Hill, Oxford
28th September 1943

[TLT; postscript TLS: BL, SPA]

Shaw had written a long letter to Lady Mary Murray on 21 September about Charlotte's death on the 12th. He gives a full account of her magical change and blessed relief on the 10th, and her 'classically beautiful' appearance six hours after her death. After saying 'All's well that ends well,' he adds: 'Some months ago I said to her one day "Why do we see so little of Gilbert Murray? Have you turned against him?" If he had heard how vehemently she repudiated this suspicion he would have been amply assured of her high regard for him. What made me ask was that she had lost her interest in another famous man; and when I asked her why, she said "I have not turned against him; but he is such *an infernal liar!"' (CL 4, 679–80). This was one of her most intimate friends, T.E. Lawrence ('Lawrence of Arabia,' 1888–1935). In early 1935 Charlotte was sick and refused to see him. Shaw asked her if there had been a quarrel, but Charlotte replied 'No unpleasantness. But he is such an INFERNAL liar' (Weintraub,* Private Shaw and Public Shaw, *269).*

My dear Shaw

Mary and I were very much touched and interested by your letter. It was kind of you to write so fully. When one gets well on in the seventies the thought of death becomes familiar and not in itself repellent, but sometimes one feels nervous about the circumstances. 'Shall I somehow disgrace myself? Shall I get intolerably cross and suspicious, or become a lingering burden and nuisance to everyone?'

I find I live contentedly from day to day, not looking forward much because there is not much to hope or fear. I see how old people become Conservative; you keep on your old opinions and habits and they grow out of date. Mary, for instance, is extreme Left in politics and early Victorian in her views of decorum and language. It is depressing how one's friends die, and how often one cannot remember who is alive and who dead.

Oddly enough, I think one of the things that has diminished our happiness a good deal is the conversion of Rosalind to extreme Catholicism and Stephen to Communism. It embarrasses M a good deal. She is a very loyal mother, and will not allow a word to be said against either -ism, which hampers intercourse with both.

I rather hope I shall die first, as I shall be more helpless alone than she will. She is full of energy but in poor health. I would get out of this house and bring her to London were it not that she is so surrounded by friends here – all the tradesmen, all the refugees, all our neighbours. She would miss them dreadfully if she went away. Meantime I potter on cheerfully with Greek and L of N. Forgive this garrulous unburdening. It is your fault. By the way, I wish there were a better Life of you. You told Hesketh Pearson all the little things you could think of to your discredit, and he had not the force of mind or imagination to bring out your greatness. No doubt someone will some day.

Yours ever, with love from both of us.
G.M.

PS I was so much living in the past that I addressed this letter to 10 Adelphi Terrace! Hence delays.

Hesketh Pearson's *G.B.S.: A Full-Length Portrait* had been published the previous year. But Archibald Henderson's second biography of Shaw, *Bernard Shaw: Playboy and Prophet*, which had come out in 1932, was much fuller and more authoritative. (His final one, *George Bernard Shaw: Man of the Century*, would be published in 1956.)

137 / To G. Bernard Shaw

Yatscombe, Boar's Hill, Oxford
14th February 1944

[TLS: BL, SPA]

On 10 February 1944 Shaw had written to Lady Mary announcing that he had reacted to his discovery that Gilbert agrees with him on spelling reform by willing all his residual estate to that cause. He commented: 'The difficulty in giving effect to my alphabetic bequest is that though the diagnostic of my intention is Labor Saving: that is, purely economic, and not Spelling reform nor Basic English nor a universal artificial auxiliary language … , and as my executor the Public Ttrustee cannot undertake the job, who can?' (Bod).

Within two weeks of the ensuing letter, Shaw – still countering anti-Nazi commentary with anti-British – published a letter in The Times *that lambasted officials for imprisoning Mohandas [Karamchand] Gandhi (1869–1948) for leading protests of 'passive resistance' to gain independence for India. Shaw calls it 'the stupidest blunder the Government has let itself be landed in by its right wing of incurable diehards. It and the unpardonable flogging business associated with it has wiped out our moral case against Hitler' (27 February, in* The Letters of Bernard Shaw to *The Times, 304).*

My dear G.B.S.

It was a pleasure to us both to hear from you. Indeed I had been thinking of sending you another Menander play which Casson thinks not much good, but a Christian spirit held me back.

About your new alphabet, I think the great and indeed insuperable difficulty lies in finding any committee that can be trusted, first, to understand what you want and next, to carry out anything like your wishes. The business men would make an awful mess of it, and the savants, as you justly say, would take some quite different view of their own.

I think the Latin (or Phoenician) alphabet is too firmly established to dislodge. It has possession of all Europe and America, the Turks have taken it over, the Japs are doing so and some parts of India. And where it fails in phonetic precision there is the Phonetic alphabet based upon it.

On the whole I come down to two requirements: a reform of English spelling and a Short-hand that can be read. For the first I should not be afraid of some diacritical marks – which can always be left out if you like – but I think the first need is a more moderate scheme than the Archer-Rippman. Roughly speaking, I should get rid of the GHs but leave the –TIONs, because they are consistent and Gemeineuropaeisch.

I agree that a legible Short-hand is badly needed. Cicero had to use one; also Pepys. I dont know about Voltaire. I use Pitman a good deal for things I have to re-read myself. You write so well you can probably manage the thick and thin strokes, the straight and curved &c. My writing is now shaky. I suspect one ought to make larger letters and, as you say, avoid the reporter's abbreviations. In course of time one might hope that the Short-hand, if really good, might supercede the Latin long-hand.

To change the subject, I am sure you are right about keeping the 'Vicar of Bray' people. I find that the Nazis actually dismissed nearly half the German school teachers. That means, half were ready to lose their jobs rather than teach what they didn't approve – a fine record; of those who complied most probably did so in order not to be made destitute. I was speaking the other day to an AMGOT Education Officer, an American professor. He had dismissed the actual Fascist officials, but said it was almost impossible among the Professors to sift out the real Fascists from those who merely wanted to be let alone and not get into trouble. He mostly contented himself with simply warning them.

Yours ever,
G.M.

The **Menander play** that Murray was working on was *The Arbitration* (*Epitrepontes*), which he published in 1945. **Lewis Casson** was an English actor and director involved in plays by both Shaw and Murray. The **Archer-Rippman** scheme of simplified spelling using phonetic principles is described in a handbook they wrote for the Simplified Spelling Society in 1911, a revision of which was still available in 2007. Walter Rippmann (1869–?) was listed as the principal author; Archer was the secretary of the society. **Gemeineuropaeisch** in this context would be common or standard European. Samuel **Pepys** (1633–1703) was a British politician best known for his diaries. **The 'Vicar of Bray' people** evokes an anonymous song about the spiritually flexible Vicar of Bray, Berkshire, who managed to keep his position by adapting his religious beliefs to the ever-changing political climate during the tumultuous sixty-seven years from the reign of Charles II to the death of George I. For the text of the song, see http://ingeb.org/songs/ingoodki.html. The opening line is: 'In good King Charles's golden days.' It was **Nazi** policy to dismiss **school teachers** and **Professors** who resisted rigid guidelines for indoctrinating students so that they would aspire to Aryan values and strength and despise other cultures, especially Jewish. **AMGOT**, the Allied Military Government for Occupied Territories, refers to the kind of military rule administered by Allied forces during and after the Second World War within occupied European territories. Murray seems to be referring to the way German teachers who were dismissed or had escaped were handled.

138 / To Gilbert Murray

Ayot St Lawrence, Welwyn, Herts.
21st June 1944

[TLS: SPA]

Send the ⅛87('4*+ thing, by all means.

May I know what the diagnosis is in case my scrappy knowledge of the latest treatments and yogas could suggest anything.

The patient sounded all right yesterday on the Brainless Trust.

G.B.S.

Line one, with its lightly veiled expletive, refers to the Menander play that Murray mentions above. The **Brainless Trust** is Shaw's joke for the 'Brains Trust,' a BBC series which, for example, had featured Wells, Max Beerbohm, and Sidney Webb on 21 May 1943 (Conolly, *Bernard Shaw and the BBC*, 113; Wilson, 397). The presumed **patient**, Murray, delivered a lecture on Tennyson's 'Ulysses' on 19 June. Since many programs were repeated, and Murray's were extremely popular, this one might well have been repeated on **'yesterday,'** the 20th. In the next letter Murray seems to mean that participating in the program is good exercise for his brain.

139 / To G. Bernard Shaw

Yatscombe, Boar's Hill, Oxford
24th June 1944

[TLS: BL, SPA]

My dear Shaw

Many thanks for reading the thing. It is going in a separate envelope, with an introduction which must be rewritten and without some Notes which you will not need.

I think part of the fun is seeing some of the oldest and stalest of stage dodges at a time when they were lively and fresh; another part is the apparent freedom with which the playwright moves though you know he is really dancing in fetters – bound by his ritual.

My brain symptoms are pretty serious. I nearly wrote your address as 'Lawrence St Eyot'; I started eating my soup with a fork; and I go to the Brains Trust. Yogi seems called for. Talking of which, I received the other day two magnificent volumes of Poetry by Arabindo [*sic*] Ghose, and on inquiry find that: he got a first at Cambridge; published a book of verse (good) together with Binyon; came out second in the India Civil Exam but was ploughed (probably quite unjustly) on the riding test; became a Nationalist agitator; accused of terrorism; retired to French territory; discovered that he was the god Siva and a perfectly respectable French lady the goddess Kali; they now live in a gorgeous seclusion, but receive the faithful on golden thrones three times a year. What times we live in!

Yours ever,
G.M.

Sri **Aurobindo Ghosh** (1872–1950) was the first Indian poet to publish most of his works in the English language. He was a leader in the Indian independence movement and a prominent religious theorist, developing concepts of the evolution of the spirit to its ultimate in 'Supermind.' His *Collected Poems and Plays* were published in 1942. Laurence **Binyon** became known for his poems about the First World War.

140 / To Gilbert Murray

Ayot St Lawrence, Welwyn, Herts.
4th July 1944

[TLS: CL 4]

My dear Murray

It is a great relief to learn that nothing is the matter with you except the troubles of the incipient Struldbrug. I, ten and a half years farther on the declivity, exceed you in blunders and forgetfulness by the square of that distance. Ibsen at last forgot how to write, and spent hours making pothooks and hangers in vain efforts to learn over again. I shall come to that presently; but I am a little consoled by discovering that though my childish acquirements are perishing, my very latest developments are still young.

Now as to Les Plaideurs (Racine's title, wasnt it?). It is enormously better than The Rape, just as Twelfth Night is better than The Comedy of Errors, Menander being more accomplished in his maturity than he was as a beginner. It is almost a XIX century Parisian 'well made' play. The only difference is that in Scribe and Sardou the five acts have been compressed into three, the unity of place has been discarded, and the long lost babes have been sidetracked by adulteries and duels. But the interest is not technical except for playwrights: it is important as evidence that bourgeois society is just what it was in 320 B C: it makes me feel as I did 45 years ago, when Grant Allen read to me a page of history and challenged me to guess who the hero was. I said 'Obviously Napoleon III.' It was not Badinguet: it was Pisistratus. So much for Progress!

After reading a few pages of your translation I automatically began scrawling alternative scansions all over it as if it were my own, but in pencil so that you can rub them out. I am very sensitive to any flaw in blank verse: I really have Shakespear's ear. For some reason or other people who have much Latin and more Greek always take contemptuous liberties with blank verse as if they did not matter in so easy a metre. But they do matter, because the metre is so easy and elastic that on the very slightest trifling with it it ceases to be verse at all. Take these lines from Hamlet

GHOST. The serpent that did sting thy father's life
Now wears his crown.
HAMLET, Oh, my prophetic soul!
My uncle!

Can you imagine Shakespear writing

GHOST. The serpent that did sting thy father's life
Now wears his crown and weds his wife
HAMLET, Oh my!
Prophetic soul: my uncle!

Yet you do this and similar things unblushingly. To end a line with a possessive pronoun and begin the next with its object is a literary crime. It is not verse; and its intrusion into verse is unbearably unpleasant. Shakespear, who exhausted the possibilities of blank verse, never did it. Take another trick. In the Four Years War the American soldiers improvised a marching song which began

Mister
McKinlay
he aint done
no wrong

He went down
to Buffalo
way Michigan
along

in the last verse this became

Cholgosh
They took him
and puthiminthėėlec-
tric chair

They shocked him
so hard that
they shocked off all
his hair

Now a very sparing use of this verbal ellipse is tolerable in blank verse. Beethoven in a bar of 16 semiquavers sometimes got in an extra one or two by grouping 3 as 2 or 7 as 5; but the effect is always musical and is never frequent. But you do it again and again in successive lines, though to do it twice in succession makes stumbling prose of the passage. You not only torture the line: you torture me.

You will now understand my scrawls. They are mostly attempts to get a caesura in the right place. Forgive them if you can.

What Greek grammar would you recommend to a beginner in that language? Is there such a thing as a good one? Schoolbooks are the worst books in the world: they make education a hated torment.

I am greatly pleased with Eisenhower's military disregard of Churchill's unconditional surrender slogan in his offer of a detailed list of conditions to the German soldiers.

My Whitehall flat has been blasted again, this time by a Robot. A window in my study was shivered into smithereens, my front door blown in, the grandfather clock prostrated, one of Charlotte's Tang horses shattered, and – *comble de malheur!* – Strobl's bust of Lady Astor done in.

Our devastation of Europe is almost beyond endurance. And they call it a Savings Campaign!

My book is printed, and will be published presently if the binders can get the necessary labor.

G. Bernard Shaw

PS I could not in any passage draw the line between Menander and Murray. The translation is perfectly homogeneous. It would act quite well.

In Swift's *Gulliver's Travels,* the term **struldbrug** is given to humans in the nation of Luggnagg who are born seemingly normal, but are in fact immortal. Although they do not die, they do continue aging, thus dramatizing the anguish of immortality without eternal youth. **Ibsen**'s final years were marked by strokes in 1900 and small apoplectic fits beginning in 1900. The latter paralysed his right side including his face, which made writing difficult and left his speech slurred. He wrote his last word on 14 February 1904, and survived until 23 May 1906. Edmund Gosse, his earliest English biographer, states in chapter 8 of *Henrik Ibsen* (Gutenberg ebook edition, unpaged) that Ibsen, 'troubled by aphasia,' sat at the table where he 'wrote the works of his maturity, ... persistently learning and forgetting the alphabet. "Look! he said, ..." pointing to his mournful **pothooks**, "See what I am doing! I am sitting here and learning my letters – my *letters*! I who was once a Writer!" Shaw's use of this detail, in conjunction with **hangers**, might have derived from a long-enduring metaphor for loss of dexterity in forming letters. In *Cashel Byron's Profession* Byron comments that in his childhood, 'as to writing, I couldn't make **pothooks and hangers** respectably' (195). And in a letter composed when he was 92, Shaw noted that he had to type letters 'because I write like a child making pothooks and hangers, very slowly' (CL 4, 820).

Shaw is apparently likening the 1668 play ***Les Plaideurs*** (*The Litigants* or *Arbiters*) by Jean **Racine** (1639–99) to the play he had worked on, Menander's *The Arbitration.* Eugène **Scribe** (1791–1861), with Victorien Sardou, were the most prominent of the French practitioners of the 'well-made play.' **Grant Allen** (1848–99) was a journalist, author of several books, and early neighbour of Shaw, plus an irresponsible Fabian (see Shaw's admonishing letter of 6 July 1894 in CL 1, 449). **Badinguet** was Napoleon III's surname. **Pisistratus** (dates unknown) was a 6th-century BC Athenian ruler who behaved as a tyrant during his three periods in power. Shaw's quotation from **Hamlet** is from act 1, scene 5. The **marching song** that Shaw recites exists in several versions, most dating from before 1915. He recalls the one entitled 'Mr. McKinley.' The relevant lines are: 'Mister McKinley he ain't done no wrong; / He went down to Buffalo, way Michigan along ... / Sholgosh, they took him and put him in the electric chair, / and shocked him so hard that they shocked off all his hair ...' William **McKinley** (1843–1901), 25th president of the United States, was shot by the Polish anarchist Leon **Czolgosz** (1873–1901).

In 1944 Dwight D. **Eisenhower** (1890–1969) was Supreme Commander of the Allied Forces in Europe. Shaw had encouraged Nancy Astor to engage Sigmund de **Strobl** (1884–1975) to do a **bust** of her in May 1933. It was finished in June. Shaw wanted it to be housed in a place of honour, and kept it in his Whitehall flat. He refrained from telling her that the bust was '**done in**' until it was repaired, and it was finally accepted by the House of Commons in honour of her having been the first elected woman to take a seat in the House. See *Bernard Shaw and Nancy Astor*, letters 46, 47, 162, 165, and 225–8.

141 / To G. Bernard Shaw

Yatscombe, Boar's Hill, Oxford
7th July 1944

[TLS: BL, SPA]

Shaw describes at length the 'new alphabet' that Murray refers to in a public letter about the terms of his will appended to 'The Author as Manual Laborer,' a summer 1944 article published in The Author (Shaw on Language, *78–86), which Murray must have seen by this time. Shaw urges that a committee be established to deal with his appeal for a 'new British alphabet' which would save writers and transcribers from unnecessary manual labour and thus reap huge economic benefits.*

My dear Shaw

Many thanks. It was kind of you to read the pseudo-Menander through, and I am very glad that you find it much better than the Rape. Casson, for some reason, thought it less interesting. It is, as you say, curiously like a nineteenth century French comedy. Among other things, I think the nineteenth century French and the third century B.C. Greeks had the same feeling towards the injustices of society. They understood them and were sorry for them, but knew there was nothing particular to be done about it!

I am much interested and pleased by your metrical comments. I really love correct metre, and my irregularities were only attempts to be conversational. I am accepting your suggestions for keeping the pause at the end of the line, but mostly leaving things inside the line which look irregular but seem to me to be phonetically correct.

As to Greek Grammars, it depends on the beginner. I rather like Sonnenschein's in the Comparative Grammar series, but there is an amusing little book called 'Eulalie, ou le Grec sans Larmes' which Salomon Reinach wrote for a granddaughter or something. I have tried it on granddaughters with moderate success, and could send you a copy if you liked.

I am sorry about your Whitehall flat. Rosalind's bedroom has been rather smashed up, but the rest of her flat not hurt. Her son, Lawrence ought to have been in the Guards' Chapel, but being an R.C., was attending Mass in a safe place; so by the way was Rosalind when her bedroom was hit. The moral is obvious. I vehemently agree with you about the devastation of Europe and the demand for unconditional surrender. I must send you a little sermon that I preached in Conway Hall about it, with a reference to you and the Bishop of Chichester.

About your new alphabet: I have been trying Pitman longhand, i.e. with no abbreviations. The difficulty that I find is that my handwriting is not good enough; with short and uncomplicated characters you have to be so exact. Your handwriting is one of the things that I envy you most. Mine is becoming very senile. However, the idea is really important. Don't you think Pitman and Daniel Jones together could form the nucleus of a committee? The present Pitman is a very intelligent man.

You mention your book being printed, but do not say what it is. It is a grand thing for us Struldbrugs to be still able to work.

Yours ever,
G.M.

*Greek Grammar for Schools, Based on the Principles and Requirement [*sic*] of the Grammatical Society*, by Edward Adolf **Sonnenschein** (1851–1929), was first published in 1892–4 (two volumes); there were several later editions. **Eulalie, ou le Grec sans Larmes**, by **Salomon Reinach** (1858–1932) was first published in 1911 and reissued as late as 1990. **Daniel Jones** (1881–1967) was one of the most distinguished English phoneticians of the twentieth century. His 2001 edition of *An English Pronouncing Dictionary, Containing 54,860 Words in International Phonetic Transcriptions* was an enlargement of a work first acclaimed in 1917. A German biography of Jones (only two copies sold; thus a co-authored dissertation?) argues that he was the actual model for Higgins in Pygmalion: Beverley Collins and Inger M. Mees, *The Real Professor Higgins: The Life and Career of Daniel Jones* (Berlin: Mouton de Gruyter, 1998); see 97–103 (*Wikipedia*). Shaw's **book being printed** was *Everybody's Political What's What?*, finally published on 15 September.

142 / To Gilbert Murray

Ayot St Lawrence, Welwyn, Herts.
16th July 1944

[TL; last 8 lines ALS: Bod, SPA]

In 1937 Shaw had supplied a final act to Shakespeare's Cymbeline *when the Shakespeare Memorial Theatre's governing committee decided not to present it because of the weakness of the last act, and Shaw idly proposed to rewrite it. Even though the original version was performed in Stratford that season after all, Shaw's version,* Cymbeline Refinished, *was presented at the Embassy Theatre in Swiss Cottage later that year (Mander and Mitchenson,* Theatrical Companion to Shaw, *247). A printed version was not available at the time of Shaw's offer to send the play to Murray.*

My dear Murray

Your Moncure Conway lecture was entirely hidden from me by the newspapers. Meanwhile the jingo romance of Churchill and the rancorous explosions of Vansittart were shoved down my throat, and the war atrocities rubbed into me by the wireless most sedulously.

Even Geoffrey Crowther, who has made The Economist a much more advanced paper than The Daily Worker, in a passionate exordium in praise of you at the Brains Trust, could find nothing better to say of you than that you had been Regius Professor of Greek (which might have happened to any pedant) and that 'above all' you had been President of the League of Nations Union! Not a word about your resuscitation of the ancient Greek drama in immortal verse which will survive all the Regius professors and all the presidents (except yourself) that ever walked.

As it happened, just before your lecture arrived I had finished a Credo of my own for the 1945 Rationalist Press Annual. The title is 'What is my Religious Faith?' I will send you a proof when I get one.

As to The Arbitrators, I have a word more to say on the point of rubatos within the line in blank verse: 5 syllables as 3, 7 as 5, puthiminthe as 2, etc. etc. They are allowable once in a way; but I should make it a rule not to do it oftener than once in 50 lines, and then always between two lines in which the metre is strongly marked. If you do it in two successive lines the verse becomes prose annoyingly.

'Conversational' is a dangerous word, like 'natural' or 'realistic.' Blank verse, or any other sort of verse, is neither natural nor conversational nor realistic in the ordinary slipshod sense: the moment it becomes so it ceases to be verse, and your artistic form is gone. Readers and listeners either accept this form as pleasurable or they dont, in which case they neither read nor listen: they get another book. But if they do, they rightly resent every lapse into unmusical prose. None the less every speech must have a 'natural' and intelligible cadence so as not to worry or puzzle the customer. Henry James made his later plays impossible by filling them with speeches that no listener could understand, though a grammarian could gather the meaning from the printed page.

Did I ever send you the fifth act I wrote for Cymbeline, Shakespear's ending having been spoiled by the passing fashion which obliged him to introduce a masque at all costs, just as a ballet was indispensable at the Paris Opera, and Wagner had to perpetrate the Venusberg atrocity in his Tannhauser? The Stratford people funked it; but it came off all right in the theatre at Swiss Cottage. It contained 70 lines of Shakespear; and when I read it to Charlotte she protested, whenever I came to an original passage, that I must cut that out. But then one day at Stratford when we were at a performance of Lear, Charlotte rose at the interval, as I thought for tea, and when I said 'Remember you have only 15 minutes,' countered with 'Havent you had enough of this drivel? I am not coming back.' And she meant it too. She didnt come back. She never read Shakespear nor spoke of him.

Casson may be right about The Rape from the point of view of popular audiences. They prefer East Lynne to The Trojan Women. And all that can be said for The Arbitrators is that it is more workmanlike and fully metered. It is no deeper.

G. Bernard Shaw

PS As Pitman's shorthand has to [be] drawn, not written, I can make it legible in a joggling train when longhand is impossible. Many of my immortal lines have been penned between King's Cross and Hatfield. A ticket collector once burst out at me with 'Are you ALWAYS workin?'

Murray's **Moncure Conway lecture** was the most recent of a long-standing series, delivered on 19 March 1944. Its full title was 'Myths and Ethics; or, Humanism and the World's Need.' Sir Robert [Gilbert] **Vansittart** (1881–1957) was best known for his hard-line attitude towards Germany, manifested in **rancorous** public **explosions.** In his 1941 book *Black Record: Germans Past and Present* he exposed what he considered an instinctive German attitude of aggression throughout history. Murray agreed with Shaw, later calling Vansittart 'rampageously anti-German' (Wilson, 404). As editor of *The Economist* from 1938 to 1956, **Geoffrey Crowther** (1907–72) greatly increased its circulation and prestige. Shaw's article appeared in the ***Rationalist Annual** for the Year 1945* (London: C.A. Watts, 1945), 3–7; repr. in *Sixteen Self Sketches,* 73–9. A **rubato** is a fluctuation of tempo within a musical phrase. The word **puthiminthe** is a compression of 'put him in the,' as in Letter 140: 'puthiminthéélec- / tric chair.' Shaw had made his point about the dialogue in the later plays of **Henry James** in 1923, when he said it lacked 'audible intelligibility' (see Shaw, *The Drama Observed,* 1396–7, and Martin Meisel, 'Shaw, Stoppard, and "Audible Intelligibility,"' *SHAW* 27 [2007]: 42–3). The **Venusberg atrocity** in Wagner's *Tannhäuser* was the result of his violating the rigid convention in the Paris Opéra of requiring a ballet in the second act to accommodate members of the aristocratic Jockey Club, whose custom was to dine first and arrive only in time for the ballet. Wagner deigned to provide a ballet – a bacchanalia set on the mountain of Venus – but he put it in act 1 (*Wikipedia*). **East Lynne** was a stage sensation in England from 1863 through the Victorian period. Adapted in several versions from a novel by Ellen Wood (1814–87), it features an unfaithful wife who has a child by her aristocratic lover. **King's Cross** and **Hatfield** are 'overground' stops.

143 / To G. Bernard Shaw

Yatscombe, Boar's Hill, Oxford
24th July 1944

[TLT: BL, SPA]

Since the late Victorian period, actor-managers such as Henry Irving and William Poel had truncated or otherwise altered the final act of Cymbeline. *When Shaw agreed to write a better one, he had confused these performances with Shakespeare's act itself. In his 'Foreword' to the play, he admits his misconception and asserts that the act 'is genuine Shakespear to the last full stop.' He explains the eccentricities as the product of a required masque to be performed with appropriate music and scenic splendour. Citing the Charringtons, he then singles out the characterization of Posthumus as 'Shakespear's anticipation' of Ibsen, and declares that he rewrote the act 'as Shakespear might have written it if he had been post-Ibsen and post-Shaw instead of post-Marlowe' (CP 7, 180, 183). In his letter of 3 August (no. 145), Murray says that he 'can't quite agree with your defence of Shakespeare's attempt at it!'*

My dear Shaw

I should immensely like to see your fifth act of Cymbeline. The existing ending is idiotic. Mary, by the way, agrees fully with Charlotte. We went to Macbeth some time ago – a poorish performance, with Edith Evans as Lady Macbeth, and I was consoling myself with the sheer beauty of the lines when Mary whispered to me 'Surely this is very silly – so utterly improbable!'

You are profoundly right, I am sure, about the mistake of trying to write verse so as to please those who do not like verse at all. You just can't do it; you can only spoil the verse. Curiously enough, I remember Kipling once saying to me almost the opposite. When he read an unfavourable review, he said to himself: 'I have not got that man; what must I do to get him?'

I also have sometimes practised writing Pitman in the train, but never for anything continuous – only bits of verse, or notes for a speech, when one can snatch the opportunity to draw clear lines.

I get more and more anxious about the post-war Settlement. The Settlement in 1920 was made by a generation which had been brought up in peace, and took for granted that peace was the normal condition for civilised man, and war a passing madness; but the next Settlement will be made by a generation, most of whom will have lived in an atmosphere of war all their conscious lives. We are laying down excellent principles, e.g. Roosevelt's Acceptance Speech; but I wonder greatly how they will be translated into fact. So much depends on the wisdom and self-control of several hundred millions of stupid people.

Yours ever,

G.M.

I greatly liked your letter in the Times about [*unintelligible*]

Edith (Mary) **Evans** (1888–1976) was a noted Shakespearean actress who also took two woman's roles in *Back to Methuselah* and played Hesione in *Heartbreak House*. The **acceptance speech** of Franklin Delano Roosevelt (1882–1945), his fourth, was delivered on 20 July 1944. By no means one of his most memorable speeches, the '**excellent principles**' that Murray says it sets forth must be those that follow his question, 'What is the job before us in 1944?' He lists three: 'to win the war – to win it fast, to win it overpoweringly'; 'to form world-wide international organizations, and to arrange to use the armed force of the sovereign nations of the world to make another war impossible within the foreseeable future'; 'to build an economy for our returning veterans and for all Americans which will provide employment and decent standards of living' (Roosevelt, 403). However, it may be that Murray confused this speech with a much longer and more imposing one delivered earlier in 1944: his 'Annual Message to Congress.' This one proposes implementing an 'economic Bill of Rights' and lists eight 'rights' that are more easily construed as 'principles,' from 'The right to a useful and remunerative job in the industries or shops or farms or mines of the nation' to 'The right to a good education' (ibid., 396). The **unintelligible** postscript almost surely refers to Shaw's letter of 21 July entitled 'Bringing up the Child: A Contrast in Method: Connemara and Berlin' (*Letters of Bernard Shaw to* The Times, 245–6).

144 / To Gilbert Murray

Ayot St Lawrence
29th July 1944

[APCS: Bod, SPA]

CYMBELINE REFINISHED

My dear Murray

I think I managed to make a fairly decent job of this, as there was really a story to finish; but when I re-read The Two Gentlemen of Verona I found not only the last act hopeless, but the first and second too silly for words. The *genre* is silly: the whole play is not good enough even for an early XIXth century Italian opera libretto. It is the work of a beginner who had not found his proper field – like my five novels.

G. Bernard Shaw

145 / To G. Bernard Shaw

Yatscombe, Boar's Hill, Oxford
3rd August 1944

[TLS: BL, SPA]

My dear Shaw

I much enjoyed your Fifth Act of Cymbeline, though I can't quite agree with your defence of Shakespeare's attempt at it! The story, like that of the 'Two Gentlemen' is morally monstrous, and W.S. does not seem to care a bit. I suppose he takes his Renaissance Italians as quite fanciful and incalculable people, much as Boccaccio does, only Boccaccio leaves them inhuman all the time and Shakespeare, as soon as he gets interested, makes them human and real, and then the story becomes intolerable. What amazingly bad plays the Elizabethans could write when they tried!

It is interesting to compare the Italian and English treatment of the villain. The Italian takes a positive pleasure in flaying him and having him stung to death; the Englishman seems to say 'Oh, don't bother, old boy. Come and have a drink.' – rather like the English Soldier in the Epilogue to St. Joan.

I like Dowden's emendation in Act V: 'Think that you are upon a *l*ock.' I also like your 'noisy and dirty children' – in literature.

Yours ever,
G.M.

Giovanni **Boccaccio** (1313–75) was an Italian poet and storyteller, best known for his collection of stories *The Decameron* (1353). Edward **Dowden** (1843–1913) edited *Cymbeline* for the Methuen series *The Works of Shakespeare*, in 1903. The phrase '**noisy and dirty children**' does not occur in Shaw's act 5, or anywhere in a standard text of Shakespeare's *Cymbeline*.

146 / To G. Bernard Shaw

Yatscombe, Boar's Hill, Oxford
1st October 1944

[TLS: BL, SPA]

Everybody's Political What's What? *was published on 15 September 1944 lacking the subtitle listed in advance announcements,* Machiavelli Modernized *(Laurence,* Bibliography, *1, 245). Its hardback edition sold over 85,000 copies within a year. In its final chapter, 'Envoy,' Shaw states: 'The present book, written in my second childhood, is not meant for people who want to know how far political thought can reach: it is just a Child's Guide to Politics' (364). He told a friend in a letter of 1 September that 'there's nothing really new in it … At my age one has nothing fresh to say' (quoted in Holroyd, 3, 481).*

Commentators have agreed that the book is little more than a reworking of material from The Intelligent Woman's Guide to Socialism and Capitalism, *and Holroyd characterizes it as 'a ragged patchwork of autobiography, sociology, history and political economy, a rambling narrative of almost 200,000 words that repeats ideas he had given better elsewhere and then repeats itself.' But he continues, 'this summary of a life's teaching was a prodigious achievement for a man ... in his eighty-ninth year.'*

Shaw's sparring exchange in the Spectator *with his error-prone friend Walter Elliot is fun and illuminating; see 'Everybody's Political What's What?: A Review and a Reply,'* SHAW *11 (1991): 213–17.*

My dear Shaw

Many thanks for the Political What's What, I am browsing on it with great enjoyment. Our main difference is that I, on the whole, think the present or at least the pre-war English civilization about the best there has ever been and you think it almost the worst. But I agree with most of what you say about its absurdities, and particularly about the hopeless absurdity with which people use political terms like 'democracy,' 'freedom,' 'Fascism' 'capitalism' &c. The words change their meaning every week. I will try to get a copy of my Anchor of Civilization to send you; it is only a lecture and seems to my muddled brain amusing.

Walter Eliot was witty about you but missed the points a good deal. You were not writing a handbook for students but something to wake people up and make them think.

I agree warmly with you about the difficulty of reading the sort of stuff one puts out oneself. I cannot read books about the influence of the Greeks and suchlike; nor yet about peace – with some exceptions. I suspect there is something physiological about it: if you breathe out carbonic acid gas it makes you sick to breathe it in.

Unwin wont send me any proofs of the Menander, but I am pegging away at another Sophocles, the Trachiniae. I shall call it the Wife of Hercules; it shows what an awful fate it is for a woman to be married to Nietzschian [*sic*] Supermen of a primitive type. A woman once said to me of her husband: 'It was like being married to a thunderstorm.'

Yours ever,
G.M.

Murray's ***Anchor of Civilization*** was the Philip Maurice Deneke lecture delivered at Lady Margaret Hall on 24 November 1942; it was published in 1943 by Oxford University Press. His next letter comments that it was 'much goaded by Leftists.' **Walter Elliot** (1888–1958), a Conservative of the Liberal wing in Parliament, served in several ministerial positions.

147 / To G. Bernard Shaw

Yatscombe, Boar's Hill, Oxford
8th October 1944

[TLT: BL, SPA]

My dear Shaw

I am enjoying What's What greatly. I like particularly The Aesthetic Man; it raises some real problems which I dont see my way through. Nor do I see my way through the puzzle of the Medical Man. It is such a magnificent profession, and the individual doctors – like a young niece of mine whose hospital was blitzed and who went on operating and removing patients from burning or falling rooms the whole night – do rise to its demands. Yet I quite agree with you that they have a tendency to become morally insane, both in vivisection and in experiments on human beings. I knew a South African doctor – a very pleasant intelligent fellow – who loved his practice in S Africa because he had such opportunities for research by infecting blacks with various diseases. 'They dont mind a bit. They dont understand infection' he explained when some protest was jerked out of me. And I agree strongly about the half of Education that is left out being the political half. We did learn some in Greats, from working at Plato and Aristotle. And a pupil of mine runs a Newspaper Reading Class for the WEA; take two papers of different views and analyze their treatment of news.

I could not find an Anchor of Civn, so I am stealing Mary's copy and sending it. I had been much goaded by Leftists when I wrote it.

Yours ever,
G.M.

What a very interesting set of letters you have sent us at the British Museum!

WEA stands for Workers' Education [or Educational] Association, a British group with many outlets that provides access to education and lifelong learning for adults from all backgrounds.

148 / To G. Bernard Shaw Yatscombe, Boar's Hill, Oxford
9th March 1945

[TLT: BL, SPA]

Shaw had published an 85-page treatise entitled Imprisonment *in 1925, first printed in 1922 as the preface to the Webbs'* English Prisons under Local Government *(vii–lxxiii); repr. in* Doctors' Delusions, Crude Criminology, Sham Education *(vol. 22 in the 'Collected Edition' of his works, 1931). The article that Murray refers to was 'Sentence of Death: The State and the Murderer,'* The Times, *5 March 1945, 5: 5, on the execution of Karl Hutton and Elizabeth Maud Jones (Laurence,* Bibliography, *2, 784).*

After having been worked on since 12 June 1944, the film version of Cæsar and Cleopatra *had opened in London on 13 December 1945. Conditions even worse than those which delayed the film of* Major Barbara *prevailed: as Dukore describes them, 'Four days after filming started, the Nazis began their German V-2 rocket attacks on London, which interrupted the shooting schedule, damaged one of the sets, destroyed dressmaking workrooms, cracked the windows and ceiling of Pascal's home, and nearly killed several members of the production unit'* (Collected Screenplays, *135; see also the first-hand account of Marjorie Deans [1901–82], Pascal's assistant and script writer, in* Meeting at the Sphinx, *89–90). Shaw and Murray must have exchanged letters on this subject, but none seem to be extant.*

My dear Shaw

This is merely an act of homage from Menander & Co. You are not expected to read the thing again, though I have adopted a number of your metrical amendments.

You have started an interesting little controversy about the death penalty. Odd, how people go on saying with confidence that the abolition of capital punishment always leads to an abundance of murders, when the evidence is all the other way. However, a matter on which I have suddenly come round to your view is the Reformed Alphabet.

I have always felt that our SSS scheme could never be adopted and therefore wanted D.J. to have a compromise scheme in reserve. But it seems impossible to get a satisfactory compromise, and I am now inclined to think that we want a really scientific phonetic alphabet, rather on Pitman principles, to exist together with the traditional alphabet and spelling. The new one would be used by professional writers and suchlike, as it happened to be found useful, and also for teaching foreigners, until possibly after a century or two it became popular.

Why do most Englishmen write so badly, as if unable to guide a pen? The Chinese have many weaknesses but they can write.

Mary has been ill, pneumonia, and given us a bad time for some four or five days, but she is much better; definitely round the corner, I think.

Yours ever,
G.M.

In Letter 140 Shaw noted that when he received Murray's draft translation of **Menander**'s *Epitreponte*s, or *The Arbitration*, he 'automatically began scrawling alternative scansions all over it.' **SSS**: Simplified Spelling System. **D.J.** must be Daniel Jones (see Letter 41).

149 / To Gilbert Murray Ayot St Lawrence, Welwyn, Herts.
16th March 1946

[TLT: SPA]

I am sending you back the magnificent play straight away; but my letter (in shorthand) must go up to London to be typewritten for you, as unless I write very slowly, like a child learning, I am illegible.

G.B.S.

150 / To Gilbert Murray 4 Whitehall Court (130), London SW1
26th March 1946

[TLS: Bod, SPA]

My dear Murray

You cannot imagine what a treat it is for me to get another translation from you of one of the Greek plays of the great Greek period. You should never touch anything else: the Latin rubbish is a wicked waste of your time. What you have achieved is not a translation among so many unreadable ones, but a collaboration in which two dramatic poems are compounded into one, producing something greater than either, and unique as far as I know. Its possibility was suggested, perhaps by Archer's translations of Ibsen; but Ibsen was always on top of Archer and was one man and not a whole school or period. You have brought the whole national drama to life again and added a music of your own to it without being in the least dwarfed by its greatest. In this last play your ear has not failed for a syllable. Sophocles-Murray is more than Sophocles, not Sophocles adulterated with the reigning Regius professor and spoilt.

Sophocles is difficult to date because he never developed as a technician, but stuck all through to stage convention because he could do the scholastic thing so superbly well. (Napoleon never changed, but fought his last battle by the book exactly as he had fought his first one, and estimated Wellington and the rest of his enemies as a pack of amateurs.) What we call construction did not exist then: theatrical art had only just emerged from the stage in which it was a recitation in the market place by a single poet who took his hat round. Change to having the parts played by separate speakers on a stately tribunal in a theatre with stone seats must have seemed a tremendous revolution; but the old street corner technique still persisted: the play consisted of recitations by messengers coming in successively to the principal characters to tell them what had just happened off stage. Horror was piled on horror until the principal worked the horrors all up into a climax of emotion on hearing the news. Sophocles had such a command of this game that he never tried to get beyond it. It was always the same string of coincidences, each messenger turning up punctually with the one on the stage finishing until it was time for the principals to discharge their full load of agony. Heracles and Deianira do not appear on the stage together, obviously because they were originally played by the same single performer in the market place.

The play is remarkably complete and perfect in its form. If there is another such, for heaven's sake add your English to it before you die.

We are both going the same way, at the legs. Shakespear was right: old men have most weak hams. I shall soon forget my own name; but except for that I keep enough of my wits about me to be able to write a bit. And I am developing a positive taste for business. No plum tree gum as yet.

Love to Lady Mary.

Get that play safely into print as soon as possible.

G. Bernard Shaw

I cannot verify what Shaw means by Murray's '**Latin rubbish**'; the noted Latin dramatists wrote several adaptations of Greek plays, but I have not come across a reference to his translating them in his letters or the scholarship about him. The **Sophocles** play that Murray had translated was *The Trachiniae*, which he will call *The Wife of Heracles* when it is published in 1947. Arthur Wellesley **Wellington** (1769–1852) was a military leader most noted for defeating Napoleon I at Waterloo. In Hamlet's 'mad scene' with Polonius (2, 2) he quotes from a book (or pretends to): 'the satirical rogue says here that **old men have** grey beards, that their faces are wrinkled, their eyes purging thick amber and **plum-tree gum**, and that they have a plentiful lack of wit, together with **most weak hams**' (*The Works of Shakespeare: Hamlet*, ed. John Dover Wilson, 2nd ed. [Cambridge: University Press, 1936], 45).

151 / To G. Bernard Shaw Yatscombe, Boar's Hill, Oxford
31st March 1946

[TLT: BL, HRC, SPA]

By 1948, Murray's translations of Greek plays had indeed become quickly superseded in the literary world; for example, the University of Chicago's editions of the complete Greek tragedies, edited by David Grene and Richmond Lattimore, sold over three million copies from 1942 to 1959. In academe, the strictures of the reigning English man of letters T.S. Eliot were highly influential on almost any topic, especially to younger students. In Letter 170, Murray comments that his young secretary treated him with 'severe doses of T S Eliot & Co, and explained how antiquated all my taste in literature is.' Still, the translations were very favourably received by BBC listeners in the wartime period and after (see the endnote for Letter 123), and in 2005 his translations of five plays of Euripides were reprinted, with their introductions and notes, in the 'Classic Translations' series of Bristol Phoenix Press (courtesy of Martin Bidney).

My dear Shaw

Your letter naturally gives me very great pleasure. It has been one of my permanent satisfactions in life that you cared about my Greek translations and thought them worthwhile, especially when the young – particularly those who don't know Greek – are explaining that they are the 'worst possible.'

One effect of your letter is to make me look up a half-written attempt to do the Oedipus at Colonus. I did it because Martin Harvey wanted a finish to the Oedipus story, but the plan fell through. Did you ever hear the queer story of Harvey's Oedipus? A man – name I forget – called on me and said his principal, whose name he must not divulge, wanted to do my Oedipus in grand style, with Rheinhardt [*sic*] as producer, and would give me carte blanche about cast and production; money no object. The thing went ahead, till after some months he came again and said it was all off. I said I had a contract. He then explained that his principal was dead, burnt in attempting to save a favourite lion from a burning circus in Edinburgh! He was 'The Great Lafayette,' the successor of Barnum in the circus world. He had all the success he wanted in the circus world, but that was not really high art, and he felt a need of doing something artistic and high-brow, and had been advised to do the Oedipus with Murray and Rheinhardt. Then his circus happened to catch fire at Edinburgh and he died in trying to rescue his lion. Later on Harvey took up the idea.

I had a real treat yesterday, taking a party to The Applecart. It is more topical now than when it first came out, and in the evening we heard Bevin dropping all his aitches in an excellent speech on Foreign Policy. The King (David Markham) was splendid, and Boanerges (Richard Cuthbert) very good; Orinthia not right in personality (Jane Henderson) though a good actress.

Yours ever,
G.M.

Sir John **Martin-Harvey** had played **Oedipus** in the 1912 staging of *Oedipus Rex*, translated by Murray. He encouraged Murray to translate ***Oedipus at Colonus*** after this performance, but he delayed until 1948, when it was published. **'The Great Lafayette'** was the noted German-American illusionist Sigmund Neuberger (1872–1911). In 1911, with his double performing 'the **Lion**'s Bride,' a lamp caught fire and the flames spread quickly, killing Neuberger and his assistant – who was first identified, and buried, as his employer (*Wikipedia*). There was no postwar revival of **The Apple Cart** in London until 7 August 1946. Murray and his friends must have seen it elsewhere. Ernest **Bevin** (1881–1951), a British labour leader, was in Churchill's war cabinet from 1940–5, then became foreign secretary in the postwar Labour government from 1945–51. **David Markham** (1913–83), **Richard Cuthbert**, and **Jane Henderson** (perhaps the film actress, 1925–60) were British professional actors.

152 / To G. Bernard Shaw

Yatscombe, Boar's Hill, Oxford
24th August 1946

[TLT: BL, SPA]

My dear Shaw

You will be sorry to hear that Mary has been seriously ill – a thrombosis, or stoppage of a small blood vessel in the brain. The brain, having some pretensions to sense, after making a fuss finds another bloodvessel which does just as well, so now she seems to be recovering. I thought you would like to know. She has always had a special place in her heart for you.

I greatly enjoyed your few words on the radio and indeed the whole of your national celebrations. It reminded me of Voltaire's apotheosis in Paris in 1778 – not that I was present at the time. But he was only eighty-four.

Yours ever,
Gilbert Murray

Shaw was 90 on 26 July. A major celebratory event was Shaw's Ninetieth Birthday Exhibition held by the National Book League from 26 July to 24 August (Gibbs, *Chronology*, 328). **Voltaire's apotheosis** occurred in February 1778 when he triumphantly returned to Paris after twenty years in exile and was driven across the city amid cheering crowds.

153 / To Gilbert Murray

Ayot St Lawrence, Welwyn, Herts.
24th August 1946

[APCS: Bod, SPA]

My dear Murray

Sidney Webb had the same experience a few years ago. It destroyed his very bold and legible handwriting; and he says he can neither write nor think. And his Scottish nurse goes out with him lest if he fell he would not get up unaided.

But he reads enormously, and talks as he always did, and is as happy and companionable.

Wells (his son tells me) was in one of his blithe and active moods all the morning. After lunch he lay down as usual for a nap, went to sleep, and presently died without waking, quite peacefully.

Mary is not for me like anyone else. I must think of her happily.

G.B.S.

Sidney Webb had suffered a stroke in January 1938, which left him partly paralysed and his speech impaired (CL 4, 492). H.G. **Wells** had died on 13 August 1946. His son (G.P. or 'Gip') wrote to Shaw on 21 August and described his father's last day (*Bernard Shaw and H.G. Wells*, 209–10).

154 / To G. Bernard Shaw Yatscombe, Boar's Hill, Oxford
24th April 1947

[TLS: BL, SPA]

My dear Shaw

It was a great and unexpected pleasure to both Mary and me to get your last volume, and I have read it over with constant chuckles. I think you have partly rewritten 'Geneva' since I saw it. Begonia Brown is splendid! I think the new U.N.E.S.C.O. will be more absurd than the C.I.C. and, I greatly fear, more disappointing because it has raised much larger hopes. Huxley of course is good, and they are being very civil to me, putting up a bust of me – I hope in some remote and obscure place.

'Cymbeline' I have read before, but cannot get over my feeling that Shakespeare's play on the subject is really too bad to be worth troubling about. He really *could* be bad when he tried but his worshippers never see it.

King Charles is the best of the lot. What an extraordinary period it was. I remember reading ages ago, I think in Taine, that the chief characteristic of Charles II's reign was the great activity of religion and next to that in science, and the 'fable convenue' has almost forgotten both.

A funny state the book trade is in. I have a book of Essays printing, of which I have seen nothing for about a year, and a translation of Sophocles' Trachiniae called 'The wife of Heracles,' of which I received one advance copy about two months ago, but nothing more. The binders must have struck or been drowned in the floods.

We are both feeling rather old but your book has rejuvenated us.

Yours ever,
Gilbert Murray

Shaw's **last volume**, published in the Constable edition of his works on 17 April, was *Geneva, Cymbeline Refinished, & Good King Charles.* **The new U.N.E.S.C.O.** (United Nations Educational, Scientific and Cultural Organization, established 16 November 1945) had absorbed and expanded the League of Nations' **C.I.C.** (International Commission on Intellectual Co-operation). Julian (Sorell) **Huxley** (1887–1975) was its first director. The **bust** of Murray is almost surely that done by Oscar Nemon (1906–85), a Croatian sculptor living in Oxford at this time. It was probably made in 1942, kept somewhere at Oxford University, and then moved to a display room at UNESCO. A photograph of the bust is the frontispiece of Stray's volume. The **King Charles** that Murray refers to is Shaw's play, not the English king who reigned from 1660–85. Hippolyte **Taine** (1828–93) was a French scholar who wrote a three-volume book on English history. A **'fable convenue'** derives from Voltaire's short tale, 'Jeannot et Colin.' Its statement, 'Toutes les histoires anciennes, comme le disait un de nos beaux esprits, ne sont que des fables convenues,' translates as 'All the old histories, as one of our great minds used to say, are only fables agreed upon.' Murray's **book of Essays**, *From the League to U.N.* (London: Oxford University Press), was published in 1948.

155 / To G. Bernard Shaw

Ayot St Lawrence, Welwyn, Herts.
14th July 1947

[TLS: BL, SPA]

My dear Shaw

It is a shame to trouble you with books to read, but I send 'The Wife of Heracles' as an act of homage to one who has always been so kind and sympathetic to my translations.

The first fifty pages, especially 25–46, seem to me a bit of very good play in the midst of a rather bad play. The character of Deianira is one of Sophocles' best achievements but, like Phaedra, she goes and dies in the middle of the play and leaves the others to storm along as best they can.

Yours ever,
G.M.

The Wife of Heracles*, being Sophocles' Play, The Trachinian Women* (London: Allen & Unwin) was published some time in the spring of 1947. **Phaedra** is a tragic figure in Euripides' *Hippolytus.*

156 / To Gilbert Murray

Ayot St Lawrence, Welwyn, Herts.
21st July 1947

[ALS: BL, SPA]

An article in The Daily Worker *by J.B.S. Haldane about the type of frogs 'which provided the chorus for Aristophanes' play "The Frogs" which is well known in Murray's English translation' prompted Shaw to paste this note on it and send it to his friend.*

The only place where I heard really vocal frogs was at Pitfold half way up the hill from Haslemere to Hindhead. There was no brekekekex: they simply roared, loud enough to be a serious nuisance at night.

G.B.S.

The gist of this note is that the **frogs** in the play were outdone vocally by the local frogs.

157 / To Gilbert Murray Ayot St Lawrence, Welwyn, Herts.
23rd July 1947

[TLS, ALS: Bod, SPA]

My dear Murray

What a relief and delight to have you back to the Greek again! Heracles is as good as ever, old as we are. A fashion has sprung up lately to describe me as the Shakespear *de nos jours*. But anyone with ears should transfer that honour to you; for Shakespear's magic now lies in the magic of his English hardly ever failing. Yours never does. It is all through Heracles. Reading it has given me extraordinary pleasure.

Sophocles has always raised the question with me whether his arrant conventionality was put on for the market, or was really a quality of his mind. Apparently he would have thirdrated us two because we have never killed anybody, nor appalled the world with wholesale cruelties. But neither did he; yet he ranked himself as a great dramatic poet. I conclude that he really did believe that 'the Lord is a man of war' [Exodus 15:3, KJV].

In your short preface to the Europa volume, line 17, you have abolished an accusative. Was this an intentional act of war on Lindley Murray grammar or a slip of the pen? The second who should be whom.

In the Capital Punishment Symposium in the Police Gazette nobody has got rid of the obsession of punishment except you and I. Without this riddance judicial killing can be nothing but vulgar and cruel revenge.

The Intellectual Co-operation Committee is an imposing title; but it never meant anything but Gilbert Murray.

I have just written to Roy Limbert, manager of the Malvern Festival Theatre, that when the Festival is resumed next year he should produce Heracles, as yours is the only name and reputation that can give his program the dignity that Shakespeare gives to Stratford.

G. Bernard Shaw

The **Europa volume** was *The World of Learning* (London: Europa Publications, 1947), which had a one-page introduction by Murray. For **Lindley Murray**, see endnote to Letter 46. On **Roy Limbert**, see the headnote to Letter 98. I found no evidence that he took Shaw's advice.

158 / To G. Bernard Shaw Yatscombe, Boar's Hill, Oxford
30th July 1947

[TLS: BL, SPA]

The departure from conventionality in Shaw's plays that Murray brings up in this letter was strategic as well as natural to Shaw. He perceived that works of art, including plays, evolve to higher levels when they depart from conventional subject matter and techniques which have catered to popular demand. Thus his statements such as 'I had to create my audiences as well as my plays' (Pearson, 170n.) and 'The theatre is my battering ram as much as the platform or the press' (CL 1, 722). Differentiating the worthy from the great artist in The Sanity of Art, *he declares: 'The great artist is he who goes a step beyond the demand, and, by supplying works of a higher beauty and a higher interest than have yet been perceived, succeeds after a brief struggle with its strangeness, in adding this fresh extension of sense to the heritage of the race' (316). In short, such a work of art 'creates new mind' (CP 2, 558). Applying this to his own school of drama in 1906, he declares that in their plays 'the author's indignation and disapproval – his moral reflections – passed over the characters on the stage and hit the audience.' In achieving this they were 'doing the highest constructive work in the world'; they were 'creating mind' ('Mr. Bernard Shaw on the Drama,' 10).*

My dear Shaw

I had not received your delightful letter about The Wife of Heracles when I started on my visit to the Frogs. It is an enormous pleasure to me that you like my Greek versions and think them worth while.

I feel the same doubts as you about Sophocles. If he was really as conventional and unthinking as he seems to be, how does he get his extraordinary flashes of insight? Is n't there much the same problem about Shakespeare? Or is it, perhaps, that most dramatists, having to make an immediate appeal to an audience of average people, feel compelled to accept the average conventional background. People like you and Euripides have somehow to establish a reputation for not doing so, and then you are free, but unless a man can somehow get his audience prepared, he has either to accept their conventions or fail to get into touch with them.

As to birthdays and suchlike, I once saw a burlesque in which an aged King refuses to dance, on the ground that 'I've lost the habit, which is not surprising, / At eighty-two, of eighty-twodinizing' (Attitudinizing).

Yours ever,
G.M.

Murray's comment about his 'visit' to the ***Frogs*** is baffling, since he had already translated it before 1902, had published a book on Aristophanes in 1933, and the play had been broadcast twice recently by the BBC. It must have been an error for *The Birds*, which his next letter says he was presently translating.

159 / To G. Bernard Shaw Yatscombe, Boar's Hill, Oxford
23rd August 1948

[TLT: BL (only final third in transcription), SPA]

My dear Shaw

One of the difficulties in your Dictionary of political terms is that so many of them are meaningless, or only get a meaning from the context in which they are used. Another is that most people in diplomacy or party politics would be ashamed to confess what their real aims were. In the old CIC days we did have a Committee to get the names of drugs and medicines agreed, also, I think, the words for doses. That was much simpler.

Mary, I am sorry to say, has been breaking her leg. She was 'gathering rosemary, dreadful trade,' and fell. Not a bad fracture; no displacement; but some four or five weeks in hospital. We are more or less servantless – a great relief for the time being – but an old retainer has come to look after me in the house, and I sponge on my neighbours for lunch or dinner. I believe the old Irish kings had a right to exact hospitality from their subjects: wasn't it called Right of Cossher?

I am doing a translation of The Birds, which is a very lovely and nonsensical thing. I need hardly say that we constantly think of you and from time to time re-read you.

Ever yours affectionately,
G.M.

By Shaw's '**Dictionary of political terms**,' Murray is referring to his article 'Rebuilding Babel' in *The Times*, 6 (19 August): 5. Laurence notes that it deals with 'the need for a political dictionary.' A continuation will appear on 30 August (*Bibliography*, 2, 801); see the next letter. The phrase **'gathering rosemary, dreadful trade'** is almost surely Murray's adaptation of Edgar's 'half way down, / Hangs one that gathers samphire, dreadful trade!' in *King Lear*, 4, 6: 14–15. **Right of Cossher**: 'Coshering' was a custom in feudal Ireland whereby a lord was entitled to feasts for himself and his retinue at tenants' houses. Murray's translation of Aristophanes' ***The Birds*** will be published in 1948.

160 / To Gilbert Murray

Ayot St Lawrence, Welwyn, Herts.
26th August 1948

[TLS: BL, SPA]

My dear Murray

Of course the glossary wont be produced: My Times letter (another coming) was only a trick to call attention to Babel.

A few weeks in hospital will probably do Lady Mary a lot of good; but I wish she hadnt had to pay so painful a price for it. My own unbroken legs are none too serviceable. Otherwise my age doesnt bother me much.

I am lucky in having for my housekeeper an able and formidable Scotswoman, and for my office boy a German Jew, Doctor of Philosophy, bibliographer, and devoted Shaviomaniac.

I live on chopped raw vegetables, having concluded that the conventional vegetarian diet of beans, maccaroni, cereals *ad lib*, cheese, eggs &c, produces protein poisoning, and am interested in a Russian woman, a vegetarian athlete who is experimenting in living on air, which Einstein regards as a form of matter.

I enclose a final revision of my latest completed play. I have pretty nearly drafted another, which I call provisionally FARFETCHED FABLES or Shawsop's Fables.

I am greatly delighted at you doing The Birds. The best thing Swinburne ever did was his translation 'Come on then ye dwellers by nature in darkness and like to the leaves' generations Who are fashioned of dirt and are moulded in mire, unenduring and shadowless nations' (I quote recklessly from memory). The combination of Swinburne's ear with the brains of Aristophanes was ideal; but you will be able to supply the best of both.

That is all for today.
G.B.S.

Shaw's **housekeeper** as of July 1947 was the **Scotswoman** Alice Laden (1901–79), known locally as 'St George's dragon.' When Dr Fritz Erwin Loewenstein (1901–69) became a relentless visitor in the early 1940s and soon Shaw's authorized '**bibliographer** and remembrancer,' Laden followed her predecessor, Blanche Patch, in harshly trying to control him. See Laurence's commentary on them in CL 4, 693–5. Shaw had completed *Buoyant Billions,* a play he had begun in 1936 and abandoned a year later, on 13 July 1947 (see next letter). He had begun ***Farfetched Fables*** on 17 July 1948. The two were published with *Shakes vs Shav* in 1951. The lines from Algernon Charles **Swinburne** (1837–1909) are from his translation of *The Birds*; the exact quotation is 'Come on then, ye dwellers by nature in darkness, and like to the leaves' generations / That are little of might, that are moulded of mire, unenduring and shadowlike nations ...' See the next letter.

161 / To G. Bernard Shaw

Yatscombe, Boar's Hill, Oxford
30th August 1948

[TLT: BL, SPA]

My dear Shaw

Thanks for 'Buoyant Billions,' which I have read three times with great enjoyment. There is a lot that one does not appreciate at first reading. I know many specimens of young 'world-betterers,' both the amiable sort and the others. In Act II you have greatly improved on Shakespeare's 'Exit, followed by a bear.' I think the conversation, or dialectic, in Act III and IV is as good as ever, and more many-sided. What fun it must be writings these things! It pleases me, too, to see how scepticism increases upon you, just as it does on me, as we reach real years of discretion. One cannot help seeing that all political generalisations are inaccurate, partly because the terms themselves are inaccurate, and partly because all the sweeping generalisations are attempts to formulate a cure for some particular temporary evil.

I enclose my shot at the parabasis of 'The Birds.' I did my best to forget Swinburne, and tried to get a little closer to the meaning of the Greek, but his version is quite magnificent. On his own lines it cannot be touched.

Mary sends her love. She is looking a good deal better for the rest, though she does not like the boredom.

Yours ever,
G.M.

PS I met an American in the train the other day who told me in a melancholy voice that he was suffering from Potts' disease. I asked what it was, and he said, 'I forget names, owing to lack of sugar in my diet.' I wonder if a diet of air would cure him and his millions of fellow sufferers?

Act I of *Buoyant Billions* is entitled **'The World Betterer**,' the occupation that the young protagonist has chosen. The finale of **Act II** is '*Hissings and rattling in the bush. An alligator crawls in. The two men fly for their lives*' (CP 7, 333). The (correct) well-known stage direction in *The Winter's Tale* is '**Exit,** ***pursued*** **by a bear**.' The **parabasis** in Greek drama is a recurring conventional address of the Chorus, here delivered by the birds after their earthly visitors have been transformed. **Pott's disease** is a kind of tuberculosis that affects the spine. It is named after Percival Pott (1714–1788), a London surgeon (*Wikipedia*).

162 / To Gilbert Murray Ayot St Lawrence, Welwyn, Herts.
31st August 1948

[TLS: Bod, SPA]

Midnight

Swinburne's version is splendid, but so Swinburnian that Euripides is forgotten, and the air smells of Bedford Park. You, as always, impersonate Euripides and recall Athens, never Oxford, because you are a dramatic poet, which S was not.

Dare I suggest a few verbal changes?

Line 6, after the cesura, 'the source of the stars and the sky' because the *source* is the great secret.

Line 10 'neither earth nor its firmament heaven swings better.'

Lines 13–14, to avoid the repetition of whirling as whirlwind, and store, which suggests something very stationary, 'his heart like a burning mountain embracing Chaos the wingéd and dark, aflame in that fiery fountain.' This is awful; but I can think of nothing else to get rid of store.

I had better go to bed. My wits are forsaking me.

G.B.S.

By '**the air smells of Bedford Park**,' Shaw probably means an upscale environment such as Bedford Park in west London, once known as the world's first 'garden suburb' (*Wikipedia*).

163 / To G. Bernard Shaw

Yatscombe, Boar's Hill, Oxford
19th October 1948

[TLS: BL, SPA]

My dear Shaw

I wonder if the enclosed would at all amuse you? It amused me when I was writing it, and gave me an opportunity of polite protest against some of the modern fashions.

I went to a Jubilee performance of 'Heartbreak House' at the Playhouse last night, well acted and a tremendous success. It took me back to a forgotten world when we were comparatively young. The house laughed delightedly throughout the first act, and listened with growing apprehension to the Jeremiads in the second and third. There is a real sense of apprehension and of possible doom hanging over our present-day students; they came in immense crowds this week to hear Toynbee, in the hope that he would tell them whether civilisation was really going to crash or not. I never saw such crowds in the Schools.

Mary's leg is mending well, but she does not think highly of the world.

Yours ever,
Gilbert Murray

I could not determine what **the enclosed** might have been. Don Chapman's ***Oxford Playhouse****: High and Low Drama in a University City* (Hatfield: University of Hertfordshire, 2008) confirms that there was an October performance of ***Heartbreak House*** for the Jubilee (133). Arnold **Toynbee** was Murray's son-in-law, now divorced from Rosalind.

164 / To G. Bernard Shaw

Yatscombe, Boar's Hill, Oxford
26th November 1948

[TLS: BL, SPA]

My dear Shaw

Here is another of them. The fact is that I cannot stop translating Greek plays just as you cannot stop writing English ones. I often think how easy it must be to write a play of your own, when you can just say what you like, instead of bothering about what somebody else meant – and then making it rhyme!

I have a letter to-day from Edwyn Bevan's daughter, Christina, ending with the sentence: 'The grandmother of my gardener's wife had fourteen children, all boys, all over 6ft 3 in hight, and all policemen.' Who can doubt the greatness of the Victorian Age?

Yours ever,
G.M.

The last of the **Greek Plays** that Murray translated was *Oedipus at Colonus*, published this year. Edwyn [Robert] **Bevan** (1870–1943) was a family friend from the time he was a student of Murray's. He became a theologian. I was unable to track down the name of **Christina**'s **grandmother**'s **gardener's** prolific **Victorian wife**, much less the ID's of her **fourteen policemen**.

165 / To G. Bernard Shaw Yatscombe, Boar's Hill, Oxford
1st May 1949

[TLT: BL, SPA]

Most likely prompted by his disgust at the liberties taken in Noël Coward's short plays, and finding an occasion by supporting a Platonic rejection of democracy, Murray emitted what his biographer calls 'his only recorded use of a four-letter word' (Wilson, 95). The ancient Greek proverb 'Corcyra is free! Shit wherever you like!' (Erasmus's Latin for it is 'Libera Corcyra, caca ubi libet') derived from the threat Corinth posed to that island in the Ionian Sea (now Corfu) during the 'Peace' after the first Pelopponesian War. Corcyra thwarted it first by defeating Corinth in a battle, then by forming an alliance among the two and Athens. The proverb, generally employed to mean 'do whatever you like,' has reappeared in many variations, most of them circumlocuting the vulgar verb.

Coward had written a cycle of ten short plays in 1936 entitled Tonight at 8:30. *These were rotated in threes each night, and the production was occasionally revived. Wearing's* The London Stage *lists no original offerings by Coward in early 1949, but Philip Hoare's biography states (vaguely) that a performance of three of the short plays were 'planned' for 1949 (379–80), and the updated Mander/Mitchenson* Theatrical Companion to Coward *states that two others were actually presented that year at the Ambassadors Theatre (301–2). One of these,* Fumed Oak, *includes an unpleasant girl who is sent off after breakfast to get ready for school (an event that does not occur in any of the other nine plays in the cycle), but is delayed not by lack of toilet paper but by having to search for her sheet music. This is the version printed in 1936, however, and it might have been retooled to evoke 'roars of laughter!' from postwar audiences.*

My dear Shaw

I write to you for sympathy, because you and I and Archer were good respectable Victorians and I am disgusted with this modern world. The immediate occasion for this outburst is that I went last night to see three Noel Coward plays. They were all a series of vulgar sneers at the old-fashioned ideas that you and I learnt from Shelley, and the special hits were such as: an ugly school girl is sent off after breakfast to 'get ready for school' and comes back snivelling that 'There was no paper. She had to use a bit of cardboard.' Roars of laughter! We and Shelley did not make that sort of attempt at being funny. Aristophanes did, but not in that snivelling way. You have always been suitably severe on democracy. It is very much what Plato said it was, a refusal to see that anything is better than anything else. Do you know the Greek saying: 'Corcyra is free! Shit wherever you like!'

I am making some notes about my father. He was, of course, Irish, Catholic, Liberal and aristocratic in his manners. He was made a frontier magistrate in the bush about the age of 23, and given some ticket of leave convicts for servants. He found one of them stealing some of the books that he had sent out to him, with great trouble, from England. The convict went for him and my father knocked him senseless. For a moment he thought the man was dead. 'That was a lesson to me, my boy,' he said. 'After that I never struck them, I always took them by the throat.' Very rum, the effort he made to keep up his culture and his manners in that rough atmosphere. This has nothing much to do with Noel Coward and Co except to make one think how utterly shocked my father (born 1810) and Shelley wd be by them. So, I think, would Stalin and Hitler and the Pope!

I wish I sometimes saw you, but one becomes rather immoveable after eighty. However I have nice grandchildren.

Yours ever,
G.M.

I was so sorry for Hammond's death. I shall miss him greatly.

Plato's most basic political principle was that only a philosopher who understands the harmony of all parts of the universe with the idea of the Good is capable of ruling the just state (*Concise Columbia Encyclopedia*, 656), which implies more tolerance for a benevolent dictator than for a democratic ruler. In *The Republic*, he says '**Democracy** passes into despotism.' Murray recorded a few memories of his **father**, Sir Terence Aubrey Murray (1810–73), in

Gilbert Murray: An Unfinished Autobiography (1960), but none of the above are included. (The Murray papers in the Bodleian include 'Unpublished Memoirs,' which are apparently quite ample.) A **ticket of leave** was a document of parole issued to trusted convicts. John Lawrence [Le Breton] **Hammond** (1872–1949) was a journalist, classical scholar, and writer of many books on social history and politics, several in collaboration with his wife Barbara and one with Arnold J. Toynbee. He had been one of Murray's intimate friends for over fifty years.

166 / To G. Bernard Shaw Yatscombe, Boar's Hill, Oxford
10th September 1949

[TLT: BL, SPA]

The following letter provides an occasion for detailing Murray's (and Lady Mary's) fortunes and misfortunes as siblings, parents, and grandparents. Gilbert had one brother, Hubert, who rarely left Australia and New Guinea. Mary (1865–1956) had six brothers and three sisters, frequently present at her former home, Castle Howard. She and Gilbert had five children: Rosalind, Denis, Agnes, Basil, and Stephen. Rosalind (1890–1967) married Arnold J. Toynbee in 1913, and they had three children: Tony, Philip, and Lawrence, before they were divorced in 1946. Tony was to commit suicide in 1939 (see Letter 115). Denis (1892–1930) suffered psychosomatic damage as a prisoner of war; married Phyllis Keller in 1918 and had a daughter, Pamela, in 1920; but died prematurely. The most sickly and beloved child, Agnes (1894–1922), died of peritonitis. Basil (1902–37) married Pauline Newton in 1927 and they had two daughters, Venetia and Ann Paludan, but he died of pneumonia contracted as a correspondent in the Spanish Civil War. Stephen (1908–94) married Margaret Gillett in 1931 and they had four children: Gilbert, Alexander (Sandy), Robin, and Hubert. Basil's daughter Ann was affiancéd to John Powell Jones at the time of this letter.

My dear Shaw

I do admire your little message about the Irish Delegation at the United Europe Assembly. It is what we all think, but have 'ne'er so well expressed.' You seem to illustrate the remark of a doctor at the Athenaeum the other day, that we had bodies calculated to last 70 to 80 years but brains good for 300. My own experience does not bear him out.

We have two small grandsons staying with us. Attractive creatures, but strangely aggressive and arrogant. Little girls are much easier. They try to get what they want by pleasing you, not by bullying you. We shall have a granddaughter also for the week end, with her fiancé. His name is Jones, and I have begun by calling him Smith. These things have to be lived down, so I have spent this afternoon at the Dog Gymkhana, trying to forget the world. She is Basil's daughter, Ann; has got a Second in 'Modern Greats' at St Hugh's and has got a place in the FO. Indeed she met her young man at the 'Country House,' where they were both being examined. He was considered the best candidate in. She, poor child, is ecstatically in love.

I have been reading the proofs of my version of The Birds, and am disgusted to find how dull most of it is. Not exactly incompetent, but just dull – like most translations of the classics.

Should I be a nuisance if I came to see you some afternoon? I should greatly like to see you again and speak of old times. I saw Masefield the other day. He was in bed but very cheerful and bright in conversation, full of the wrongs of Amy Robsart.

Ever your admiring old friend,

G.M.

Shaw's comment on **the Irish Delegation at the United Europe Assembly** (or Council of Europe), 'The Irish at Strasbourg,' had just appeared in *European Affairs* 1 (September): 27. Murray's quotation is from Alexander Pope's 'An Essay on Criticism': 'What oft was thought, **but ne'er so well expressed.'** Perhaps unconsciously, the **doctor at the Athenaeum** echoed the 'Gospel of the Brothers Barnabas' in *Back to Methuselah*, the leading proposition of which is that 'men must live three hundred years if civilization is to be saved' (CP 5, 459). The **Dog Gymkhana** was a competitive dog show. **Ann** Paludan (1928–) was a specialist in China connected to the Foreign Office (**FO**). **Masefield** (see headnote to Letter 51) may have been contemplating the possible suicide of **Amy Robsart** (1532–60), who married Lord Robert Dudley, a favourite of Queen Elizabeth, and rarely lived with her husband. She fell down a staircase and died in unexplained circumstances.

167 / To G. Bernard Shaw Yatscombe, Boar's Hill, Oxford
28th October 1949

[TLT: BL, SPA]

My dear Shaw

I nearly invaded your privacy on Monday as I had a UNA meeting at Letchworth on Sunday night – a noble though hardly very large audience who struggled through the appalling rain. I had thoughts of telephoning to you to see if you were visible, but I had to go off to another meeting at Horsham, also UNA: so you see I am clinging to my youthful errors as pertinaciously as you are to yours.

Have you ever read Euripides' ION? It is a singularly bad play, but very interesting. The subject of the child of a god by a mortal mother was quite a common subject for tragedy. Originally, no doubt, it was Spring born of the sky god and mother earth, but was made anthropomorphic. The ION has that plot, but treats it almost satirically. Apollo has committed a ruffianly rape on Creusa with the most frightful consequences, and dares not appear at the end of the play to defend himself, but sends Athena in his place, and it is arranged that Creusa's husband is to go on thinking that he is the boy's father. The interesting thing is that, as far as I can make out, this killed that type of tragedy. There are no more sons-of-god tragedies, but curiously enough the new comedy takes on the same idea. There is always a mysterious foundling brought up as a slave or poor peasant who turns out to be the child of a prince or at least a rich, free citizen. The facts of the change are, I think, clear: one can only guess at the explanation.

Mary sends her love. She is grateful to you for remaining, like her, obstinately Socialist, while I still cling to the noble, if extinct, tribe of Liberals.

Yours ever,
G.M.

The **UNA** was the United Nations Association, the successor since 1945 of the League of Nations Union (see the headnote for Letter 94). Murray had begun as co-president and remained active from then on. In *Euripides and His Age*, Murray had called ***Ion*** one of his most 'ironical and enigmatic' plays, and also 'the most definitely blasphemous against the traditional gods' (120–1). Before Shaw had met the Murrays, he wrote to Lady Mary: 'I pledge you my word … that Liberalism is immoral. For the last 20 years Liberalism has done nothing but make Liberals unhappy, whilst Fabianism has been spreading joy and insufferable self conceit on all its votaries. Don't be Liberal, I implore you' (letter of 1 September 1898, Bod).

168 / To Gilbert Murray Ayot St Lawrence, Welwyn, Herts.
5th November 1949

[TLS, postscript ALS: Bod, SPA]

Shaw's capsule summary of the development of his economic thinking in the nineteenth century in the ensuing letter strikingly contrasts with the complacent

Liberalism that Murray managed to sustain, with occasional moments of doubt, until he died. Shaw found reason, through Marx, to rid himself of Manchester School doctrine, which originated with Richard Cobden and John Bright in 1820, flourished primarily because of opportunistic businessmen during the industrial revolution, and dominated the British Liberal Party in the mid-nineteenth century. To Shaw, Marx's 'jeremiad against the bourgeousie' early in Das Kapital *exposed the actual consequences of laissez-faire economic theory, 'with its dreams and dogmas of Free Trade, Liberty, Equality and Fraternity,' its convenient assumption that poverty is inevitable, and its fruits in huge economic imbalances. It is symptomatic that Murray's main exposure to the downside of the era came through reading 'Hammond's books – horrifying stories, published and attested, which in previous ages noone would have known about.' How this turns out to be the reason why people like Shaw 'go wrong about the century' is difficult to grasp.*

My dear Murray

I should have been glad to see you on your day at Letchworth; but we are getting too old to be good for oneanother. Whitely when he died left a beautiful estate in Surrey to old ladies who had saved a little to provide for their old age, but not enough to make them comfortable or keep them in their class. Everything was as perfect as money could make it. The old ladies had nothing to complain of. But to the astonishment of all philanthropists the mental hospital filled up; and the villas were left empty. The old ladies had all gone mad.

Then somebody had the bright idea of inviting all the young people in the neighborhood to come into the place and play lawn tennis and croquet and have tea with the insane inhabitants, who promptly recovered their wits and became normal again. They had in fact driven oneanother mad, and needed only contact with young people to keep them in mental health.

I do not fear that you and I will drive oneanother mad yet, old as we are; but when elderly strangers propose to visit me now I always say 'Dont: make young friends.'

I never read nor heard of ION; but I certainly will if you translate it.

By the way, do you know German enough to translate Goethe's Faust? If you know only 100 words you could make a better version than any other poet with the whole German dictionary at his fingers' ends.

ION will interest me because Jesus is the last protagonist who is still believed to be the son of a mortal mother by a god. The Catholic Herald has just launched a furious criticism of my play Buoyant Billions because in it I imply that Stalin and Jesus are alike mortal. I am denounced as an obsolete dotard gabbling the shibboleths of 50 years ago.

One of the differences between our retrospect of the nineteenth century is that you still accept the Whig view that it was a period of prosperity and happiness, hideously broken up by the wars of the twentieth. My outlook was much the same as yours until at the beginning of the 80ties Marx changed the mind of Europe and, for me, snatched the lid off hell and convinced me that the Manchester School, with its dreams and dogmas of Free Trade, Liberty, Equality and Fraternity, which satisfied Macaulay and Gladstone, blinded them to the horrors of the nineteenth century as the most damnably wicked and ruinous episode in human history. I had been quite pleased with Gladstone's Midlothian speeches, and admired those of John Bright. I was full of Mill's Essay on Liberty, Spencer's Data of Ethics, and Darwin. I was intensely anti-clerical; called myself publicly an Atheist at a meeting of the Shelley Society; and mistook that reaction for genuine Freethinking.

The moment Marx got his knife into me, all this faded into an obsolete past; and I was henceforth hated by the Liberals whom I discarded as fossils, and, with Sidney Webb, made the old Socialism, with its Liberal barricaders, constitutional by Fabianism, which is now, by the way, Stalinism in Russia.

The revolutionary change in my Anschauung makes what difference there is between you and me. You are pre-Marx in my estimate of the nineteenth century; but as you are not also pre-Plato or pre-Euripides, we get on pretty well together.

An article of mine on Election Prospects is in today's Daily Mail, of all papers! It was refused by The Times and The Sunday Express. I did not send it to the Labor papers because in their ignorance and uncertainty they are so mortally afraid of me that when they publish anything of mine for its circulation value they preface it with a note to say that they dont believe a word of it.

I was driven to write this article by my fear that if Stalin dies (he is 70) we shall be at war with the U.S.S.R. in a fortnight. Vichinsky, Gromyko and Co. are as jingo as Bevin, McNeill, Shawcross & Co. Stalin alone knows that the U.S.S.R. cannot afford another war, and that he himself would be shot if he threatened one instead of being merely kicked upstairs into a House of Lords. That is real responsibility. I saw Stalin in 1931, and liked him.

G.B.S.

PS There is a radical contradiction in Whig Liberalism. It is founded on the Deism of Voltaire and Adam Smith, who believed that God, always watching and guiding human affairs, would overrule all mankind's sins and mistakes for good. Hence Laissez-faire: all's well that ends well.

Yet it is Atheist, Agnostic, Rationalist, Broad Church, and anti-clerical: in short, godless.

My god, the Life Force, proceeds by Trial & Error.

The universally known founder of Whiteley's chain of stores, William **Whiteley** (1831–1907), amassed a huge fortune by treating his working-class employees as slave labour and by offering such a variety of goods that he dubbed himself 'The Universal Provider.' Shaw remarked to Louis Calvert that he is 'a comic Undershaft' (Holroyd 2, 245). Whiteley was shot to death in 1907 by a man who claimed to be his illegitimate son; for details on the incident and its adaptation in *Misalliance*, see CL 2, 675–6. His generous bequest of a retirement compound to be named Whiteley Village had a radically different history from the one Shaw describes; Andrew Etherington, who served as a catering consultant there for several years, contradicts most of his assertions in a personal letter, including the one that only women were housed there. The poetic drama ***Faust*** by Johann von Wolfgang **Goethe** (1749–1832) is considered one of the great works of world literature. Part 1 was published in 1808, part 2 after his death. Murray had felt comfortable with the German language since he began reading and corresponding with the German classicist Ulrich von Wilamowitz-Moellendorff (1848–1931) in the mid-1890s, but he never found time to translate *Faust*. William Ewart **Gladstone** (1809–98) was the dominant personality of the Liberal Party from 1868–94, and served as prime minister four times. **Anschauung** means point of view or perception. Shaw's article in the day's **Daily Mail** (3:4) was '**Election Prospects** as I See Them' (Laurence, *Bibliography*, 2, 806). **Stalin** lived until he was 74. Andrei **Vishinsky** (1883–1954), a lawyer and diplomat, served as the Soviet foreign minister from 1949–53. He had become the 'legal mastermind' of Stalin's campaign of political repression and persecution during the 'Great Purge' of 1936–8. Andrei **Gromyko** (1909–89) was Soviet ambassador to the United States from 1943–6, then 'Permanent Representative' to the United Nations, where his frequent nays gained him the nickname 'Mr. Nyet.' **McNeill** is probably Hector McNeil (1907–55), vice-president of the United Nations General Assembly in 1947 and leader of the British delegation to the Economic Commission for Europe in 1948. Hartley **Shawcross** (1902–2003) was a British barrister and politician who served as attorney-general from 1945–51. He was the chief prosecutor at the Nuremberg War Crimes tribunal of 1945–6. **Voltaire**, who proclaimed himself a **deist**, was a French philosopher and wit who advocated free trade as well as freedom of religion. His *Dictionnaire philosophique* (1764) contains various critiques of religious beliefs and behaviour. Adam **Smith** (1723–90) was a Scottish social philosopher whose *An Inquiry into the Nature and Causes of the Wealth of Nations* (1776), was widely welcomed for its argument that free market policies are more productive and beneficial to their societies than other policies. His **Deism** is a brand that postulates something more than a creator who then absented Himself; God's presence subtly manifests itself as 'an invisible hand' that guides **laissez-faire** economies to success.

169 / To G. Bernard Shaw

Yatscombe, Boar's Hill, Oxford
12th November 1949

[TLS: BL, SPA]

My dear Shaw

I much enjoyed your letter. You are perfectly right in saying that we old people need the presence of the young to keep us sane and cheerful. That is one of the great advantages of a university town, and explains why people like A.L. Smith played all sorts of games – parlour games as well as outdoor – when far on in the seventies.

And there is another important and paradoxical thing in which, I think, you are absolutely right. The old-fashioned Liberals who often called themselves atheist had a strong unconscious and unquestioning faith in some higher law which they did not explicitly admit. Think of Morley's great speech condemning the Boer War with the refrain 'It will still be wrong.'

What they believed in was what the middle ages called 'The Law of God which is above princes.' It is the great issue now between what I call the civilised nations and your supposed friends Hitler's National Socialists and Stalin's Communists. Our quarrel with them is not about economics, it is about some mystical things that we call 'justice,' 'truth,' and 'human freedom' – though we never can define what we mean by those words. We don't really believe in Bentham, much as we admire him. Of course you have always insisted on the need for a certain mysticism, and no doubt you are right.

I think the reason you people go wrong about the nineteenth century is a fairly simple one. It was the first century which had an active and efficient social conscience, so that it made searching enquiries into the conditions of all 'the desolate and oppressed.' Consequently one found – e.g. in Hammond's books – horrifying stories, published and attested, which in previous ages noone would have known about. Of course there was also the new problem of the industrial revolution, which nobody knew how to tackle.

My proofs of the BIRDS, which have been about a year at the printers, have just turned up. I suppose in another year they will be corrected.

Yours ever,
G.M.

A.L. Smith remains unidentified. John **Morley** (1838–1923) was a British Liberal statesman whose model was Gladstone, about whom he wrote the official biography (1903). He became one of the party's leading pro-Boers partly on moral grounds, but also with his focus on the war as an inordinately expensive imperialist adventure. He later resigned from the government when it declared war in 1914. A close friend and ally of Murray's for years, and a fellow 'intellectual in politics,' he was unique for basing his political stands on principles rather than party allegiance. Jeremy **Bentham** (1748–1832) was an English philosopher and political theorist, founder of the school of utilitarianism. His *Introduction to the Principles of Morals and Legislation* (1789) held that human beings apply a 'hedonic calculus' to any activity they undertake, which weights its potential for causing happiness against the unhappiness that might result (Goldwag, 141). Murray's translation of Aristophanes' *The Birds* was published in 1950.

170 / To G. Bernard Shaw Yatscombe, Boar's Hill, Oxford
30th April 1950

[TLT: BL, SPA]

Lewis Lett (1878–1967) was an English engineer who moved to Papua New Guinea in 1910 and became a friend of Gilbert's older brother Hubert. He turned to journalism and then to biography, and published Sir Hubert Murray of Papua: Statesman and Empire Builder *in 1949. The 1968 biography by Francis West,* Hubert Murray: The Australian Pro-Consul, *describes Lett's work as 'eulogistic,' and notes many errors in it. Hubert's progressive and effective administration of Papua earned him kudos from the League of Nations, and his resistance to threatened absorption into the Consolidated Territories was successful until five years after his death in 1940. Hubert was a formidable physical specimen who preferred boxing to exploiting his academic talents at Oxford University in the mid-1880s. In 1886 he won the Queensbury heavyweight medal, after having come in second the year before.*

My dear Shaw

I think you remember my big brother in Cashell Byron days, when he got the Queensberry heavy-weight medal. Have you seen his Life, by a man called Lett? Such a curious story. First a wild Irishman, a heavy drinker and an unsuccessful barrister in Sydney – with a double first at Oxford behind him. Then a turn to teetotalism – with a whiskey bottle on the table in front of him to show he was not afraid of it. Always a contempt for juries and for conventions, and a sort of discontent until he got at last – in a small out of the way island – a position of supreme power, when he became a sort of model 'father of his people' quoted all over the world. Lived in his shirt-sleeves, neglected all ceremonies, and read Faust and the Iliad through every year. Was a devout Catholic – 'not because the doctrines were true but because men had to have some religion.' It brings back to me old days, before the Deluge.

You will be sorry to hear that Mary has begun to lose her memory and to become a little helpless. I think Charlotte had much the same experience. M is not unhappy, but it is a sad thing, seeing a fine mind waste away.

I have been having as secretary a daughter of Faber the publisher, who treated me with severe doses of T S Eliot & Co, and explained how antiquated all my taste in literature is. She had no success, I fear.

Yours ever,
G.M.

Shaw completed his novel about a pugilist, ***Cashel Byron's** Profession*, in 1883. Two years later it was serialized in the progressive magazine *To-Day*. The figurative term '**before the Deluge**' refers directly to the flood described in Genesis (the 'antediluvian' era), and indirectly to any analogous period. Lady **Mary** Murray would die in September 1956 at the age of 90; Murray will survive her by eight months, dying at 91. On **Eliot**, see headnotes to Letters 51 and 158.

171 / To Gilbert Murray Ayot St Lawrence, Welwyn, Herts.
6th May 1950

[TLS: Bod, SPA]

Shaw was deepy interested in the art of pugilism, and took boxing lessons in the early 1880s. He even enrolled to compete in the 1883 Queensbury Amateur Boxing Championships, but his name was not drawn (Peters, 79). Cashel Byron's Profession *contains a boxing scene between Cashel and Billy Paradise that anticipates his description of the fight between Hubert Murray and Anthony Diamond below. His memories supplement and clarify West's brief biographical account: 'turning the scale at over fourteen stone,' Hubert was defeated by an unnamed but clearly smaller opponent, to his brother Gilbert's 'incredulous disappointment'*

(24–5). Benny Green's Shaw's Champions *quotes a man who interviewed Shaw in 1929 and recorded his description of Diamond's victory: 'The big man hadn't a chance. Being a gentleman, he wouldn't make a bull rush and commit murder: and Diamond was so much too quick for him that it was a relief to everyone when one of his gloves came off and had to be replaced.' Diamond won the competition easily and impressed G.B.S. as being 'among the best boxers he had ever seen' (171).*

This is the last extant letter between Shaw and Murray.

My dear Murray

I do not see where your Irishman comes in *à propos* of your brother the pugilist, nor always which is which. But one of them anticipated my declaration in my recent view of Inge's autobiography, that if my lot were cast as a parish priest in Ireland I would not preach Creative Evolution to my peasant flock, but give them what they were capable of, elevating the Host, binding and loosing, confessing and absolving, teaching the women to form their characters on the Blessed Virgin, and impressing on them that Holy Writ was handwritten by a god in the image of man, all of which, though incredible to me and leading such as I straight to atheism, would be better for them than no religion at all, which would make them quite ungovernable.

I witnessed the defeat of your brother (I forget his Christian name) by a man half his weight and girth, named Anthony Diamond. It was like Sayers's one and only defeat by Nat Langham, after which poor Tom went home blind and crying with mortification. Diamond, like Nat, had a lightning straight left, which nobody was quick enough to get away from or duck and counter. It hit you and he was out of reach in the hundredth of a second. Your brother was too much of a gentleman and too little of a ruffian to tackle him effectively. He should have charged in, ducking to 'ride' a possible counter, and just murdered him by sheer weight and savage hammering. But he was too amiable and sportsmanlike to do this, and put up a classic defence, which was useless, instead of 'in fighting' like ten devils. He did not score a single point; and Diamond scored all the time, though without marking him noticeably in the 3 rounds. In those days champions were all middle weights, not heavies.

Loss of memory is not an unhappy deficiency. It is memory that torments. I remember old Lady Lytton, wife of the second Earl, who kept her good looks and dressed gaily and was quite happy when her memory failed. She would swing around a heavy chair for me; and I was careful not to help her, as I knew she was doing it to shew how strong she was, like Queen Bess dancing where the Spanish Ambassador could see her.

Rutland Boughton asked me the other day whether it did not make me very happy to look back on all the successes and triumphs of my long life. I told him that these were what I never thought about: it was the failures and fooleries and humiliations and cowardices that kept cropping up inopportunely.

I am for the moment tormented, not by reminiscences, but by a ghastly bout of lumbago. I have to go to the hospital every day to be Radiant heated.

G. Bernard Shaw

By '**Inge's autobiography**,' Shaw must refer to Dean Inge's *Diary of a Dean: St Paul's, 1911–1934* (London: Hutchinson, 1949). Laurence's bibliography and its supplement do not list a review of it. Shaw's view of how he would **preach** to a **peasant flock** is paralleled by his long-held pragmatic attitude towards preparing working-class people for conversion; step one is arousing their interest in Marxist revolutionary ideas, which will give them a hopeful cause and make some of them ready to consider less impossibilist, more practical Fabian means to social renovation. Stephen **Nat**haniel **Langham** (1820–71) was the only boxer to defeat Thomas **Sayers** (1826–65), who fought an American to a draw in what was billed as the 'world championship.' **Lady** Betty Bulwer-**Lytton** Balfour (1867–1942) was the wife of Gerald [William] Balfour, 2nd earl of Balfour (1853–1945). The reference to Elizabeth I showing off before the **Spanish Ambassador** pertains to a pencil drawing at Abbotsford entitled 'Queen Elizabeth dancing before the Spanish Ambassador,' by Charles Kirkpatrick Sharpe (1781–1851) (Thomas Frognall Dibdin, *A bibliographical, antiquarian and picturesque tour in the northern countries of England and in Scotland* [London: Richards, 1838], vol. 2, 581). **Rutland Boughton** (1878–1960) was an English composer in a variety of musical forms. In 1934 Shaw wrote to him, 'Now that Elgar is gone, you have the only original personal English style on the market. I find that I have a great taste for it' (Hyperion Records website; Sir Edward Elgar, 1857–1934). The **Radiant heat** treatment for severe **lumbago**, a painful muscular rheumatism in the lumbar region, involved dousing at a temperature of 210–310 degrees for thirty minutes in an upended coffin-like structure (*Wikipedia*; see Gilbert Jessop). Along with the Murrays and Charlotte, Shaw had earlier bouts with lumbago. In an amusing series of comments in letters to his wife, on 30 April 1912 he told Charlotte that he had apparently contracted lumbago – though 'Possibly it is appendicitis. Possibly spinal paralysis.' On 5 May he reported, 'As to the lumbago, every time I sit down it becomes less and less probable that I should ever straighten up again.' Three days later the degree of hope has expired: 'Every muscle in my body is racked: the lumbago is no longer perceptible because I am all lumbago from head to toe' (Cornell: letters from Shaw to Charlotte transcribed and bound from originals in BL).

Table of Correspondents

All the letters were written either by Bernard Shaw or Gilbert Murray

References

Works by Bernard Shaw

Agitations: Letters to the Press 1875–1950. Ed. Dan H. Laurence and James Rambeau. New York: Ungar, 1985.

'Authentic Shavian Democracy.' *Time & Tide,* 10 February 1945 (MS copy of article).

Bernard Shaw and Barry Jackson: Selected Correspondence of Bernard Shaw. Ed. L.W. Conolly. Toronto: University of Toronto Press, 2002.

Bernard Shaw and Gabriel Pascal: Selected Correspondence of Bernard Shaw. Ed. Bernard F. Dukore. Toronto: University of Toronto Press, 1996.

Bernard Shaw and H.G. Wells: Selected Correspondence of Bernard Shaw. Ed. J. Percy Smith. Toronto: University of Toronto Press, 1995.

Bernard Shaw and Lady Astor: Selected Correspondence of Bernard Shaw. Ed. J.P. Wearing. Toronto: University of Toronto Press, 2005.

Bernard Shaw Theatrics: Selected Correspondence of Bernard Shaw. Ed. Dan H. Laurence. Toronto: University of Toronto Press, 1995.

Bernard Shaw and the Webbs: Selected Correspondence of Bernard Shaw. Ed. Alex C. Michalos and Deborah C. Poff. Toronto: University of Toronto Press, 2002.

Bernard Shaw's Book Reviews, Originally Published in the Pall Mall Gazette from 1885 to 1888. 2 vols. Ed. Brian F. Tyson. University Park: Penn State University Press, 1991.

Bernard Shaw's Letters to Siegfried Trebitsch. Ed. Samuel A. Weiss. Stanford, CA: Stanford University Press, 1986.

The Bodley Head Bernard Shaw: Collected Plays with Their Prefaces. Ed. Dan H. Laurence. 7 vols. London: Reinhardt, 1970–4.

Cashel Byron's Profession. New York: Brentano's, 1916.

'Civilization and the Soldier.' *Humane Review* 1 (January 1901): 298–315; reprinted in *SHAW* 9 (1989): 99–112.

Collected Letters. 4 vols. Ed. Dan H. Laurence. London: Reinhardt, 1965–88.

The Collected Screenplays. Ed. Bernard F. Dukore. Athens: University of Georgia Press, 1980.

The Complete Prefaces. 3 vols. Ed. Dan H. Laurence and Daniel J. Leary. London: Allen Lane, 1993–7.

Dear Mr Shaw: Selections from Bernard Shaw's Postbag. Ed. Vivian Elliot. London: Bloomsbury, 1987.

The Diaries, 1885–1897, with Early Autobiographical Notebooks and Diaries, and an Abortive 1917 Diary. 2 vols. Ed. Stanley Weintraub. University Park: Penn State University Press, 1986.

Doctor's Delusions, Crude Criminology, and Sham Education. New York: Wise, 1932. (*Major Critical Essays* 22).

The Drama Observed. 4 vols. Ed. Bernard F. Dukore. University Park: Penn State University Press, 1993.

Essays in Fabian Socialism. New York: Wise, 1932. (*Major Critical Essays* 30).

Everybody's Political What's What? London: Constable, 1944.

Fabianism and the Empire: A Manifesto by the Fabian Society. London: Grant Richards, 1900.

'The Great War and the Aftermath.' *Fortnightly Review* 697 (January and February 1925): 1–12, 145–52; reprinted in *Table-Talk of G.B.S.: Conversations on Things in General between George Bernard Shaw and His Biographer,* 118–62. Ed. Archibald Henderson. New York: Harper, 1925.

'The Illusions of Socialism.' In Edward Carpenter, ed., *Forecasts of the Coming Century, by a Decade of Writers,* 141–73. Manchester: Labour Press, 1897.

The Intelligent Woman's Guide to Socialism and Capitalism. New York: Brentano's, 1928; reprint with introduction by Susan Moller Okin. Somerset, NJ: Transaction, 2005.

The Intelligent Woman's Guide to Socialism, Capitalism, Sovietism and Fascism. Richmond [upon Thames]: Alma Classics, 2012 (reprint of 2-vol. 1937 ed.; foreword by Polly Toynbee).

'The League of Nations: A First Visit Impression.' *English Review* 47 (November 1928): 522–31.

The Letters of Bernard Shaw to The Times, *1898–1950.* Ed. Ronald Ford. Dublin: Irish Academic Press, 2007.

Major Critical Essays: The Quintessence of Ibsenism, The Perfect Wagnerite, The Sanity of Art. New York: Wise, 1932.

'Mr. Bernard Shaw on the Drama.' Reported lecture to the Imperial Institute. *The Times,* 8 March 1906, 10.

Mrs Warren's Profession. Ed. Leonard W. Conolly. Peterborough, ON: Broadview Press, 2005.

Pen Portraits and Reviews. New York: Wise, 1932. (*Major Critical Essays* 29).
Platform and Pulpit. Ed. Dan H. Laurence. New York: Hill & Wang, 1961.
Practical Politics: Twentieth-Century Views on Politics and Economics. Ed. Lloyd J. Hubenka. Lincoln: University of Nebraska Press, 1976.
'Professor Gilbert Murray's Defence of Sir Edward Grey.' *The New Statesman* 5, 17 July 1915, 349–51.
The Rationalization of Russia. Bloomington: Indiana University Press, 1964.
The Religious Speeches of Bernard Shaw. Ed. Warren S. Smith. University Park: Penn State University Press, 1963.
The Road to Equality: Ten Unpublished Lectures and Essays, 1884–1918. Ed. Louis Crompton. Boston: Beacon Press, 1971.
Shaw: Interviews and Recollections. Ed. A.M. Gibbs. London: Macmillan, 1990.
Shaw on Language. Ed. Abraham Tauber. New York: Philosophical Library, 1963.
Shaw and Society: An Anthology and a Symposium. Ed. C.E.M. Joad. London: Odhams Press, 1953.
Shaw on Theatre. Ed. E.J. West. New York: Hill & Wang, 1958.
Sixteen Self Sketches. London: Constable, 1949.
Table-Talk of G.B.S.: Conversations on Things in General between George Bernard Shaw and His Biographer. Ed. Archibald Henderson. New York: Harper, 1925.
'That Silly Game – Disarmament.' *North Eastern Daily Gazette,* 19 March 1935; reprinted in Gibbs, ed., *Shaw: Interviews,* 358–60.
'Torture by Forcible Feeding Is Illegal.' In Rodelle Weintraub, ed., *Fabian Feminist: Bernard Shaw and Woman,* 228–35. University Park: Penn State University Press, 1977. Report of a speech reprinted from *London Budget,* 23 March 1913.
'"We Want a Five-Year Plan Here": George Bernard Shaw at the I.L.P. National Summer School,' 1931; reprinted as 'The Only Hope of the World' in *Platform and Pulpit,* 218–26.
What I Really Wrote about the War. New York: Wise, 1931. (*Major Critical Essays* 21).
What Shaw Really Wrote about the War. Ed. J.L. Wisenthal and Daniel O'Leary. Gainesville: University Press of Florida, 2006.

Works by Gilbert Murray

Andromache: A Play in Three Acts. London: William Heinemann, 1900.
Aristophanes: A Study. Oxford: Clarendon Press, 1933.
The Bacchae of Euripides. London: Allen and Unwin, 1904.
Carlyon Sahib: A Drama in Four Acts. London: William Heinemann, 1900.
'The Early G.B.S.' *New Statesman and Nation* 34 (16 August 1947): 128.
'Ethical Problems of the War' and 'Thoughts on the War.' In Viscount Bryce

et al., eds, *The War of Democracy, the Allies' Statement ...* (1917).
Essays & Addresses. London: George Allen & Unwin, 1921.
Euripides and His Age. London: Williams and Norgate, 1913.
Euripides, The Electra. New York: Oxford University Press, 1907.
Faith, War, and Policy: Addresses and Essays on the European War. Boston: Houghton Mifflin, 1917.
'A Few Memories.' *Drama,* n.s. 20 (Spring 1951): 7–9.
Five Stages of Greek Religion. New York: Columbia University Press, 1925. See *Four Stages* (below).
The Foreign Policy of Sir Edward Grey, 1906–1915. Oxford: Clarendon Press, 1915.
'A Foreword.' In Stephen Winsten, ed., *G.B.S. 90: Aspects of Bernard Shaw's Life and Work,* 13–15. London: Hutchinson, 1946.
Four Stages of Greek Religion: Studies Based on a Course of Lectures Delivered in April 1912 at Columbia University. New York: Columbia University Press, 1912.
Gilbert Murray's Euripides: The Trojan Woman *and Other Plays.* Ed. James Morwood. Exeter: Exeter Press, 2005. (Includes the introductions and notes, and an introduction by the editor.)
'Greek and English Tragedy.' In G.S. Gordon, ed., *English Literature and the Classics,* 7–24. Oxford: Clarendon Press, 1912.
Hippolytus, Bacchae, and The Frogs of Aristophanes. London: George Allen, 1902.
A History of Ancient Greek Literature. London: William Heinemann, 1897.
The Medea of Euripides. New York: Oxford University Press, 1906.
'Mr. Bernard Shaw's New Plays.' *Speaker* 3 (9 February 1901): 516–17.
'Mr. Shaw's "Geneva."' *Spectator* 161 (26 August 1938): 330–1.
Oedipus, King of Thebes. London: Grant Allen, 1911.
The Ordeal of This Generation: The War, the League, and the Future. London: Allen & Unwin, 1929.
'Presidential Address.' *Proceedings of the Society for Psychical Research* 49 (1952): 155–69.
The Trojan Women of Euripides. London: Allen and Unwin, 1905.
An Unfinished Autobiography, with Contributions by His Friends. London: George Allen and Unwin, 1960.

Other References

Notes: Essays in collections by Murray (*An Unfinished Autobiography*) and Stray (*Gilbert Murray Reassessed*) simply say 'in Murray' and 'in Stray.' Editions of the works of Shaw and Murray are not repeated below under editors' names. The abbreviation *SHAW* refers to *SHAW: The Annual of Bernard Shaw Studies.*

Albert, Sidney P. 'From *Murray's Mother-in-Law* to *Major Barbara*: The Outside Story.' *SHAW* 18 (1998): 19–65.

– 'G.B.S. in Hellas: A Resource for Classicists.' *SHAW* 23 (2003): 167–80.

– '"In More Ways than One"': *Major Barbara*'s Debt to Gilbert Murray.' *Educational Theatre Journal* 20 (1968): 123–40; reprinted in Warren Sylvester Smith, ed. *Bernard Shaw's Plays: Major Barbara, Heartbreak House, Saint Joan, Too True to be Good, with Backgrounds and Criticism*, 375–97. New York: Norton, 1970.

– 'Shaw's Advice to the Players of *Major Barbara*.' *Theatre Survey* 10 (1969): 1–17; 'More Shaw Advice ...' *Theatre Survey* 11 (1970): 66–85.

– *Shaw, Plato, and Euripides: Classical Currents in* Major Barbara. Gainesville: University Press of Florida, 2012.

Alexander, James. *Shaw's Controversial Socialism.* Gainesville: University Press of Florida, 2009.

Archer, Charles. *William Archer: Life, Work and Friendships.* London: Allen and Unwin, 1931.

Archer, William. *The Old Drama and the New: An Essay in Re-valuation.* Boston: Small, Maynard, 1923.

– *The Vedrenne-Barker Season, 1904–1905: A Record and Commentary.* London: Allen, 1905.

Augustine, Saint. *Basic Writings of Saint Augustine*, vol. 1. Ed. Whitney J. Oates. Grand Rapids, MI: Random House, 1948.

Baker, Stuart E. *Bernard Shaw's Remarkable Religion: A Faith That Fits the Facts.* Gainesville: University Press of Florida, 2002.

Barker, Dudley. *The Man of Principle: A Biography of John Galsworthy.* New York: Stein and Day, 1970.

Bentley, Eric. *Bernard Shaw: A Reconsideration.* New York: Norton, 1976 (new ed. of 1947 book).

Bentley, Michael. *The Liberal Mind, 1914–1929.* Cambridge: Cambridge University Press, 1977.

Bergquist, Gordon N. *The Pen and the Sword: War and Peace in the Plays of Bernard Shaw.* Salzburg: Institut für Englische Sprache und Literatur, Universität Salzburg, 1977.

Berst, Charles A. 'In the Beginning: The Poetic Genesis of Shaw's God.' *SHAW* 1 (1981): 5–41.

Birn, Donald S. *The League of Nations Union, 1918–1945.* Oxford: Clarendon Press, 1981.

Bowra, C.M. *Memories 1898–1939.* Cambridge, MA: Harvard University Press, 1967.

Bridges, Robert. *Selected Letters.* 2 vols. Newark: University of Delaware Press, 1984.

Carpenter, Charles A. 'Shaw and Bertrand Russell versus Gilbert Murray on Britain's Entry into World War I: The Inside Story.' *SHAW* 33 (2013): 25–54.

Cash, Arthur H. *John Wilkes: The Scandalous Father of Civil Liberty*. New Haven, CT: Yale University Press, 2006.

Ceadel, Martin. 'Gilbert Murray and International Politics.' In Stray, 217–37.

Champion, Henry Hyde. 'H. H. Champion and Bernard Shaw.' In Leslie M. Henderson, *The Goldstein Story*, 159–67. Melbourne: Stockland Press, 1973.

Chapman, John Jay. 'Professor Gilbert Murray – Oxford.' In *Greek Genius and Other Essays*, 97–124. New York: Moffat, Yard, 1915.

Chapman, Richard A. 'Official Liberality.' *Public Administration* 48, no. 2 (1970): 123–36.

Chappelow, Allan. *Shaw: 'The Chucker-Out': A Biographical Exposition and Critique, and a Companion to and Commentary on 'Shaw the Villager.'* London: George Allen and Unwin, 1969.

Chesterton, G.K. *George Bernard Shaw*. London: Bodley Head, 1909.

Clarke, Peter. *Hope and Glory: Britain 1900–1990*. London: Allen Lane; Penguin Press, 1996.

– *Liberals and Social Democrats*. Cambridge: Cambridge University Press, 1978.

Cole, Margaret. *Beatrice Webb*. London: Longmans, Green, 1945.

Cook, Chris. *The Longman Handbook of Modern British History, 1714–1987*. 2nd ed. London: Longman, 1988.

Coward, Noël. *Tonight at 8:30: Plays by Noel Coward*. New York: Sun Dial Press, 1936.

Crompton, Louis. *Shaw the Dramatist*. Lincoln: University of Nebraska Press, 1969.

Degen, Marie Louise. *The History of the Woman's Peace Party*. Baltimore, MD: Johns Hopkins Press, 1939, reprinted by Burt Franklin Reprints (New York, 1974).

Devlin, Diana. *A Speaking Part: Lewis Casson and the Theatre of His Time*. London: Hodder and Stoughton, 1982.

Dodds, E.R. *Missing Persons: An Autobiography*. Oxford: Clarendon Press, 1977.

Dukore, Bernard F. *Bernard Shaw, Playwright: Aspects of Shavian Drama*. Columbia: University of Missouri Press, 1973.

– 'Revising *Major Barbara*.' *Shaw Review* 16, no. 1 (1973): 2–10.

Dunbar, Janet. *J. M. Barrie: The Man behind the Image*. Boston: Houghton Mifflin, 1970.

– *Mrs G.B.S.: A Portrait*. New York: Harper and Row, 1963.

Egerton, George W. *Great Britain and the Creation of the League of Nations: Strategy, Politics, and International Organization, 1914–1919*. Chapel Hill: University of North Carolina Press, 1978.

Einstein, Albert. *The World as I See It*. New York: Covici, Friede, 1934.

Elton, Godfrey, ed. *The First Fifty Years of the Rhodes Trust and the Rhodes Scholarships 1903–1953*. Oxford: Blackwell, 1955.

Ervine, St John. *Bernard Shaw: His Life, Work and Friends.* New York: Morrow, 1956.

Fowler, Robert L. 'Gilbert Murray: Four (Five) Stages of Greek Religion.' In William M. Calder, ed., *The Cambridge Ritualists Reconsidered,* 79–95. Atlanta, GA: Scholars Press, 1991.

Freeden, Michael. *Liberalism Divided: A Study in British Political Thought, 1914–1939.* Oxford: Clarendon Press, 1986.

Gibbs, A. M. *Bernard Shaw: A Life.* Gainesville: University Press of Florida, 2005.

– *A Bernard Shaw Chronology.* Basingstoke: Palgrave, 2001.

Gilbert, Martin. *Winston S. Churchill, Volume VI: Finest Hour, 1939–1941.* Boston: Houghton Mifflin, 1983.

Gilbert, Martin, ed. *The Churchill War Papers, Volume III: The Ever-Widening War, 1941.* New York: Norton, 2000.

Ginden, James. *John Galsworthy's Life and Art: An Alien's Fortress.* Ann Arbor: University of Michigan Press, 1987.

Glasgow, Eric. 'The Origins of the Home University Library.' *Library Review* 50, no. 2 (2001).

Goldwag, Arthur. *'Isms & 'Ologies: The 453 Basic Tenets You've Only Pretended to Understand.* New York: Madison Park Press, 2007.

Gosse, Edmund. *Henrik Ibsen.* Gutenberg Ebook edition, unpaged.

Granville-Barker, Harley. 'On Translating Greek Tragedy.' In Murray, 237–47.

Green, Benny. *Shaw's Champions: G.B.S. & Prizefighting from Cashel Byron to Gene Tunney.* London: Elm Tree Books, 1978.

Green, Paul. *Dramatic Heritage.* New York: Samuel French, 1953.

Grey, Sir Edward. *Twenty-Five Years, 1892–1916.* 2 vols. New York: Stokes, 1925.

Griffith, Gareth. *Socialism and Superior Brains: The Political Thought of Bernard Shaw.* London: Routledge, 1993.

Hall, Edith, and Fiona Macintosh. 'The Shavian Euripides and the Euripidean Shaw: Greek Tragedy and the New Drama.' In *Greek Tragedy and the British Theatre, 1660–1914,* 488–520. Oxford: Oxford University Press, 2005.

Hansel, C.E.M. *ESP and Parapsychology: A Critical Reevaluation.* Buffalo, NY: Prometheus Books, 1980.

Hazlehurst, Cameron. *Politicians at War, July 1914 to May 1915.* London: Cape, 1971.

Henderson, Archibald. *George Bernard Shaw: Man of the Century.* New York: Appleton, Century, Crofts, 1956.

Henderson, Isobel. 'The Teacher of Greek.' In Murray, 125–48.

Hoare, Philip. *Noël Coward: A Biography.* New York: Simon & Schuster, 1995.

Holroyd, Michael. *Bernard Shaw.* 4 vols. London: Chatto and Windus, 1988–91.

Hugo, Leon H. 'Britons, Boers, and Blacks: Bernard Shaw on South Africa.' *SHAW* 11 (1991): 79–95.

– *Edwardian Shaw: The Writer and His Age.* Basingstoke: Macmillan, 1999.
– 'Shaw and the Twenty-Nine Percenters.' *SHAW* 13 (1993): 51–71.
Hutchings, W.W. *London Town Past and Present.* New York: Cassell, 1909.
Incorporated Stage Society. *Ten Years 1899–1909.* London, 1909; see also the Society's *First Annual Report.* London, 1900.
Irvine, William. *The Universe of G.B.S.* New York: Whittlesey House, 1949.
Joad, C.E.M. *Shaw.* London: Gollancz, 1949.
Joyce, James Avery. *Broken Star: The Story of the League of Nations (1919–1939).* Swansea: Christopher Davies, 1978.
Kennedy, Dennis. *Granville Barker and the Dream of Theatre.* Cambridge: Cambridge University Press, 1985.
Laurence, Dan H. *Bernard Shaw: A Bibliography.* 2 vols. Oxford: Clarendon Press, 1983; 'A Supplement to *Bernard Shaw: A Bibliography.*' *SHAW* 20 (2000): 3–128.
Leary, Daniel. '*Too True to be Good* and Shaw's Romantic Synthesis: A Religion for Our Times.' *SHAW* 1 (1981): 183–203.
Leventhal, F.M. *The Last Dissenter: H. N. Brailsford and His World.* Oxford: Clarendon Press, 1985.
Lloyd-Jones, Hugh. 'Gilbert Murray.' In *Blood for the Ghosts: Classical Influences in the Nineteenth and Twentieth Centuries,* 195–214. London: Duckworth, 1982.
Lowe, N.J. 'Gilbert Murray and Psychic Research.' In Stray, 349–70.
Luke, Kimberley. 'Order or Justice: The Denshawai Incident and British Imperialism.' *History Compass* 5, no. 2 (2007): 278–87.
MacCarthy, Desmond. *The Court Theatre 1904–1907: A Commentary and Criticism.* New ed., ed. Stanley Weintraub. Coral Gables, FL: University of Miami Press, 1966 (first published 1907).
– *Shaw.* London: MacGibbon and Kee, 1951.
Macintosh, Fiona. 'From the Court to the National: The Theatrical Legacy of Gilbert Murray's *Bacchae.*' In Stray, 145–65.
MacKenzie, Norman, and Jeanne MacKenzie. *The Life of H.G. Wells: The Time Traveller.* London: Weidenfeld and Nicolson, 1973.
Madariaga, Salvador de. 'Gilbert Murray and the League.' In Murray, 176–97.
Mander, Raymond, and Joe Mitchenson. *Theatrical Companion to Coward: A Pictorial Record of the Theatrical Works of Noël Coward.* Updated by Barry Day and Sheridan Morley. London: Oberon Books, 2000.
– *Theatrical Companion to Shaw: A Pictorial Record of the First Performances of the Plays of George Bernard Shaw.* New York: Pitman, 1955.
Marrot, H.V. *The Life and Letters of John Galsworthy.* New York: Scribner's, 1936.
McBriar, A.M. *Fabian Socialism and English Politics, 1884–1918.* Cambridge: Cambridge University Press, 1962.
McCarthy, Lillah. *Myself and My Friends.* New York: Dutton, 1933.

Meyer, Michael. *Ibsen*: A Biography. Garden City, NY: Doubleday, 1971.

Minney, R.J. *Recollections of George Bernard Shaw.* Englewood Cliffs, NJ: Prentice-Hall, 1969.

Mommsen, Theodor. *The History of Rome.* New ed. Ed. Dero A. Saunders and John H. Collins. New York: Meridian Books, 1958.

Monk, Ray. *Bertrand Russell: The Spirit of Solitude, 1872–1921.* New York: Free Press, 1996.

Morefield, Jeanne. *Covenants without Swords: Idealist Liberalism and the Spirit of Empire.* Princeton, NJ: Princeton University Press, 2005.

Morgan, Margery M. *A Drama of Political Man: A Study in the Plays of Harley Granville Barker.* London: Sidgwick and Jackson, 1961.

Morris, Mick. '"That Living Voice": Gilbert Murray at the BBC.' In Stray, 293–317. (Appendix lists all of his appearances plus the recordings that were kept.)

Morwood, James. 'Gilbert Murray's Translations of Greek Tragedy.' In Stray, 133–44.

– 'Introduction.' In Murray, *Gilbert Murray's Euripides*, xii–xxx.

Murray, Gilbert, et al. *An Unfinished Autobiography, with Contributions by His Friends.* London: George Allen and Unwin, 1960.

Murray, Hubert. *Selected Letters of Hubert Murray.* Ed. Francis West. Melbourne: Oxford University Press, 1970. (Gilbert Murray's brother.)

Newbolt, H.J. 'The Happy Warrior.' *Monthly Review* 2, no. 5 (January 1901): 1–10.

O'Leary, Daniel. 'Censored and Embedded Shaw: Print Culture and Shavian Analysis of Wartime Media.' *SHAW* 28 (2008): 168–87.

The Oxford Companion to the Theatre. 3rd ed., ed. Phyllis Hartnoll. Oxford: Oxford University Press, 1967; 4th ed., ed. Hartnoll, 1983.

Patch, Blanche. *Thirty Years with G.B.S.* London: Gollancz, 1951.

Pearce, Malcolm, and Geoffrey Stewart. *British Political History, 1867–2001: Democracy and Decline.* 3rd ed. London: Routledge, 2002.

Pearson, Hesketh. *G.B.S.: A Full-Length Portrait.* New York: Harper, 1942.

Perris, Simon. '"The Kingdom of Heaven within Me": Inner (World) Peace in Gilbert Murray's *The Trojan Women.*' *Comparative Drama*, 45 (2010): 423–40.

– 'Our Savior Dionysos: Humanism and Theology in Gilbert Murray's *Bakkhai.*' *Translation & Literature* 21, no. 1 (2012): 21–42.

Peters, Sally. *Bernard Shaw: The Ascent of the Superman.* New Haven, CT: Yale University Press, 1996.

Pilecki, Gerard Anthony. *Shaw's* Geneva*: A Critical Study of the Evolution of the Text in Relation to Shaw's Political Thought and Dramatic Practice.* London: Mouton, 1965.

Pugh, Patricia. 'Bernard Shaw, Imperialist.' *SHAW* 11 (1991): 98–118.

Purdom, C.B. *Harley Granville Barker: Man of the Theatre, Dramatist and Scholar.* London: Rockliff, 1955.

Rattray, R.F. *Bernard Shaw: A Chronicle.* Luton: Leagrave Press, 1951.

Robbins, Keith. *Sir Edward Grey: A Biography of Lord Grey of Fallodon.* London: Cassell, 1971.

Roosevelt, Franklin Delano. *Nothing to Fear: The Selected Addresses of Franklin Delano Roosevelt, 1932–1945.* Ed. B.D. Zevin. Cambridge: Houghton Mifflin, 1946.

Russell, Bertrand. *The Autobiography of Bertrand Russell, 1872–1914; The Autobiography of Bertrand Russell, 1914–1944.* Boston: Little, Brown, 1951. (Letters to and from Gilbert Murray: 1, 234–46; 2, 376–88.)

– 'A Fifty-Six Year Friendship.' In Murray, 205–11.

– *Justice in War-Time: A Reply to Professor Gilbert Murray.* Chicago: Open Court, 1916.

– *Prophecy and Dissent, 1914–16.* Ed. Richard A. Rempel. London: Unwin Hyman, 1988. (Vol. 13 of *The Collected Papers of Bertrand Russell.*)

– *Selected Letters.* 2 vols. London: Routledge, 2001–2.

Sadie, Stanley, ed. *The Norton / Grove Concise Encyclopedia of Music.* New York: Norton, 1988.

Saint, Andrew. 'Technical Education and the Early LCC.' In *Politics and the People of London: The London County Council, 1889–1965.* London: Hambledon Press, 1989.

Salmon, Eric. *Granville Barker: A Secret Life.* Rutherford, NJ: Fairleigh Dickinson University Press, 1983.

Salmon, Eric, ed. 'Gilbert Murray, 1866–1957.' In *Granville Barker and His Correspondents: A Selection of Letters by Him and to Him,* 195–298. Detroit, MI: Wayne State University Press, 1986.

Salter, W.S. *Essays on Two Moderns: Euripides and Samuel Butler.* London: Sidgwick & Jackson, 1911.

Smith, Adrian. *The New Statesman: Portrait of a Political Weekly, 1913–1938.* London: Frank Cass, 1996.

Smith, David C. *H. G. Wells, Desperately Mortal: A Biography.* New Haven, CT: Yale University Press, 1986.

Smith, Jean. 'The Committee for Intellectual Co-operation in Gilbert Murray's Papers.' In Murray, 198–204.

Stage Society. *The Incorporated Stage Society: Ten Years 1899–1909.* London, 1909.

Stevenson, Ian. *Telepathic Impressions: A Review and Report of Thirty-five Cases.* Charlottesville: University Press of Virginia, 1970.

Stray, Christopher, ed. *Gilbert Murray Reassessed: Hellenism, Theatre, and International Politics.* Oxford: Oxford University Press, 2007.

Taylor, A.J.P. *English History 1914–1945.* London: Oxford University Press, 1965.

Thompson, Paul. *Socialists, Liberals and Labour: The Struggle for London, 1885–1914.* London: Routledge and Kegan Paul, 1967.

Thomson, J.A.K. 'Gilbert Murray.' *Proceedings of the British Academy* 43 (1957): 245–70.

Thomson, J.A.K., and A.J. Toynbee, eds. *Essays in Honour of Gilbert Murray.* London: George Allen and Unwin, 1936.

Thorndike, Sybil, in collaboration with Lewis Casson. 'The Theatre and Gilbert Murray.' In Murray, 149–75.

Toynbee, Arnold. 'The Unity of Gilbert Murray's Life and Work.' In Murray, 212–20.

Trotter, W.R. *The Hilltop Writers.* Sussex: Book Guild, 1996.

Waller, Philip. *Writers, Readers, and Reputations: Literary Life in Britain 1870–1918.* Oxford: Oxford University Press, 2006.

Wearing, J.P. *American and British Theatrical Biography: A Directory.* Metuchen, NY: Scarecrow Press, 1979.

– *The London Stage, 1940–1949: A Calendar of Plays and Players, Vol. I.* 2 vols. Metuchen, NJ: Scarecrow Press, 1991.

Wearing, J.P., general ed. *G.B. Shaw: An Annotated Bibliography of Writings about Him.* 3 vols. DeKalb: Northern Illinois University Press, 1986–87.

Webb, Beatrice. *The Diary of Beatrice Webb.* 4 vols. Ed. Norman and Jeanne MacKenzie. Cambridge: Cambridge University Press, 1978.

Webb, Sidney, and Beatrice Webb. *Soviet Communism: A New Civilization?* London: Longmans, Green, 1935. 2 vols. (Reissued with retorts to critics – and without the question mark – the following year.)

Weinreb, Ben, and Christopher Hibbert, eds. *The London Encyclopedia.* London: Papermac, 1993.

Weintraub, Stanley. *Journey to Heartbreak: The Crucible Years of Bernard Shaw 1914–1918.* New York: Weybright and Talley, 1971.

– 'Shaw's Troy: *Heartbreak House* and Euripides' *Trojan Women.*' *SHAW* 29 (2009): 41–9.

Weintraub, Stanley, ed. *Saint Joan Fifty Years After, 1923/24–1973/74.* Baton Rouge: Louisiana State University Press, 1973.

Wells, H.G. *The Correspondence of H.G. Wells.* 4 vols. Ed. David C. Smith. London: Pickering and Chatto, 1998.

– *Experiment in Autobiography: Discoveries and Conclusions of a Very Ordinary Brain.* 2 vols. London: Gollancz, 1934.

West, Francis. *Gilbert Murray: A Life.* London: Croom Helm, 1984.

– *Hubert Murray, the Australian Pro-Consul.* Melbourne: Oxford University Press, 1968.

Whitebrook, Peter. *William Archer: A Biography*. London: Methuen, 1993.

Who's Who in the Theatre: A Biographical Record of the Contemporary Stage. 4th ed., ed. John Parker. London: Pitman, 1922.

Wilson, Duncan. *Gilbert Murray, OM, 1866–1957*. Oxford: Clarendon Press, 1987.

Wilson, Edmund. *Travels in Two Democracies*. New York: Harcourt, Brace, 1936.

Winsten, Stephen, ed. *GBS 90: Aspects of Bernard Shaw's Life and Works*. London: Hutchinson, 1946.

Yearwood, Peter J. *Guarantee of Peace: The League of Nations in British Policy, 1914–1925*. Oxford: Oxford University Press, 2009.

Index

Selected Correspondence of Bernard Shaw

Bernard Shaw Theatrics, edited by Dan H. Laurence

Bernard Shaw and H.G. Wells, edited by J. Percy Smith

Bernard Shaw and Gabriel Pascal, edited by Bernard F. Dukore

Bernard Shaw and Barry Jackson, edited by L.W. Conolly

Bernard Shaw and the Webbs, edited by Alex C. Michalos and Deborah C. Poff

Bernard Shaw and Nancy Astor, edited by J.P. Wearing

Bernard Shaw and His Publishers, edited by Michel C. Pharand

Bernard Shaw and Gilbert Murray, edited by Charles A. Carpenter

www.ingramcontent.com/pod-product-compliance
Lightning Source LLC
LaVergne TN
LVHW040152080826
844660LV00014B/931/J

* 9 7 8 1 4 4 2 6 4 3 8 2 6 *